THE CAMBRIDGE COM
SHAKESPEARE AND CONTEMPO

CW00554777

While Shakespeare's popularity has continued
paid to the work of his contemporaries. The contributors to this *Companion*
introduce the distinctive drama of these playwrights, from the court comedies
of John Lyly to the works of Richard Brome in the Caroline era. With chapters
on a wide range of familiar and lesser-known dramatists, including Thomas
Kyd, Christopher Marlowe, Ben Jonson, John Webster, Thomas Middleton
and John Ford, this book devotes particular attention to their personal and
professional relationships, occupational rivalries and collaborations. Their
plays are situated in their proper cultural and historical contexts, with
discussions of performance in the early modern theatre, drama and reputation
and the emergence of city comedy. Overturning the popular misconception
that Shakespeare wrote in isolation, this book offers a new perspective on the
most impressive body of drama in the history of the English stage.

TON HOENSELAARS is Professor of Early Modern English Literature and
Culture at Utrecht University.

A complete list of books in the series is at the back of this book

THE CAMBRIDGE COMPANION TO

SHAKESPEARE AND CONTEMPORARY DRAMATISTS

EDITED BY
TON HOENSELAARS
Universiteit Utrecht, The Netherlands

CAMBRIDGE UNIVERSITY PRESS
Cambridge, New York, Melbourne, Madrid, Cape Town,
Singapore, São Paulo, Delhi, Mexico City

Cambridge University Press
The Edinburgh Building, Cambridge CB2 8RU, UK

Published in the United States of America by Cambridge University Press, New York

www.cambridge.org
Information on this title: www.cambridge.org/9780521767545

First published 2012

Printed and bound in the United Kingdom by the MPG Books Group

A catalogue record for this publication is available from the British Library

Library of Congress Cataloguing in Publication data
The Cambridge companion to Shakespeare and contemporary dramatists /
[edited by] Ton Hoenselaars.
p.   cm. – (Cambridge companions to literature)
Includes bibliographical references and index.
ISBN 978-0-521-76754-5 (hardback) – ISBN 978-0-521-12874-2 (paperback)
1. English drama–Early modern and Elizabethan, 1500–1600–History and criticism.
2. English drama–17th century–History and criticism.   3. Shakespeare, William,
1564–1616–Criticism and interpretation.   I. Hoenselaars, A. J., 1956–
PR653.C27 2012
822'.309–dc23
2012014215

ISBN 978-0-521-76754-5 Hardback
ISBN 978-0-521-12874-2 Paperback

For Stanley Wells

CONTENTS

ILLUSTRATIONS

CONTRIBUTORS

CLARA CALVO, University of Murcia

WARREN CHERNAIK, King's College London

PAUL FRANSSEN, Utrecht University

DARRYLL GRANTLEY, University of Kent

ROBERT HENKE, Washington University, St Louis

CATHERINE HENZE, University of Wisconsin, Green Bay

HEATHER HIRSCHFELD, University of Tennessee, Knoxville

TON HOENSELAARS, Utrecht University

RUI CARVALHO HOMEM, University of Porto

LISA HOPKINS, Sheffield Hallam University

JEAN E. HOWARD, Columbia University

ARTHUR F. KINNEY, University of Massachusetts, Amherst

MICHELLE O'CALLAGHAN, University of Reading

ELIZABETH SCHAFER, Royal Holloway, University of London,

MATTHEW STEGGLE, Sheffield Hallam University

RICHARD WILSON, Cardiff University

PREFACE

The contributors to this volume of newly commissioned essays introduce Shakespeare and a vast range of fellow dramatists in the early modern theatre, including John Lyly, Christopher Marlowe, Thomas Kyd, John Marston, Thomas Heywood, Thomas Dekker, George Chapman, Ben Jonson, Thomas Middleton, Francis Beaumont, John Fletcher, Philip Massinger, John Webster, John Ford and Richard Brome. The essays examine the lives of these dramatists and discuss their individual achievements in detail. The essays are, however, also mindful of the fact that close personal and professional relations existed between Shakespeare and the other dramatists in the early modern theatre. Attention, therefore, is also devoted to the multiple forms of interaction between them – involving tutelage and encouragement as well as occupational rivalry and collaborative authorship. This approach to Shakespeare and his fellow dramatists enhances our appreciation of the single-authored as well as the collaborative plays that together represent the most impressive body of drama in English stage history.

The essays in this collection introduce the playwrights and a number of their works in chronological order. They range from Arthur Kinney's full account of John Lyly and the University Wits in the 1580s and 1590s – whose hyper-inventive use of the English language and experiments with dramatic representation left an indelible stamp on Shakespeare's work – to Lisa Hopkins's discussion of John Ford, whose *'Tis Pity She's a Whore* (1632) and *Perkin Warbeck* (1633) may be read as Caroline appropriations of Shakespearean models for tragedy and history. Kyd's charismatic *Spanish Tragedy*, as Clara Calvo demonstrates, was an inevitable presence, a familiar text for nearly every dramatist of the period to quote, to revise, to imitate, to emulate, to parody, but never to ignore. Richard Wilson reads the work of Marlowe and Shakespeare as closely interreflecting texts that bring into sharp focus these two colossal rivals' decidedly different personalities and world views. Rivalry between Shakespeare and Jonson was no less palpable, as Warren Chernaik shows, comparing the two dramatists as they depicted the Roman world. In his account of the life and work of John Marston, Matthew Steggle describes how around the turn of the sixteenth century conflicting ideas about the status of literary and dramatic authorship unleashed the Poets' War, or the War of the Theatres, with Marston himself, Jonson and Dekker at the militant centre. Darryll Grantley introduces Thomas Dekker and his work, and demonstrates how the commercial theatre's demand for registering the latest fashions significantly determined both Dekker's readiness to co-author and the sophistication of the end-product. By contrast to Dekker, it may be tempting to think of Shakespeare as an individual writer for the stage. However, from Ton Hoenselaars's essay Shakespeare emerges as an author who worked collaboratively throughout his writing career. Although the number of plays of which Shakespeare is the unchallenged sole author remains unusual, critics now generally agree about the hand of contemporaries like Nashe, Peele, Middleton and Fletcher in the Shakespeare canon, and assume that Shakespeare acted as one of the dramatists who revised *Sir Thomas More*. Thomas Heywood – sharing Dekker's almost un-Shakespearean interest in London as a dramatic setting – is alleged to have collaborated on more plays than any of his contemporaries. Yet, as Jean Howard demonstrates, Heywood may be recognised as a committed dramatist who effectively experimented with existing genres and sought to develop new theatrical means to heighten the emotional impact of his plays. George Chapman, introduced by Paul Franssen, may have been the most learned dramatist of his time, and he was nearly alone in his fascination with the contemporary European continent as a source and setting for his plays. His singular identity, however, did not prevent him from participating in the writing of *Eastward Ho* (with Jonson and Marston). Catherine Henze writes about Francis Beaumont and John Fletcher, devoting equal attention to their individual plays and their joint work. Interestingly, a closer look at the music in their plays also reveals unsuspected networks of collaboration between the dramatists and their theatre personnel.

Michelle O'Callaghan guides the reader through the drama of Thomas Middleton, the playwright whom some critics hail as 'our other Shakespeare'. Active as sole author, co-writer and reviser, Middleton ever worked with an eye to the fashion, and with his ingenuity and commitment managed to lift the genres of comedy and tragedy to new heights. Robert Henke looks at John Webster. An in-depth study of the playwright's career, his plays and his reflections on the art of writing reveals disparate views of single and joint authorship which, in turn, suggest a conflict between public constraint and private interiority. Rui Carvalho Homem writes of Massinger's unstable reputation since the seventeenth century. Homem suggests that we may have been confused by the incompatibility of Massinger's ideas, and have looked for a degree of coherence in the plays, whereas their very absence should perhaps be recognised as their most vital characteristic, as a feature that must appeal to our twenty-first century.

In the case of later dramatists like Webster, Ford, Massinger and Brome, it is customary to signal their often obvious debt to earlier playwrights, whom they mention by name, whose work they cite and on which they model their own new plays. Introducing Richard Brome as a playwright whose topical comedy is politically committed rather than escapist, Heather Hirschfeld duly recognises Brome as the traditional 'underservant' to Jonson, but she also demonstrates how comedies like *The Northern Lasse* and *The Antipodes* are beholden to Shakespeare as well.

What emerges from this chronological panorama of early modern drama – with so many dramatists whose rivalry, collaboration, quotation, borrowing and imitation produced the plays that continue to fascinate playgoers and readers alike – is above all a sense of variety. Focusing on familiar and less familiar play-texts, these essays introduce a wide range of dramatic genres practised on the popular stage, including romantic comedy, citizen comedy and city comedy, tragedy, revenge tragedy, domestic tragedy, tragicomedy, as well as the English and Roman history play. Introducing Shakespeare, his fellow dramatists and their plays, these essays further convey an intriguing sense of emergent individuality, while more traditional guild-like forms of collaborative writing persist. In this way, they enhance our appreciation of the individual dramatists' contribution to the history of English drama, but also capture the cohesion and dynamics of the early modern stage.

In recent years, the popularity of Shakespeare has continued to grow, but so has our interest in the fellow dramatists. Theatres have come to pursue an ever more diverse early modern repertoire beyond the plays of Shakespeare, generating a body of productions with rich stage histories. In the essay that completes this collection, Elizabeth Schafer argues that even though we have recorded stage histories for a number of playwrights, there is still a real need for more performance-centred criticism in relation to most early modern plays. Writing such criticism, however, demands a proper sense of the historian's duties and responsibilities with respect to issues of selection and perspective. Schafer illustrates her argument with reference to the stage histories of familiar plays like Webster's *The Duchess of Malfi* and Jonson's *The Alchemist*, but also breaks a lance for the considerably less canonical, anonymous *Arden of Faversham* whose stage history is fraught with gender issues.

As they are performed with greater frequency, the texts of the plays by Shakespeare's colleagues have also become more widely available. Individual plays or thematic groupings of these plays are now available in well-known series and anthologies of English Renaissance drama. Gary Taylor and John Lavagnino's *Thomas Middleton: The Collected Works* (2007) has given a significant boost to the study of early modern dramatic authorship, individual as well as collaborative. Likewise David Bevington, Martin Butler and Ian Donaldson's new *Cambridge Edition of the Works of Ben Jonson* (2012) promises to transform the field: not simply with its seven volumes already available on the shelf, but also with the editorial team's development, currently in progress, of a digital environment, which will facilitate Jonsonian research worldwide in many ways. The internet is an ideal site for concentrating interest also on the less canonical playwrights of the early modern period, and the *Richard Brome Online* project hosted by the University of Sheffield is a case in point, with its laudable objective to cross-fertilise editorial and staging practices. The plays of Shakespeare and his fellow dramatists have never been more easily available than they are today, and opportunities to approach them have rarely been more diverse. Has there ever been a more opportune moment to study to them?

CHRONOLOGY OF THE LIFE AND WORK OF SHAKESPEARE AND CONTEMPORARY DRAMATISTS

This chronology lists selected key events both in the history of the English nation and its theatre, and in the lives of Shakespeare and the contemporary dramatists discussed in this collection of essays. Dating the plays is often necessarily approximate. Where possible, the dates given refer to the first performance or the composition of the play, rather than its publication. A more detailed listing is available in Alfred Harbage, *Annals of English Drama, 975–1700*, 3rd edition, revised by Sylvia S. Wagonheim (London and New York: Routledge, 1989). The dates for Shakespeare's works are based on the 'Canon and Chronology' section in Stanley Wells and Gary Taylor, with John Jowett and William Montgomery, *William Shakespeare: A Textual Companion* (Oxford: Clarendon Press, 1987).

1533	Birth of Queen Elizabeth I
1535	Execution of Sir Thomas More
1553	Death of Edward VI and accession of Mary I
c. 1554	John Lyly born
1558	Death of Mary I. Accession of Elizabeth I
	Robert Greene born
	Thomas Kyd born
	Thomas Lodge born
	George Peele born
c. 1559	George Chapman born
1560	Henry Chettle born
	Anthony Munday born
1563	Michael Drayton born

Kyd, *The Spanish Tragedy*

1588   Spanish Armada defeated

Marlowe, 2 *Tamburlaine the Great*

Lodge, *The Wounds of Civil War*

1589   Greene, *Friar Bacon and Friar Bungay*

Lyly, *Midas*

Peele, *The Battle of Alcazar*

c. 1590   Richard Brome born

1590   Lyly, *Love's Metamorphosis*

Greene and Lodge, *A Looking Glass for London and England*

Peele, *The Old Wives Tale*

1590–1   Shakespeare, *The Two Gentlemen of Verona*, *The Taming of the Shrew*

1591   Lyly, *Endymion*

Greene, *Orlando Furioso*

Anon., *Arden of Faversham*

Shakespeare, *The First Part of the Contention* (2 *Henry VI*), *Richard Duke of York* (3 *Henry VI*)

1592   Marlowe, *Doctor Faustus*

Marlowe, *Edward II*

Greene, *Summer's Last Will and Testament*

Shakespeare, 1 *Henry VI*, *Titus Andronicus*

Plague breaks out in London, closing the theatres for two years

Chettle publishes Greene's *Groats-worth of Wit bought with a Million of Repentance*, calling Shakespeare an 'upstart crow'

Greene dies

1592–3   Shakespeare, *Richard III* and *Venus and Adonis*

1593   Marlowe, *The Massacre at Paris*

Marlowe killed in Deptford

1600	Fortune theatre built
	Marston, *Antonio's Revenge*
	First composition of Anthony Munday and Henry Chettle's *Sir Thomas More*
1600–1	Shakespeare, *Hamlet* and *Twelfth Night*
1601	Jonson, *Poetaster*
	Nashe dies
1602	Shakespeare, *Troilus and Cressida*
1603	Queen Elizabeth dies and is succeeded by King James I and VI
	Lord Chamberlain's Men become the King's Men
	Shakespeare, *Measure for Measure*
	Heywood, *A Woman Killed with Kindness*
	Jonson's *Sejanus, His Fall* is published and lists Shakespeare as one of the 'principal tragedians'
	Marston, *The Malcontent*
1603–14	Shakespeare, *A Lover's Complaint*, *Sir Thomas More* and *Othello*
1604	Chapman, *Bussy D'Ambois*
	Dekker and Webster, *Westward Ho*
	Heywood, 1 *If You Know Not Me You Know Nobody*
	Elizabeth Cary, *The Tragedy of Mariam*
1604–5	Shakespeare, *All's Well that Ends Well*
1605	Shakespeare, *Timon of Athens*
	Chapman, Jonson and Marston, *Eastward Ho*
	Dekker and Webster, *Northward Ho*
	Heywood, 2 *If You Know Not Me You Know Nobody*
1605–6	Shakespeare, *King Lear*
1606	Shakespeare, *Macbeth* and *Antony and Cleopatra*
	Whitefriars theatre built
	Middleton, *The Revenger's Tragedy*

Middleton, *Michaelmas Term*

Middleton, *A Yorkshire Tragedy*

Lyly dies

1607   Shakespeare, *Pericles*

Heywood, *The Rape of Lucrece*

Beaumont, *The Knight of the Burning Pestle*

Chettle dies

1608   King's Men lease Blackfriars theatre

Shakespeare, *Coriolanus*

Fletcher, *The Faithful Shepherdess*

Chapman, *The Conspiracy and Tragedy of Byron*

1609   Cockpit theatre built

Beaumont and Fletcher, *Philaster, or Love Lies a-Bleeding*

Shakespeare, *The Winter's Tale*

Shakespeare's *Sonnets* published

1610   Beaumont and Fletcher, *The Maid's Tragedy*

Chapman, *The Revenge of Bussy D'Ambois*

Shakespeare, *Cymbeline*

1611   Jonson, *Catiline, His Conspiracy*

Middleton, *The Second Maiden's Tragedy*

Shakespeare, *The Tempest*

1612   Webster, *The White Devil*

1613   The Globe on fire during a performance of Shakespeare's *Henry VIII (All is True)*

Middleton, *A Chaste Maid in Cheapside*

1613–14   Shakespeare and Fletcher, *The Two Noble Kinsmen*

1614   Second Globe built

Webster, *The Duchess of Malfi*

1616   Shakespeare dies

Beaumont dies

Jonson's *Works* published

I

ARTHUR F. KINNEY

John Lyly and the University Wits: George Peele, Robert Greene, Thomas Lodge and Thomas Nashe

Figures of rhetoric – figures of speech

Today John Lyly is the most neglected, underappreciated and misunderstood Elizabethan playwright. Lyly's understanding of the world, and of language, came out of his own personal heritage which he honoured throughout his uneven career. He was the grandson of William Lyly (also spelled as Lily and Lilye), High Master of St Paul's School and, with John Colet, author of the grammar school Latin text that was required at all Elizabethan schools and that survived as the fundamental Latin text well into the nineteenth century; the two men added 'Godly Lessons for Chyldren' which began with the central theme of all of John Lyly's writings: 'It is the fyrst poynte of wysedome, to know thy self.'[1] William Lyly was a member of the leading circle of humanists, including Erasmus and Thomas More, and his son – John's father – was in turn a tutor in Canterbury or at the Queen's School connected to the cathedral. John Lyly (c. 1554–1606) followed his grandfather to Magdalen College, Oxford, where he stayed an extra two years hoping for a teaching post there or for preferment under William Cecil, Lord Burghley. Instead, Burghley got him a position as secretary to his son-in-law, Edward de Vere, Earl of Oxford.

Humanism taught Lyly to love the classics. His first play, *Campaspe* (1583) came from Pliny and Plutarch's *Life of Alexander*; it was phenomenally successful, going through three editions in a single year. His second play, *Sappho and Phao*, appeared two months later; it drew on Aelian and Ovid and immediately went through two editions. Lyly's mode of writing, too – what his editor Carter A. Daniel calls 'the ornately symmetrical prose style filled with fantastic similes and constructed in rhythmic swirls of alliteration and antithesis'[2] – is also classical. Lyly imported into humanist work the antique rhetorical use of *isocolon* (successive phrases or clauses of the same approximate length), *parison* (parallel placement of grammatical units), and *paramoion* (similar sound in parallel members including alliteration but also assonance, consonance, and rhyme).[3] To these patterns of sound, G. K. Hunter has added proverbs, rhetorical questions and extended similes drawn from genuine, fantastic, traditional or invented natural history.[4] For Greek and Roman writers, as for George Puttenham in *The Arte of English Poesie* in 1589, these were known as *schemes*, figures of rhetoric. But that observation is only partially true; Lyly was just as interested in figures of thought, or *tropes*. His language is intellectually inquisitive and playful, complex and often intense. Jonas A. Barish has noted this: 'By using the anti-thetic pair "more bolde then wise" instead of the simple adverb "boldly," Lyly underscores the fact that Callimachus [in the formative *Euphues*] might have behaved otherwise than he did, that the situation contained equivocal possibilities.'[5]

Two innovations that Lyly bequeathed to his generation of playwrights and those who followed them were romantic love as the proper subject for secular comedy, and revelations through the art of rhetoric of the exercise of the mind, using examples from the natural world to reveal an individual consciousness. This is a subtle but pervasive matter. There are few outright villains in Lylian drama; the struggle is an interior one. While his language may seem at first excessive, its effects are in fact unspoken. He works not so much through exposure as through revelation, and the insights are shared, often at the same moment, by the actor and the audience. With explicit metaphors, his meaning is nevertheless nuanced. Robert Y. Turner has put this another way: 'his experiments with dialogue, guided by his sense of the limitations of language, put on stage probably for the first time conversa-tions not about love but conversations that dramatize love.'[6] The famous, many-layered dialogue between Phillida and Gallathea, for instance, builds on the love each of the women, disguised as men, have for each other, love they both want to confess and dare not reveal; it is an extraordinary and unprecedented situation that Shakespeare will imitate both in *As You Like It* and *Twelfth Night* (*Gallathea*, ed. Daniel, 125–6). Just as the undisclosed connections between series of thoughts or examples harbours a telling sig-nificance, so the asides – foreshortened, truncated soliloquies – provide what must be concealed. It is a dialogue ripe with inhibitions in which spontan-eous hypotheses stand in for silenced desires.

In his constant search for figures of speech which can convey figures of thought, Lyly, in his plays, keeps returning to the inhibited, employing lan-guage to show how language is avoided and not used. In *Campaspe*, all three main characters – Campaspe, Apelles and Alexander – share a fear of spoken disclosure. Sappho and Phao, the princess and the ferryman, are silenced by their distance in rank. In *Mother Bombie*, the prohibition of love between Maestius and Serena, falsely thinking themselves to be brother and sister, is what confounds and resolves the main plot. In each case, figures of thought reveal the sharp boundaries of figures of speech while figures of speech search for tactics that can relay figures of thought in unending patterns of schemes and tropes.

Lyly applied his innovative use of classical rhetoric to plots taken from the classical writers and cast them with classical heroes and pagan gods. This humanist compound inspired Lyly's innovations that broke Renaissance drama from earlier church drama, spectacular pageants and Lord Mayor shows and gave it inventive form and purpose that would last, in developing configurations, to the Restoration. And always there was the grounding in language. 'Whatever drawbacks of his method', Barish writes,

> Lyly effected a revolution in the language of comedy as significant as Marlowe's was for tragedy. He invented, virtually single-handed, a viable comic prose for the English stage, something which could replace the clumsy, uncertain medium of Gascoigne's *Supposes*, the shambling invertebrate language of *The Famous Victories of Henry V*, and the varieties of broken-down tumbling verse that did duty for prose in the popular theatre. For the first time, dramatic prose rested on an adequate structural foundation; for the first time, it was able to support an intricate plot without confusion and without prolixity.[7]

Lyly brought to life a classical heritage and a classical language turned into English. And he provided comedy with a rich new sense of epistemology and psychology without sacrificing playfulness and wit.

Boys' companies

In his *Discourse of English Poetrie* (1586), William Webbe writes that 'I think there is none that will gainsay, but Master *Iohn Lilly* hath deserued moste highe commendations, as he which hath stept one steppe further therein that any either before or since.' Such bold innovations were made in spite of, or because, Lyly wrote seven and perhaps all eight of his plays not for an adult company but for the boys' companies of St Paul's and the Chapel Royal.[8] Initially writing several comedies for court performance by the company of his benefactor Edward de Vere (the so-called 'Oxford Boys'), Lyly was later to provide plays for the Boys of St Paul's. With the need to secure an income, they also gave public performances, and Lyly is likely to have profited as well. The companies he wrote for consisted of choirboys – often, in his plays, given to song – and they must have continued their musicality in the sound patterns and repetitive rhythms of his euphuistic language. His audiences came to *hear* his plays; as he remarks in the Epilogue to *Campaspe* pronounced at Blackfriars, 'We hope in the ears where our travails be lodged no carping shall harbour [our] tongues' and in the Epilogue delivered at court, before the Queen, he hoped for appreciation of 'sweet notes'.[9] He was keenly aware of performance. But he was also keenly aware of spectacle. Apelles falling in love while painting the portrait of Campaspe in the play named for her led to his witnessing a beauty that also captivated Alexander, King of Macedon, and their competition for her – the king too high in rank; the painter consumed with art – is the situation unfolding before the sceptic philosopher Diogenes. The play was set forth visibly by the staging, with Apelles' studio at one end, and Diogenes' tub at the other. At the conclusion, it is royalty that is unfit for a commoner; social hierarchy is upheld. Alexander looks elsewhere for companionship: 'Diogenes, I will have thy cabin removed nearer to my court, because I will be a philosopher.' But Diogenes also knows his place: 'And when you have done so I pray you remove your court further from my cabin, because I will not be a courtier' (5.4.78–83).

'Our intent', Lyly writes for the Prologue of *Sappho and Phao* at the Blackfriars, 'was at this time to move inward delight, not outward lightness, and to breed (if it might be) soft smiling, not loud laughing, knowing it to the wise to be as great pleasure to hear counsel mixed with wit as to the foolish to have sport mingled with rudeness.'[10] The play is designed to be intellectually amusing and enlightening, without the satire and scorn portrayed in *Campaspe*, although now humans like Sappho and Phao will mingle with gods like Venus and Cupid. This intermingling of humanity and the gods in *Sappho and Phao* is prolegomenon to *Endymion, The Man in the Moon* (1591), Lyly's best known play. This 'comedy of ideas' concerns Endymion's love for Cynthia, the moon.[11] As he remarks to his close friend,

> I find, Eumenides, in all things both variety to content and satiety to glut, saving only my affections, which are so stayed, and withal so stately, that I can neither satisfy my heart with love nor mine eyes with wonder. My thoughts, Eumenides, are stitched to the stars, which, being as high as I can see, thou mayest imagine how much higher they are than I can reach.[12]

Eumenides finds this 'mad' (1.1.20), idolatrous (78), blasphemous (78), 'bewitched' (88), 'the crazed rhetoric of a lunatic'.[13] But the 'mangled and disordered mind' (2.1.27) of Endymion enhances the well-known story from Ovid or the lesser-known shepherd Endymion in Pliny's *Natural History* by acknowledging his capacity for wonder and his interest in both the physical and the metaphysical; it has been read as a study in Neoplatonism or as a tribute to Elizabeth I. Such reactions, however, fail to account for Lyly's mastery in a network of connections and reflections, dramatised in four parallel and corresponding plots. As Daniel has noted, the crossings and re-crossings of these four stories give *Endimion* a unity of plot unlike anything else in Lyly's plays. The magic spell cast upon Endimion, for example, is conceived by Tellus [his earthly lover] (level 3) and executed by the old enchantress Dipsas (level 4); later Eumenides (level 2) learns from Dipsas's husband Geron that the spell can be broken by a kiss from Cynthia (level 1).[14]

Such acts, all motivated by love, are further complicated by Eumenides' loyal friendship to Endymion and parodied by the braggart soldier Sir Tophas:

> love hath, as it were, milked by thoughts and drained from my heart the very substance of my accustomed courage. It worketh in my head like new wine, so as I must hoop my sconce with iron, lest my head break and so I bewray my brains. But I pray thee, first discover me in all parts, that I may be like a lover, and then will I sigh and die. Take my gun, and give me a gown. *Cedant arma togae.* (3.3.23–30)[15]

Shakespeare will find in Sir Tophas the suggestion for Don Adriano de Armado in *Love's Labour's Lost* and the lunary bank on which Endymion sleeps under the spell of Dipsas a source for *A Midsummer Night's Dream*, but Lyly introduces something else Shakespeare will take up: before the spell is broken by Corsites, Endymion 'hath been cast into a deep sleep almost these twenty years' according to Eumenides (3.4.18–19) and then, later, 'Thou hast slept forty years' (5.1.56) while the rest of the play follows a normal time scheme. It is the first use in English drama of double time that will reappear later in *Romeo and Juliet* and *Othello*.

Lyly's finest play is *Gallathea* (1588), and in its experiments with gender the most influential. It is one of the first English comedies making use of disguise – here boys playing girls playing boys. Like *As You Like It*, it retreats from the court to the pastoral. Like *Twelfth Night*, its plot is a response to the dangers of the sea. It concludes, like *The Taming of the Shrew* and *The Winter's Tale*, with magical transformations. Gallathea and Phillida are disguised by their fathers to protect them from being made virginal sacrifices; but the play orchestrates this situation by Cupid's disguise to gain admission to Diana's nymphs and Neptune disguises himself as a shepherd to 'mark all, and in the end will mar all'; 'destiny cannot be prevented by craft', he later adds.[16]

Once again, Lyly manages four distinct groups – gods, parents, lovers, and commoners – and integrates the plots of the two women disguised as boys, boys whose flight to the woods is the result of a shipwreck, Neptune's ritual and Cupid's scheme. The incredibility of Neptune and Cupid assuming human form is reversed by the alchemist, the astronomer and the cozener who con Rafe, Robin and Dick. Their comic exploits, alongside Cupid's

Puck-like tricks, help make the anticipation of Agar's savagery and the anxiety of Phillida and Gallathea bearable. Lyly's modulated figures of speech reverberate in his figures of thought. His final innovation is the play's incompleteness. Just as, later, it is not clear what interpretations Horatio will give to Hamlet's story or Lodovico to Othello's (if he ever tells one), so here it is unknown which disguised boy is transformed into a girl. Lyly's earlier experiments required his audience to interpret his prologues, plays and epilogues; now he asks them to complete the story as well.

Midas (?1589) displays Lyly's rare mastery of plot construction. The work is taken from two separate tales in Ovid's *Metamorphoses* XI – Midas' decision to choose the power to turn everything into gold when offered three possibilities by Martius (war and control), Mellacrites (wealth) and Eristus (love), and his judgement of a music contest between Pan and Apollo when, erroneously choosing Pan, he is awarded with the ears of an ass – and, employing sequential references, parallel themes and cross-cutting, brings the two disparate stories into a single cohesive narrative. The underlying form, drawing on the studies of the humanist classroom, is the debate, and at those pageant-like moments when all action is suspended for dialogue, his work looks forward to the court masque. Critics commonly assert that the play takes on more force as a guarded analogy between Midas and the aggressive Philip II of Spain whose Armada had only just been defeated by the English.

A Pleasant Conceited Comedy Called Mother Bombie (1588–91) is named for a minor character, a prophetess who is an outgrowth of Sibylla in *Sappho and Phao*, but the play, drawing on Plautus and foreshadowing *The Comedy of Errors*, has four fathers – Memphio and Stellio, wealthy landowners, and Prisius and Sperantus, two men of modest means – seeking marriage partners for their children. What is at stake is money – the fortunes of the children are determined by the fortunes of the families. 'Marriage among them', Candius, Sperantus' son, remarks, 'is become a market.'[17] T. W. Baldwin has seen the farcical placement of fathers and children as both balanced and contrasting.[18]

Love's Metamorphosis: A Witty and Courtly Pastoral (1595) is Lyly's last play and his shortest (1,150 lines) with the fewest characters (fifteen) in the fewest scenes (eleven). It now seems a deliberate signature piece, bringing together all his interests and contributions to Elizabethan drama: a love comedy mixing gods and humans in parallel situations that is dense, choric, and so transparent, memorably unfolding in pattern, structure and tone that give even its moral candour a haunting sense of beauty: 'it surely must be', Daniel judges, 'one of the most unjustly neglected plays in English literature'.[19] The play appeals to sight and to sound, to spectacle and to language, from the moment Ceres' sacred tree speaks in Fidelia's voice to the moment her three nymphs are transformed into their symbolic counterparts. Such magical moments, in this work, are psychologically sound and intellectually suggestive.

University Wits

Lyly's sense of classical learning, already popularised in court performances and public pageantry such as the Lord Mayor shows, inspired him to write for a career. He was by far the most successful of the Oxford and Cambridge graduates who, in the 1580s, shared his ambition, a group now labelled the 'University Wits'. According to G. K. Hunter, they

> revolutionized Elizabethan popular literature by bringing to its aid interests and expectations that had not previously been seen to be relevant, but which were close enough to the tradition to combine with it and create new wholes. The position of the university wits, caught between a lively vernacular culture that could be despised intellectually but not disregarded economically, and a humanist ideal of literary excellence that remained obstinately an ideal rather than a reality – this position is reflected in their lives, humble in origin and straitened in circumstances, continuously involved in the vernacular realities of earning, and not earning, a living. But at the same time they remained caught intellectually by the dream of the poet as a god on earth, the dream of eloquence as the key to power, the dream of a civilization in which the learning was the heart of kingship.[20]

After Lyly, the best of these University Wits writing drama was George Peele, the son of the clerk and teacher at Christ's Hospital, London, and the author of two works on bookkeeping, who as a student first at Broadgates Hall (now Pembroke College), Oxford, until he moved across the street to Christ Church, translated Euripides' *Iphigenia* plays from Greek, earning the praise of the Latin scholar William Gager. He took his BA in 1577 and his MA two years later. In 1589, Thomas Nashe would write of Peele in a letter 'To the Gentlemen of Both Vniuersities' prefacing Robert Greene's *Menaphon* (1589) that 'I dare commend him vnto all that know him, as the chiefe supporter of pleasance now liuing, the *Atlas* of Poetrie, and *primus verborum artifex*: whose first increase, of the arraignement of *Paris*, might pleade to your opinion, his pregnant dexteritie of wit, manifold varitie of inuention, wherein (*me iudice*) hee goeth a step beyond all that write' (sig. B3v).

Peele's best work is *The Old Wives Tale*, probably written in 1591, about the time he and Shakespeare were composing *Titus Andronicus*. Its plot construction is stunning, the most ingenious of all plays of the English Renaissance, although, as A. R. Braunmuller writes, 'In style, subject matter, construction, and even in its very short length, the play seems to be utterly *sui generis*'.[21] The work begins when three pages – Anticke, Frolicke and Fantasticke – are lost in the woods until there appears out of the blackness the blacksmith Clunch who invites them to spend the night at his cottage, where his wife Madge offers them cheese and pudding and then, at their request, offers 'to drive away the time with an old wives winters tale', such as Mamillius will request in Shakespeare's late romance.[22] Madge brings a story of a conjuror who turned himself into a dragon and abducted a fair daughter, but here she falters: she was the daughter of 'a King, or a Lord, or a Duke',[23] she is unsure which. The girl's two brothers go to seek her – and at this point, the two brothers come on stage and take over the story themselves. They introduce an old man who takes over the story himself. And so begins a plot in which nine successive stories unfold from their individual precedents, adding new characters, new plot twists and moments of magic and spectacle until the end, when, in reverse order, the scenes pile up to make a whole narrative: the daughter is sought by both her brothers and Eumenides, the 'Wandering Knight' who is her lover,[24] and finally rescued. The separate episodes turn out to be interlocking parts of the same winter's tale. But during the intervening period, time itself is interrupted and fragmented, uprooting customary linearity, turning fluid. Moreover, the present narrators recall individual portions of the past in their present retelling which involve unrealistic spectacles (a man changes nightly into a bear; two furies appear out of the conjuror's cell; two heads are pulled out of a well), and various prophecies come true, mixing past, present and future, suspending chronology. All of life's reference points are removed, unmooring events to give the play an increasing magicality. The presentation ends when Madge, who has fallen asleep in the course of it, awakes and offers her departing guests some bread and cheese. Along the way all forms of popular writing – romance, folktale, chivalric adventure, ghost story, witchcraft, pageantry and, most of all drama itself – are parodied and particular works, like the anonymous play *Mucedorus*, are subjects of burlesque. No other English Renaissance play is so complex or asks so much of its audience, while at the same time providing frequent intervals of song and dance that give playgoers time for reflection.

Peele's first play, *The Araygnement of Paris* (1584), taken from Ovid, reaches a level of poetic mastery he was not to match again. In this his most Lylian work, the theme is love and loyalty, bringing together on stage Olympic and country gods and pastoral characters. The play concerns Paris' award of a golden apple to Venus (love) as the most beautiful goddess rather than to Juno (majesty) or to Athena (wisdom) and begins with a prologue by Ate (discord) who likens Paris' disastrous choice to 'the Tragedie of

Troie'.[25] The remarkable centrepiece is '*Paris oration to the Councell of the gods*' (III, 102–4) which Braunmuller demonstrates is a classical declamation complimenting the court, offering self-deprecation, promising brevity, admitting the deed but then excusing himself, suggesting others might do the same, rejecting partiality, making concessions and offering extenuating arguments.[26] Asked to tell a story, he tells one much as Othello will before the Venetian senate:

> And thus, thryse reverend, have I tolde my tale,
> And crave the torment of my guiltless soule
> To be measured by my faultles thought.
> If warlicke Pallas, or the queene of heaven
> Sue to reverse my sentence by appeale,
> Be it as please your majesties devine,
> The wronge, the hurte not mine, if anie be,
> But hers whose beauty claymed the prize of me. (III, 104)

Venus surrenders the apple to Diana who in turn awards it to Queen Elizabeth:

> This Paragon, this onely this is shee,
> In whom do meete so manie gifts in one,
> On whom our countrie gods so often gaze,
> In honour of whose name the Muses singe. (III, 111–12)

The Children of the Chapel, in performing this play with its songs and several dumb shows, must have been at court in the Queen's presence.

Peele's history play *The Battle of Alcazar* (?1589) comes down to us in a mutilated text that introduces, for the first time in English drama, a Presenter to open each act, anticipatory of the Choruses in Shakespeare's *Henry IV, Part Two* and especially *Henry V*. The play traces Muly Mahamet's bloody rise to the crown beginning with a dumb show in which two murderers smother the young prince in bed and then strangle their uncle, the staging of such crimes looking forward to events in *Richard III* and to the dumb show in *Hamlet*, and concluding with the title battle bringing down Sebastian, King of Portugal; Abdelmelec, King of Morocco; and his nephew, Muly Mahamet, the Moor. Following Lyly's practice of subplots, the English gentleman adventurer Thomas Stukeley, having aborted a papal mission to fight in Ireland in order to join a Portuguese expedition to Africa, is stabbed by an unidentified Italian and 'Dies in these desert fields of Africa' (5.1.122). Sebastian fails to enlist the aid of King Philip of Spain in the battle with the Moors. Shakespeare may also have recalled Muly Mahamet's final lines – 'A horse, a horse, a villain, a horse / That I may take the river straight and fly' (5.1.96–7) – when writing *Richard III*.

The most prolific of the University Wits was Robert Greene (1558–93): in his thirty-five years, he produced an unusually large number of romances and pamphlets, four single-authored plays, and one in collaboration with Thomas Lodge. He was born in Norwich where he attended grammar school before entering Corpus Christi College, Cambridge, as a sizar in 1573; at Michaelmas term 1575 he transferred to St John's College, Cambridge, where he was awarded a BA in 1580, followed by an MA from Clare Hall, Cambridge, in 1583 and an MA from Oxford in 1588. He proudly put on the title-pages of his publications 'Master of Arts in both universities'. His best-known play is *The Honorary History of Friar Bacon and Friar Bungay* which brings together the historic Roger Bacon, a thirteenth-century Oxford philosopher and alchemist whose name was connected with magic and heresy, and the wholly imaginary Friar Bungay, an underplot (following Lyly) with an overplot about the historic Edward, Prince of Wales, son of Henry III, and the wholly imaginary fair Margaret of Fressingfield, a country milkmaid and daughter of the Keeper of Fressingfield, Suffolk. The two narratives are stitched together as studies in the vanity of human wishes, of human presumption, and of intolerance with patient understanding.

In his visit to England, Emperor Frederick of Germany praises Oxford to King Henry:

> The town gorgeous, with high-built colleges,
> And scholars seemly in their grave attire,
> Learnèd in searching principles of art.[27]

This follows (as with Lyly) a similar, echoing observation by Edward Lacy, Earl of Lincoln, Prince Edward's friend who praises the Surrey landscape:

> Alate we ran the deer, and through the launds
> Stripped with our nags the lofty frolic bucks
> That scudded 'fore the teasers like the wind,
> Ne'er was the deer of merry Fressingfield
> So lustily pulled down by jolly mates,
> Nor shared by the farmers such fat venison,
> So frankly dealt, this hundred years before;
> Nor have I seen my lord more frolic in the chase. (scene 1, 3–10)

This is a pastoral land of peace, plenty, and community. When the Prince asks Lacy to court Margaret for him, he turns euphuistic when writing to her:

> The blooms of the almond tree grow in the night and vanish in a morn; the flies hemerae, fair Peggy, take life with the sun and die with the dew; fancy, that slippeth in with a gaze, goeth out with a wink; and too timely loves have ever the shortest length. I write this as thy grief and my folly. (scene 10, 123–8)

Lacy pretends to be Edward, acting as his proxy, but when the Prince is betrothed to Elinor of Castile, the distressed Margaret puts on nun's clothing and prepares to enter a convent until Edward confesses the disguise, and she sheds her Lylian 'metamorphosis' (scene 14, 66). Meantime, Friar Bacon's overreaching is intellectual, not social. He dabbles in black magic:

> I have framed out a monstrous head of brass,
> That, by the enchanting forces of the devil,
> Shall tell out strange and uncouth aphorisms,
> And girt fair England with a wall of brass. (scene 11, 17–20)

But the brass head speaks while Bacon is sleeping and his other accomplishment, a magical perspective glass, displays to two sons their fathers murdering each other and they kill each other in response. Selfish overreaching punishes Bacon, while Friar Bungay is reduced to conjuring a tree which is destroyed by a dragon, the sort of spectacle Lyly employed and Peele uses in *The Old Wives Tale*.

Noteworthy, too, is Greene's *Historie of Orlando Fvrioso, One of the Twelve Peeres of France* (1592), based on Ariosto's epic, and concentrating on Orlando's madness when the poems which Sacrepant pins on trees convince him of the infidelity of a loyal Angelica:

> For Sacrepant must haue Angelica,
> And with her Sacrepant must haue the Crowne:
> By hooke or crooke I must and will haue both.[28]

In his fits of insanity, Orlando mistakes a fiddle for a sword and rips off a man's leg for a club. But this is Greene's most consistently entertaining play. It ends happily with the reunion of Orlando and Angelica, and Sacrepant, stricken with shame – 'O, thats the sting that pricks my conscience!' (5.1.1255) – confesses to Orlando:

> I tel thee, knight, for thou doest seeme no lesse,
> That I ingraude the rundelaies on the trees,
> And hung the schedules of poore Medors loue,
> Intending so to breed debate
> Between Orlando and Angelica:
> O, thus I wrongd Orlando and Angelica! (5.1.1257–62)

As hyperbolic now as Orlando has been – 'The highest mountaines swimme in streames of bloud' (5.1.1289) – he takes his own life. Throughout *Orlando Fvrioso*, Greene creates the kind of orderly world transformed into madness that will later characterise *A Midsummer Night's Dream*.

Greene also collaborated with Thomas Lodge on *A Looking Glasse for London and England*, the only extant play by two of the University Wits.[29]

The play was exceptionally popular; it played four times at the Rose theatre in 1592 and went through five editions by 1594. Following Lyly's examples, the play establishes a parallel between the sin and corruption of biblical Nineveh and late sixteenth-century London but avoids censorship by enacting the earlier reign of Rasni and only prophesying Elizabethan London through predictions of Oseas (Hosea) and, later, Jonah. Both speak from a higher stage looking on the action below. Oseas warns,

> Looke, London, look, with inward eies behold,
> What lessons the euents do here vnfold.
> Sinne growne to pride, to misery is thrall;
> The warning bell is rung, beware to fall.
> Ye worldy men whom wealth doth lift on hie,
> Beware and feare, for worldly men must die.[30]

There are memorable moments of Lylian spectacle when Jonah is thrown out of the whale, for example (p. 191); or a tree rises from the trap (p. 150); or fire from below swallows Radagon, counsellor to Rasni, King of Nineveh (p. 181); or, at the close, he and his nobles appear penitent in sackcloth and ashes: 'I haue vpholden incest, rape, and spoyle, / 'Tis I that wrought the sinne, must weepe the sinne' (p. 220). Occasionally the biblical persons call on pagan gods, as Lyly's characters do (p. 130); occasionally, the language is Lylian: 'Lockt are the Iems of ioy in dens of death' (p. 152). Lodge is thought to have supplied only the scenes of biblical usurers, which closely follow his earlier work entitled *An Alarvm against Vsurers* (1584) as their practices are revealed by their victims. Thus in *A Looking Glasse*,

> [I pray you] sir consider that my losse was great by the [commoditie I took]e vp, you knowe sir I borrowed of you fortie [pounds, whereof] I had ten pounds in money, and thirty pounds [in Lute strings], which when I came to sell againe, I could get [but fiue] pounds for them, so had I sir but fifteene poundes for [my fortie:] In consideration of this ill bargaine, I pray sir [giue me a] month longer. (pp. 140–1)

Ionas concludes the play relating the 'Corruption, whordome, drunkennesse, and pride' of the biblical past to the present time of the audience, 'Repent O London' (p. 232), resting the play, as Lyly did, with the playgoers.

Thomas Lodge (1558–1625) was the son of an alderman and Lord Mayor of London who was a member of the Grocers' Company and the Muscovy Company. The son studied at the Merchant Taylors' School, London, before earning a BA in the Catholic-leaning Trinity College, Oxford, around 1573, after which he studied law at Lincoln's Inn and, decades later, medicine in Avignon. He died of the plague which he contracted when he refused to leave his patients during the epidemic in London. His single-authored play,

The Wounds of Civil War: The Most Lamentable and True Tragedies of Marius and Scilla (c. 1586), is a humanist product, the first English play based on classical history; his source was *Appian's History of Rome*, translated by W. B. in 1578, and Plutarch's *Life of Marius*.

The play begins when the aristocratic Scilla is unexpectedly appointed general rather than the democratic Marius in the Mithridatic War. Both rivals are bloodthirsty. Early on Scilla remarks that those

> whose presentations reign on earth,
> This Capitol wherein your glories shine
> Was ne'er so press'd and throng'd with scarlet gowns
> As Rome shall be with heaps of slaughter'd souls
> Before that Scilla yield his titles up. (1.1.213–17)

Later, when Marius is victorious on the battlefield, he tells his men, 'Go, soldiers, seek out Bebius and his friends, Atilius, Numitorius, and the rest: Cut off their heads, for they did cross me once' (4.1.55–7). Both fight for the honour of Rome. Marius finds this the basis for leading Roman forces (1.1.134–7); for Scilla, it is also a matter of competition: 'Senators, I hammer in my head / With every thought of honour some revenge' (2.1.187–8). Both leaders call on fortune, seen both as fate and as a reward from the gods. Marius, capturing Scilla's wife and daughter, releases them and, in the end, takes his life. Scilla is more fortunate. Early in the play, Granius advises him, 'Scilla, my years hath taught me to discern / Betwixt ambitious pride and princely zeal' (2.1.81–2). Outliving Marius, he tells his wife:

> Cornelia, man hath power by some instinct
> And gracious resolution of the stars
> To conquer kingdoms, not to master fate;
> For when the course of mortal life is run,
> Then Clotho ends the web her sister spun. (5.5.339–43)

But fortune warns both men when their lives are closing in, Marius through 'Seven mighty eagles' (3.2.99–103; 4.2.183) while the spirit of Genius addresses Scilla (5.5.301–8). Despite the alternation of victory in their rivalry, the play builds on parallelisms and correspondences much as Lyly had and, like Lyly, explores the ways in which differing perspectives on events can be justified.

The last of the University Wits, Thomas Nashe (1567–?1601), brought his unabashedly sharp social satire and his enormous rhetorical and lexical energy to drama. His boyhood was spent in East Anglia – Lowestoft and West Harling, Norfolk – before matriculating as a sizar of St John's College, Cambridge, in 1582. Two years later the university appointed him a scholar of the Lady Margaret Foundation. He received his BA in

1586 and stayed on until moving permanently to London in early autumn 1588. He has been given credit for eight plays (along with a novel and many pamphlets), including the ill-fated *Isle of Dogs* in collaboration with Ben Jonson, called in by the authorities and causing him to flee temporarily to Yarmouth. His only extant drama is *A Pleasante Comedie, called Summer's last will and Testament* (?1592; published 1600), an occasional work performed in 1592 in the Great Hall of Archbishop Whitgift's palace at Croydon.

The Presenter, who also delivers a long prologue, is Will Summer, the historic jester at the court of Henry VIII; his entertainment of the seasons – ''tis no Play neyther, but a sheew'[31] – is a double pun on *summer* sustained throughout. It provides a bifocal perspective on the Henrican years now irrevocably dead and gone and the summer season now dying, while keeping alive on the margins the threatening plague that caused people to gather at Croydon. This is not merely allusion. 'What can be made of a Summers last will & Testament?' Will asks and answers:

> Forsooth, because the plague raignes in most places in this latter end of summer, Summer must come in sicke: he must call his officers to account, yeeld his throne to Autumne, make Winter his Executour, and tittle tattle Tom boy: God giue you a good night in Watling street.[32]

What follows is a series of pageant-like episodes that veer between literary and social satire, with thoughts and memories of the plague making life fragile despite Will's robustness, and prepare for Winter's diatribe which makes the ideals, practices and achievements of humanism – of education itself – tendentious and fragile, too. Summer first calls on Ver, or Spring, who brings in the hobby-horse and Morris dancers as his accomplishments before delivering a sophistic sermon on improvidence, mocking Lyly's style with his use of parison, repetition and rhetorical questions. Orion follows with a mock encomium on dogs taken from Sextus Empiricus, a popular university text. Harvest appears as a yeoman farmer and soldier, one who is reliable, earnest and self-taught, in contrast to Bacchus who, looking forward to Sir Toby Belch, quotes Plato and Aristotle in justification of drinking.

Summer decides, amidst such noise, to make Autumn his executor and heir before Winter, but Winter objects:

> He and the spring are schollers fauourites.
> What schollers are, what thriftles kind of men,
> Your selfe be iudge. (III, 273)

His rancour seems unstoppable: 'Poets, which, for a meales meat or two, / Would promise monarchs immortalitie' (III, 273):

Young men, yong boyes, beware of Schoolemasters,
They will infect you, marre you, bleare your eyes:
They seeke to lay the curse of God on you,
Namely, confusion of languages,
Wherewith those that the towre of *Babel* built
Accursed were in the worldes infancie,
Latin, it was the speech of Infidels.
Logique hath nought to say in a true cause.
Philosophie is curiositie:
And *Socrates* was therefore put to death,
Onely for he was a Philosopher:
Abhorre, contemne, despise these damned snares. (III, 279)

Summer rejects such sentiments: 'I haue attended thy inuectiue tale: / So much vntrueth wit neuer shadowed' (III, 280) and leaves his goods to Autumn, making Winter his executor. All this saddens Summer and he asks Will Summer for 'some dolefull ditty to the Lute' (III, 282). The song, now bringing death in the form of plague onto the stage, is the best of Nashe's writing:

Beauty is but a flowre,
Which wrinckles will deuoure,
Brightnesse falls from the ayre,
Queenes haue died yong and faire,
Dust hath closde Helens eye.
I am sick, I must dye,
Lord, haue mercy on vs. (III, 283)

For a full appreciation of the song it is vital, certainly, to recall that its last line is also the phrase required at the time to be put on doors of houses infected with plague. Winter's sons now appear – Christmas who is known for snow and ice; Back-winter (delayed winter) whose impudence forces Summer to imprison him. At the entertainment's end, Summer is carried off singing, but he sings of his own death, and the world's: '*Gone is our sport, fled is poore* Croydens *pleasure*' (III, 292). With Nashe, more than a decade on, Lyly's innovations in the drama are still at work but little of their gentle spirit remains.

No Shakespeare without Lyly

'Lyly enjoyed the high regard of his contemporaries – Jonson included him, alongside Chaucer, Spenser, Marlowe, Kyd, and Beaumont, in his poem in praise of Shakespeare – but even more because he exerted a major influence on Shakespeare's dramatic technique.'[33] Lyly introduced love as the appropriate concern of comedy – something Shakespeare would execute from *Two Gentlemen of Verona* to *Troilus and Cressida* and the late romances. He saw comedy based in the human shortcomings in self-knowledge – in ignorance, not innocence, as foreground in *Love's Labour's Lost, Much Ado About Nothing* and *All's Well that Ends Well*. He saw disguise as a means to self-knowledge, particularly gendered disguise as in *The Merchant of Venice, As You Like It, Twelfth Night* and *The Merry Wives of Windsor*. Lyly envisioned comedy based in family relationships, as Shakespeare would in *The Comedy of Errors, The Taming of the Shrew* and *A Midsummer Night's Dream*. He constructed comedies in deliberate patterns of groups of characters and locations, such as Venice and Belmont or inside and outside the walls of Troy; or as a journey as in *The Two Gentlemen of Verona* and *All's Well that Ends Well* or the romances; or by the groups of characters as in *A Midsummer Night's Dream* or *Twelfth Night*; and he further constructed plays by linking overplots with underplots as in *The Merchant of Venice* and *A Midsummer Night's Dream*. Lyly experimented with fixed stations contrasting on stage throughout a play, as in *The Comedy of Errors*. He introduced incomplete plots that Shakespeare would also use in *The Comedy of Errors* and *All's Well that Ends Well*.

There are more local connections as well. Take the single instance of *Endymion*. Endymion's bewitchment foreshadows Bottom. The obscene pun on 'Twit, twit' (3.4.145) by Sir Tophas is repeated by Winter at the close of *Love's Labour's Lost* (5.2.901). The watches in 3.2 of *Endymion* are refashioned by Dogberry and Verges in *Much Ado About Nothing* (4.2). When Endymion says to Cynthia, 'Silence, madam, consents. That is most true' (5.4.215) he anticipates Hermione in *The Winter's Tale* (5.3). No other Renaissance English playwright matches Lyly's pervasiveness in Shakespeare's work. Inhabiting a humanist legacy, Lyly created one of his own.

NOTES

1 William Lily and John Colet, *A Short Introduction of Grammar, 1549*, Sholar Press Facsimile 262 (Menston, UK: Scolar Press, 1970), sig. A2.
2 Carter A. Daniel, 'Introduction' to *The Plays of John Lyly* (Lewisburg, PA: Bucknell University Press, 1998), 11–24 at 11.
3 This was first pointed out by Morris William Croll in his edition of Lyly's *Euphues: The Anatomy of Wit & Euphues and His England*, ed. Morris William Croll and Henry Clemons (London, 1916), quoted by Peter Saccio, *The Court Comedies of John Lyly* (Princeton University Press, 1969), 40.
4 G. K. Hunter, *John Lyly: The Humanist as Courtier* (London: Routledge & Kegan Paul, 1962), 265.
5 Jonas A. Barish, 'The Prose Style of John Lyly', *English Literary History* 23 (1956), 14–35 at 18.

6 Robert Y. Turner, 'Some Dialogues of Love in Lyly's Comedies', *English Literary History* 29 (1962), 276–88 at 276.

7 Barish, 'Prose Style of John Lyly', 34.

8 For further information see also Michael Shapiro, 'Early (Pre-1590) Boy Companies and their Acting Venues', and Mary Bly, 'The Boy Companies, 1599–1613', in *The Oxford Handbook of Early Modern Theatre*, ed. Richard Dutton (Oxford University Press, 2009), 120–35 and 136–150 respectively.

9 John Lyly, *Campaspe*, ed. G. K. Hunter (Manchester University Press, 1991), 136, lines 3–4; 138, line 2.

10 John Lyly, *Sappho and Phao*, ed. David Bevington (Manchester University Press, 1991), 201, lines 5–11.

11 Joseph Houppert, *John Lyly* (Boston: Twayne Publishers, 1975), 94.

12 John Lyly, *Endymion*, ed. David Bevington (Manchester University Press, 1996), 1.1.1–7.

13 Michael Pincombe, *The Plays of John Lyly: Eros and Eliza* (Manchester University Press, 1996), 90.

14 *Plays of John Lyly*, ed. Daniel, 195.

15 'Let military give way to civilian' (Cicero, *De Officiis*, 1.xiii.77). Sir Tophas also parodies William Lily's *Grammar*.

16 *Gallathea*, in *Plays of John Lyly*, ed. Daniel, 119, 138.

17 *Mother Bombie*, in *Plays of John Lyly*, ed. Daniel, 248.

18 T. W. Baldwin, *Shakespeare's Five-Act Structure* (Urbana, IL: University of Illinois Press, 1947), 530–1.

19 Daniel, *Plays of John Lyly*, 314.

20 G. K. Hunter, *Lyly and Peele* (London: Longmans, Green & Co., 1968), 9.

21 A. R. Braunmuller, *George Peele* (Boston: Twayne Publishers, 1983), 46.

22 *The Old Wives Tale*, ed. Frank S. Hook, in *The Dramatic Works of George Peele* (New Haven: Yale University Press, 1970), III, 391.

23 *Old Wives Tale*, ed. Hook, III, 391.

24 *Old Wives Tale*, ed. Hook, III, 402ff.

25 *The Araygnment of Paris*, ed. R. Mark Benbow, in *Dramatic Works*, III, 65.

26 Braunmuller, *George Peele*, 40.

27 Robert Greene, *Friar Bacon and Friar Bungay*, ed. David Bevington and Eric Rasmussen in *English Renaissance Drama: A Norton Anthology*, ed. David Bevington, Lars Engle, Katharine Eisaman Maus and Eric Rasmussen (New York: W. W. Norton & Co., 2002), scene 9, 5–7.

28 *Orlando Furioso*, *The Plays and Poems of Robert Greene*, ed. J. Churton Collins, 2 vols. (Oxford: Clarendon Press, 1905), I, 1.1.240–2.

29 A second collaboration is that of Thomas Nashe who in 1596 supplied additions to *Dido, Queene of Carthage* by Christopher Marlowe (1564–93), a graduate of King's School, Canterbury (attached to the cathedral) and in attendance at Christ's College, Cambridge. He is the one University Wit treated elsewhere in this volume. See Chapter 3, pp. 34–53.

30 Thomas Lodge and Robert Greene, *A Looking Glasse for London and England*, ed. George Alan Clugston (New York: Garland Publishing, 1980), 206.

31 Thomas Lodge, *The Wounds of Civil War*, ed. Joseph Houppert (Lincoln, NE: University of Nebraska Press, 1969), 12–13.

32 Thomas Nashe, *A Pleasant Comedie, called Summers last will and Testament* in *The Works of Thomas Nashe*, ed. Ronald B. McKerrow, 5 vols. (Oxford: Basil Blackwell, 1958), III, 235.

33 Daniel, *Plays of John Lyly*, 11.

Further reading

Ardolino, Frank, 'The Protestant Context of George Peele's "Pleasant Conceited" *Old Wives Tale*.' *Medieval and Renaissance Drama in England* 18 (2005), 146–65.

Ashley, L. R. N., *George Peele*. New York: Twayne, 1970.

Cartwright, Kent, 'The Confusions of *Gallathea*: John Lyly as Popular Dramatist.' *Comparative Drama* 32:2 (1998), 207–30.

Connolly, Annaliese, '"O Unquenchable Thirst of Gold": Lyly's *Midas* and the English Quest for Empire.' *Early Modern Literary Studies* 9 (2002), available online at http://extra.shu.ac.uk/emls/08–2/conngold.html.

Dooley, Mark, 'Inversion, Metamorphosis, and Sexual Difference: Female Same-Sex Desire in Ovid and Lyly', in *Ovid and the Renaissance Body*, ed. Goran V. Stanivukovic. University of Toronto Press, 2001, 59–76.

Geller, Sherri, 'Commentary as Cover-Up: Criticizing Illiberal Patronage in Thomas Nashe's *Summer's Last Will and Testament*.' *English Literary Renaissance* 25 (1995), 148–78.

Hibbard, G. R., *Thomas Nashe: A Critical Introduction*. London: Routledge & Kegan Paul, 1962.

Hutson, Lorna, *Thomas Nashe in Context*. Oxford: Clarendon Press, 1989.

Jankowski, Theodora A., '"Where There Can Be No Cause for Affection": Redefining Virgins, Their Desires, and Their Pleasures in John Lyly's *Gallathea*', in *Feminist Readings of Early Modern Culture*, ed. Valerie Traub, M. Lindsay Kaplan and Dympna Callaghan. Cambridge University Press, 1996, 253–74.

Lamb, Mary Ellen, 'Old Wives' Tales, George Peele, and Narrative Abjection.' *Critical Survey* 14 (2004), 28–43.

Melnikoff, Kirk, '"That Will I See, Lead and Ile Follow Thee": Robert Greene and the Authority of Performance', in *Writing Robert Greene: Essays on England's First Notorious Professional Writer*, ed. Kirk Melnikoff and Edward Gieskes. Aldershot: Ashgate, 2008, 39–51.

Neufeld, Christine M., 'Lyly's Chimerical Vision: Witchcraft in *Endymion*.' *Forum for Modern Language* 43 (2007), 351–69.

Reynolds, Bryan, and Henry S. Turner, 'From *Homo Academicus* to *Poetica Publicus*: Celebrity and Transversal Knowledge in Robert Greene's *Friar Bacon and Friar Bungay* (c. 1589)', in *Writing Robert Greene: Essays on England's First Notorious Professional Writer*, ed. Kirk Melnikoff and Edward Gieskes. Aldershot: Ashgate, 2008, 73–93.

Vanhoutte, Jacqueline A., 'Sacrifice, Violence and the Virgin Queen in Lyly's *Gallathea*.' *Cahiers Élisabéthains* 49 (1996), 1–14.

Walsh, Brian, '"Deep Prescience": Succession and the Politics of Prophecy in *Friar Bacon and Friar Bungay*.' *Medieval and Renaissance Drama in England* 23 (2010), 63–85.

2

CLARA CALVO

Thomas Kyd and the Elizabethan blockbuster: *The Spanish Tragedy*

Six years older than Shakespeare and Marlowe, Thomas Kyd (1558–94) shares with them the honour of being among the first writers of tragedy in English. Together, Kyd, Marlowe and Shakespeare turned the decasyllabic blank verse into the form of expression that gave English Renaissance drama its unique character. It is impossible to say if Kyd's *The Spanish Tragedy* precedes or postdates Marlowe's *Tamburlaine*, but the more than generous attention it was soon to receive in revivals, editions, quotations, allusions and parodies, suggests that it was the first early modern blockbuster.

Kyd's early life had much in common with Shakespeare's. Both playwrights were born into a middle-class background, and their fathers enjoyed a good social status. Kyd's father, a scrivener or court notary, served as Warden of the Company of Scriveners in 1580 and Shakespeare's held municipal offices as alderman and bailiff. They differ, though, in one respect: whereas Kyd's father was highly literate, Shakespeare's signed legal documents with an illiterate man's mark. Marlowe, George Peele, Robert Greene, Thomas Nashe and Thomas Lodge all had an academic background, but there is no indication that Kyd or Shakespeare attended university, even though they received a good secondary education. At the King's New School in Stratford, Shakespeare was taught by two learned schoolmasters: Simon Hunt – who left Stratford in 1575 for the Catholic seminary at Douai and became a Jesuit – and Thomas Jenkins. Kyd attended one of the most advanced educational centres in London, Richard Mulcaster's Merchant Taylors' School, which also had Edmund Spenser and Thomas Lodge among its pupils. Both Kyd and Shakespeare may have done some play-acting at school, because performing Latin plays was part of the curriculum. Before becoming playwrights for some of the most successful companies of their time, they may also have worked as players, and both, without permanent success, looked for the patronage of a noble lord. Both have been suspected of Catholic sympathies without conclusive evidence.[1] Like Shakespeare's, Kyd's biography has its 'lost years', the years between the school and the playhouse, so we can only guess that Kyd took up his father's profession and became a scrivener. Kyd's handwriting in autograph documents looks neat and professional, and he may well have found employment as a secretary or tutor at the household of a nobleman.

In spite of the auspicious beginnings that they had in common, the later lives of Kyd and Shakespeare could not have been more dissimilar. Kyd's premature death at the age of thirty-six prevented his dramatic talent from developing fully. Unlike Shakespeare, who left a substantial patrimony at his death, Kyd left debts and no property. Shakespeare's grave in Stratford is still a site of pilgrimage today, whereas Kyd's burial place in St Mary Colechurch disappeared in the Great Fire of London in 1666. Thanks to Heminges and Condell, the 1623 First Folio prevented the loss of many of Shakespeare's plays. Kyd was not so lucky. Few plays can be ascribed to him with certainty, even though shortly after his death he was granted the epithet 'industrious', possibly because of the sheer number of his works. Around 1585, Kyd was writing plays, now lost, for the Queen's Men, but aside from *The Spanish Tragedy*, we only know for certain that he produced another play, the closet tragedy *Cornelia* (1594), which was a translation of *Cornélie* (1574) by the French playwright Robert Garnier, and that he translated Torquato Tasso's *Padre di Famiglia* as *The Householder's Philosophy* (1588). The anonymous tragedy of *Soliman and Perseda* (1592) has been attributed to Kyd, mostly because of its correspondence with the playlet staged as the play-within-the-play in *The Spanish Tragedy* (4.4).[2] Kyd is also believed to have written at least two other plays now lost, the old *Hamlet* (also known as Ur-*Hamlet* by analogy with Goethe's Ur-*Faust*), which Shakespeare may have used as a source, and *Don Horatio*, the play that Philip Henslowe records in his *Diary* as 'spanes comodye donne oracioe' [Spanish comedy Don Horatio] or 'the comodey of doneoracio' [comedy of Don Horatio], a play possibly written after *The Spanish Tragedy*, as a prequel and companion piece. Unlike Shakespeare, who had his name on an edition of *Hamlet* as early as 1603, Kyd did not see his name on the title page of any printed copy of *The Spanish Tragedy*. The play, extremely popular in its time, went through eleven editions between 1592 and 1633, but none carries the author's name.[3]

'Industrious', 'sporting', 'famous'. Beyond these three epithets, it is difficult to know what Kyd's contemporaries really thought of the man. In *A Knights Conjuring* (1607), Thomas Dekker described Kyd as 'industrious' and critics have read into this a backhanded compliment meaning 'prolific but prosaic'. Ben Jonson praising Shakespeare in the First Folio ('To the memory of my beloued, The Avthor', 1623), called the maker of *The Spanish Tragedy* 'sporting Kid'. Thomas Heywood, in *The Hierarchie of the Blessed Angells* (1635) refers to him as 'famous Kid'. A small canon of works may be attributed to

Kyd today, but in his time he nevertheless enjoyed an important reputation as literary author. Four years after Kyd's death, Francis Meres included him amongst 'our best for Tragedie' (*Palladis Tamia*, 1598), and he figures in two anthologies of poetry dating from 1600, namely *Bel-vedere* and Robert Allott's *England's Parnassus*. Debate still surrounds Thomas Nashe's allusion to the 'Kidde in *AEsop*' in his Preface to Robert Greene's *Menaphon* (1589), which is often read as a direct taunt. In one passage, where bad translators and hack writers come under attack, a series of obscure allusions have been interpreted as references to Kyd: 'to leave the trade of *Noverint*, whereto they were born' (*Noverint* refers derogatorily to Kyd's probable profession of scrivener, which certainly was his father's); 'English *Seneca*' (acknowledging Kyd's borrowings from the Roman playwright); 'thrust Elisium into hell' (a possible reference to the Ghost's narration of his descent into the underworld in *The Spanish Tragedy* [1.1.63–75]); 'to bodge up a blank verse with ifs and ands' (echoing Lorenzo's 'What, villain, ifs and ands?' in *The Spanish Tragedy* [2.1.77]) and 'turning over French *Doudie*' (looking for inspiration in French books). We may not be able to determine with absolute certainty if Nashe in the preface to Greene's *Menaphon* wanted to direct his satire directly against Kyd, but his invective brings to mind the objection to 'an upstart Crow, beautified with our feathers' in *Greenes Groats-Worth of Witte*, attributed to Henry Chettle.[4] Like this well-known passage, in which Shakespeare is called 'the onely Shake-scene in a countrie' and 'an absolute Johannes fac totum', Nashe's preface – addressed 'To the Gentlemen Stvdents of Both Vniversities' – points to a certain anxiety about literary competitors and superciliously sneers at parvenu playwrights stealing the limelight of public favour. In both texts, the target is an author of popular plays who is not university-trained. In spite of Nashe's possible snub and of back-handed, qualified praise from other playwrights, Kyd was firmly established in the canon of English drama by the reign of James I. Besides calling him 'industrious', Dekker imagined Kyd amongst other famous poets in the Elysian 'Grove of Bay Trees'. As Lukas Erne has pointed out, Dekker placed Kyd sitting next to Thomas Watson and Thomas Achelley, away from Marlowe, Greene, Peele and Nashe, as if to suggest that Kyd did not belong to Shakespeare's generation, but to an intermediate generation, after Chaucer and Spenser.[5]

Kyd's early death was probably brought on by his imprisonment and likely torture in Bridewell. In April 1593, a series of libels against foreigners appeared posted on several London buildings, including the Dutch Church, and the Privy Council was eager to find culprits. Kyd was arrested on 12 May 1593 and charged with the possession of heretical papers denying the deity of Christ. Since Marlowe was arrested and examined by the Privy

Council on 18 May, it is suspected that Kyd may have informed against him. The methods of the Privy Council were certainly persuasive – the Catholic priest Edmund Campion, trained on the Continent for the Jesuit crusade against Lutheranism and fanatically bent on martyrdom, seems to have revealed the names of his hosts in Lancashire when tortured on the rack at the Tower of London. The suspicion that Kyd may have informed against Marlowe is based on two letters addressed by Kyd to the Lord Keeper, Sir John Puckering, hoping to regain his former patron's favour by exculpating himself. Kyd argued that the heretical papers belonged to his room-mate Marlowe and that they got mixed up with his own papers when they were sharing lodgings. Kyd also accused Marlowe of being an atheist and of having a dreadful character. It is unfortunate that the letters to Lord Puckering, written long after Marlowe had been killed at Deptford, are our only tangible biographical clues to Kyd's character. They turn Kyd into a bad colleague and worse friend. He comes across as mean, cowardly, self-righteous and sanctimonious.

For the history of English drama it is nevertheless a happy occurrence that these letters exist, because they reveal other useful information. At some point prior to his arrest, Kyd was not only sharing accommodation with Marlowe; they were working for the same patron. Unfortunately, Kyd does not mention his patron's name, but three candidates have been proposed: (1) Ferdinando Stanley, Lord Strange (later Earl of Derby); (2) Henry Radcliffe, Earl of Sussex; and (3) Henry Herbert, Earl of Pembroke. Marlowe is not known to have written a play for such a minor touring company as Sussex's Men, but he did write *The Jew of Malta* for Strange's Men and *Edward II* for Pembroke's Men. If Kyd was employed by either Lord Strange or the Earl of Pembroke, he would have worked for a nobleman who gave his patronage and livery to one of the two most famous companies of Shakespeare's time: the Admiral's Men (previously Strange's Men) and the King's Men (earlier Pembroke's Men and the Chamberlain's Men). Kyd's close contact with Marlowe during the latter part of his career (writing for the same patron and company, sharing accommodation, possibly sharing or exchanging reading matter) explains how difficult it is to determine if Marlowe influenced Kyd or Kyd inspired Marlowe. Together, Kyd and Marlowe shaped English drama's unique, malleable blank verse, which Shakespeare would so fully exploit later.

The Spanish Tragedy is one of the most important plays in the development of English drama. It could be the first extant English tragedy in blank verse since *Gorboduc* (1561), *Jocasta* (1567) and *Horestes* (1567). All the early editions up to 1633 printed *The Spanish Tragedy* anonymously, until Richard Farmer (1766), and shortly after Thomas Hawkins (1773), recorded that Thomas Heywood had attributed the play to Thomas Kyd in his *Apology for Actors* (1612).[6]

Trying to fix the date of the play has not proved as easy. *The Spanish Tragedy* was written between 1582 and 1592: it derives material from Thomas Watson's *Hekatompathia* (entered in the Stationers' Register in 1582) and, according to Philip Henslowe, Strange's Men had performed the play at the Rose on 23 February 1592. Henslowe did not record *The Spanish Tragedy* as 'ne' [or 'new'], so it is unlikely that it was a new play in 1592 when, on 6 October, it was entered in the Stationers' Register for Abel Jeffes. As *The Spanish Tragedy* mentions the island of Terceira, one of the Azores where the Battle of Terceira between Spanish and Franco-Portuguese forces was fought on 27 July 1583, it is not likely to have been written before this date. Ben Jonson – who parodied the play, may have played Hieronimo and was at one point paid to revise and add to the text of *The Spanish Tragedy* – would seem to have dated the play in the Induction to his *Bartholomew Fair* (1614). Here, Jonson mocks audiences who still like *The Spanish Tragedy*, and presents it as old-fashioned, perhaps exaggerating its age:

> Hee that will sweare, *Ieronimo*, or *Andronicus* are the best playes, yet, shall passe vnexcepted at, heere, as a man whose Iudgement shewes it is constant, and hath stood still, these fiue and twentie, or thirtie yeeres.[7]

According to Jonson, *The Spanish Tragedy* would have been performed in a London playhouse between 1584 and 1589. Critics tend to date the composition of the play between 1585 and 1589 but it remains uncertain whether it was written before or after the failed invasion attempt of the Spanish Armada in 1588. The absence of even the slightest reference to the Armada is considered odd, particularly when other plays written immediately after 1588 – like George Peele's *Battle of Alcazar* – mention it. This silence seems the more remarkable when we see that Hieronimo's masque in 1.4 deals with English victories over the Spanish and the Portuguese. Although these victories are mostly legendary, the jingoistic tone of the masque and the anxiety it conveys seem to capture the spirit of the years preceding the frustrated invasion. If *The Spanish Tragedy* were to be a pre-Armada play, written in or around 1587, it would also be the first revenge tragedy and the first play to contain a Machiavellian villain as well as a play-within-the-play.

There is no known source for *The Spanish Tragedy*. Some, including F. S. Boas and Lukas Erne, think that it is quite unlikely that Kyd invented its story line from beginning to end, and assume that the play had a source which is now lost. Arthur Freeman believes that Kyd assembled his play's plot from a variety of minor sources and mixed it with the inspiration afforded by contemporary events.[8] Several sources for incidents in the play have been identified. Andrea's descent to the netherworld (1.1) closely follows Book VI of Virgil's *Aeneid*, and other borrowings from Virgil, Ovid and Seneca have been identified. Another Roman author, Lucian, and his *De Calumnia*, may have provided Kyd with material for the character and actions of Villuppo (1.3). The description of the battle won by the Spanish forces (1.2) was in all probability taken from Garnier's *Cornélie*. Two semi-contemporary events may have provided the inspiration for this battle, namely the Battle of Alcazar (1578) – when the young Portuguese King Sebastian's death gave rise to the legend that he had disappeared during the fight – and the Battle of Alcantara (1580), in which Philip II's army defeated the Portuguese troops raised by Don António Prior de Crato.[9] Lorenzo's Machiavellian disposal of his servant Pedringano, after enlisting him as his ally in a murder, has been traced to *The Copie of a Leter*, a tract about Leicester's machinations to get rid of a thief called Gates by pretending to be his protector. This tract, printed in Paris, was forbidden in England, but multiple manuscript copies circulated in London. Thomas Watson's *Hekatompathia* also provided material for Balthazar's lover's discourse in 2.2, and the story behind the playlet 'Soliman and Perseda' comes, with an altered ending, from a tale in Sir Henry Wotton's *Courtlie Controuersie of Cupids Cautels* (1578), a translation of Jacques Yver's collection of short narratives. These sources show that Kyd had already found the formula for assembling a play that would be immensely popular with other playwrights for decades to come: this well-made play mixed borrowings from Latin authors with plots and episodes from French and Italian novellas in translation, adding the occasional topical reference for good measure.

The Spanish Tragedy is a highly innovative play, which is something we can only realise once we remind ourselves that it was composed when practically none of the masterpieces of Elizabethan drama that we now know had yet been written. It is remarkable for the sophistication of its plot and the complexity of its internal structure, for its thematic richness, for the moral, philosophical and political issues that it raises, and for its characterisation and use of language. The complex, convoluted, suspense-filled plot of the play revolves around a series of interconnected revenge drives: the Ghost of Don Andrea expects revenge on Balthazar for his unfair death in battle; Hieronimo decides to obtain retribution for the death of his son Horatio personally, as neither King nor Heaven gives him justice; Bel-Imperia wants revenge for the deaths of her two lovers, Andrea and Horatio; Lorenzo and Balthazar kill Horatio to avenge themselves on a social inferior who has humiliated them and risen above his rank by courting Bel-Imperia.

The Spanish Tragedy presents an unusual division into four acts, instead of the five-act structure common to later plays. This division, present since the earliest extant edition of 1592, could be Kyd's or the printer's, but it may also be the result of textual corruption. Since Act 3 is twice as long as Act 1, it has been suggested that Act 3 could be divided into two acts with a break at 3.6 or 3.7. In this case, the current Act 4 could become Act 5. This rather irregular structure could be related to the chorus-like function of the Ghost of Andrea and Revenge who remain on stage after 1.1 to watch the play (the 'mystery' as Revenge says [1.1.90]) and comment on the action at the end of each act. The play's thematic depth partly derives from the tension between predetermination and free will arising from the conflicting viewpoints provided by (a) the outer frame of the play, from which the Ghost of Don Andrea and Revenge see the action as the predetermined destiny of human beings, and (b) the inner frame of the play, in which Hieronimo freely examines different courses of action and eventually settles for revenge.

The complexity of the play owes much to its self-reflexive nature. The play is highly metatheatrical, as it contains three different types of embedded 'entertainment': Hieronimo's masque at the banquet (1.4), the premonitory dumb show that Revenge explains (3.15), and the play-within-the-play entitled 'Soliman and Perseda' (4.4). The central action – Hieronimo's revenge – is in fact a spectacle watched by the Ghost and Revenge and the hanging of Horatio and Pedringano, too, have spectators, much like Elizabethan executions at the first permanent scaffold in England, the 'Triple Tree' at Tyburn. *The Spanish Tragedy* shows a fascination with spectacles of death or near-death. To the hangings of Horatio and Pedringano, the play adds the shooting of Serberine, the stabbings of Lorenzo and Balthasar, and the suicides of Isabella, Bel-Imperia and Hieronimo. To this, one may add Hieronimo's contemplation of suicide in 3.12, his attempted hanging in 4.4 and Alexandro's last-minute release from being burned at the stake (3.1).

With *The Spanish Tragedy*, Kyd succeeded in recreating Senecan tragedy for the English stage. The play's thematic richness, though, extends beyond revenge and justice, its intertwined central themes, to the dismal prospects of a monarchy devoid of an heir, as the play ends with the total destruction of the houses of Spain and Portugal. Hell and Heaven are omnipresent in the play and the preoccupation with life beyond death is enacted in the speeches by the Ghost and Revenge that open and close the play. Surprisingly, a story concerned with one of the most Catholic of Renaissance courts is markedly pagan in tone, and the Ghost's descent to the underworld is more mythological than Christian. Other important thematic concerns of the play include the relationship between parents and offspring, and the complex power relations between a brother (Lorenzo) and his sister (Bel-Imperia) that John Webster and John Ford were to develop later. The play is also centrally concerned with the representation of grief and madness and contains a political exploration of current issues in Elizabethan England, such as nationalistic feeling and imperial dreams.

The Spanish Tragedy presents an impressive panorama of stage characters who were to prove both memorable and influential for the development of English drama. Besides the impressive Hieronimo as the grief-stricken father turned absolute avenger, we encounter Bel-Imperia, the formidable, sexually alert, verbally articulate, determined lady who would serve as a prototype for female characters from Queen Margaret (in Shakespeare's first tetralogy of Histories), Lear's elder daughters and Lady Macbeth, to Webster's Duchess or Ford's Annabella. Lorenzo, the clever, selfish and sly courtier who interacts with the audience through asides and soliloquies served as model for dozens of Machiavellian villains in English drama. The clumsy and ineffectual Balthazar prefigures Polonius in *Hamlet* and Roderigo in *Othello*, whereas the comic/tragic servant Pedringano points to Falstaff. Even minor characters, like Horatio's mother, Isabella, a forerunner of Ophelia, make a strong impact with little more than one or two scenes. Hieronimo, to whom Hamlet owes much, and Lorenzo, who might have inspired Richard III and Iago, are still more prototypes than fully developed individual characters. Bel-Imperia, instead, is a fully fledged female character, powerful and attractive, who lives up to her name and in dialogue with her slick, artful brother comes across as sharp-thinking and quick-witted.

Hieronimo, however, is the play's core, and with his soliloquies he provided a model that went beyond Hamlet, serving as inspiration for a whole generation of tragic heroes in English drama. Hieronimo's soliloquies often combine the best and the worst of Kyd's blank verse with its tendency to express intense feeling in cliché-ridden, over-emphatic language. The artificial, highly rhetorical ring that is a feature of many of Kyd's pentameters – so different from Marlowe's bombastic, mighty line and Shakespeare's fluent, naturalistic verse – triggered multiple parodies. Kyd's artificial style, with its frequent alliterative patterns and parallel structures, co-exists with a supple, almost conversational mould that is convincing and flows naturally in the stichomythia of Bel-Imperia's dialogue with her brother in 1.4, her impatience in 3.9, and Hieronimo's response to Bazulto's supplication in 3.13.

The title page of the 1602 quarto of *The Spanish Tragedy* announces that it has been 'Newly corrected, amended, and enlarged with new additions of the Painters part, and others, as it hath of late been divers times acted'. The five so-called 'additions' of unequal length (340 lines in total) do not only add to but also, in some cases, replace the text of the 1592 quarto. Although there seems to be no consistent pattern, it is worth noting that some of the additions further explore Hieronimo's mental condition. The first addition (inserted between 2.5.45 and 46) shows Hieronimo in a state of intellectual confusion, reluctant to accept the fact that the hanged man is his son Horatio. The second addition (replacing 3.2.65–6) consists of twelve lines, and the object again seems to be to show Hieronimo's madness, feigned or real, as, in front of his son's murderer, he vouchsafes that the murder of a son is 'an idle thing', a 'thing of nothing' (second addition, lines 5, 8). The third addition (inserted between 3.11.1 and 3.11.2) largely consists of an extended, moving set speech in which Hieronimo broods on 'what is a son'. The fourth addition (between 3.12 and 3.13), by far the longest, amounts to almost a new scene (also known as the Painter Scene), and is centrally concerned with Hieronimo's lunacy. The fifth addition (replacing 4.4.168–90) is an attempt to provide Castile and the Viceroy with reasons for the death of their children, which inconsistently ignores Hieronimo's vow of silence.

The anonymous additions in the 1602 quarto testify to the popularity of *The Spanish Tragedy*. The Induction to Jonson's *Cynthia's Revels*, probably composed in 1600, refers to '*the old Hieronimo*, (as it was first acted)', indicating that the play had already undergone revision.[10] A decade after its first staging, then, some of the play's features were felt to be out of date, but on probably more than one occasion it was considered worth the time and the money to have it revised. The authorship of the additions has been tentatively attributed to Jonson. This was done on the basis of two entries in Henslowe's diary, indicating that Henslowe made two advance payments to Jonson, the first in September 1601, for 'writtinge of his adicians in geronymo', and the second in June 1602, 'for new adicyons for Jeronymo'.[11] There are strong objections to Jonson's authorship of the 1602 additions on the grounds of both style and metrical deficiency, and there is no certainty that Jonson actually wrote any additions. If he did, they are probably lost. The fourth addition, the Painter Scene, seems to predate Henslowe's payments to Jonson, since it was parodied in John Marston's *Antonio and Mellida* (5.1.1–51).[12] Other candidates have been proposed for the authorship of the revisions, including Shakespeare, Dekker and Webster, but the evidence is not conclusive. Attribution to Shakespeare rests on stylometric tests which show that function and lexical words found in the additions indicate a proximity to Shakespeare's plays. Although evidence is far from conclusive, the additions, particularly the fourth, resemble Shakespeare more than Jonson, Dekker or Webster.[13]

Intriguingly, of course, there is an additional motive behind the various attempts to date the additions more accurately. It could help determine whether they were penned before or after the Ur-*Hamlet*, or Shakespeare's *Hamlet* even. Whether *Hamlet* was inspired by the additions to *The Spanish Tragedy* or the additions capitalise on *Hamlet*'s success, what seems clear is that around 1600 playhouse audiences paid to watch and hear lengthy explorations of the psyche on stage and were attracted to representations of the most extreme experiences of the human mind, such as grief, despair and madness. The 1602 additions fascinated the Romantics – Samuel Taylor Coleridge and Charles Lamb thought that they were better than the play itself.[14]

The Spanish Tragedy was probably performed before 1592, but there is no record for the date, venue or company of its premiere. Henslowe's diary tells us that it was performed twenty-nine times between 1592 and 1597, thus making it only slightly less popular than Marlowe's *Jew of Malta* but more in demand than his *Doctor Faustus*. Between 1592 and 1604, the play was performed by four different companies: Strange's Men, the Admiral's Men, Pembroke's Men and the Chamberlain's Men (later the King's Men). It was performed at the Rose and the Fortune and perhaps also at the Theatre, the Cross Key Inn, Newington Butts, the Curtain and the first Globe.[15] Hieronimo was played by the leading actors of the time, certainly by Edward Alleyn and, possibly, also by Richard Burbage. If Dekker's *Satiromastix* (1602) is right, Jonson performed Hieronimo with a company of strolling players in 1597.[16] We have no record of performances at court but, around 1619–20, the Master of the Revels, Sir George Buc, was considering *The Spanish Tragedy* for the Christmas entertainments, as it would pair up nicely with *Hamlet*. Throughout the seventeenth century, it was performed on the European continent, in cities including Frankfurt (as early as 1601), Dresden, Lüneburg and Prague, with other performances recorded in Bohemia, Denmark and the Low Countries. On 24 February 1667/68, Samuel Pepys saw the play performed at the Nursery but was not enthusiastic about it. Surprisingly, perhaps, given the play's immense popularity during the sixteenth and seventeenth centuries, Pepys's *Diary* also recorded the last professional performance before the Mercury Theatre's London production in 1973 (directed by Philip Allen-Morgan). Since 1973, there have been only a handful of professional productions: it was staged by the Citizens' Theatre, Glasgow (directed by Robert David MacDonald, 1978), the National Theatre in London (directed by Michael Bogdanov, 1982), the Royal Shakespeare Company (directed by Michael Boyd, 1987), and more recently at London's Arcola Theatre (directed by Mitchell Moreno, 2009), and at the Rose theatre on Bankside (directed by Adrian Brown, 2010).

In spite of its extraordinary popularity during the sixteenth and seventeenth centuries – or, perhaps, because of it – *The Spanish Tragedy* soon became outdated. The development towards psychological realism in the 1590s rendered its characters deficient and laughable. Its dramatic structure, resting on parallelisms, analogy and scenes echoing previous scenes, quickly came to be seen as artificial, and its highly rhetorical style and long set speeches provided much fodder for parody. The list of authors who echoed or parodied *The Spanish Tragedy* is long and includes Beaumont and Fletcher, Dekker, Jonson, Middleton and Shakespeare. Jonson alluded to the play disparagingly in at least seven plays: *Every Man in His Humour*, *Cynthia's Revels, Poetaster, The Alchemist, A Tale of a Tub, The New Inn* and *Bartholomew Fair*. Its lasting popularity is suggested by frequent parodies in Caroline plays up to the 1630s – James Shirley alone parodied it in *The Bird in a Cage, Changes, or Love in a Maze* and *The Constant Maid*. Most parodies generally revolved around the same four scenes: the Ghost's opening speech ('When this eternal substance of my soul / Did live imprison'd in my wanton flesh, / Each in their function serving other's need, / I was a courtier in the Spanish court', 1.1.1–4); Hieronimo's speech when he finds his son's body ('What outcries pluck me from my naked bed', 2.5.1–33), Hieronimo's highly rhetorical speech ('O eyes, no eyes, but fountains fraught with tears', 3.2.1), and Balthazar's rhymed lover's complaint ('No, she is wilder, and more hard withal, / Than beast, or bird, or tree, or stony wall', 2.1.9–28). The speeches of the Ghost and Hieronimo are notably satirised in Thomas Rawlins's *The Rebellion* (1640). Here, a group of tailors, like the mechanicals in *A Midsummer Night's Dream*, plan to stage a play at court, and initially settle for *The Spanish Tragedy*. Even though in the end the play is not performed, the incident involving Kyd's tragedy does indicate how well known it was before the closing of the theatres in 1642.

Attribution of the Ur-*Hamlet* to Kyd mostly relies on Nashe's Preface to Greene's *Menaphon*. Those who accept that Nashe had Kyd in mind when he wrote his attack on the trivial translators who, knowing little Latin, can read Seneca at night and produce whole *Hamlet*s the following morning, also assume that Kyd must have written a tragedy about the Danish prince. Nashe editors, including Ronald McKerrow, have challenged this association, arguing that Nashe did not refer to Kyd or *The Spanish Tragedy* in his preface to *Menaphon*. Attribution of the Ur-*Hamlet* to Kyd also rests on internal evidence, as there are similarities between *The Spanish Tragedy* and the first quarto of *Hamlet*. In particular, parallels may be found in the scene between Gertrude and Horatio that is missing from Q2 and F, and in passages from the closet scene that are unique to Q1. Kyd may or may not have written the Ur-*Hamlet*, but Shakespeare probably used *The Spanish Tragedy* as a source of inspiration for his own revenge tragedy situated at the court of Denmark.[17]

Extraordinarily popular, *The Spanish Tragedy* is likely to have left a deep impression on Shakespeare's mind. Echoes from Kyd abound in his work. Lear's grief and despair on the heath are anticipated by Hieronimo's anguished discovery of his son's dead body. Also, Hieronimo's lengthy speech in this scene (3.2) may, as Stanley Wells suggests, have inspired Young Clifford's 'rhetorical outburst' upon the discovery of his father's corpse in *The First Part of the Contention* (*Henry VI, Part 2*).[18] The opening of *Macbeth*, with the hero returning triumphant from a battle described in detail, echoes Horatio's victorious entry and the General's narration of the defeat of the Portuguese forces. Also *Titus Andronicus* bears signs of influence from Kyd.[19] The masque performed by Tamora and her sons in 5.2, like Hieronimo's court theatricals in 4.4, requires courtiers turned actors. By having Tamora impersonate Revenge, Shakespeare may well have sought to capitalise on the success of Kyd's play. In *Henry VI, Part 3*, the napkin dipped in Rutland's blood that Queen Margaret uses to torture York (1.4.80–4) recalls the handkerchief Hieronimo dips in his son's blood (2.5.51), and York's speech in the play's opening act (1.4.138–48) resorts to the same rhetorical question–answer pattern that Hieronimo's uses in 2.5.51–4.[20] Verbal parallels between *The Spanish Tragedy* and plays by Shakespeare have indeed been identified:

'O speak, if any spark of life remain' – *The Spanish Tragedy* (2.5.17)
'If any spark of life be yet remaining' – *Henry VI, Part 3* (5.6.66)

'So hares may pull dead lions by the beard' – *The Spanish Tragedy* (1.2.172)
'Whose valour plucks dead lions by the beard' – *King John* (2.1.138)

Beyond verbal parallels like these, Shakespeare perhaps picked up from Kyd dramatic solutions for complicated staged situations. In *Othello*, when Iago's villainy has been exposed, Shakespeare echoes the ending of *The Spanish Tragedy*. Pressed to produce an explanation for his motives, Iago replies:

Demand me nothing. What you know, you know.
From this time forth I never will speak word. (5.2.309–10)

Iago's refusal echoes Hieronimo's determination to remain silent: 'Sufficeth I may not, nor I will not tell thee' (4.4.182). In both plays, the response of the authorities is identical. The King of Spain commands:

Fetch forth the tortures.
Traitor as thou art, I'll make thee tell. (4.4.183–4)

'Torments will ope your lips' (5.2.312), proclaim the officials from the Venetian state. Neither Hieronimo nor Iago speaks again – to do so would spoil the tragic momentum, as Shakespeare must have learnt from Kyd.

The Spanish Tragedy also influenced *Hamlet* in many ways. The Ghost, returning from beyond the grave to demand revenge, purgatory as a 'middle path', and the use of the soliloquy are some of them. Hieronimo's soliloquies of hesitation, particularly when he is contemplating suicide with either poniard or halter (3.12), must have triggered the formulation of the dilemma as 'To be, or not to be'. Shakespeare also developed variations on what he learnt from Kyd: Hamlet walking on stage with a book must have made contemporary audiences expect a soliloquy like Hieronimo's *Vindicta mihi!* (3.13) when, instead, they were treated to a comic dialogue with a foolish old man. Kyd's attention to decorum and his inclination to suit the word to the action may even have inspired Hamlet's advice to the players. Claudius's attempt to murder Hamlet by proxy recalls Lorenzo's hiring of Pedringano to kill Serberine. Also the cameos of feigned and real madness between Hieronimo and his wife Isabella return in Hamlet and Ophelia, showing once again Shakespeare's debt to the genius of sporting Kyd. The intrigue-like, suspense-ridden plot of *Hamlet* no doubt owes more to Kyd and *The Spanish Tragedy* than to Marlowe or any other of Shakespeare's predecessors.

The impact of Kyd's tragedy of revenge on early modern drama and beyond was pervasive. Many of its distinctive features were soon ridiculed, and the play as a whole was felt to be outmoded. Yet, its formative influence on later revenge or domestic tragedies, and also on English history plays, including *Henry VI* and *Richard III*, is unmistakable. Kyd's combination of revenge and madness involving the destruction of dynastic lines links *The Spanish Tragedy* directly to *Hamlet*, and beyond, to Jacobean tragedies like John Webster's *Duchess of Malfi*. Like these two no less canonical plays, *The Spanish Tragedy* transcends the orbit of domestic revenge, showing how the state itself is ultimately threatened when justice fails and the individual feels impelled to resort to revenge. The compelling narrative about the fall of two Iberian royal houses that the play articulates, together with its exploration of nationalistic energy and colonial aspirations, make Kyd one of the earliest Elizabethan playwrights explicitly to engage with European politics. Kyd also stands out amongst Shakespeare's contemporaries because he owes his place in the canon to a single play, but then again it happens to be a play that functioned as a fulcrum in the development of two of the most successful genres of English drama, revenge tragedy and the history play.

NOTES

1 For the suggestion that Thomas Kyd may have been a Catholic see Lukas Erne, *Beyond 'The Spanish Tragedy': A Study of the Works of Thomas Kyd* (Manchester University Press, 2001), 55.

2 See Thomas Kyd, *The Spanish Tragedy*, ed. Philip Edwards (London: Methuen, 1959). All further quotations from the play will be taken from this edition, and reference will be given in the text.

3 Early editions of *The Spanish Tragedy* appeared in 1592, 1594, 1599, 1602 (containing the additions), 1603, 1610, 1615 (containing a woodcut illustrating

two scenes, 2.4 and 2.5), 1618, 1623 and 1633. On the evidence of the title page in the earliest extant edition, it is generally believed that there was another edition before Q1592 of which no copies survive.

4 *Greenes Groats-Worth of Witte, Bought with a Million Repentance* (London: for William Wright, 1592), sig. F1v.

5 Erne, *Beyond 'The Spanish Tragedy'*, 1.

6 Arthur Freeman, 'Thomas Hawkins, Richard Farmer, and the Authorship of *The Spanish Tragedy*', *Notes & Queries* 50:2 (June 2003), 214–15. Before Richard Farmer and Thomas Hawkins, the bookseller Edward Archer had listed *The Spanish Tragedy* as by 'Tho. Kyte' in 1656.

7 *Ben Jonson*, ed. C. H. Herford, and Percy and Evelyn Simpson, 11 vols. (Oxford: Clarendon Press, 1925–52), VI (1938), 16.

8 Arthur Freeman, *Thomas Kyd: Facts and Problems* (Oxford: Clarendon Press, 1967), 50–70.

9 The Battle of Alcácer Quibir gave occasion to George Peele's *The Battle of Alcazar* (1594), performed by Strange's Men in 1592–3.

10 *Cynthia's Revels*, in *Ben Jonson*, ed. Herford *et al.*, IV (1932), lines 9–19.

11 R. A. Foakes and R. T. Rickert, *Henslowe's Diary* (Cambridge University Press, 1961) 182, 203.

12 Arthur Freeman discusses Marston's parody of the Painter Scene at length in his *Thomas Kyd: Facts and Problems*, 126–9 (acknowledging F. G. Fleay, L. L. Schücking and Harry Levin).

13 Hugh Craig, 'The 1602 Additions to *The Spanish Tragedy*', in *Shakespeare, Computers, and the Mystery of Authorship*, ed. Hugh Craig and Arthur F. Kinney (Cambridge University Press, 2009), 163–80 at 179–80. Brian Vickers thinks that the 320 lines added by Q1602 'should in future be included in the Shakespeare canon'. See Brian Vickers, 'Shakespeare and Authorship Studies in the Twenty-First Century', *Shakespeare Quarterly* 62:1 (Spring 2011), 106–42 at 111.

14 Freeman, *Thomas Kyd: Facts and Problems*, 138.

15 In John Webster's 'Induction' to John Marston's *The Malcontent*, we read that the King's Men appropriated this play for the Globe in retaliation for the appropriation of a played entitled 'Jeronimo' by one of the children's companies. If Webster's 'Jeronimo in Decimo sexto' refers to *The Spanish Tragedy*, Kyd's tragedy would also have been played by the Children of the Chapel at Blackfriars. It is now believed that the play Webster refers to is *The First Part of Hieronimo*, a burlesque version of a prequel to *The Spanish Tragedy*. See Erne, *Beyond 'The Spanish Tragedy'*, 22–3; and Lucy Munro, *Children of the Queen's Revels: A Jacobean Theatre Repertory* (Cambridge University Press, 2005), 135.

16 In Thomas Dekker's *Satiromastix*, Jonson (alias 'Horace') is told: 'thou hast forgot how thou amblest (in leather pilch) by a play-wagon, in the high way, and took'st mad Ieronimoes part, to get seruice among the Mimickes'. See *The Dramatic Works of Thomas Dekker*, vol. 1, ed. Fredson Bowers (Cambridge University Press, 1953), 4.1.130–2.

17 For the numerous dramatic elements shared by *Hamlet* and *The Spanish Tragedy* see Stanley Wells, *Shakespeare & Co.: Christopher Marlowe, Thomas Dekker, Ben Jonson, Thomas Middleton, John Fletcher and the Other Players in His Story* (London: Penguin, 2006), 74; and Philip Edwards, 'Shakespeare and Kyd',

in *Shakespeare, Man of the Theater: Proceedings of the Second Congress of the International Shakespeare Association, 1981*, ed. Kenneth Muir, Jay L. Halio and D. J. Palmer (Newark, DE: University of Delaware Press, 1983), 148–54.

18 For a discussion of the parallelism between these two scenes see Wells, *Shakespeare & Co.*, 74.

19 According to Stanley Wells, Shakespeare wrote *Titus Andronicus* in 'direct emulation' of Kyd's *Spanish Tragedy* (*Shakespeare & Co.*, 75). For the relation between these two revenge tragedies see also Jonathan Bate, 'The Performance of Revenge: *Titus Andronicus* and *The Spanish Tragedy*', in *The Show Within: Dramatic and Other Insets: English Renaissance Drama (1550–1642)*, vol. II, ed. François Laroque (Montpellier: Université Paul-Valéry, 1992), 267–84.

20 All Shakespearean references in the text are keyed to *The Norton Shakespeare. Based on the Oxford Edition*, ed. Stephen Greenblatt, Walter Cohen, Jean E. Howard and Katharine Eisaman Maus, 2nd edn (New York and London: W. W. Norton, 2008).

Further reading

Ardolino, Frank, *Apocalypse and Armada in Kyd's 'Spanish Tragedy'*, Sixteenth Century Essays and Studies 29. Kirksville, MO: Sixteenth Century Journal, Northeast Missouri State University, 1995.

Boas, Frederick Samuel, ed., *The Works of Thomas Kyd*. Oxford: Clarendon Press, 1901, rpt. 1955.

Bowers, Fredson, *Elizabethan Revenge Tragedy 1587–1642*. Princeton University Press, 1940.

Díaz-Fernández, José Ramón, 'Thomas Kyd: A Bibliography, 1966–1992.' *Bulletin of Bibliography* 52:1 (1995), 1–13.

Kline, Daniel T., 'The Circulation of the Letter in Kyd's *The Spanish Tragedy*', in *Tudor Drama Before Shakespeare, 1485–1590: New Directions for Research, Criticism, and Pedagogy*, ed. Lloyd Edward Kermode, Jason Scott-Warren and Martine Van Elk. Basingstoke and New York: Palgrave, 2004, 229–47.

Levin, Michael Henry, '"Vindicta Mihi!": Meaning, Morality and Motivation in *The Spanish Tragedy*.' *Studies in English Literature* 4 (1964), 307–24.

McAlindon, Thomas, '*Tamburlaine the Great* and *The Spanish Tragedy*: The Genesis of a Tradition.' *Huntington Library Quarterly* 45 (1982), 59–81.

Shapiro, James, '"Tragedies Naturally Performed": Kyd's Representation of Violence, *The Spanish Tragedy* (c. 1587)', in *Staging the Renaissance: Reinterpretations of Elizabethan and Jacobean Drama*, ed. David S. Kastan and Peter Stallybrass. London and New York: Routledge, 1991, 99–113.

Siemon, James, 'Sporting Kyd.' *English Literary Renaissance* 24 (1994), 553–83.

3

RICHARD WILSON

'The words of Mercury': Shakespeare and Marlowe

Sick of fear

Shakespeare was haunted by Christopher Marlowe more than by any other Elizabethan writer. He may even have imagined their relation as a literal haunting, blaming this for his late start, and in the Sonnets asking whether it was 'his spirit, by spirits taught to write / Above a mortal pitch, that struck me dead'.[1] Any account of Shakespeare's debt to his almost exact contemporary therefore has to begin, according to Harold Bloom in *The Anatomy of Influence*, with his inferiority complex as an 'unlettered clerk' crying 'Amen' (85) while Marlowe's 'great verse ... my verse astonishèd' (86), in his own words, and he exerted 'all his might, / To make me tongued-tied' (80). Bloom identifies the author of *Tamburlaine* and *Faustus* as the Rival Poet of the Sonnets because no other writer held such uncanny power over an audience as 'that able spirit' (85): 'I imagine the young Shakespeare attending a performance of *Tamburlaine* with fascination. The possibility of the sublime of power was born at the moment of Marlowe's impact.'[2] With its hyperbolic rhetoric and exotic nouns, Marlowe's writing fits the description of 'variation or quick change ... new-found methods' and 'compounds strange' (76) that the Sonnets attribute to the poet said to be 'by all the muses filed' (85). But in lines that may allude to Marlowe's shadowy circle of backers, these poems also picture the unnamed writer with 'his compeers by night / Giving him aid' (86), as if Shakespeare sensed and resented something extra-literary about such superhuman empowerment.

Shakespeare's 'tongued-tied muse' is too polite (85) for him to name his opposite, but he gives a clue: 'Who is it that says most ...?' (84). And if it simplifies their *agon* to call it rivalry, the theory that Marlowe is the 'better spirit' (80) of the Sonnets is persuasive, since these poems keep applauding the other writer's rhetorical *flights* for adding 'feathers' to learning's wing (78), in the signature Marlovian metaphor for literary aspiration, which proved his 'modern quill' (83) a 'worthier pen' (79), and made 'his style admirèd everywhere' (84). And when dumbstruck Shakespeare blames his precursor's 'golden quill / And precious phrase' (85) for 'my silence' (86), these texts further hint at the contrasting effect of self-effacing reticence we associate with the writer of *King Lear*. For it was because he was stunned by Marlowe's authorial personality, Bloom infers, that this 'unlettered clerk' became 'the major master of ellipsis in the history of theatre', with 'dumb thoughts, speaking in effect' (85), so 'we have to interpret what he leaves out'.[3] The Sonnets reveal a poet 'sick of ... fear' (86) at his predecessor's towering 'pitch' (86); but by insisting 'silence ... shall be most my glory, being dumb' (83), they thus outline Shakespeare's tactic to overtake 'the full proud sail of his great verse' (86), and remind the reader of fate of the 'invincible' Armada:

> But since your worth, wide as the ocean is,
> The humble as the proudest sail doth bear,
> My saucy barque, inferior far to his,
> On your broad main doth wilfully appear. (Sonnet 80)

In 1588 England's little boats defied Spain's galleons by sneaking *under* their fire; and in these sonnets the poet appears to mock his Cambridge-educated superior as one of those top-heavy ships 'of tall building and of goodly pride' that sailed so careless of 'being wrecked' (80). Shakespeare always values 'tongue-tied simplicity' over the 'rattling tongue / Of saucy and audacious eloquence' (*MND* 5.1.102–3).[4] But if it refers to the *Tamburlaine* phenomenon, it is this undercutting which is 'saucy', as Marlowe's drama had been the great morale-booster on the eve of the invasion. With *Tamburlaine the Great, Part One* Londoners thrilled to the victory of 'a great and thund'ring speech' (1.1.3) over the armies of Asia, as if watching the Armada defeated.[5] Like Elizabeth in her Tilbury speech, Marlowe's play made light of England's 'Dad's Army' and scant resources, by mobilising a new cult hero, who does no real fighting, but whose self-aggrandising 'words are swords' (*Tamburlaine 1*, 1.1.74). A piratical Robin Hood, Tamburlaine is a patriotic poster-boy for the 'inglorious crew' (*Tamburlaine 1*, 4.3.67) of playgoers, who with 'a little spoil / Durst, in disdain of wrong and tyranny, / Defend his freedom 'gainst a monarchy' (*Tamburlaine 1*, 2.1.54–6). 'You see ... what working words he hath', says Theridamas, 'But when you see his actions top his speech' you will be speechless yourself (*Tamburlaine 1*, 2.3.25–6). For wielding his 'well-refinèd pen' (Sonnet 85) to redraft the map 'Tamburlaine is Marlowe', too, as a poet soliciting backers: 'What will he do supported by a king ... And stuffed with treasure for his highest thoughts?' (*Tamburlaine 1*, 2.1.57–9).[6] Between the playhouse and the palace, Marlowe would be torn apart by these opposing sources of authority. But what Shakespeare, a Johnny-come-lately by his account, who lost years to writer's block, learned from the 'high astounding terms' (*Tamburlaine 1*, Prologue, 5) of this hyped-up drama, his Armada verse implies, was the 'soft power' of theatre itself:

> Where kings shall crouch unto our conquering swords
> And hosts of soldiers stand amazed at us,
> When with their fearful tongues they shall confess,
> 'These are the men that all world admires.' (*Tamburlaine 1*, 1.2.220–3)

Marlowe brought Machiavelli on stage to lecture how 'Might first made kings' (*Jew of Malta*, Prologue, 20); yet his own message for Shakespeare was that to be king requires 'but a jest' (*Tamburlaine 1*, 2.5.98), for what an actor 'swears shall be performed' (*Tamburlaine 1*, 5.1.107). So *Tamburlaine the Great, Part One* keeps performing the simplest speech act, a coronation investiture, as its hero pronounces himself or followers kings: 'I speak it, and my words are oracles' (*Tamburlaine 1*, 3.3.102). Within the audience's lifetime Oliver Cromwell would prove it was indeed possible 'to make him king' who 'came up of nothing' (*Tamburlaine 2*, 3.1.72–5), by supplanting Charles I. So to the monarchs he deposes by speaking ''gainst a world of kings' (*Tamburlaine 1*, 4.2.81), this actor-manager is a 'monster turned to a manly shape' (*Tamburlaine 1*, 2.6.16). And in the sequel, 'murd'rous Fates throw all his triumphs down' (*Tamburlaine 2*, Prologue, 4) as if, having used him to repel the Armada, the authorities turned against the dramatist. In fact, a preface tells how 'gentlemen readers' censored the 'fond and frivolous' episodes theatregoers loved: a reference to a crack-down in 1589. Likewise, Marlowe's rulers fear the entertainer's box-office draw: 'He brings a world of people to the field' (*Tamburlaine 2*, 1.1.67). In *Tamburlaine the Great, Part Two* the emphasis therefore shifts from power to the *limit* of words, as the old stager realises 'raging cannot make her live' (2.4.120) when his wife Zenocrate dies, gags royal slaves with horses' bits, and is finally struck down after burning the Koran. Shakespeare had settled in London at this time, and so was able to absorb from the two-part *Tamburlaine* not only soaring verbal power, but the catch in the repetition compulsion of this inflated hyper-drama, which was how, in Marlowe's other signature figure of entrapment, even language is in its 'confine immurèd' (Sonnet 84):

> If all the pens that ever poets held
> Had fed the feeling of their master's thoughts …
> Yet should there hover in their restless heads,
> One thought, one grace, one wonder at the least,
> Which into words no virtue can digest. (*Tamburlaine 1*, 5.1.161–73)

A savage spectacle

Marlowe began by writing for boys of the queen's Chapel Royal, but ended his first neoclassical play, *Dido, Queen of Carthage*, with the queen committing suttee on a pyre of his love poems as Aeneas sails to Rome on orders of Mercury, and sailors formerly 'clapped under hatches ... merry-make for joy' (5.1.240–59). Shakespeare recalls this jubilant liberation from court culture at the end of his career, when he closes *The Tempest* with mariners 'clapped under hatches' then 'Cap'ring' with joy to be released' (5.1.234–41). 'Dido and Aeneas shall want troops', he also has Antony boast, when hoping to take a bow with Cleopatra in the underworld (*Ant.* 4.15.53); as though the 'unlettered' gatecrasher could not help admiring Marlowe's escape from the dead-end of classical decorum into that 'world of people' (*Tamburlaine 2*, 1.1.67) in the city's amphitheatres. For there the 'scum of men', a 'monster of five hundred thousand heads', roared assent as 'if the gods had held a parliament' (*Tamburlaine 1*, 4.3.7; 2.6.106) at the cynical medley of tragedy and comedy, sadism and sarcasm, with which Marlowe stamped his ego on the play. Critics call Marlovian ambition purposeless; as Faustus says he desires nothing 'but mine own fantasy, / That will receive no object' (*Faustus*, 1.105–6). But if an impressionable Shakespeare was in the Shoreditch crowd, the tyro must have learned how, starting when Aeneas acts out the massacre at Troy, Marlowe's processional plots do give his protagonists an object, which is not to be some 'petty' king, in this age when kings are weak (*Tamburlaine 2*, 3.5.64), but to 'ride in triumph' (*Tamburlaine 1*, 2.5.50) on stage:

> Why, this 'tis to have an army in the field ...
> As ancient Romans over their captive lords,
> So will I triumph over this wanton king
> And he shall follow my proud chariot's wheels. (*Massacre*, 21.49–53)

Stephen Greenblatt proposes that Marlowe was driven by 'the will to absolute play'.[7] But this was, in fact, never a will to *free* play, being fixated on the crushing circus of the imperial triumph, which editors connect to Renaissance pictures like Andrea Mantegna's *Triumph of Caesar*, and victory parades like Elizabeth's into London in 1588. It was a pageant mode he shared with Edmund Spenser, whose court poem *The Faerie Queene* he trumped, however, to show how courtiers 'themselves shall make our pageant' (*Tamburlaine 2*, 4.3.90). Tamburlaine's cry, 'Holla, ye pampered jades of Asia!' (*Tamburlaine 2*, 4.3.1), as he whips the kings yoked to his pageant-wagon, thus trumpets the drive of all these Marlovian tableaux: *to annexe sovereign power to the poet*. Shakespeare seems to have been both awed and appalled by this tyrannical author-centred theatre, judging by the Marlovian playmakers he made hero-villains. In his own first Roman triumph, for instance, Titus Andronicus opens festivities ordering 'fire straight' (Marlowe's favourite gimmick) for human sacrifice, and ends baking the victim's brothers in a pie, but the mother's interjection introduces Shakespearean disquiet: 'O cruel irreligious piety!' (*Tit.* 1.1.130). So while critics explain how much Shakespeare owed to the 'red, sticky blood' of Marlowe's sensationalism, his projection of it onto amoral schemers like Aaron, the Moorish lover of the empress, suggests he recognised that this affectless 'will to play' was an imposition on the paying public of a craving for personal power:[8]

> Now climbeth Tamora Olympus' top,
> Safe out of fortune's shot, and sifts aloft,
> Secure of thunder's crack or lightning flash,
> Advanced above pale envy's threat'ning reach ...
> I will be bright, and shine in pearl and gold
> To wait upon this new-made empress.
> To wait, said I? – To wanton with this queen ... (*Tit.* 2.1.1–21)

Marlowe's loudest message for Shakespeare was how performers 'that seem but silly country swains / May have the leading of so great an host' (*Tamburlaine 1*, 1.2.47–8). But it seems the grudging admirer also heard the megalomania in this declamatory metatheatre: 'The god of war resigns his room to me, / Meaning to make me general of the world' (*Tamburlaine 1*, 5.1.450–1). Shakespeare's unease at the fatal attraction of 'a savage spectacle' (*JC* 3.1.225) thus accounts for the ambivalence of his most Marlovian theatrical impresario, the homicidal Richard III, who weaves 'Plots' and 'inductions' (*R3* 1.1.32) to compel the silence of the lambs. To invent a 'mounting spirit' like the Bastard in *King John* (1.1.206) was, to be sure, a homage to Marlowe's updating of the figure of the medieval Vice. Antony, Iago, Edmund and Macbeth all display the same will to rhetorical power over a collusive audience by staging 'a pageant / To keep us in false gaze' (*Oth.* 1.3.19–20). But the Bastard is himself 'amazed' (*John* 4.3.141) by the 'suiciding' of young Prince Arthur; and, like the composer Salieri mesmerised by Mozart, Shakespeare clearly found something *demonic* in the magic of Marlowe's stagecraft. So if he continued to be haunted by the mirthless laughter of Marlowe's theatre of cruelty, his concerned response was not to compete with such 'spirited' histrionics, but to project his discomfort through a novel type of anti-theatrical character, such as Brutus, whose thoughtful abstention from the parade of power registers audience resistance:

CASSIUS: Will you go see the order of the course?
BRUTUS: Not I.
CASSIUS: I pray you, do.
BRUTUS: I am not gamesome; I do lack some part
Of that quick spirit that is in Antony. (*JC* 1.2.27–31)

The messenger of death

Watching the audience watch *Tamburlaine* Shakespeare conceived a far more consensual theatre than Marlowe's producer's one, and a different literary system, in which playgoers were kingmakers. So in Shakespeare's self-denying drama the recurring story would be that the best, such as Edgar in *King Lear*, lack conviction, while the worst, like Edmund, are full of Marlowe's passionate intensity. As Bloom writes, 'Shakespeare swerved from Marlowe, to found a new freedom of distance, unlike any other stance in literature.' But the theorist of 'the anxiety of influence' recognises exceptional reasons for aversion in this case, as Shakespeare, 'a cautious person dedicated to self-conservation, must have been careful to steer clear of Marlowe, a quick man with a dagger, murdered by the Elizabethan CIA, which he served'.[9] And it is true that *fear* seems to be the emotion whenever Marlowe's double life is alluded to in Shakespeare's writing, even when it insists that neither 'He nor that affable familiar ghost / Which nightly gulls him with intelligence' was frightening (Sonnet 86). The latecomer was obviously traumatised by the fate of his unlucky predecessor, and anxious to disengage from Marlowe's spectral hold on audiences through the ambiguating of fact and fiction, the living with the dead, heightened by unnerving asides about having been 'taught by spirits' to write a 'damnèd book' (*Faustus*, 1.72).

Suspicions of Marlowe's activities in the 'School of Night', a secret scientific society around the 'Wizard Earl' of Northumberland, shadowed responses to his writings, in which he was said to be 'damning God out of heaven with that Atheist Tamburlaine'.[10] Elizabethans scrambled atheism with Satanism. So, 'Prosecute it to the full', rasped the queen, when Marlowe's 'Damnable Judgement of Religion and scorn of God's word', were reported; and whether or not this was his death sentence, many agreed with the informer Richard Baines that it was necessary 'the mouth of so dangerous a member may be stopped'.[11] If his own references to 'our actors' as 'all spirits' (*Temp.* 4.1.148–9) are believed, Shakespeare must himself have taken it half seriously when Marlowe boasted of being 'a divine in show' (*Faustus*, 1.3), and of theatre as necromancy, 'By which the spirits are enforced to rise' (*Faustus*, 3.13). For 'Heaven's winged herald, Jove-born

Mercury', was how the shoemaker's son introduced himself in his poem *Hero and Leander* (386), mystifying his double agency among spooks and spectators by identifying with the messenger of the gods. It was an equivocal tribute, then, when Shakespeare's reaction to Marlowe's murder on 30 May 1593 was to bring him back as the queen's messenger he had been in life. In *Love's Labour's Lost* the great survivor established the pattern for his belatedness when he attempted to detoxify the deceased's final frenzied work, *The Massacre at Paris*, as a romantic comedy, with the same cast out of France's Wars of Religion converted from agents of hate to 'ambassadors of love', and St Bartholomew's Day replayed as planned, not with mass murder, but 'like a merriment' (*LLL* 5.2.760, 766). Yet even here the entry of the messenger Mercadé freezes the laughter on stage, as if the fiction of the play is engulfed in the brutal facts of the violent docudrama Marlowe staged:

PRINCESS: Welcome, Mercadé,
                      But that thou interrup'st our merriment.
MERCADÉ: I am sorry, madam, for the news I bring
                      Is heavy in my tongue. The King your father –
PRINCESS: Dead, for my life.
MERCADÉ: Even so. My tale is told. (*LLL* 5.2.699–703)

'The words of Mercury are harsh after the songs of Apollo' (*LLL* 5.2.903–4): in the end Shakespeare identifies Mercadé explicitly with 'herald Mercury'. So if Marlowe's ghost returns in the shape of macabre Mercadé, as 'the messenger of death' (*Massacre*, 13.3) from his own drama, that underlines how alarming Shakespeare found the Marlovian confusion of life and literature, real time with the time of the play. He shuts down *Love's Labour's Lost*, in any case, by separating the actors from the audience, 'You that way, we this way' (5.2.904), as though chary of the way Marlowe tempted fate by intruding himself in Hitchcockian cameo roles which pushed to the limit the thrill of *acting* for both the state and stage. For as his biographer Charles Nicholl remarks, the troubling question about Marlowe is not how spying shaped his writing, but how writing shaped his espionage.[12] So if Shakespeare keeps staging the death of the author, that might be because of the eerie way Marlowe foretold his end in scenes like the one in *The Massacre at Paris* of the murder of the professor Ramus, stabbed as he frets over the Companion to Literature he has written, which the dramatist studied at Cambridge for its thesis that the life is irrelevant to the work; to 'contradict which', jeers Guise, 'I say: Ramus shall die' (*Massacre*, 9.35). In *Julius Caesar*, a play of emulation haunted by Guise's brag, 'Yet Caesar shall go forth' (*Massacre*, 21.65), the episode is rerun, with the poet Cinna butchered 'for his bad verses' (*JC* 3.3.29–30). Thus Marlowe's ghost beckons Shakespeare as a phantasmal figure for the pathos of the real, the Faustian fascination with power that lures the artist to his nemesis:

CINNA:　I dreamt tonight that I did feast with Caesar,
　　　　And things unlucky charge my fantasy. (*JC* 3.3.1–2)

A grave man

In *Romeo and Juliet*, the tragedy Shakespeare began after Marlowe's murder, the uncanniness of 'Things … fall'n out … unluckily' (*Rom.* 3.4.1) emanates from Mercutio, a prankster who thinks soldiers dream of cutting throats (*Rom.* 1.4.72–103). In a play where 'What's in a name' (*Rom.* 2.1.85) is the desire to live after death, Mercutio's ties him directly to the dead poet; and with his quicksilver wit, recklessness and homosexuality, he looks like a portrait of Shakespeare's Mercurial colleague. Marlowe and poet Tom Watson stabbed a boy to death in just such an affray as Mercutio incites. When canny Shakespeare kills off uncanny Mercutio, therefore, he is doing more than suppress a champion of male bonding. Some think he is expressing guilt at subconsciously murdering his rival. But in fact he is exploiting the classic trope of *apophrades* – the literary return of the dead – to turn Marlowe's untimely concept of the play as a real *event* on itself, and exorcise the idea of performative language as a Faustian séance 'To raise a spirit' (*Rom.* 2.1.24):

　　　O Romeo, Romeo, brave Mercutio is dead!
　　　That gallant spirit hath aspired the clouds,
　　　Which too untimely here did scorn the earth. (*Rom.* 3.1.111–13)

Like the interruption of Mercadé, Mercutio's auto-destruction is a warning about the 'too untimely' mixing of personality with performance. The 'deadly point to point' of his stabbing, as in 'martial scorn' he deflects the 'piercing steel … back to Tybalt', who 'Retorts it' in an 'envious thrust' (*Rom.* 3.1.154–62), therefore reads so much like reports that Marlowe pushed his 'dagger into his own head', it is hard not to feel Shakespeare shared the belief that 'this barking dog called Marlin' had with poetic justice 'compelled his own hand'.[13] Thus the Friar's sermon that 'These violent delights have violent ends, / And in their triumph die like fire and powder' (*Rom.* 2.5.9–10) seems as much aimed at Marlowe's pyrotechnic theatre as lovers in Verona. With his phallocentric fantasy about 'the bawdy hand of the dial … upon the prick of noon' (*Rom.* 2.3.99–100), Romeo's friend personifies the Marlovian drive to make the time of the play identical to that of the playgoers. But by depicting 'bold' Mercutio (*Rom.* 3.1.153) as so *forward*, Shakespeare seems to judge Marlowe's getting ahead of himself as a comparable death-wish, a killer instance of the theatrical bad timing which ruins the illusion of the play, and is therefore known as 'corpsing':

> ROMEO: Courage, man. The hurt cannot be much.
>
> MERCUTIO: No, 'tis not so deep as a well, nor so wide as a church door, but 'tis enough. 'Twill serve. Ask for me tomorrow, and you shall find me a grave man. (*Rom.* 3.1.91–4)

By making Mercutio suddenly 'grave', Shakespeare portrays Marlowe like the joker shouting 'fire' in the theatre, astonished to be taken seriously. Mention of a church door may even refer to his arrest, days before he was killed, for nailing a poster signed 'Tamburlaine' on a London church threatening another 'Paris massacre'.[14] Like Leander, the poet was out of his depth; but Shakespeare scorns the cover-up, that he died fighting over some 'lewd love', when in *As You Like It* Ganymede says Leander drowned from cramp: 'Men have died from time to time, and worms have eaten them, but not for love' (*AYLI* 4.1.91–2). Earlier Phoebe fell for this boy, quoting the contrary idea from *Hero and Leander* (176): 'Dead shepherd, now I find thy saw of might: / "Who ever loved that loved not at first sight?"' (*AYLI* 3.5.82–3); which would be a fine tribute to Marlowe's great hit, his song 'The Passionate Shepherd', if Ganymede were not Rosalind in disguise! Taking the poem literally, the country girl confuses a persona with the person. So Touchstone surely voices Shakespeare's own misgivings at his forerunner's pushiness when he notes the peril of misreading: 'When a man's verses cannot be understood, nor a man's good wit seconded with the forward child, understanding, it strikes a man more dead than a great reckoning in a little room' (*AYLI* 3.3.9–12). Before putting himself forward, a poet should pause for a *second*, the fool puns. According to the inquest, the genius who dreamed of 'Infinite riches in a little room' (*Jew of Malta*, 1.1.37) died unseconded in a brawl over 'the reckoning' in a Thames-side pub. What must, then, have shocked his literary seconder, who in his portrait of the artist as a young man gave himself a backward role as bumpkin William, was how gravely a poet's words might be mistaken.[15]

Thinking his prattle to be tedious

> My father is deceased; come, Gaveston,
> And share the kingdom with thy dearest friend.

The first words of Marlowe's *Edward II* (1.1–2) gloss his own lyric in 'The Passionate Shepherd', 'Come live with me and be my love', as an irresistible offer from a perfect patron. Gaveston's plan to 'draw the pliant king which way I please' (*Edward II*, 1.52) with poetry and music thus hints how Marlowe's idea of theatre came to be bound up with his pursuit of power, specifically that of Elizabeth's heir, King James of Scotland, where 'when I last saw him', playwright Thomas Kyd told investigators, 'he meant to be'.[16] 'As for the multitude', the favourite therefore sneers, 'These are not men for me' (*Edward II*, 1.20, 49). Evidently Marlowe was sailing away from the London playhouse as Shakespeare's career in it was taking off. Gaveston sounds in fact to be speaking for the writer when he plots an 'Italian' masque (*Edward II*, 1.54) for his lover, in which the spectator Actaeon is punished for leering at a boy dressed as the Virgin Queen by seeming to be mauled to death by dogs. 'Such things as these best please his majesty', smirks the playmaker (*Edward II*, 1.70). This sounds like a manifesto for the new style of theatre funded by absolute monarchs, the court masque, in which Marlowe's vision of merging actors with the audience would be realised. References to the real play's backer, James's fixer the Earl of Pembroke, as a master of revels whose keeper (named James) abandons Gaveston, in fact key this scenario to the author's own precarious proximity to power in the earl's library in Wiltshire. 'Do not spurn this poor priest of Apollo', he begged the countess, Mary Sidney.[17] Shakespeare was an actor in Pembroke's troupe, as 'With garish robes' (*Edward II*, 6.183) they scandalised the country folk. But his first script for the company, *The Taming of the Shrew*, parodied Gaveston's Italian masque in the 'flatt'ring dream' (*Shr.*, Induction, 1.40) wasted on a drunken tinker, Christopher Sly. So if *Edward II* was about the staging of real power, it is significant that with *Richard II* Shakespeare's reply was a play which affirmed the virtual reality of theatre itself.

Edward II is Marlowe's most Shakespearean play, where he copies his imitator by adopting the weak king narrative from the popular *Henry VI* cycle. But his own choice of the royal road of patronage here produced an un-Shakespearean fixation on the body of the king, possession of which makes his upstart lover 'as great / As Caesar riding in the Roman street' (*Edward II*, 1.171–2). Gaveston's pornographic Actaeon masque is indeed actualised in Edward's murder with the obscene immediacy of a snuff movie, when the king is sodomised with a '*red-hot spit*' (*Edward II*, stage direction, 25.112). Tellingly, this horrific scene was never censored, for Edward's Christ-like suffering 'in mire and puddle' (*Edward II*, 25.59) simply sanctions the 'kingly regiment' (*Edward II*, 1.165), or sacred monarchy, which is reasserted by his son. The result is a drama that defies sexual and social norms even as it embraces royalty. By contrast, in *Richard II* the divine right dogma that not all 'the rough rude sea / Can wash the balm from an anointed king' (*R2* 3.2.50–1) is belied by rumours that the king is himself the murderer of a ruler, his uncle, whom he bathed in 'streams of blood' (*R2* 1.1.103). Thus Shakespeare exploits the legal fiction of the King's Two Bodies to imply that the office is greater than the man; and his critique of his rival for infatuation with personal power becomes obvious when the poeticising Richard associates his patronage with the most hyperbolic of Marlowe's speeches, Faustus's paean to Helen of Troy, 'Was this the face that launched a thousand ships?' (*Faustus*, 13.90):

> Was this the face
> That every day under his household roof
> Did keep ten thousand men? Was this the face
> That like the sun did make beholders wink? (*R2* 4.1.271–4)

Richard's identification with Helen is all that survives in Shakespeare's history of Gaveston's 'frolics', in which he travesties 'the Greekish strumpet' (*Edward II*, 9.15) or garbs 'outlandish cullions' (*Edward II*, 4.408), in 'women's favours' (*Edward II*, 6.182–6). Shakespeare's bookish king is instead an inept performer, who aborts the 'stately triumph' (*Edward II*, 6.12) that Edward relishes when a trial-by-combat threatens to expose his crime, but is then permitted only 'a little scene, / To monarchize' (*R2* 3.2.160–1). Shakespeare thereby decouples the play from patronage. So in *Richard II* not only are the sex and sadism of *Edward II* suppressed, but the ruse of 'the wasteful King' (*R2* 3.4.56) to present a Gavestonian masque, in which he will ascend like the sun as his 'bare and naked' subjects quake (*R2* 3.2.42), is eclipsed by Bolingbroke's wooing of 'poor craftsmen with the craft of smiles' (*R2* 1.4.27). Marlowe's 'murmuring commons' are the same 'vulgar peasants' (*Dido*, 4.4.73) who resent 'masques [and] lascivious shows' (*Edward II*, 6.156–9) in all his works, the 'rude and gross people' he despised himself.[18] But Shakespeare's commons are a carnival crowd of 'young and old' (*R2* 3.2.115), who cheer the usurper's histrionics, as 'Off goes his bonnet to an oysterwench' (*R2* 1.4.30). What is rejected in *Richard II*, then, is not theatre, but the 'flattering sounds' of Marlowe's projected royal revels, in which 'Lascivious metres' mimic 'fashions in proud Italy' (*R2* 2.1.19–21). Shakespeare, who wrote no masques, seems to have considered the Italianate shows sponsored by the Stuarts a dead-end. So as Bolingbroke announces in his play, 'Our scene is altered from a serious thing' (*R2* 5.3.77), like a political masque, to a 'courtship to the common people' (*R2* 1.4.23), that is pure theatricality:

> As in a theatre the eyes of men,
> After a well-graced actor leaves the stage,
> Are idly bent on him that enters next,
> Thinking his prattle to be tedious ... (*R2* 5.2.23–6)

By placing time-waster Richard *after* 'well graced' Bolingbroke, Shakespeare reverses his own belatedness in an act of triumphant substitution. In this play which 'sets the word ... against the word' (*R2* 5.3.120) Marlowe's project to abolish the space between reality and representation with 'high astounding terms' is emptied out, as 'the breath of kings' (*R2* 1.3.208) is reduced to tedious 'prattle' (*R2* 5.2.26) by 'breath of worldly men' (*R2* 3.2.52). The author of *Edward II* had impudently insinuated himself in the way 'The mightiest kings', such as the homosexual James, 'have had their minions' (*Edward II*, 4.390). 'Like Leander gasped upon the sand' (*Edward II*, 1.8), Marlowe pushed his luck. By contrast, when *Richard II* was put on in 1601 as a fanfare for Essex's Revolt, its symbolism of the King's Two Bodies made it hard to tell whose side its author was on, and the play may have been repeated for the queen. Dissociated from anything topical, such detachment could not look less like self-promotion; but it ensured that while Marlowe was murdered, Kyd tortured and Jonson imprisoned, Shakespeare was never questioned by the authorities, and always had the last word.

Writ in blood

As on reality TV, Marlowe's exhibitionism was the flip-side of a sadistic animus towards the spectators, and the violence of this performativity is distilled in a legend which tells of an audience of his *Doctor Faustus* petrified by the apparition of an extra devil. The story testifies to the demonism of the idea conjured in the play, that language breaks the barrier between the real and symbolic when it binds the future in a contract. This textual irrevocability was Marlowe's addition to the Devil's Pact, as if he was stoking fears that words could metamorphose things into hypothetical phantasms, like the ghost of Helen. So it is suggestive that Shakespeare's sharpest engagement with Marlowe's material word should be a deconstruction of the hypothecation of a written bond. *The Merchant of Venice* is, of course, a response to *The Jew of Malta*, where Barabas conjures the diabolic spectrality of paper credit, as 'From little unto more, from more to most' (*Jew of Malta*, 1.2.107), 'Without control' he 'pick[s] his riches up' (*Jew of Malta*, 1.1.22). But because they read it with the hindsight of modern anti-Semitism, critics overlook the way the play also valorises the Jew as the hero of Marlowe's theatre of intention, whose texts are 'So neatly plotted and so well performed' (*Jew of Malta*, 3.3.2) they prevail over the 'scripture' (*Jew of Malta*, 1.2.111) with which Catholics tax his profits. Barabas loses the plot when he gives away his scam. But his Judaic cult of textuality aligns him with the Protestant Faustus as a magician of the performative language inscribed in contracts. *The Merchant of Venice* seems a reaction as much to Faustus's capitalistic pact, in any event, as to Barabas's Mephistophelean hedge fund instruments:

> Why, this bond is forfeit,
> And lawfully by this the Jew may claim
> A pound of flesh, to be by him cut off
> Nearest the merchant's heart. [*To Shylock*] Be merciful.
> Take thrice thy money. Bid me tear the bond. (*MV* 4.1.225–9)

Marlowe uses the term 'perform' twenty times, but ten of these are in *Doctor Faustus*. In all earlier versions of the pact the bond is torn, and Satan robbed of satisfaction, after some feudal figure like the Virgin intervenes. That Faustus's avatars burn the document confirms how vampiric society found the idea he embraces, that once signed, texts are lost to phantoms of exchange: 'Here, Mephistopheles, receive this scroll, / A deed of gift' (*Faustus*, 5.89–90). Marlowe, who saw how words give hostages to fortune, was fascinated by writing on the body. But in *Faustus* the text inscribed in the signatory's blood cancels even 'Christ's blood' (*Faustus*, 14.75) as an instrument of irredeemable linguistic power. Marlowe's plot thus literalises the demonic law of contract when, despite offering to burn his books, Faustus learns 'no end is limited' (*Faustus*, 14.101) to such textual forms. Three years on, in 1595, however, Shakespeare's take on the blood pact rehearses the old solution when Portia offers to pay Shylock 'and deface the bond' (*MV* 3.2.298). This version sets out to redeem both *Faustus* and *The Jew* by reverting to their common source, in which a Jewish usurer was Satan's broker. It ends not with Portia's annulment of the bond, however, but her glee that if the Devil quotes scripture, he can be crushed by his own devices, and the last we hear of Shylock is that he is being harried to sign away his wealth: 'give him this deed, / And let him sign it' (*MV* 4.2.1–2). 'He shall have merely justice and his bond' (*MV* 4.1.334): Shakespeare concedes that Lady Bountiful can never free us from our words. But such textual literalism betrays an anger over agency that surfaces when Portia quotes some acid lines of Ovid's about the dawn that Marlowe translated and gave to Faustus, at the point when he realises 'The stars move still, time runs, the clock will strike, / The devil will come, and Faustus must be damned', 'O lente, lente currite noctis equi!' (*Faustus*, 14.72–3, 71):

> Hold in thy rosy horses that they move not …
> Thou mak'st the surety to the lawyer run,
> That with one word hath nigh himself undone.
> The lawyer and the clerk hate thy view,
> Both whom thou raisest up to toil anew …

The moon sleeps with Endymion every day;
Thou art as fair as she, then kiss and play.[19]

If Elizabeth, whose symbol was the moon, had personally condemned Marlowe, Shakespeare's comment on her favouritism was bitter indeed: 'The moon sleeps with Endymion, / And would not be awaked' (*MV* 5.1.108–9). So the lawyer and the clerk, Portia and Nerissa, throw at the dead poet the *Schadenfreude* that 'When the moon shone we did not see the candle' (*MV* 5.1.91). In this play about a legacy, the living writer struggled to eclipse the dead one by ridiculing Marlovian rhetoric in Portia's suitors: Aragon who 'will not jump with common spirits' (*MV* 2.9.31), and Morocco who offers to 'make incision' in his arm 'To prove whose blood is reddest' (*MV* 2.1.6), like Tamburlaine scoffing how 'Blood is the god of war's rich livery' (*Tamburlaine* 2, 3.2.116). So it is simplistic to read Shakespeare's prejudices into *The Merchant of Venice*, when it is Marlowe's orientalism it mocks. Its contradictions seem rather to betray the frustration that to compete with the dead is to play their game, the Oedipal knot Nerissa highlights by reminding Portia about her father's will. So this story of an unbreakable bond can be read as Shakespeare's chafing at the dead hand of intention his precursor instituted, when the creator of Faustus signed his own text: '*terminat author opus*' (*Faustus*, Epilogue, 9): the author ends the play. That Shakespeare broke this testamentary bondage by citing Marlowe's lines about debtors undone by sureties confirms how he took to heart the lesson of Faustus torn to pieces by controllers, and recoiled from an agency aspiring to the reality of words that were 'like the Draco's' in being 'writ in blood' (*Jew of Malta*, Prologue, 21).

So empty a heart

'Mountains and hills, come, come and fall on me' cries Faustus at the end (*Faustus*, 14.81), echoing 'Come live with me'. Thus, from Jupiter's cringing 'Come, gentle Ganymede, and play with me' (*Dido*, 1.1.1), to Edward's pledge to 'live or die with Gaveston' (*Edward II*, 1.137), Marlowe's self-quotation from 'The Passionate Shepherd' plays with fire in a way that is opposite to Shakespeare's secrecy, a symbolic suicide made explicit when Ithamore trashes the lyric with the prostitute Bellamira (*Jew of Malta*, 4.2.91–101), or when Tamburlaine's enemy Callapine bribes his jailer Almeda to 'depart from hence with me' (*Tamburlaine* 2, 1.2.11). If Shakespeare prefigures modernism by dissolving his personality in art, Marlowe thus flaunts a postmodern cult of celebrity when he pokes his head into the work, as it were, to have it cut off; like his other contemporary Caravaggio, who paints his own decapitated head in history paintings 'to prevent us from reading the work *as* history'.[20] When Shakespeare makes his entry on the veritable poetic Facebook generated by Marlowe's song, it is suggestive, then, that his clearest allusion to its dead author is in the context of a self-annihilating Thames-side duel. In *The Merry Wives of Windsor* the Welsh clergyman Hugh Evans is anathema to Huguenot Doctor Caius, who is paranoid about conspiracies. Moreover Windsor's hotels are full of 'Doctor Faustuses' (*Wiv.* 4.5.56) from Reformation Germany. So with the Protestant fanatic swearing 'de herring is no dead so as I vill kill him' (*Wiv.* 2.3.10), and the popish priest itching to 'knog his urinals' (*Wiv.* 3.1.10–11), the English town comes close to restaging *The Massacre at Paris* when these religious warriors square up beside their River Styx, and to steel his courage the Welshman remembers Marlowe's song:

> To shallow rivers, to whose falls
> Melodious birds sing madrigals.
> There will we make our peds of roses,
> And a thousand fragrant posies ...
> Mercy on me! I have a great dispositions to cry. (*Wiv.* 3.1.13–18)

'Whenas I sat in Pabylon' (*Wiv.* 3.1.20–1), blubs Evans, recollecting Psalm 137, a text set for Catholics by composer William Byrd. So, what are we to make of this mockery of sectarian tears, as 'shallow rivers' evoke that other riverside rendezvous, when the doomed poet awaited the tide? That Shakespeare had heard enough madrigals by 'melodious' Byrd and rejected this 'great dispositions to cry'. For if *Love's Labour's Lost* was propelled into mourning by words of Mercury, there is no doubt here about Shakespeare's refusal to mourn any more: 'Let the sky rain potatoes', exclaims Falstaff (*Wiv.* 5.5.16), dressed 'like Sir Actaeon' (*Wiv.* 2.1.105) and deriding Faustus's apostrophe to 'mountains and hills' (*Faustus*, 14.81). The 'passionate shepherd' had turned sex to violence with his 'astounding terms'. But his successor turns the men of violence back to sex, to 'Let them keep their limbs whole, and hack our English' (*Wiv.* 3.1.66–7).

While Shakespeare would rather hack words than limbs, and even offers to shake hands with his audience (*MND*, Epilogue, 15), Marlowe's aggression towards the public is epitomised by a story, similar to the stunt about the devil, that on the order of Tamburlaine to shoot the Governor of Babylon, bullets flew 'at random' (*Tamburlaine* 2, 4.1.52) in the playhouse, and 'killed a woman great with child'.[21] Just before, Olympia tricked Theridamas into testing on her a potion to ensure no pistol 'can pierce your flesh' (*Tamburlaine* 2, 4.2.66). So the loaded gun actualised the linguistic instrumentalism that ricochets through Marlovian theatre, in scenes like the sadistic one where the virgins of Damascus are exposed to 'Death' on 'the slicing edge' of Tamburlaine's steel (*Tamburlaine 1*, 5.1.112). Considering how Marlowe's scaremongering about massacres backfired in both life and art, it was this sensational instance of the pathos of the real that provoked Shakespeare's most salutary divergence, therefore, when in *Henry V* he had the king promise to re-enact the Damascus atrocity at the siege of Harfleur:

> Take pity of your town and of your people ...
> If not – why, in a moment look to see
> The blind and bloody soldier with foul hand
> Defile the locks of your shrill-shrieking daughters. (*H5* 3.3.105–12)

Henry's threat to have 'naked infants spitted upon pikes' (*H5* 3.3.115) tops Tamburlaine's terror with Aeneas' report in *Dido* of 'infants swimming in their parents' blood', virgins flung on pikes and old men 'Kneeling for mercy to a Greekish lad, / Who with steel pole-axes dashed out their brains' (*Dido*, 2.1.198–9). The warlord's mania to 'reduce' the world with his pen (*Tamburlaine 1*, 4.4.81) had been mimicked in Hotspur's mapping of England (*1H4* 3.1.111); as his bequest of a map would be copied by Lear. But Henry's saving grace is that his massacre of innocents remains imaginary, as *his words are never actualised*. Instead Marlowe's 'killing tongue' (*H5* 3.2.32) is displaced onto the king's shadow, Pistol, for from the instant he enters with 'How now, Mephistopheles?' (*Wiv.* 1.1.109), every utterance of 'this roaring devil i'th' old play' (*H5* 4.4.63–4) parrots the playwright. 'I did never know so full a voice issue from so empty a heart' (*H5* 4.4.60), regrets his Boy, in an aside that might be Shakespeare's epitaph for Marlowe. But Pistol's '*Coup' la gorge*' (*H5* 4.6.39) does for this servant when his manic 'word' to cut the prisoners' throats provokes French retaliation. After such crimes against humanity, the return to London is therefore framed within the canniest of Shakespeare's anachronisms, a back-handed compliment to his heartless progenitor:

> The Mayor and all his brethren, in best sort,
> Like to the senators of th'antique Rome
> With the plebeians swarming at their heels,
> Go forth to fetch their conqu'ring Caesar in. (*H5* 5.0.25–8)

In *Henry V* the picture of Romans panicked by Caesar is lifted from Marlowe's translation of Lucan's *Pharsalia*, where citizens hurry out in 'terror' of the dictator (*Poems*, lines 484–92), and it is this allusion which darkens the next lines about traitorous Essex 'Bringing rebellion' home (*H5* 5.0.32), as if the shade of Marlowe is making a topical point. Yet to grasp this, the Chorus comments, needs the 'working-house of thought'

(*H5* 5.0.23); for it is here that Shakespeare makes his break with the spookiness of Marlowe's 'working words' when he says 'The flat unraisèd spirits' of his 'unworthy scaffold' are 'ciphers' without 'your imaginary forces' (*H5*, Prologue, 8–18). From the author's 'working words' to the audience's 'working thought': there is a false modesty in this apology that Shakespeare lacks the trailblazer's 'muse of fire' to 'ascend / The brightest heaven', as the labour he initiates is the 'working-house' of modern theatre (*H5*, Prologue, 1–2). Marlowe had rendered spectators speechless, conjuring the real presence of kings with a performativity uncannily like the cult of the dead. But by crediting audiences with power to think for themselves Shakespeare was initiating the age of representation: 'For 'tis your thoughts that now must deck our kings' (*H5*, Prologue, 28).

As a painted tyrant

'One speech in it I chiefly loved, 'twas Aeneas' tale to Dido', Hamlet avers (*Ham.* 2.2.426–7). By making the Prince of Denmark a fan of *Dido*, Shakespeare posthumously awarded Marlowe the fame in that northern court for which he longed. But Hamlet's perverse taste for lines Henry eschews, where Aeneas 'speaks of Priam's slaughter' (*Ham.* 2.2.427–8), is of a piece with his callous intention to 'speak daggers' (*Ham.* 3.2.366), and use theatre to probe the audience 'to the quick', the hostility to 'creatures sitting at a play' (*Ham.* 2.2.574, 566) he terms 'poison in jest' (*Ham.* 3.2.214). In fact, Hamlet's elitist advice to the Players to privilege 'the judicious' over 'a whole theatre' of 'barren spectators' (*Ham.* 3.2.24–37) sounds like Gaveston commissioning 'wanton poets' (*Edward II*, 1.50) to create works which are similarly 'caviare to the general' (*Ham.* 2.2.418). Thus, when the Prince bullies the actors to 'speak no more than is set down for them' (*Ham.* 3.2.35), or denigrates the playhouse as a 'foul and pestilent congregation' (*Ham.* 2.2.293), we can perhaps hear Marlowe's 'notes to the actors', for Shakespeare seems to associate this authorial dictatorship with psychopathic exhibitionism:

> Roasted in wrath and fire,
> And thus o'er-sizèd with coagulate gore,
> With eyes like carbuncles the hellish Pyrrhus
> Old grandsire Priam seeks. (*Ham.* 2.2.441–4)

In *Dido, Queen of Carthage* the 'Greekish lad' figured the author's phallic power, as he 'whisked his sword about, / And with the wind thereof the king fell down' (*Dido*, 2.1.253–4). Shakespeare therefore seizes on this annihilating wind as a metaphor for Marlovian theatre by making it the fire which 'burnt the topless towers of Ilium' (*Faustus*, 13.91), in its author's famous words, as Troy 'with flaming top / Stoops to his base' (*Ham.* 2.2.455–6). Yet it is at this point of maximum verbal violence that the Player interposes the most momentous of all breathing spaces, when he recounts how Pyrrhus' sword, 'Which was declining on the milky head … seemed i'th' air to stick' (*Ham.* 2.2.458–9). Marlowe's murdering idol 'stood stone still' (*Dido*, 2.1.263) after the massacre, contemplating genocide with the pitilessness that excites Hamlet. But here 'Pyrrhus' pause' (*Ham.* 2.2.467) *precedes* the act, extending the life-saving interim 'Between the acting of a dreadful thing / And the first motion' (*JC* 2.1.63–4) into the eternal stasis of a picture, like the contemporary painting by Rembrandt of Abraham with the sacrificial blade suspended over Isaac:

> So, as a painted tyrant, Pyrrhus stood,
> And, like a neutral to his will and matter,
> Did nothing. (*Ham.* 2.2.460–2)

Shakespeare wrote much about creation *ex nihilo*. But the *nothing* stalling Marlowe's will to power in *Hamlet* is truly *naughty*, for it invokes the zero of the 'Wooden O', where, the Player reports, 'we often see … The bold winds speechless, and the orb below / As hush as death' (*Ham.* 2.2.463–6). The stillness of 'this distracted globe' (*Ham.* 1.5.97) is very far from Marlowe's blood and thunder. Rather, Pyrrhus' hesitation opens space for the *aesthetic*, as a hiatus within which a reckoning is endlessly deferred. Its caesura is not, then, just a signal for the prince of indecision, but a template for art itself. 'Silence', predicted Shakespeare in the Sonnets, 'shall be most my glory' (Sonnet 83); and here he silences the loudest voice by rendering windy prattle speechless. And the dramatist who dreams that art might 'give delight and hurt not' (*Temp.* 3.2.131) refers to his hurtful rival directly only once again. Set in the same Virgilian seas, Shakespeare's final play reprises Marlowe's first, as though rewinding to make a study, a courtier groans, of 'Widow Dido' (*Temp.* 2.1.80). Like Faustus, Prospero knows actors are 'all spirits' (*Temp.* 4.1.149), and opens graves to 'let 'em forth' (*Temp.* 5.1.49) by his Marlovian art. But when he calls up the goddesses from *Dido* to authorise a different outcome to 'Aeneas' tale', the magus wrecks his own masque, and instead *The Tempest* concludes with Shakespeare's grandest refusal of the 'rough magic' of Marlowe's Faustian pact with power:

> I'll break my staff,
> Bury it certain fathoms in the earth,
> And deeper than did ever plummet sound
> I'll drown my book. (5.1.54–7)

NOTES

1 *The Sonnets* in *The Norton Shakespeare. Based on the Oxford Edition*, ed. Stephen Greenblatt, Walter Cohen, Jean E. Howard and Katharine Eisaman Maus, 2nd edn (New York and London: W. W. Norton, 2008), Sonnet 86. All further quotations from the plays and poems of Shakespeare are taken from this edition, and reference is given in the text.

2 Harold Bloom, *The Anatomy of Influence* (New Haven, CT: Yale University Press, 2011), 49.

3 Bloom, *The Anatomy of Influence*, 55.

4 Abbreviations for titles of Shakespeare's plays follow those used in the New Cambridge Shakespeare series.

5 All quotations of Marlowe's plays are from Christopher Marlowe, *The Complete Plays*, ed. Frank Romany and Robert Lindsey (London: Penguin, 2003).

6 Bloom, *The Anatomy of Influence*, 49.

7 Stephen Greenblatt, *Renaissance Self-Fashioning: From More to Shakespeare* (University of Chicago Press, 1980), 200.

8 M. C. Bradbrook, *Themes and Conventions of Elizabethan Tragedy* (Cambridge University Press, 1935), 147.

9 Bloom, *The Anatomy of Influence*, 50.

10 Robert Greene, *Perimedes the Blacke-Smith* (London: 1588), quoted in David Riggs, *The World of Christopher Marlowe* (London: Faber and Faber, 2004), 222.

11 Queen Elizabeth quoted in Riggs, *The World of Christopher Marlowe*, 330; Richard Baines, 'The Baines Note', reprinted in Marlowe, *The Complete Plays*, xxxv.

12 Charles Nicholl, *The Reckoning: The Murder of Christopher Marlowe* (London: Jonathan Cape, 1992), 201–2.

13 Thomas Beard, *Theatre of Gods Judgements* (London: 1597), quoted in Nicholl, *The Reckoning*, 77–8.

14 'The Dutch Church Libel', reprinted in Nicholl, *The Reckoning*, 43–4.

15 Inquisition taken at Deptford Strand, 1 June 1593, reprinted in Frederick S. Boas, *Christopher Marlowe: A Biographical and Critical Study* (Oxford University Press, 1940), 270–1.

16 Thomas Kyd quoted in Riggs, *The World of Christopher Marlowe*, 139.

17 Christopher Marlowe, 'Dedicatory Epistle to Mary Sidney Herbert, Countess of Pembroke', in *The Collected Poems of Christopher Marlowe*, ed. Patrick Cheney and Brian Striar (Oxford University Press, 2006), 292.

18 'The Baines Note', in Marlowe, *The Complete Plays*, xxxiv.

19 Christopher Marlowe, *The Complete Poems and Translations*, ed. Stephen Orgel (London: Penguin, 2007), 'Elegy XIII', lines 10, 19–22, 43–4.

20 Leo Bersani and Ulysse Dutoit, *Caravaggio's Secrets* (Cambridge, MA: MIT Press, 1998), 1 and 91.

21 Letter of Philip Gawdy, 16 November 1587, reprinted in Boas, *Christopher Marlowe*, 71.

Further reading

Bednarz, James P., 'Marlowe and the English Literary Scene', in *The Cambridge Companion to Christopher Marlowe*, ed. Patrick Cheney. Cambridge University Press, 2004, 90–105.

Bloom, Harold, *The Anatomy of Influence*. New Haven, CT: Yale University Press, 2011.

Bradbrook, M. C., 'Shakespeare's Recollections of Marlowe', in *Shakespeare's Styles: Essays in Honour of Kenneth Muir*, ed. Philip Edwards, Inga-Stina Ewbank and G. K. Hunter. Cambridge University Press, 1980, 191–204.

Cartelli, Thomas, *Marlowe, Shakespeare, and the Economy of Theatrical Experience*. Philadelphia, PA: University of Pennsylvania Press, 1991.

Charney, Maurice, 'The Voice of Marlowe's Tamburlaine in Early Shakespeare.' *Comparative Drama* 31:2 (Summer, 1997), 213–23.

Hillman, Richard, *Shakespeare, Marlowe and the Politics of France*. New York: Palgrave, 2002.

Logan, Robert A., *Shakespeare's Marlowe: The Influence of Christopher Marlowe on Shakespeare's Artistry*. Aldershot: Ashgate Publishing, 2007.

Shapiro, James, *Rival Playwrights: Marlowe, Jonson, Shakespeare*. New York: Columbia University Press, 1991.

Wilson, Richard, 'Tragedy, Patronage, and Power', in *The Cambridge Companion to Christopher Marlowe*, ed. Patrick Cheney. Cambridge University Press, 2004, 150–72.

'"Writ in Blood": Marlowe and the New Historicists', in *Constructing Christopher Marlowe*, ed. J. A. Downie and J. T. Parnell. Cambridge University Press, 2000, 116–32.

4

WARREN CHERNAIK

The dyer's hand: Shakespeare and Jonson

The tradition of contrasting Shakespeare and Jonson as exemplifying nature and art, usually to Jonson's disadvantage, began in the seventeenth century and remained critical orthodoxy throughout the eighteenth and nineteenth centuries. To Milton in 'L'Allegro', Jonson is 'learned', where 'sweetest Shakespeare fancy's child' can spontaneously 'warble his native woodnotes wild'.[1] Dryden includes an extensive comparison of these two 'Rivalls in Poesie' in his 'Essay Of Dramatic Poesy' (1667): Jonson is 'the most learned and judicious Writer which any Theater ever had', 'deeply conversant in the Ancients, both Greek and Latine', and 'a most severe Judge of himself as well as others', while Shakespeare, in contrast, 'needed not the spectacles of Books to read Nature; he look'd inwards, and found her there'. Dryden continues:

> If I would compare him with *Shakespeare*, I must acknowledge him the more correct Poet, but *Shakespeare* the greater wit. *Shakespeare* was the *Homer*, or Father of our Dramatick Poets; *Johnson* was the *Virgil*, the pattern of elaborate writing; I admire him, but I love *Shakespeare*.[2]

Jonson's own remarks on his rival and contemporary are decidedly mixed. In his *Discoveries*, he says he 'loved the man, and [does] honour his memory, on this side idolatry, as much as any', but here and elsewhere Jonson also complains 'that Shakespeare wanted [= lacked] art', having a copious imagination that 'flowed with such facility that sometimes it was necessary that he should be stopped':

> I remember the players have often mentioned it as an honour to Shakespeare, that in his writing, whatsoever he penned, he never blotted out line. My answer hath been, 'Would he had blotted a thousand'.[3]

Jonson's tribute to 'My Beloved, the Author' in the Shakespeare First Folio (1623) is unstinting in its praise of him as a dramatist and poet excelling all his English predecessors and fully equal to the best authors of Greece and Rome: in a phrase often quoted, 'He was not of an age, but for all time.' To some extent Jonson in this 1623 poem tries to accommodate Shakespeare to his own classical ideal of the conscious, calculating artist who 'must sweat' to produce his effects, reconciling nature, the source of 'the poet's matter', with art: 'For a good poet's made, as well as born.'[4] His incidental remarks on Shakespeare in prefaces attached to his own plays are in keeping with Jonson's general critical principles, and associate the plays of Shakespeare with practices in the popular theatre that cater to what Jonson considers debased popular taste, pleasing the theatrical audience. Thus, in the Induction to *Bartholomew Fair* (1614), he includes a dig at the 'servant-monster' of *The Tempest*, saying he is 'loth to make Nature afraid in his plays, like those that beget Tales, Tempests, and such like drolleries', and the verse Prologue to *Every Man in His Humour* takes a swipe at the stage conventions followed in the *Henry VI* plays, *Henry V* and *The Winter's Tale* as examples of 'the ill customs of the age'.[5] His own plays, Jonson says, will not 'make a child, now swaddled, to proceed / Man', or depict the wars of York and Lancaster with 'three rusty swords', or include a chorus that 'wafts you o'er the seas'.[6]

In these prologues, prefaces and dedications to printed versions of his plays, Jonson is consistently hostile towards his audience, with what Jonas Barish has described as 'a deeply rooted antitheatricalism', as a dramatist 'at loggerheads with his "calling"', suspicious of the medium he has chosen to work in.[7] There are no such authorial addresses, attempts to educate the audience and correct the deficiencies in public taste, in Shakespeare. His prologues and epilogues, relatively few, are spoken by actors, and are generally appeals for applause, like the Epilogue at the end of *A Midsummer Night's Dream*, spoken by Puck:

> Give me your hands, if we be friends,
> And Robin shall restore amends.[8]

Jonson's paratexts are addressed to the reader, and make a distinction between Pretenders and Understanders, the 'unskilful' who allow themselves 'to be cozened' and 'the Reader extraordinary', able to appreciate 'Art' and immune from 'so thick and dark an ignorance, as now almost covers the age'. In at least two of his plays, *Sejanus* and *Every Man out of His Humour*, Jonson specifically tells his readers that the play before them differs from the text 'as acted on the public stage'.[9] The title page of *The New Inn* (1631), bristling with indignation, neatly sums up Jonson's distrust of actors and spectators, appealing over their heads to more discerning readers: 'As it was never acted, but most negligently play'd, by some, the Kings Servants. And more squeamishly beheld, and censured by others, the Kings Subjects. 1629. Now, at last, and to set at liberty to the Readers ... to be judg'd.'[10]

Jonson differs from Shakespeare most strongly in his preference for the medium of print over the ephemeral, unreliable stage. Shakespeare appears to have been indifferent to publication of his plays, leaving the greater part of them to be 'collected ... onely to keepe the Memory of so worthy a Friend, & Fellow alive' by his fellow actors Heminges and Condell in the First Folio seven years after his death.[11] Jonson, in contrast, carefully supervised the publication of a Folio *Works* in 1616, a volume of over a thousand pages, including texts of nine plays, thirteen masques and two groups of poems, under the headings 'Epigrammes' and 'The Forrest'. In many respects, Jonson's *Works* follows the model of Renaissance editions of classical authors, and Jonson took great care in overseeing details of the printing. Contemporaries criticised Jonson for immodesty and pretension in publishing such a volume. Suckling, in his satiric *Session of the Poets*, has Jonson claim that 'he deserv'd the Bayes, / For his were calld Works, where others were but Plaies'.[12] Where Shakespeare, according to Jonson, had 'small Latin, and less Greek', Jonson had an extensive 'well-furnisht' library of classical and Renaissance texts and took pride in his learning. *Sejanus* is as heavily indebted to Tacitus as *Julius Caesar* and *Antony and Cleopatra* are to North's Plutarch, but the 1605 quarto of Jonson's play, unlike Shakespeare's text, is full of marginal annotations identifying his sources, for the benefit of 'the learned' among his readers.[13]

Though Shakespeare and Jonson followed a similar trajectory as actors and dramatists in the early part of their careers, their paths diverged later on. Both came from relatively humble backgrounds (Jonson was 'brought up poorly') and left school early, at fifteen or sixteen. Jonson was apprenticed as a bricklayer – he hated the trade, though he retained his membership in the bricklayers' guild until 1611 – and served briefly as a soldier in the Netherlands before, in his mid-twenties, beginning a career as an actor and playwright. Virtually none of Jonson's early plays, most of them written in collaboration, have survived. He apparently began his career as an actor with Pembroke's Men in 1595–7 (he is said to have played Hieronimo in *The Spanish Tragedy* for this company), and between 1597 and 1602 received payment from Henslowe for at least five collaborative plays, as well as 'additions' to *The Spanish Tragedy*.[14] Shakespeare, whose 'lost years', between 1585 and 1592, are shrouded in uncertainty, is likely to have begun acting with the Queen's Men and Pembroke's Men, touring companies. In 1592–3, the repertory of Pembroke's Men included versions of several early plays by Shakespeare as sole author or co-author: *Titus Andronicus*, *2 Henry VI* (*The First Part of the Contention of the Two Famous Houses of York and Lancaster*), *3 Henry VI* (*The True Tragedy of Richard Duke of*

York and the Good King Henry the Sixth), *Edward III*, and the mysterious *Taming of a Shrew*.[15]

In 1594, Shakespeare became a sharer in the Lord Chamberlain's Men, from which he received a steady income in return for writing an average of two plays a year and acting in some of the company's plays. We know that Shakespeare acted in two of Jonson's plays performed by the Chamberlain's Men/King's Men: *Every Man In* (1598), where he played Lorenzo Senior or possibly Bobadillo, and *Sejanus* (1603), where he played Tiberius to Burbage's Sejanus. Jonson, unlike Shakespeare, was a freelance, with no permanent arrangement with a particular company. Six of his plays were performed by the Chamberlain's Men/King's Men, with Burbage in the principal role: *Every Man In* (1598), *Every Man Out* (1599), *Sejanus* (1603), *Volpone* (1606), *The Alchemist* (1610), and *Catiline* (1611). Burbage thus in all probability played Sejanus for the King's Men in the same season as Othello, Volpone in the same season as Macbeth, Face in the same season as Leontes. Four further plays by Jonson, *The Devil Is an Ass* (1615) and the late plays *The Staple of News* (1626), *The New Inn* (1629), and *The Magnetic Lady* (1632), were performed by the King's Men after Shakespeare had left the company. *Bartholomew Fair* (1614) was written for Queen Henrietta's Men and performed at the Hope. Four plays by Jonson were written for a children's company (Children of the Queen's Chapel/Children of Blackfriars): *Cynthia's Revels* (1600), *Poetaster* (1601), *Eastward Ho* (1605) and *Epicoene* (1609), and two earlier plays, *The Case Is Altered* and the ill-fated *The Isle of Dogs* (1597), were apparently written for Pembroke's Men. Jonson complained to William Drummond of Hawthornden that poetry had 'beggared' him and that 'of his plays he never gained two hundred pounds' altogether.[16] In 1616, he abandoned the public stage entirely, and for the next ten years he found a more reliable source of income, as well as preferment as a courtier, as the principal writer of masques for James I.

Jonson differed from Shakespeare, then, in not being a full-time writer for the public stage. In the 1616 Folio *Works*, the plays make up roughly two-thirds of the volume and poems, 'Masques at Court' and 'Entertainments' written for James I make up one-third. Far more than Shakespeare, Jonson was dependent on patronage, both from James I, who gave him an annual pension of 100 marks beginning in 1616, and from the prominent courtiers to whom he addressed poems and dedications. In Shakespeare's sonnets, many of which were written in the 1590s, the relationship between Poet and Fair Youth is in part that of poet and patron, and the poems *Venus and Adonis* (1593) and *The Rape of Lucrece* (1594) are both dedicated to the Earl of Southampton as patron. The 'rival poet' sonnets – the sequence from 76 to 86 – present a contest for preferment between the speaker and an

'alien pen' who has been successful in gaining the 'prize' of material assistance from the young nobleman addressed in these poems.[17] Sonnet 111,
though very different in tone from Jonson's splenetic attacks on the taste
of the theatrical audience, expresses dissatisfaction with the status of actor
and dramatist in the public theatre, a sense of unworthiness, almost one of
pollution by the medium the poet 'works in':

> That did not better for my life provide
> Than public means which public manners breeds.
> Then comes it that my name receives a brand,
> And almost thence my nature is subdued
> To that it works in, like the dyer's hand. (3–7)

But Shakespeare, unlike Jonson, for most of his career remained outside
patronage networks and the world of the court. The preface 'To the great
Variety of Readers', introducing the First Folio, urges readers: 'judge your
six-pen'orth, your shillings worth', as they had done in seeing the plays
at the Globe and the Blackfriars, illustrating how Shakespeare stands 'on
the fault line between past and future, between aristocratic and commercial
support'.[18]

Jonson, for all his expressed disdain for the theatrical audience, was a practical dramatist, whose plays only fully come alive when realised in performance. Sam Mendes, who directed *The Alchemist* for the Royal Shakespeare
Company in 1991, comments on how leaden and 'difficult' the play seemed
on the first day of rehearsal – 'I've never had such a terrible read-through in
my life, and such an appallingly depressed group of actors'. Until suddenly
'something clicks':

> They begin to understand the rhythm of it and it becomes suddenly incredibly
> translucent, and very easily understandable … There's a rhythm not just in
> specific scenes but throughout the whole play … We had to sort of decode it
> as a series of moves, a series of journeys, a series of stage shapes. The moment
> they were up on their feet and playing with each other they realized how alive
> the language was and how many options it gave them. I think it is very, very
> difficult to judge straight off the page.[19]

The Alchemist is a play about theatricality, about the alchemy of imagina-
tive transformation. The most effective modern productions of this play,
as of *Every Man In* and *Volpone*, have all used minimal sets, a bare stage
space, with strategically placed doors to allow rapid exits and entrances. As
Mendes says in the interview:

> For me *The Alchemist* is about the alchemy of making something out of noth-
> ing in an empty room; Face and Subtle creating something out of language
> itself. I deliberately set it in an empty room with nothing onstage but a table

and the three people. It was up to them to make everyone who walks into that room believe it's what they say it is, to create the pictures in the minds of the gulls and in the minds of the audience.[20]

The base materials out of which Face and Subtle's dream factory is fashioned, as they create illusions appropriate for each of the characters lured into the house, are made apparent in the opening scene, in which the two confederates quarrel, each abusing the other.

FACE: When you went pinned up in the several rags
           You'd raked and picked from dunghills, before day,
           Your feet in mouldy slippers, for your kibes,
           A felt of rug, and a thin threadbare cloak,
           That scarce would cover your no-buttocks.
...
SUBTLE: Thou vermin, have I ta'en thee, out of dung,
           So poor, so wretched, when no living thing
           Would keep thee company, but a spider, or worse?
           Raised thee from brooms and dust and watering pans?

                                        (1.1.33–7, 64–7)

The insistent materiality of these passages is characteristic of Jonson, as is the colloquial energy of the verse. Masters of disguise and improvisatory skills, the play's fraudsters and magicians are, unlike their gullible, self-deceiving victims, aware of the power of illusion, through which they hope to exercise control. The opening scene serves as a reminder that the 'venture tripartite' of Subtle, Face and Dol Common can dissolve at any moment, in a reverse of the alchemical process by which, according to Subtle's claim, 'lead, and other metals … would be gold, if they had time' (1.1.135; 2.3.135–6). In the play's wonderfully complex comic plot, the success of the multiple scams depends on each of the dupes remaining ignorant of the existence of any of the others.[21]

It is characteristic of the moral ambivalence of Jonson's comedies that here, as in *Bartholomew Fair*, we do not want his rogues to be found out. Subtle and Face are artists as well as criminals, and the audience response is likely to be like that of Justice Clement towards the clever servant Brainworm at the end of *Every Man in His Humour*, or Winwife and Quarlous observing the skill of the pickpocket in *Bartholomew Fair*: it 'deserves to be pardoned for the wit o'the offence' (*Every Man in His Humour*, 5.3.97–8); ''fore God he is a brave fellow; pity he should be detected' (*Bartholomew Fair*, 3.5.149–50). In *The Alchemist*, unlike *Volpone*, the gulls are ruled not by selfish greed but by the desire to transform their lives. Disguise in Jonson's plays, as Peter Womack says, is 'the recurring form of a rooted opposition of desire and law'. The house of illusion in *The Alchemist*, to which a cross-section of aspiring Londoners is drawn as if by magnetic attraction, is, like the fair in *Bartholomew Fair* and the bedchamber of Volpone, shrine to the gold Volpone and his suitors worship, 'a space where stable identities dissolve in proliferating forms of desire'.[22] In the 1977 Royal Shakespeare Company production of *The Alchemist*, at the curtain call Ian McKellen and John Woodvine, playing Face and Subtle, revealed by removing their masks that each, in yet another quickfire transformation of theatrical magic, was wearing the other's clothing.

Shakespearean and Jonsonian comedy are traditionally distinguished as romantic and satiric comedy, differing in tone and in characteristic setting: 'This is Illyria, lady' (*Twelfth Night*, 1.2.2) as against 'Our scene is London' (Prologue, *Alchemist*, 5). In the Prologues to *Every Man In* and *The Alchemist*, Jonson sets out the artistic credo of a critical realist offering 'fair correctives' and 'wholesome remedies' to viewers who can expect to see their own society anatomised:

> Deeds, and language, such as men do use;
> And persons, such as Comedy would choose,
> When she would show an image of the times,
> And sport with human follies, not with crimes.[23]

Romantic love, so central to Shakespeare's comedies, is virtually absent from Jonson's. Bonario and Celia, thinly characterised, are the least interesting figures in *Volpone;* Grace Welborn in *Bartholomew Fair* is a cipher, willing to accept either of two suitors she scarcely knows to escape marriage with the foolish Cokes, choosing a winner by lot; and the naïve, nubile Dame Pliant, treated as an item of property, is handed over to the elderly Lovewit, with no say in the matter, at the end of *The Alchemist*. According to Northrop Frye's 'The Argument of Comedy', Shakespearean comedy characteristically contrasts a 'green world', embodying the anarchic freedom of the imagination, with the constricted, rule-bound world of everyday existence: the Duke's court and the Forest of Arden, Athens and the wood of Titania and Puck. Jonson's comedies, in contrast, tend to be set in confined spaces, often claustrophobic: Morose's house, unsuccessfully fortified against intrusion; Volpone's room, in which, like a spider in his web, he waits for victims and is himself imprisoned in the role he has chosen to play; the house in which Corvino has imprisoned his wife Celia, threatening her with violence.[24] The one play by Jonson that approaches the Shakespearean pattern is *Bartholomew Fair*, in which various groups of characters, independently of each other, leave their ordinary pursuits in Act 1 to experience the pleasures of the Fair in Acts 2–5, willingly or unwillingly embracing the spirit of carnival.

Of all Jonson's comedies, the most harshly corrective, the most savage and unrelenting in its satire is *Volpone*. The Venice of *Volpone* is a world where the judges are no less corrupt than the criminals brought before them, where the greedy suitors after Volpone's wealth, men with no redeeming qualities, include a lawyer willing to 'use his tongue' (4.4.11) to lie and to persecute the innocent, a father eager to disinherit his son, and a husband who oscillates between obsessive jealousy and a desire to prostitute his wife for gain. Voltore, the doddering Corbaccio and the furious Corvino are all utterly despicable, unlike the relatively harmless gulls of *The Alchemist* and *Bartholomew Fair*. The endemic corruption of Volpone's Venice resembles that of Tiberius' Rome in *Sejanus*, and the two plays are similar in tone, though one is a comedy and the other a tragedy. Volpone and Mosca are in no way superior morally to those they exploit, though distinguished from them by their greater cleverness, resourcefulness and performing skills.

Volpone, like *The Alchemist*, illustrates Jonson's great skill in constructing a comic plot, finding unity in multiplicity. As Dryden says, praising Jonson:

> If then the parts are manag'd so regularly that the beauty of the whole be kept intire, and that the variety become not a perplex'd and confus'd mass of accidents, you will find it infinitely pleasing to be led in a labyrinth of design, where you see some of your way before you, yet discern not the end till you arrive at it.[25]

Yet in *Volpone*, there is a double or false ending at the end of Act 4, in which Volpone and Mosca, abetted by the corrupt lawyer Voltore, appear to have triumphed, in a victory of deceit and injustice, only for new complications to arise in Act 5. As Dryden says, 'there appears two actions in the Play; the first naturally ending with the fourth Act; the second forc'd from it in the fifth'.[26] After having narrowly escaped exposure in Act 4, Volpone assumes one disguise too many, away from the safety of his own 'private' chamber, and 'out of mere wantonness' succeeds only 'to make a snare for [his] own neck' (5.1.3; 5.11.1–4). Mosca takes the opportunity to cheat his master by seizing all of Volpone's property, and Volpone then, in open court ('My ruins shall not come alone'), removes his disguise and reveals the imposture (5.12.86).

The justice doled out at the end of *Volpone* is extremely harsh. Mosca, 'being a fellow of no birth or blood', is sentenced to 'live perpetual prisoner' as a galley-slave, and Volpone, as well as having all his property confiscated, is sentenced, since he has feigned sickness to gain that wealth, 'to lie in prison, cramped with irons, / Till thou be'st sick and lame indeed' (5.12.112–14, 122–4). In his prefatory epistle, Jonson defends his ending as consonant with 'the office of a comic Poet, to imitate justice, and instruct to life', showing that drama can 'punish vice'.[27] But the savagery of the sentences, which critics and audiences have found unsettling, gives the play a darkness of tone closer to tragedy than to the characteristic denouement of Shakespearean comedy, where problems are resolved amid general 'revelry' celebrating 'the good of our returnèd fortune': 'Jack shall have Jill, / Nought shall go ill, ... and all shall be well.'[28]

In the endings of *The Alchemist* and *Bartholomew Fair*, there is no element of retributive justice, with strict punishment of offenders. In *The Alchemist*, Surly's attempts to 'find the knaveries' of Subtle and Face, revealing the deception, come to nothing. When Lovewit, master of the house, whose name describes his character, returns in Act 5, he is 'indulgent to [his] servant's wit'. Face, pleased at having 'clean / Got off', dissolves his former partnership to enter a new one with Lovewit, and the two retain the 'pelf' gained from the gulls, as Subtle and Dol Common are forced to flee the house, to practise their trade elsewhere (*Alchemist*, 4.6.9; 5.5.150, 159–60, 163). *Bartholomew Fair*, as critics have often noted, is more 'genial' in tone than Jonson's other comedies, more indulgent of the folly displayed by its characters. In this play, as Womack says, 'the persistent opposition of theatre and authority is for once resolved by the unconditional surrender of the latter in the general amnesty of carnival'.[29] Those characters who try to assert authority or impose their moral standards on others are repeatedly found wanting. As the cantankerous Wasp, guardian of the foolish Cokes, admits in Act 5, once his fallibility has been made evident, 'the date of my authority is out; I must think no longer to reign, my government is at an end. He that will correct another, must want fault in himself' (*Bartholomew Fair*, 5.4.85–7). Of the would-be censors and arbiters of conduct, the one who is most strongly satirised is the Puritan Zeal-of-the-Land Busy, grotesque, hypocritical, abusing language and rhetoric in outpourings that approach redundant vacuity. Justice Adam Overdo, like the Duke in *Measure for Measure*, sets out in disguise to spy on malefactors, 'disguised (as the careful magistrate ought) for the good of the republic ... and the weeding out of enormity'. But the moralist's efforts to detect and correct the abuses he purports to find everywhere he sees are frustrated and rendered ridiculous. Repeatedly beaten and placed in the stocks, humbled by learning that the 'enormities' he inveighs against are the ordinary lot of humanity, Overdo at the end of the play is cautioned, 'remember you are but Adam, flesh and blood! You have your frailty' (5.2.81–3; 5.6.89–90, 100).

Jonson's two tragedies, *Sejanus* (1603) and *Catiline* (1611), like *Julius Caesar* (1599), *Antony and Cleopatra* (1606) and *Coriolanus* (1609), draw in considerable detail on classical historians – Tacitus and Sallust in Jonson,

Plutarch and Livy in Shakespeare. Shakespeare's Rome encompasses the early Roman republic in *Coriolanus* and his poem *The Rape of Lucrece* (1594) and its dying moments in *Julius Caesar* and *Antony and Cleopatra*, with various aspects of the Roman empire treated in *Titus Andronicus* (1593) and *Cymbeline* (1610). Jonson treats the late republic in *Catiline* and the early empire, the reign of Tiberius, in *Sejanus*. Neither *Sejanus* nor *Catiline* seems to have been a success at its initial performance. In combative prefaces to *Catiline*, Jonson complains, 'against all noise of opinion', about the faulty taste and 'ignorance' of censurers, and says of *Sejanus*: 'It is a poem that ... suffered no less violence from our people here, than the subject of it did from the rage of the people of Rome .... For this hath out-lived their malice.' *Sejanus* displeased powerful figures at court, and Jonson was questioned by the Privy Council, accused of 'popery and treason', and a year later was imprisoned for having aroused the king's displeasure by another play, *Eastward Ho*.[30]

There are passages in *Sejanus* that might have made James I and prominent courtiers distinctly uncomfortable. Tiberius, the reigning emperor, is depicted as a tyrant, a master of dissimulation, indifferent to the public interest, the fount of corruption and injustice. What is potentially incendiary in *Sejanus* is the play's depiction of the symbiotic relationship between unscrupulous monarch and unscrupulous favourite. In Act 2, Sejanus advises Tiberius to have no compunction about ruling tyrannously: might makes right.

SEJANUS: The prince, who shames a tyrant's name to bear,
           Shall never dare do anything, but fear
           ...
           It is the license of dark deeds protects
           Even states most hated: when no laws resist
           The sword, but that it acteth what it list. (2.178–9, 183–5)

The villainous Sejanus is presented as the instrument of Tiberius' tyranny, carrying out the emperor's unspoken desires, and when Sejanus outlives his usefulness, the emperor ruthlessly discards him, replacing him as favourite with Macro, whom he knows to be no less vicious and unprincipled than Sejanus. Macro's response is that of a true Machiavel and servant of arbitrary power: a prince's command overrides all considerations of morality.

MACRO: I will not ask why Caesar bids do this:
         But joy that he bids me. It is the bliss
         Of courts to be employed; no matter how:
         A prince's power makes all his actions virtue. (3.714–17)

What is under attack in *Sejanus* is not simply the influence of self-seeking, ambitious court favourites, but tyranny, the reduction of free-born Romans to the condition of slavery.[31]

What most clearly differentiates *Sejanus* from *Julius Caesar* is the play's apparent political stance and its relationship to the republican tradition. When Cassius, in speeches addressed to Brutus, attacks the adulation of 'one only man' (*Julius Caesar*, 1.2.158), using the *topos* of a decline from the age of 'our fathers' (1.2.159), a 'breed of noble bloods' (1.2.152), his appeal to republican values is calculated, aimed at persuading Brutus to join the conspiracy.

CASSIUS: Why, man, he doth bestride the narrow world
          Like a Colossus, and we petty men
          Walk under his huge legs, and peep about
          To find ourselves dishonourable graves. (*Julius Caesar*, 1.2.136–9)

Cassius is simultaneously invoking the principle of egalitarianism and patrician snobbery, in an appeal to family tradition and an idealised Roman past. Republican principles, however strongly held, are in this passage intermingled with resentment.

In *Sejanus*, the dissident republican Arruntius makes a number of similar assertions, but as an indication of shared allegiances, republican principles that his friends and associates accept as axiomatic: he has no persuasive end in mind.

ARRUNTIUS: The men are not the same: 'tis we are base,
            Poor and degenerate from the exalted strain
            Of our great fathers. (*Sejanus*, 1.87–9)

To Arruntius, 'the constant Brutus' and 'brave Cassius', like 'godlike Cato', are heroes of liberty, and Caesar, who 'sought unkindly to captive his country', is a 'monster' intent on doing 'evil' (1.90–1, 93, 95–6, 104). In *Julius Caesar*, Caesar's potential tyranny is open to debate: Shakespeare's Caesar is enigmatic and opaque, a blank sheet for others to write on. In *Sejanus*, the tyranny of Tiberius and Sejanus is demonstrated again and again in the action of the play. 'Th'abuse of greatness is when it disjoins / Remorse from power' (*Julius Caesar*, 2.1.18–19) is an axiom equally applicable to *Julius Caesar* and to *Sejanus*, but there is a difference between what might or might not happen and what has already happened, with damaging consequences.

Though *Sejanus* is a tragedy, its tone is often that of dark comedy, as reviewers commented when the Royal Shakespeare Company produced the play in 2005–6. In his programme notes for this production, Martin Butler characterises *Sejanus* as one of several plays by Jonson 'to build on the

Machiavellian dictum that men are driven by self-interest and crooks tend to prevail'. Paul Taylor, reviewing the production for *The Independent*, called the play 'a grimly sardonic take on realpolitik' with a mood 'closer to satire than to tragedy'.[32] The relationship between Volpone and Mosca is similar to that between Tiberius and Sejanus: initially united in an amoral pursuit of power, exploiting and domineering over others, the compact between the two is broken when the servant tries to supplant his master, over-reaching himself. In many ways, *Sejanus* is a deeply pessimistic play. Though, more than in Jonson's comedies, it presents a group of virtuous characters to contrast with the amoral rogues, it shows them to be utterly powerless, unable to influence the course of events, as Tiberius and his henchmen pick them off, one at a time.

The characteristic approach of Shakespeare in his Roman plays is argument *in utramque partem*, the juxtaposition of contrasting perspectives, both sides of a case, doing justice to each. In *Coriolanus*, *Antony and Cleopatra* and *Julius Caesar*, contending forces – Coriolanus and the disgruntled Roman citizens, Antony and Octavius, Brutus and Antony – are motivated by incompatible assumptions, and none can lay claim to the exclusive possession of truth. In *Sejanus* and *Catiline*, the moral dividing lines are clear-cut: Tiberius, Sejanus and Macro are unequivocally evil, and so are Catiline and his followers Lentulus and Cethegus. Unlike the rogues in Jonson's comedies, there is nothing attractive about these figures, no moral ambivalence.[33]

Jonson's principal sources for *Catiline* are Sallust's *Bellum Catilinae* and two speeches by Cicero, *In Catilinam* I and IV. In Jonson's play, Catiline is consistently base in his actions and motivations, bent on destruction, 'the ruin of [his] country' (1.45). Exulting in his evil, Jonson's Catiline openly appeals to the hitherto frustrated 'longings', sexual and acquisitive, of his supporters:

> Is there a beauty, here in Rome, you love?
> An enemy you would kill? What head's not yours?
> Whose wife, which boy, whose daughter?[34]

Jonson departs from Sallust in two respects: he gives greater prominence than Sallust to Cicero, making him the hero of the play, the saviour of Rome, and he presents Julius Caesar as deeply involved in Catiline's conspiracy.[35]

Jonson's Caesar is an advocate of Machiavellian 'policy', scornful of moral considerations, advising Catiline, 'Let 'em call it mischief; / When it is past and prospered, 'twill be virtue' (3.504–5). He is no less ruthless than Catiline, whom he encourages in his rebellion and then, once it is clear that Catiline's attempt to seize power has failed, cynically abandons. Caesar, as Jonson presents him, is a dangerous man, ambitious, envious and unscrupulous, much closer to the Caesar of Lucan's *Pharsalia* than to Shakespeare's *Julius Caesar*. In Jonson's play, Caesar, like his protegé Catiline, represents a disease eating away at the Roman republic. In potential, as yet unfulfilled, Jonson's Caesar is the Caesar of the classical republican tradition, the bold and turbulent man who destroyed Roman liberty, plunging the Roman world into the darkness of tyranny. If the 'careful magistrate' Cicero, by his vigilance, manages to preserve the Roman commonwealth from destruction, the play suggests that this victory is only a temporary one.

If there is an element of ambivalence in *Catiline*, it lies in the treatment of Cicero. Cicero is praised in choral odes for his 'wisdom, foresight, fortitude' and concern for 'the public good' (2.376, 2.401), and he is shown as acting resolutely and efficiently to defeat Catiline and his conspirators. At the same time, he can be accused of using morally dubious means to attain his ends, using 'vile' intermediaries, base and selfish, as spies and informers. In an imperfect world, he comments,

> some men will do well, for price:
> So few are virtuous, when the reward's away. (3.456, 479–80)

Critics are divided as to whether Cicero's actions in defence of the commonwealth are justified. Jonson himself in a choral ode comments on how the names assigned to the deeds of public figures bear no absolute, unchanging significance, but are open to widely divergent interpretations, as what one man calls 'diligence', another 'deceit', and a statesman's 'watchfulness' can be construed as a sinister 'lying in wait' to entrap one's enemies (4.884, 886). In both *Catiline* and *Sejanus*, the Roman world depicted is corrupt, and the tone is darkly satiric. Reviewers of the Royal Shakespeare Company production of *Sejanus* commented again and again on how the play not only 'uses ancient Rome to comment on the political climate of Jonson's own age', but had immediate relevance to 'our own political landscape', 'with its encroaching surveillance': the production 'allows us to deduce the modern parallels for ourselves'.[36] The world of Machiavellian intrigue in Jonson's two Roman tragedies is not one in which tragic grandeur or transcendence is possible.

NOTES

1   John Milton, *Complete Shorter Poems*, ed. John Carey (London: Longman, 1997), 132–4.
2   D. H. Craig, ed., *Ben Jonson: The Critical Heritage* (London: Routledge, 1990), 251–3.
3   *Ben Jonson*, ed. Ian Donaldson (Oxford University Press, 1985), 539, 596.
4   *Ben Jonson*, ed. Donaldson, 29–43 and 55–64.

5 Ben Jonson, *Complete Plays*, ed. G. A. Wilkes, 4 vols. (Oxford: Clarendon Press, 1981–2), respectively IV, 10, lines 112–15 ('Induction', *Bartholomew Fair*) and 1, 83, line 4 ('Prologue', *Every Man in His Humour*). The 'Prologue' to *Every Man in His Humour*, not included in the 1601 quarto, was first included in *Works* (1616), and was probably written *c.* 1612.

6 'Prologue', *Every Man in His Humour*, lines 7–11, and 15.

7 Jonas Barish, 'Jonson and the Loathèd Stage', in *A Celebration of Ben Jonson*, ed. William Blissett and R. W. Van Fossen (Toronto: University of Toronto Press, 1973), 27–31.

8 *A Midsummer Night's Dream* in *The Norton Shakespeare. Based on the Oxford Edition*, ed. Stephen Greenblatt, Walter Cohen, Jean E. Howard and Katharine Eisaman Maus, 2nd edn (New York and London: W. W. Norton, 2008), 'Epilogue', lines 15–16. All further quotations from the plays of Shakespeare are taken from this edition, and reference is given in the text.

9 'To the Reader', *The Alchemist*; Dedication and prefaces 'To the Reader in Ordinary' and 'To the Reader extraordinary', *Catiline*; 'To the Readers', *Sejanus*, in *Complete Plays*, ed. Wilkes, III, 228, 359–60; II, 234.

10 *Complete Plays* IV, 365.

11 'Epistle Dedicatory', First Folio.

12 *Ben Jonson*, ed. C. H. Herford and Percy and Evelyn Simpson, II vols. (Oxford: Clarendon Press, 1925–52), IX (1950), 13, 45–7.

13 *Ben Jonson*, ed. Donaldson, 31; 'To the Readers', *Sejanus*, *Complete Plays*, ed. Wilkes, II, 234.

14 W. David Kay, *Ben Jonson, A Literary Life* (Basingstoke: Macmillan, 1995), 1, 12–17. On Jonson's lost early plays and his dealings with Henslowe, see Anne Barton, *Ben Jonson Dramatist* (Cambridge University Press, 1984), 8–28.

15 On Shakespeare, the Queen's Men, and Pembroke's Men, see Scott McMillin and Sally-Beth MacLean, *The Queen's Men and Their Plays* (Cambridge University Press, 1998), 160–4; and Andrew Gurr, *The Shakespearean Stage, 1579–1642*, 3rd edn (Cambridge University Press, 1992), 38–47.

16 *Ben Jonson*, ed. Donaldson, 607, 609. On *The Isle of Dogs*, for which Jonson was imprisoned because of its 'seditious and slanderous matter', see Kay, *Ben Jonson*, 17–20.

17 Sonnet 78, 3; Sonnet 86, 2. The rival poet may be a composite figure, though one possible candidate is George Chapman. See the introduction to *Shakespeare's Sonnets*, ed. Katherine Duncan-Jones (London: Thomas Nelson and Sons, 1997), 57–69; and MacDonald P. Jackson, 'Francis Meres and the Cultural Contexts of Shakespeare's Rival Poet Sonnets', *Review of English Studies* 56 (2005), 224–46.

18 First Folio, sig. A3; David Bergeron, 'The King's Men's King's Men: Shakespeare and Folio Patronage', in *Shakespeare and Theatrical Patronage in Early Modern England*, ed. Paul White and Suzanne Westfall (Cambridge University Press, 2002), 23–48 at 46.

19 Interview with Sam Mendes, in *Ben Jonson and Theatre*, ed. Richard Cave, Elizabeth Schafer and Brian Woolland (London and New York: Routledge, 1999), 79–80.

20 Mendes in *Ben Jonson and Theatre*, 80.

21 On the skill with which Jonson links 'seven quite different comic plots all running unsuspectingly parallel to one another', see Barton, *Ben Jonson Dramatist*, 143. For a discussion of *The Alchemist* on stage in recent years see also Elizabeth Schafer, 'Troublesome Histories: Performance and Early Modern Drama', Chapter 16 in this volume, pp. 244–68.

22 Peter Womack, *Ben Jonson* (Oxford: Basil Blackwell, 1986), 119, 145.

23 Prologue, *Alchemist*, 15, 18; Prologue, *Every Man In*, 21–4.

24 Northrop Frye, 'The Argument of Comedy', in *English Institute Essays 1948* (New York: Columbia University Press, 1949), 58–73. Cf. Ian Donaldson, *Jonson's Magic Houses* (Oxford: Clarendon Press, 1997), 71–84.

25 Craig, *Ben Jonson: The Critical Heritage*, 249.

26 'Of Dramatic Poesy', in Craig, *Ben Jonson: The Critical Heritage*, 249. On the double ending in *Volpone*, see Donaldson, *Jonson's Magic Houses*, 113–14, 118–24.

27 Dedication to *Volpone*, 107, 112–13.

28 *As You Like It*, 5.4.163–6; *A Midsummer Night's Dream*, 3.3.45–7.

29 Womack, *Ben Jonson*, 157–8. See also Jonas Barish, *Ben Jonson and the Language of Prose Comedy* (Cambridge, MA: Harvard University Press, 1960), 195–213; and Ian Donaldson, *The World Upside Down* (Oxford: Clarendon Press, 1970), 51–8.

30 *Complete Plays*, ed. Wilkes, II, 233; III, 359–60; *Ben Jonson*, ed. Donaldson, 602; Kay, *Ben Jonson*, 74–6.

31 The discussion of the politics of *Sejanus* is partly based on my discussion of the play in *The Myth of Rome in Shakespeare and His Contemporaries* (Cambridge University Press, 2011). See also Curtis Perry, *Literature and Favoritism in Early Modern England* (Cambridge University Press, 2006), 229–52.

32 Martin Butler, programme notes, 2005; Paul Taylor, *The Independent*, 24 January 2006. Cf. reviews by Michael Billington, *The Guardian*, 28 July 2005; Charles Spencer, *The Telegraph*, 20 January 2006; and Victoria Segal, *Sunday Times*, 31 July 2005, emphasising Jonson's 'comedic skills' and his fascination with 'the dynamics of power'.

33 Cf. Ian Donaldson, '"Misconstruing Everything": *Julius Caesar* and *Sejanus*', in *Shakespeare Performed*, ed. Grace Ioppolo (London: Associated University Presses, 2000), 88–107.

34 *Catiline*, respectively 1.480, 1.474–6.

35 See also Blair Worden, 'Politics in *Catiline*: Jonson and his Sources', in *Re-Presenting Ben Jonson*, ed. Martin Butler (Basingstoke: Macmillan, 1999), 152–73.

36 See reviews by Charles Spencer, *The Telegraph*, 20 January 2006; Michael Billington, *The Guardian*, 28 July 2005; Ian Johns, *The Times*, 28 January 2005, and Dominic Cavendish, *The Telegraph*, 28 July 2005.

Further reading

Harp, Richard, and Stanley Stewart, eds., *The Cambridge Companion to Ben Jonson*. Cambridge University Press, 2000.

Kahn, Coppélia, *Roman Shakespeare: Warriors, Wounds, and Women*. London and New York: Routledge, 1997.

Kernan, Alvin, ed., *Two Renaissance Mythmakers: Christopher Marlowe and Ben Jonson*. Baltimore, MD, and London: Johns Hopkins University Press, 1977.

Maus, Katharine Eisaman, *Ben Jonson and the Roman Frame of Mind*. Princeton University Press, 1984.

McDonald, Russ, *Shakespeare and Jonson, Jonson and Shakespeare*. Lincoln, NE: University of Nebraska Press, 1988.

Miola, Robert S., *Shakespeare's Rome*. New York: Cambridge University Press, 1983.

Shapiro, James S., *Rival Playwrights: Marlowe, Jonson, Shakespeare*. New York: Columbia University Press, 1991.

Yachnin, Paul. *Stage-Wrights: Shakespeare, Jonson, Middleton, and the Making of Theatrical Value*. Philadelphia, PA: University of Pennsylvania Press, 1997.

5

MATTHEW STEGGLE

Urbane John Marston: obscenity, playfulness, co-operation

The work of John Marston (1576–1634) has often been treated as if it possessed an almost solipsistic independence from and antagonism to, not just the dramatic establishment of his day, but the world at large. Marston is best known for a hostile attitude to an audience exemplified by the narrator's declaration, in *Certain Satires*, that he will only write in the hope of causing offence:

> If thys displease the worlds wrong-iudging sight,
> It glads my soule, and in some better spright
> I'le write againe. But if that this doe please,
> Hence, hence, Satyrick Muse, take endlesse ease.[1]

This hostility is further exemplified by *The Scourge of Villainy* (1598), dedicated 'To everlasting oblivion', by the dedication of *Antonio and Mellida* (1602) to 'the most honorably renowned No-body', and by the contemporary description of Marston himself in *The Parnassus Plays* as '*Monsieur Kinsayder*, lifting up [his] leg and pissing against the world'.[2] Such comments have set the tone for much of Marston's critical history.[3] And yet, as writer, collaborator and theatrical shareholder, the 'real' Marston had complex constructive links to the theatrical culture of his day. Indeed, he also wrote for that most public, decorous and community-conscious of forms, the City of London civic entertainment. While aggressive hostility to all and sundry is undeniably part of the persona of what one might call the Marston brand, the factual reality is more complex, as this chapter will explore.

John Marston was born in 1576 in Oxfordshire. His father, John Marston Senior, was a prominent and successful lawyer who had studied law at the Middle Temple in London, and who had served, among other roles, as chief lawyer to the city of Coventry. After a period of study at Oxford, Marston followed his father to the Middle Temple. Marston seems to have had little time for the law, but there was more to the Middle Temple than that: as Philip Finkelpearl and others have explored, the Inns of Court were fertile territory for a young writer, filled as they were with well-heeled and ambitious young men revelling in intellectual display and artistic competition.[4] An adversarial, lawyer-like interest in debate and counter-argument remains, arguably, one of the keynotes of Marston's work.

In 1598, Marston ventured into print, publishing *The Metamorphosis of Pygmalion's Image. And Certain Satires*. The former piece is a specimen of that favourite form of late Elizabethan England, the epyllion, whose best-known representative is Shakespeare's *Venus and Adonis* (1593). Marston's version dramatises the story of Pygmalion, who creates a beautiful naked statue which comes to life: and it finds her far more interesting, and in a way far more desirable, when she is a statue than when she is a living woman. Pygmalion's lingering gaze travels down the statue's body, heading inexorably for the groin and prompting the narrator to comment admiringly:

> He wondred that she blusht not when his eye
> Saluted those same parts of secrecie:
> Conceiting not it was imagerie
> That kindly yeelded that large libertie.
> O that my Mistres were an Image too,
> That I might blameles her perfections view. (*The Poems*, 54)

This is typical of Marston's writing in its almost teenage fascination with the hidden and taboo, especially, obsessively, around matters of female sexuality. Typical, too, and a feature of Marston often overlooked, is the way in which the statement seems to rebound upon the narrator. 'Blameless' is the word that does the damage. Hitherto omniscient and impersonal, his position is undercut by the reference to his own love life, evidently not entirely satisfactory, leading to the rather comic desire that his mistress might be transformed from a living woman into a sort of sex doll. The reader, in turn, is caught up in the break of concentration. Throughout the poem and its aftermath the 'narrator' bounces, with typical inconsistency, between voyeuristic pleasure, attacks on the wickedness of voyeuristic pleasure, and vague hints of personal inadequacy; and somewhere in the background there is, implicitly, a certain detached amusement about the terms of reference of the debate.

And the 'narrator' of Marston's satires is just that – a narrator: a character by the name of 'W. Kinsayder', the surname meaning dog-castrator, being a pun on Marston's own name with its implicit pun, 'mar' (= destroy) 'stone' (= testicle). While the satires delivered in this persona certainly are angry and violent in the style of Juvenal, full of neologisms and deliberately ugly images as they attack contemporary abuses, the narrator of them should not simply be identified with the author.

As a verse satirist Marston was successful and notorious enough to be referred to by name in the Bishops' Ban, the order issued by Archbishop

Whitgift on 1 June 1599 to ban, and indeed to burn, a number of contemporary books of a satirical nature. At about this time Marston started to be recorded as a writer for the professional stage, and it has often been suggested that the Bishops' Ban was a motive impelling him to switch genres, although, as Richard McCabe and others have suggested, the truth is probably more complex. At any rate, Marston entered into theatrical writing with a background in formal verse satire.[5]

In particular, Marston specialised in writing for the boys' companies, whose actors were mostly aged between twelve and fourteen, with a rigorous musical training behind them. Acting in indoor playhouses for an audience who fancied themselves slightly more socially elite than the audience of the public amphitheatres, the boys' companies possessed a distinctive house style: excellent music, occurring between the acts and also integrated into the action, and an intense, self-referential interest in contemporary cultural and literary fashion. They also – although the exact extent of this is disputed – seem to have revelled in the disparity between the obviously immature young actors and the 'adult' material they were called upon to perform. Boys' company plays frequently pushed at the limits of cultural acceptability, especially around sexuality, being fascinated both by adult sexuality, and by sexual activity involving children. They also tested the boundaries of personal satire. In the words of *Hamlet*'s Rosencrantz, the boy actors 'are now the fashion, and so berattle the common stages – so they call them – that many wearing rapiers are afraid of goose-quills, and dare scarce come hither', and the boys' companies do seem consistently to have cultivated a reputation for the sharply, personally, satirical.[6] On all of these counts, they meshed well with the persona that Marston was establishing.

T. F. Wharton provides a useful overall summary of what one might call the 'traditional' view of Marston's career as a dramatic writer:

> His first play, *Histriomastix* (1598) was written … for his peers at the Middle Temple, but then, in two brief creative bursts, first for the playhouse at Paul's, then for the Blackfriars, he wrote eight sole-authored plays: for Paul's playhouse, between 1600 (possibly 1599) and 1601, *Antonio and Mellida*, *Jack Drum's Entertainment*, *Antonio's Revenge*, and *What You Will*; for the Blackfriars, between 1604 and 1606, *The Malcontent*, *The Dutch Courtesan*, *The Fawn*, and *Sophonisba*. The silent two- or three-year interim marks Marston's virtual obliteration by Jonson in the 'War of the Theatres'.[7]

Let us consider in more detail the plays and events mentioned in the above account.

Histriomastix is a strange and unwieldy six-act play, an allegory about the relationship between prosperity and society. It seems to have been performed at the Middle Temple around 1598. The first explicit ascription of the play to Marston was not made until the nineteenth century, and then only on the basis of a seeming allusion to it in Jonson's *Every Man out of His Humour*, in the context of a passage attacking contemporary neologisms (including several associated with Marston). In recent years Roslyn L. Knutson has argued that the play, untypical of Marston on many counts, should be taken out of the Marston canon altogether, and debate continues about whether or not the play can in fact be linked to Marston at all.[8]

The so-called *Antonio* plays – *Antonio and Mellida* (c. 1599) and *Antonio's Revenge* (1599–1600) – are a 'revenge musical', in Rick Bowers's pregnant phrase.[9] The first of the pair is a play of Venetian ducal intrigue that appears to be on the pattern of *The Spanish Tragedy*, Thomas Kyd's great contemporary success, building up to a bloody climax which then defeats expectations by springing a happy ending. Senecan elements combine in it with Marston's usual satirical energy and vim. Its sequel, *Antonio's Revenge*, then turns audience expectation on its head again, taking the characters from the previous play and killing them off, for real this time, in ways both gruesome and inventive. Here, for instance, Antonio kills the Duke's son Julio, shortly before sprinkling his blood as an oblation and then serving him to the Duke as sweetmeats:

ANTONIO: O that I knew which joint, which side, which limb
          Were father all, and had no mother in't,
          That I might rip it vein by vein and carve revenge
          In bleeding rases! But since 'tis mixed together,
          Have at adventure, pell-mell, no reverse –
          Come hither, boy. This is Andrugio's hearse.
                    [Antonio *draws his dagger.*]
JULIO: O God! you'll hurt me. For my sister's sake,
          Pray you do not hurt me. And you kill me, 'deed,
          I'll tell my father.[10]

The blood-and-thunder rhetoric is made hollow by the at first pathetic and then ridiculous reply, and the incongruity, for a moment, breaks the dramatic illusion – almost a Brechtian *Verfremdungseffekt*.

The *Satires* and *Antonio's Revenge* have always tended to be the dominant items in setting the agenda for Marston criticism. But Marston's other plays, while they share elements of the playful cruelty discussed so far, are more various than this model would suggest. *Jack Drum's Entertainment* is a comedy of love, lust and mistaken identity, set in Highgate, a village on the outskirts of London. Far from being an exercise in Senecan continental darkness, it is a sunny play that even includes an appearance from that set-piece of English pastoral, a troupe of Morris dancers. *What You Will* is also a happy-ending love-comedy of marital reunion, particularly interesting because of its connections to Shakespeare.

What You Will is set in Venice, and revolves around the unfortunate merchant Albano, believed drowned at sea. Albano's wife is on the point of remarrying to a foolish Frenchman, Laverdure, and Albano's friends, in a bid to prevent the marriage, arrange for a man to impersonate Albano in the hope of causing confusion. The impostor is able to mimic Albano's costume, his appearance, even his characteristic stammer. At this point Albano himself appears in Venice, having at last made his way home after shipwreck, and finds that nobody believes that he is Albano. The farcical confusions escalate into a stand-up argument between the two Albanos, conducted of course in the medium of stammering, until eventually order is restored. *What You Will* has many rare forms of engagement with Shakespeare. Revolving as it does around doubles and shipwreck, it has a flavour of *The Comedy of Errors*, and interesting links with *Twelfth Night, or What You Will*, with which it partially shares a title (perhaps as a result of Marston having accidentally anticipated Shakespeare's intended main title for the play we now know as *Twelfth Night*). It is also a play notably interested in the poetics of satire and comedy, and the role of the satirist. For instance, the Induction of the play, in which an onstage audience discuss the play to come, offers a dialogue about different models of dramatic satire which challenges the usual pieties about literary merit and unfit audiences. Doricus argues that audience reception *is* literary merit:

> *Musike and Poetry* were first approu'd
> By common scence; and that which pleased most,
> Held most allowed passe: no, rules of Art
> Were shapt to pleasure, not pleasure to your rules[11]

In the play itself, Lampatho Doria and Quadratus, a feuding pair of writers, argue about the nature of poetic inspiration, the place of the satirist, and the role of drama, while flitting in and out of the play's main love-plot.

This brings us to the lacuna at the heart of Marston's theatrical career, or at least at the heart of the usual construction of that career: the Poets' War, or War of the Theatres. Briefly: in the years between 1599 and 1601, the plays of Jonson, Marston and Dekker, in particular, are repeatedly interested in the character and persona of the satirist, and in the intellectual and ethical implications of stage satire as a form. Since *What You Will* seems to respond in particular to discussions of these matters on Jonson's near-contemporary play *Every Man out of His Humour*, the play becomes part of a series of plays that James Bednarz has called a 'major debate in the English Renaissance on the nature and function of drama'.[12]

Furthermore, at least some of these plays tipped over into personal satire. In his comedy *Poetaster*, performed in 1601, Jonson personally satirised Marston as the ambitious, clueless poet-satirist Crispinas, who spends the play first trying to impress, and then trying to cause trouble for, the long-suffering poet Horace (who is, in some sense, a representation of Jonson himself). Crispinas vomits on stage in the final scene of the play, having been given an emetic to purge him of the complex and uncouth words he loves to use in his poetry. One by one, he throws up words and phrases including 'lubrical', 'glibbery', and 'spurious snotteries'.[13]

Jonson himself, in conversation with William Drummond of Hawthornden many years later, confirmed that this play was personally satirical, describing the events as follows: 'He had many quarrels with Marston, beat him, and took his Pistol from him, wrote his Poetaster on him; the beginning of them were that Marston represented him in the stage.'[14]

Taking their cue from Jonson's remark, many scholars have looked at Marston's early output searching for possible satirical personations of Jonson. Candidates include the scholar Chrisoganus of *Histriomastix*; the foolish Brabant Senior of *Jack Drum's Entertainment*; and *What You Will*'s Lampatho Doria. However, none of these is entirely obviously or uncomplicatedly a personation of Jonson. Arguably the best candidate is the unsuccessful satirist Lampatho, but Lampatho also has some traits which seem to allude to Marston himself. MacDonald P. Jackson and Michael Neill describe Lampatho as a 'teasing anamorphic double-portrait' combining elements of Jonson and of Marston: a useful formulation which suggests that these plays are more complex than mere *romans à clef*.[15]

But the play which finished the War of the Theatres offers a more complex contemporary personation of Marston to set against the intemperate Crispinas of *Poetaster*. The play is Thomas Dekker's *Satiromastix*, a response to *Poetaster* in which the whole action is translated from the Rome of the Emperor Augustus to the England of King William II. Crispinas and Demetrius (Jonson's version of Dekker in *Poetaster*) are reinvented as modest and reasonable writers trying to do a job. As for 'Horace' – detached from his Roman context, and now an obvious and detailed parody of Jonson – he is presented as a talented but petulant *enfant terrible* who suffers various indignities in the course of learning that he must behave more considerately to those around him.[16] This is Dekker's Crispinas [= Marston]:

> Doe we not see fooles laugh at heauen? and mocke
> The Makers workmanship; be not you grieu'd
> If that which you molde faire, vpright and smooth,
> Be skewed a wry, made crooked, lame and vile,
> By racking coments, and calumnious tongues,
> So to be bit it ranckles not: for innocence
> May with a feather brush off the foulest wrongs.
> But when your dastard wit will strike at men
> In corners, and in riddles folde the vices
> Of your best friends, you must not take to heart,
> If they take off all gilding from their pilles,
> And onely offer you the bitter Coare.[17]

While this Crispinas is still a writer of satire, he is more detached from it, able to step back from that writing rather than being immersed in its persona, and seeing satire as taking place within mutually improving bonds of friendship. His intervention with Horace is more constructive than one might expect:

> We come like your Phisitions, to purge
> Your sicke and daungerous minde of her disease. (*Satiromastix*, 1.2.247–8)

As Dekker's alternative personation of Marston shows, the easy caricature of Marston is by no means the whole story, and it is by no means clear that in the course of the War of the Theatres, Marston, as has been proposed, suffered virtual obliteration.

Indeed, around 1603, Marston became a shareholder in the Children of the Queen's Revels, as they now became – the former Children of the Chapel, the company which had staged *Poetaster*. Marston continued to work with Jonson, dedicating to him the printed edition of *The Malcontent*, and collaborating with him on *Eastward Ho* (1605). The four plays itemised by Wharton from this later part of Marston's career comprise the sober and serious tragedy *Sophonisba*, whose eponymous heroine is an African queen and an exemplar of Stoic constancy; *The Fawn* and *The Malcontent*, two 'disguised Duke' tragicomedies whose outcomes are definitely happy; and *The Dutch Courtesan*, a lively and realistic city comedy set in London.

In 1606, King James's brother-in-law, King Christian VI of Denmark, came to visit England. The two kings visited London together on 31 July 1606, and were provided with entertainments at the expense of the City of London. These included a procession, a *tableau vivant*, a dramatic 'eclogue' performed at the Fleet Conduit, a Latin speech by the Recorder of the City of London, as well as an allegorical Latin entertainment. Marston wrote the Latin speech; a signed presentation manuscript of it survives. Marston can also be linked to the 'eclogue', since he later borrows material from it. It is unclear how much further, if at all, his involvement in the day extended beyond these two elements, but for Marston to be involved in the event at all indicates the extent of his cultural capital. In 1607, Marston again appears as an occasional writer, commissioned to provide an entertainment to celebrate the August 1607 visit of Alice, Dowager Countess of Derby, to her daughter and son-in-law Lord and Lady Huntingdon at their house, Castle Ashby, in Leicestershire. The *Entertainment at Ashby* is a masque-like confection, drawing on elaborate scenic effects and imagery from Edmund Spenser's *Faerie Queene* and, arguably, Shakespeare's *Midsummer Night's Dream*. Again, it looks almost totally unlike the work usually associated with the Marston persona.[18]

Thereafter, Marston seems to have simply retired from writing. He married the daughter of one of King James I's chaplains and entered the church, being ordained in 1609 and living quietly, as a priest, for the next twenty-five years. He left behind – in addition to the sole-authored plays already mentioned – contributions to a number of collaborative dramas, including *The Insatiate Countess*, a lurid tragedy about nymphomania (believed to have been started by Marston and completed by Lewis Machin and William Berkstead), and *Lust's Dominion*, a darkly comic tragedy set in Spain, whose hero is Eleazer the Moor (and in which Thomas Dekker, too, is thought to have had a hand). In recent work stressing Marston's collaborative modes, Charles Cathcart has plausibly suggested that yet another play, *The Family of Love*, generally attributed to Thomas Middleton, might have to be considered on the edge of the Marston canon.[19]

This is the paradox of Marston: he is an author whose best-known persona is as a solitary, snarling satirist, but at the same time one whose work is frequently collaborative and deeply enmeshed in the theatrical culture of its time. Marston's best-known play, *The Malcontent*, is particularly interesting from this point of view.

The Malcontent as we possess it is a complex, multi-layered text, full of signs of collaboration. The early printings bear a Latin dedication by Marston to Jonson, 'AMICO SVO CANDIDO ET CORDATO' – to his candid and good-hearted friend (3). Some of those printings also contain extra material, written by John Webster for an occasion when the play transferred – under circumstances that are still not entirely clear – from the Children of the Chapel to the adult players of the King's Men, Shakespeare's own company. In the Induction, some of the great names of early modern drama, including Shakespeare's leading man Richard Burbage, as well as Henry Condell, the eventual compiler of the First Folio, both play versions of themselves, defending their acquisition of the play from the children: as 'Condell' remarks,

> Why not Malevole in folio with us, as Jeronimo [from Kyd's *The Spanish Tragedy*] in decimo-sexto with them? They taught us a name for our play: we call it *One for another*. ('The Induction', 78–80)

In dialogue like this, one begins to see a picture of early modern drama in general in terms of exchanges, swaps and constructive competition. This is particularly the case since, around 1604, the King's Men were also performing *Measure for Measure*, the latest work of their chief playwright Shakespeare. This is a play with obvious similarities to *The Malcontent* in its use of what has been described as the 'disguised Duke' motif, and its dark sexual tragicomedy, although it is Marston's play, not Shakespeare's, that seems to have enjoyed the greater contemporary impact.

The Malcontent revolves around Malevole, a foul-mouthed and discontented hanger-on at the court of Duke Pietro of Genoa. Pietro himself has only recently come to power, having usurped the previous Duke, Altofront. Pietro himself is being conspired against, although he does not know it, by his favourite Mendoza who (having already seduced Pietro's wife Aurelia) now seeks to take over also the ducal throne. It soon becomes apparent to the audience, though, that Malevole is in fact the deposed Altofront in disguise. Hence, when Mendoza tells Malevole to murder Pietro – 'kill him, hurle him i' the main, and proclaim thou sawest wolves eat him' (3.3.105–6) – Malevole/Altofront actually spares Pietro's life and puts him into hiding. The plotting and counterplotting continue at a frantic pace, resembling nothing so much as 'The Courier's Tragedy', that hilariously accelerated parody of a Jacobean tragedy offered by Thomas Pynchon in *The Crying of Lot 49*, until the play comes to its climax in a dance of disguised avengers. Set as it is in a corrupt court, and exploring ideas of disguise, feigning and delay, *The Malcontent* has obvious connections not just with contemporary revenge tragedies; not just with Shakespeare's *Measure for Measure*; but also with the greatest revenge tragedy of them all, *Hamlet*.

But the most important thing about *The Malcontent* is that it is a very funny play. Fast-moving and verbally freewheeling, there is an exuberance about its accumulation of detail which constantly surprises the reader. Here, for instance, is Malevole, addressing Maquerelle and letting his imagination run wild on the subject of possible aphrodisiacs that the court ladies could apply to their elderly husbands:

> Lady, ha' ye now no restoratives for your decayed Jasons? Look ye, crab's guts baked, distilled ox-pith, the pulverized hairs of a lion's upper lip, jelly of

cock-sparrows, he-monkey's marrow, or powder of fox-stones? ... Fried frogs
are very good, and French-like, too. (2.2.19–21, 33–4)

The comic list of aphrodisiacs is something of a staple of Renaissance comedy,
also used, for instance, in Jonson's *The Alchemist*. This, though, is a particularly amusing example. Through the first part of this list, humour is gained
from the lovingly varied rhythms of each phrase and the diverse images and
textures evoked: but it is that final, unexpected appeal to fashion which is
particularly winning. The humour also points up some of the play's recurring concerns, which take us back to the stanza from *The Metamorphosis of
Pygmalion's Image* discussed above. Like the poem, this play is almost obsessive in its interest in sexuality, especially female sexuality, and that interest
destabilises the position of the satirist-narrator. Malevole is, or ought to be,
a monitory voice condemning inappropriate sexual behaviour. And yet his
sarcastic recommendations have the unexpected effect of encouraging such
behaviour, to the point of him being almost an *agent provocateur*. In this
case, for instance, the attentive Maquerelle proceeds to ask him to find her a
suitable fox (from which to prepare the powdered fox testicles). In any case
it is inevitable that, given the nature of his underlying disguise, Malevole
is encouraging the very kinds of behaviour he hates, so that the tone of his
speech is always shifting.[20]

Throughout *The Malcontent*, the intrigues are driven by the twin and
interrelated forces of lust and will-to-power. Even Mendoza, the play's arch-
politician, is driven to his machinations – as he admits in soliloquy – specifically by the sexual advantages he gains from political power:

O blessed state, what a ravishing prospect doth the Olympus of favour yield!
Death, I cornute the Duke! Sweet woman, most sweet Ladies, nay Angels!'

(1.5.32–4)

Indeed, in Mendoza's world view, sexual desire dominates human will, and
introduces an almost clockwork determinism into the world:

Lust's like the plummets hanging on clock-lines,
Will ne'er 'a done till all is quite undone. (2.1.9–10)

It is important to remember, though, that Mendoza's view is not necessarily one
endorsed by the play itself. Among the female characters, Maria, Altofront's
wife who now believes him dead, remains steadfastly true to his memory:
Altofront, on being reunited with her, calls her 'more lovèd than my breath'
(5.6.71). The hero of this play is, much more obviously than his Shakespearean
relatives Duke Vincentio in *Measure for Measure* or Duke Prospero in *The
Tempest*, a man in love, and this love, in counterpoint to the sordidly mechanical desires of Mendoza and the rest, is arguably central to the play.

In particular, in spite of the misanthropic tone of many of Malevole's utterances in character, the ending that he engineers enacts not the carnage of a revenge tragedy but a masque-like finale. Mendoza is set upon by those whom he believes he has killed, and they in turn appear to kill him, but only in pretence. Pietro is spared and given a new chance. Perhaps even more surprisingly, so is Pietro's wife Aurelia: the play's reaction to female adultery is not to demand the death of the adulteress, but to have her sorry for what she did and with a chance to rebuild her marriage together with her husband. *The Malcontent* may start as playful and disturbing farce, but it ends with reunions and reaffirmations of the power of marriage, and that is part of the complexity of the play.

Each era has tended to see Marston in the image of its own preoccupations. Thus, for a generation of twentieth-century critics, Marston was an Absurdist born before his time. In the most recent iteration, he has been reclaimed again: 'De-centered and de-stabilizing, anarchically playful, constantly transgressing boundaries of literary convention, politics, or gender, Marston's vexing transactions with his audience always challenge us, not least by the jagged shifts of tone, characterization, and meaning which are not merely his protective coloration but his very essence. This is exactly the voice of post-modernism.'[21] This essay perhaps starts towards another version: of Marston as a sophisticated, collaborative, creative literary professional. Sexually frank, satirically daring, both modern and yet deeply of his time, Marston remains one of the most puzzling, and appealing, of early modern dramatists.

NOTES

1   *The Poems of John Marston*, ed. Arnold Davenport (Liverpool University Press, 1961), 92.

2   See John Marston, *The Malcontent*, ed. George K. Hunter (Manchester University Press, 1975), xix–xx.

3   For a more detailed discussion, see T. F. Wharton, *The Critical Fall and Rise of John Marston* (Columbia, SC: Camden House, 1994).

4   Philip J. Finkelpearl, *John Marston of the Middle Temple: An Elizabethan Dramatist and His Social Setting* (Cambridge, MA: Harvard University Press, 1969).

5   Richard A. McCabe, 'Elizabethan Satire and the Bishops' Ban of 1599', *Yearbook of English Studies* 11 (1981), 188–93.

6   *Hamlet* in *The Complete Works*, ed. Stanley Wells and Gary Taylor (Oxford University Press, 1986), 2.2.341–4.

7   T. F. Wharton, 'Introduction' to *The Drama of John Marston: Critical Re-Visions*, ed. T. F. Wharton (Cambridge University Press, 2000), 1.

8   Roslyn L. Knutson, '*Histrio-Mastix*: Not by John Marston', *Studies in Philology* 98 (2001), 359–77.

9   Rick Bowers, 'John Marston at the "Mart of Woe": The *Antonio* Plays', in *The Drama of John Marston*, ed. Wharton, 14–26: see also Rick Bowers, *Radical Comedy in Early Modern England: Contexts, Cultures, Performances* (Aldershot: Ashgate, 2008), 71–82.

10 *Antonio's Revenge*, ed. W. Reavley Gair (Manchester University Press, 1978), 3.3.20–8.

11 *What You Will*, in *The Plays of John Marston*, ed. H. Harvey Wood, 3 vols. (London: Oliver and Boyd, 1934–9), 11, 'Induction', 232.

12 James P. Bednarz, *Shakespeare and the Poets' War* (New York: Columbia University Press, 2001), 5. See also Matthew Steggle, *Wars of the Theatres: The Poetics of Personation in the Age of Jonson* (Victoria, BC: English Literary Studies, 1998).

13 Ben Jonson, *Poetaster*, ed. Tom Cain (Manchester University Press, 1995), 5.3.271, 277.

14 *Ben Jonson's Conversations with William Drummond of Hawthornden*, ed. R. F. Patterson (London, Glasgow, and Bombay: Blackie and Son, 1923), 26–7.

15 *The Plays of John Marston*, ed. MacDonald P. Jackson and Michael Neill (Cambridge University Press, 1986), xiv.

16 Marston is often thought to have had some role in writing *Satiromastix*, but external evidence is lacking: for a recent contribution, see James P. Bednarz, 'Between Collaboration and Rivalry: Dekker and Marston's Coactive Drama', *Ben Jonson Journal* 10 (2003), 209–34.

17 Thomas Dekker, *Satiromastix*, in *The Dramatic Works of Thomas Dekker*, ed. Fredson Bowers, 4 vols. (Cambridge University Press, 1953–61), 1, 1.2.212–23.

18 For fuller bibliography on both of these, see Matthew Steggle, 'John Marston's *Entertainment at Ashby* and the 1606 Fleet Conduit Eclogue', *Medieval and Renaissance Drama in England* 19 (2006), 249–55.

19 Charles Cathcart, *Marston, Rivalry, Rapprochement, and Jonson* (Aldershot: Ashgate, 2008).

20 For more work on Marston and sexuality see the essays in Wharton's collection of essays, *The Drama of John Marston*. The volume marks one of the new frontiers of Marston studies.

21 Wharton, *The Drama of John Marston*, 10.

Further reading

Axelrad, A. José, *Un Malcontent Elizabéthain: John Marston, 1576–1634*. Paris: Didier, 1955.

Caputi, Anthony, *John Marston, Satirist*. Ithaca, NY: Cornell University Press, 1961.

Cathcart, Charles, *Marston, Rivalry, Rapprochement, and Jonson*. Aldershot and Burlington, VT: Ashgate, 2008.

Finkelpearl, Philip J., *John Marston of the Middle Temple: An Elizabethan Dramatist in His Social Setting*. Cambridge, MA: Harvard University Press, 1969.

Geckle, George L., *John Marston's Drama: Themes, Images, Sources*. Rutherford, NJ: Fairleigh Dickinson University Press, 1980.

Gibbons, Brian, *Jacobean City Comedy*, 2nd edn. London and New York: Methuen, 1980.

Ingram, R. W., *John Marston*. Boston: Twayne, 1978.

Tucker, Kenneth, *John Marston: A Reference Guide*. Boston: G. K. Hall, 1985.

Wharton, T. F., *The Critical Fall and Rise of John Marston*. Columbia, SC: Camden House, 1994.

Wharton, T. F., ed., *The Drama of John Marston: Critical Re-Visions*. Cambridge University Press, 2000.

6

DARRYLL GRANTLEY

Thomas Dekker and the emergence
of city comedy

In the trilogy of university plays known as *The Parnassus Plays*, produced at
St John's College, Cambridge, between 1589/9 and 1602/3, a recurrent concern is expressed about the professional fate of the growing number of graduates the universities were turning out by the end of the sixteenth century.
This includes a worry about the popularisation of modes of discourse that
are considered in the plays more properly to be the province of the social
and educational elite and, these being university plays, the drama comes in
for specific attention. Gullio, a fool in *The Second Part of the Return from
Parnassus*, is an admirer of Shakespeare and he draws his 'shreds of poetrie'
from the theatre.[1] It is a source of discomfort in the play that drama as a
mode of literary writing that is ultimately the product of learning should
be indiscriminately peddled in the marketplace of the public theatres. The
play also contains the dramatisation of real figures from that theatre – Will
Kempe and Richard Burbage – who in their turn criticise the dramatic writing of scholars:

> Few of the vniuersity [men] pen plaies well, they smell too much of that writer
> *Ouid*, and that writer['s] *Meta-morphoses*, and talke too much of *Proserpina*
> & *Iuppiter*. Why heres our fellow *Shakespeare* puts them all downe, I and *Ben
> Ionson* too. O that *Ben Ionson* is a pestilent fellow, he brought vp *Horace* giu-
> ing Poets a pill, but our fellow *Shakespeare* hath giuen him a purge that made
> him beray his credit. (1766–7)

The play seems to be reflecting an anxiety on the part of scholars about
the advent of a profession that required some learning but involved indiscriminately both men who had been to university and men who had not.
There is some regret that university men should be getting involved with
this profession at all – 'But ist not strange these mimick apes should prize
/ Vnhappy Schollers at a hireling rate?' (1918–19) – not only because the
scholars had to work for actors, but because of the prostitution of their
talents and learning that was involved. There is an implicit recognition of a

new type of profession here, one that makes use of learning but caters to the taste of the multitude.

One member of this new profession was Thomas Dekker, of whose early life little is known except that he was born in London in the early 1570s. It is highly improbable that he went to university, and he is thus more likely to be among the first crop of non-graduates to start making plays for the commercial theatre, one of the new breed of dramatists who would succeed the University Wits who had formed the first cohort of playwrights. As such he helped to usher in a vigorous period of playwriting populated by names that have become the beacons of early modern drama, including Shakespeare, Ben Jonson and Thomas Middleton. The success of these writers for the theatre did not depend on their education, but on their ability to gauge the tastes of audiences and to craft products to appeal to those tastes. That Dekker was highly attuned to these conditions is abundantly demonstrated not only by his plays but also by the large number of other publications he produced for the popular market.

Dekker's professional life was in many ways indicative of the thrusting spirit of the growing metropolis, and in his attempts to exploit a variety of opportunities to make money through his writing he demonstrated the sort of adaptability and proteanism that were an advantage for a successful life in the complex and sprawling urban environment, the rapid growth of which had produced a new demographic phenomenon in England. In the course of his career he wrote verse, religious tracts and other popular pamphlets as well as his varied output for the theatre. Dekker was very much a working writer, and completely in the spirit of the new commercial theatre.

He appears to have started his professional life working for the Lord Chamberlain's company, but from 8 January 1598 he begins to be mentioned in Philip Henslowe's diary and he was probably working for Henslowe and his Admiral's Company even before this date. Between 1598 and 1600 Dekker worked to a varying extent on over thirty plays for this company, of which only eight were singly authored. In the early part of his career, he is recorded as having been paid for making alterations to several plays, and he appears to have been something of a hack, for which Jonson would later satirise him in his *Poetaster* (1601) as a 'dresser of plays about town'.[2] However, the sheer range of his work, his collaborations and long, if interrupted, working life give him a significant part in the theatre writing culture of early modern England from the late Elizabethan to the Caroline periods.

The prominence of Shakespeare and, to a lesser extent, Marlowe and Jonson as individual writers for the stage tends to distort perception of the realities of early modern playwriting. The commercial theatre demanded a steady turnover of new plays geared to the prevailing fashions in audience taste, and this left relatively little room to accommodate the literary *auteur* where non-closet drama was concerned. In his numerous collaborations, Dekker's career in theatre writing more readily exemplifies the reality of this commercial marketplace. Henslowe's first entry for him records the purchase from Dekker of a 'book' or play manuscript, and he evidently was not short of theatre work in the early years, in 1599–1600 being paid for work on at least ten plays, though only four of these are in his name alone. Most of Dekker's work for theatre, including two of these early single-authored plays, has now been lost, a fact that is likely to have significantly reduced his visibility to subsequent centuries. Aside from those for which he was paid to make alterations – like *Sir Thomas More* to which Shakespeare also contributed[3] – he had a hand as collaborator or sole author in over forty-five plays, but only around eighteen of his plays survive, of which eight are known to have been written by him alone, with three further ones usually ascribed to him as sole playwright.

The probably inadequate extant records for the years 1598 to 1602 show Dekker to have been very active, not only as single author, but in a wide variety of collaborative combinations. In 1598 he wrote nine plays with Henry Chettle and Michael Drayton, four of them also including Robert Wilson as a contributor. In 1599 he wrote three plays with Chettle, one with Jonson and one with both. In 1600 he produced five in various combinations including Chettle, Robert Wilson, Michael Drayton, John Day, William Haughton, Richard Hathway and Anthony Munday, and in 1601 he is recorded as writing one play with Chettle. In 1602 he wrote five in widely differing collaborative arrangements with Chettle, Drayton, Munday and new partners Thomas Heywood, Wentworth Smith, John Webster and Thomas Middleton. Dekker thus cut his teeth working with several of the Elizabethan playwrights, but his career and collaborations stretched through the Jacobean to the Caroline period although, with some notable exceptions, later mostly in two-man combinations. A relatively frequent and long-standing collaborator was Webster with whom he continued to work in 1624 even after he had spent seven years in debtors' prison for a debt to Webster's father. In the case of Jonson, Dekker has the distinction of being the only playwright to have worked as a sole collaborator with him on any play, the work being *The Page of Plymouth* (1599). Though Jonson went on to attack Dekker in *Cynthia's Revels* (1600) and *The Poetaster* (1601) as part of the 'War of the Theatres' at the turn of the century, to which Dekker responded rather less viciously in *Satiromastix* (1601), the two worked together a couple of years later on the royal entry for James VI and I, for which Dekker wrote *The Magnificent Entertainment given to King James* (presented in 1604).

Dekker's extensive non-dramatic writing shows him to have been able to turn his hand to a wide range of writing, and his apprenticeship as partly a 'dresser of plays' and a collaborator appears to have helped him to considerable versatility in respect of the range of dramatic genres that he tackled. He also proves to have absorbed influences from writers with whom he did not work, like those of John Lyly and Christopher Marlowe discernible in his 1599 comedy *Old Fortunatus*. In the early years, working with Chettle and Drayton he wrote a large number of chronicle plays, a genre popular in the nationalistic post-Armada decade of the 1590s. By 1598 he had written enough tragic drama for Francis Meres to name him in *Palladis Tamia, Wit's Treasury* as among the 'best for tragedy'. His early work even includes *Jephthah*, a now lost biblical play that he wrote with Anthony Munday in 1602. He also turned his hand to public celebratory drama, writing, aside from the collaboration with Jonson on the royal entry mentioned above, a contribution to the festivities for the installation of a new Lord Mayor in 1612, entitled *Troia Nova Triumphans*. There was clearly also an element of opportunistic pragmatism shaping Dekker's oeuvre for the stage, another respect in which he helps define what it was to be a commercial playwright in early modern London. One instance of this is the case of the plays with directional titles, discussed below, but it is possible that Dekker and Middleton wrote *The Honest Whore* with an eye to a provocative title, since a year later, in 1605, Marston wrote *The Dutch Courtesan* and a year after that Dekker produced *The Whore of Babylon*. Topicality is also of potential relevance; Dekker and Ford wrote *The Witch of Edmonton* in 1621 following publication of an account of a recent witch trial, and he collaborated with Rowley, Ford and Webster in 1624 on the now lost *A Late Murder of the Son upon the Mother, or, Keep the Widow Waking*, based on actual recent crimes.

Dekker's responsiveness to the demands of the medium and the public mood equips him well as a writer of a mode that was of perennial popularity in the growing metropolis, city comedy. Prior to the commercial theatre era, the principal target audiences to which dramatists catered had been academic communities including the Inns of Court, the hall audiences in country houses and at court, and public outdoor audiences in urban contexts. With the advent of purpose-built commercial theatres in London in the 1570s, playwrights became increasingly aware of the fact that there was another dimension to the audiences for which they were catering – geographical localisation and a developing metropolitan consciousness in what was a rapidly growing city. This was also a relatively brief moment in history when playwrights wrote their plays for such a geographically specific audience. Prior to the establishment of the London commercial theatres, apart from the great cycles of scriptural plays in provincial towns, most of the drama on offer had been by itinerant companies. After the end of the seventeenth century, an ever broadening base of audiences was created principally by the establishment of provincial theatres. In Dekker's period, however, playwrights could be assured that the audiences they needed to be concerned about were those who inhabited the same city as they did. Dekker's dramatic and non-dramatic work shows a particular aptitude for and interest in evoking the everyday life of this metropolis in its many aspects. In two of his plays set in London we see a number of his attributes as a playwright come together. These are *The Shoemakers' Holiday* (1600) one of the earliest extant works that was entirely authored by him, and the later *Roaring Girl* (1610), written in collaboration with Thomas Middleton. These plays demonstrate at once Dekker's ability to dramatise London life in his plays, to contribute to the development of new genres in dramatic writing and to respond to changes in audience taste. Dekker and Middleton are both playwrights who stand out as having a particular fascination with London. In this respect they contrast with Marlowe and Shakespeare who tended only to set narratives in London when their historical material obliged them to do so. Significant changes and developments occurred in audience tastes over the seventy or so years between the establishment of the first commercial theatres and their suppression in 1642. The emergence of city comedy in the first place was arguably a response to the London audiences' desire to see the life of their city represented on stage, and perhaps is also the reason for the occurrence of London's name in several plays of the late sixteenth century.[4]

This genre would evolve over the following decades, but many of its enduring elements are already present in *The Shoemakers' Holiday*. The way in which the narrative of the play is set in the capital reflects the ethos of the 1590s, a period following the Armada scare which was characterised by an emerging sense of national identity. This found its way into various forms of writing including the drama, manifesting itself in the several chronicles that appeared in this period, and on the popular stage in chronicle and history plays. Though *The Shoemakers' Holiday* is very loosely based on historical material and is set against the backdrop of Henry V's French wars, Dekker caters specifically to his London audience by choosing not to emphasise the broader nationalist implications of those wars, but to focus instead on a glorification of London artisans and citizens. This is done with an insistence on a rollicking comic tone driven by the figure of Simon Eyre himself. Potentially serious issues such as the desertion of young Lacy from the army during the French wars, his cross-class marriage to the Lord Mayor's daughter, Rose, against the strong opposition of both their families, and Hammon's almost successful attempt to trick Ralph's wife into marrying him, are all handled with little sense of the potential consequences that could ensue. Instead, the tone is celebratory. When the King appears, he is not presented as a military hero, albeit that he is fresh from the battlefields of France, but as a benevolent figure more interested in being entertained by Eyre, and helping him in his endeavour to create harmony and social cohesion. It is not so much national as civic pride that is foregrounded here, Eyre repeatedly emphasising the significance and power of the role of Lord Mayor and making the purpose of the King's presence the inspection of the newly completed Leadenhall, as one of the great new buildings of London.

What Dekker successfully manages to do is create a sense of the texture of everyday life in London. This is partly effected by a clear grounding of the action in the built environment of London. By the end of the first scene Eyre is identified as living in Tower Street and there are several references to locations in the conurbation such as the musters at Mile End, Tuttle Fields and Finsbury, as well as the shoemakers of St Martin's Ward, the area adjacent to Bedlam, Fleet Street, Tower Street and Whitechapel. The audience of Londoners is easily enabled to move imaginatively around the terrain in which the narrative is set, and the geography of London is more actively brought into play at various points, such as the fact that the whereabouts of Ralph's wife is initially unknown. This is, in the period, a phenomenon that would have been unique to London as it was the only city in the realm large enough easily to allow for such anonymity. Geography also contributes to the stage action, such as when Lincoln and Oatley are told by Firke that the location of the marriage by the errant lovers is 'Saint *Faiths* Church vnder *Paules*', whereas they are actually being married in the Savoy.[5] Lincoln and Oatley arrive at St Faith's church to find another illicit marriage, between Hammon and Ralph's wife Jane, but one that is foiled at the last minute. The movement of characters around London not only intensifies the realism of the narrative but adds to its dramatic energy and this geographical materiality would become an integral part of many later city comedies. The glorification of the artisan class is also manifest in aspects of the London geography, and one that involves a blatant telescoping of the narrative. The building that the King comes to see, the Leadenhall, is a 'great new hall in Gratious streete corner, which our Maister the newe lord Maior hath built' (5.2.181–2). Eyre has hardly had time, since his accession as Lord Mayor or indeed his recent acquisition of wealth, to have completed this building but its inclusion in the play is characteristic of the impulse to celebrate the growing metropolis, a tendency evident in several plays in the 1590s.[6] As such it testifies to Dekker's acute response to the taste of the times.

Because of its focus on everyday transactional culture, city comedy as a genre often yields intriguing details of the texture of middle class and artisanal life in London in the period, and Dekker's play is a good example of this. Two consecutive scenes show people at work in shops: in the fourth scene of Act 3, Jane is in her sempster's shop when she is accosted by Hammond, and in the following scene the shoemakers are in their workshop, the dialogue indicating that the process of shoemaking is actually being represented. Though there may be some idealisation here, in this latter scene and others involving Eyre's workmen, a considerable overlap is suggested between family and professional life in such pre-industrial enterprises, and the play's narrative also connects these to the broader arenas of urban and national life. Material and social preoccupations in the capitalist society of early modern London are also exemplified, especially by Eyre's wife, who betrays much more eagerness for social ascendancy than Eyre himself, though Dekker does moderate this quality in comparison with Eyre's wife in his source for the story, Thomas Deloney's *Pleasant and Princely History of the Gentle Craft* (c. 1597/8). She is also attracted by the material trappings of advancement, such as clothing, and Eyre mockingly talks of her having 'couerd [her] Saracens head with this french flappe' and 'loaden [her] bumme with this farthingale, tis trash, trumpery, vanity' (5.1.14–16). Despite the mockery here, there is a clear degree of celebration of the acquisition of wealth, power and the means to display it among certain members of the artisan class. The play opens with the Lord Mayor's assertion that,

> Poore Cittizens must not with Courtiers wed,
> Who will in silkes, and gay apparrell spend
> More in one yeare, then I am worth by farre. (1.1.12–14)

But the play also implicitly sanctions the access of artisans to the products of the plethora of luxury trades that sprang up in London in the later sixteenth century. One example of this is the fine pair of shoes that the shoemaker Rafe makes for his wife before his departure for France:

> Rich men at parting, guie their wiues rich gifts,
> Iewels and rings, to grace their lillie hands,
> Thou know'st our trade makes rings for womens heeles:
> Here take this paire of shooes cut out by *Hodge*,
> Sticht by my fellow *Firke*, seam'd by my selfe,
> Made vp and pinckt, with letters for thy name. (1.1.225–30)

A prominent tendency in later city comedy is to represent Londoners as canny, opportunistic and streetwise, qualities necessary for the negotiation of the metropolitan jungle they inhabit. These qualities are often contrasted with those of hapless country folk, who are recurrently prey to the wiles of more unscrupulous Londoners. Morality in these plays sometimes takes second place to a wily sophistication which is more necessary for success in the harshly competitive world portrayed. Jonson's *The Alchemist* (1610) is perhaps one of the best examples of this, but it is found in varying degrees across this genre of comedy. These qualities are less in evidence in the principal figures of earlier, Elizabethan city comedies and this is certainly true of Dekker's protagonist here. Though Eyre gains his sudden wealth through the cheap windfall purchase of a shipment of goods from a distressed skipper, an element derived from his source, there is no sense of urban one-upmanship and trickery in evidence here. The figure of Eyre is much more one of madcap fun, though he is constantly aware of both the responsibilities and the possibilities of his power. He is consistently genial, benevolent towards his workmen and wife and protective of Lacy and Rose, and his principal acts are perhaps his beneficence towards the apprentices and artisans of his craft. Dekker endows Eyre with dramatic energy largely through his rich use of language, often in mock castigation of his wife and employees, as in:

> Where be these boyes, these girles, these drabbes, these scoundrels, they wallow in the fat brewisse of my bountie, and licke vp the crums of my table, yet wil not rise to see my walkes cleansed: come out you powder-beefe-queanes, what *Nan*, what *Madge-mumble-crust*, come out you fatte Midriffe-swagbelly whores, and sweepe me these kennels, that the noysome stench offende not the nose of my neighbours. (1.4.1–7)

Dekker's interest in language here would later be developed in another strand of his popular writing, his 'coney-catching' pamphlets, in which he shows great interest in 'thieves' cant'.[7] *The Shoemakers' Holiday* is rather clumsily constructed, its success depending largely on its colourful language and on Eyre as a vibrant dramatic character. This is indicative of Dekker's general mode of playwriting, which strongly tends to rely for its success on characterisation rather than structure.

Another of Dekker's city comedies, *Westward Ho* (*c.* 1604), appeared a few years later, and was a product of one of his numerous collaborations, this time with John Webster. Though written no more than five years after *The Shoemakers' Holiday*, it shows a real development of the genre, and while the earlier play is very Elizabethan in tone and character, *Westward Ho* is solidly Jacobean. Though it has the same looseness of structure and dependence on character that typifies much of Dekker's work, there is greater emphasis on intrigue, and its comedy depends upon this. The various strands of narrative involve sexual intrigue, animated by a central character, an Italian resident in London called Justiniano, who is motivated by an unjustified doubt about of his wife's fidelity. There is plentiful suggestion of the opportunities and even encouragements to sexual errancy afforded by the capital. Mistress Justiniano is approached on behalf of an earl who wishes to woo her by a bawd called Mistress Birdlime, masquerading as a seller of cosmetics and a laundress. Justiniano himself masquerades as a tutor to three citizen wives in order to facilitate access to them by lovers. Both disguises – and these are not the only instances of concealed identities in the play – help to suggest the unreliability of apparent identity in a metropolis that is large enough to afford easy anonymity. But more of a danger to marriage and morality is London as a free market: not only do Birdlime and Justiniano peddle sexual wares under the guise of more legitimate business, but the lines between commodity consumption and sexuality are blurred in Justiniano's observation, 'Why should I long to eate of Bakers bread onely, when theres so much Sifting, and bolting, and grynding in euery corner of the Citty?'[8] He goes on to point out the range of sexual choice offered by the city and particularly the freedom permitted to women by the fact that their normal business of household purchases gives them the liberty to roam at will and unremarked. This is illustrated when the three city wives go to Brentford, one of the notorious 'outleaps' of London used for sexual trysts, ostensibly on a legitimate errand but actually to meet their suitors. The whole intrigue narrative in its various strands suggests a willingness to cater to prurient appetites, and Dekker has been accused of a lax attitude to morality, though all attempts at transgression in the play actually come to nothing. It turns out that the wives were tricking the suitors rather than their husbands, and Mistress Justiniano also remains steadfastly faithful. The play is, however, one of the earliest Jacobean city comedies to usher in a rather different perspective on London life from that in the Elizabethan ones, one that would admit much more cynicism and emphasis on the primacy of strategy over moral values than had been the case before.

The play was enough of a success to provoke George Chapman, Ben Jonson and John Marston to capitalise on the idea of a directional and geographic title and write *Eastward Ho* the following year, while Dekker and Webster followed up their own play with *Northward Ho* that year too.[9] Rather as each of the two competing patent theatres later in the Restoration period would seek to copy the formula of successful productions by their competitor, a similarly opportunistic impulse seems to be at work here. That all three plays were products of collaborations tends to underscore this as a process of nakedly commercial production, very much the basis, in fact, on which Dekker entered the profession in the first place. But if formulae of theatrical writing are involved here, Dekker is certainly in the forefront of evolving those formulae. While *Westward Ho* is a city comedy of a rather different type from *The Shoemakers' Holiday*, *Northward Ho* in its turn takes a further move towards the harsh urban and even dangerous world that is the milieu of most Jacobean examples of the genre (as, indeed, does

Eastward Ho). In Dekker and Webster's second play, two gallants called Greenshield and Featherstone attempt to seduce the wife of a citizen and to give her husband the false impression that she has capitulated. This sets up a process of revenge in which it is revealed that Featherstone has, in fact, committed adultery with the wife of Greenshield, and he is tricked into marrying a whore. The play thus ends with some bitter revelations and consequences, unlike the more benign conclusion of *Westward Ho*.

In both these later city comedies the embedding of the narratives in the geographical and metaphorical frame of reference provided by the capital is even greater than in *The Shoemakers' Holiday*. In that play locations in London tend to be identified to the extent that the narrative requires them to be. But in *Westward Ho* and *Northward Ho* there is much more incidental filling out of geographical detail, an example of the first of these being Birdlime's claim to 'keepe a Hot-house in Gunpowder Ally (neere crouched Fryers)' (*Westward Ho*, 1.1.8–9). This is information not essential to the narrative but suggests the greater extent to which Dekker and Webster attempt to give their dramatic narratives a material location recognisable to the audience. This is sometimes used to suggest the knowingness of characters, as in *Westward Ho* when Mistress Wafer and Sir Gosling Glow-worm are talking about setting up an assignation with the help of Justiniano:

> JUSTINIANO: Where will you meet ith morning?
> GOSLING: At some Tauerne neere the water-side, thats priuate.
> JUSTINIANO: The Grey-hound, the Greyhound in Black-fryers, an excellent *Randeuous*. (*Westward Ho*, 2.3.102–5)

The presence of London as a setting is also to be found in the reference to places in the city in metaphoric constructions, as in, 'as stale as Wenches that trauaile euery second tyde betweene Graues ende and Billingsgate' (1.1.147–9), 'as dark as a roome in Bedlam' (1.1.156), or 'as hungry as euer came a Countery Atturny from Westminster' (3.2.36–7) from *Westward Ho*, and 'as melancholy ... as Fleete-Street in a long vacation' (1.1.51), or 'tame as a fray in Fleetestreete' (2.2.142) from *Northward Ho*.[10] This not only draws upon the London audience's knowledge of and associations with their urban environment but is part of a growing self-consciousness in city comedy of the cultural, moral and material distinctness of London and its uniqueness as a metropolis.

The titillating rascality of several figures in city comedy is often commensurate with the extent to which they are identified with the urban milieu in which they operate. This involves both knowingness and mobility around the terrain. *Westward Ho*'s Justiniano is a good early example of this, making Dekker and Webster among the first writers to develop this aspect of the city comedy genre. However, it is in a later collaboration with Thomas Middleton – *The Roaring Girl* – that Dekker is involved in creating a work that luxuriates in the seamier side of London life and celebrates the city's sophistication in accommodating alternative ways of behaving and living. In discussing a collaboration such as this, the problem inevitably arises about which writer wrote what part of the plays. Though several opinions have been offered on the issue and the tendency has been to assume that Middleton was responsible for the writing of the Moll Cutpurse episodes, there is no absolute basis to exclude this, the principal strand of the play, from a discussion of Dekker's work. It is very likely, in any case, that the writers would have discussed and had some hand in the overall conception of the work and the characters that populate it.[11] It appeared in 1611, though was probably written earlier, and it might be regarded as the result of a bit of professional opportunism on the part of Dekker and Middleton. It may also have been inspired by Dekker's clear fascination with the more transgressive elements of the life of the capital, evident also in his coney-catching pamphlets. The play fictionalises an actual cross-dressing woman of some notoriety in London, Mary Frith, who is recorded as performing a song at the Fortune theatre in the same year as the play appeared there. The London of the play is in fact a more tolerant place for such a figure to exist than the reality, as Mary Frith was made to do public penance at St Paul's, and was later sent to Newgate for graver offences.

In the play, the writers are careful to balance Moll Cutpurse's sexually provocative roguishness with the overall sympathy with which she is constructed since the conceit is that she collaborates in a pretence that she is in a match with a young gentleman, Sebastian Wengrave, in order that his father might drop his opposition to his son's actual choice, and so Moll has to function both as bugbear and heroine. Her characterisation helps create a mould for a particular sort of figure that populates city comedies, theatrically attractive but often somewhat reprobate, whose strategic skill in negotiating the complex urban environment is more important than straightforward moral conformity. Though she flouts convention and even the law, Dekker and Middleton take care to build in a sort of heroism that endears her to the audience. In a duel she bests her would-be lover, Laxton, a sleazy, self-serving creature with nothing to recommend him, so that her actions automatically carry the approval of the audience. At another point she rescues the roistering son of a city grandee from a sergeant, an act at once transgressive and bespeaking courageous defence of a young friend. She also manages to outwit Trapdoor, a devious individual sent by the old Wengrave to entrap her. The audience is implicitly invited to view her most explicit challenge to convention – her subversion of her traditional gender role – with fascination more than condemnation, and she is described as

> mad *Mol*, or merry *Moll*, a creatur
> So strange in quality, a whole citty takes
> Note of her name and person.[12]

The idea that she is part of London's criminal underworld (like her real equivalent) has to be maintained in the interests of audience titillation and the use of her reputation in the narrative, though her criminal connections are only obliquely suggested, such as in her assertion that 'I lye about chicke lane' (3.1.167). This was a known haunt of thieves, but the assertion is made in circumstances that might reflect bravado rather than veracity. Her identity as a *rouée* comes more from her ducking and diving around London, suggesting a lack of containment that unsettles Trapdoor who remarks,

> I like you the worse because you shift your lodging so often,
> Ile not meddle with you for that tricke sir. (3.1.168–9)

A lack of geographical fixity, along with their knowingness about the urban terrain, was becoming one of the features of city comedy rake figures.

As might be expected from Dekker and Middleton, the play also abundantly renders the texture of citizen life in London, in its social, moral, economic and even administrative aspects. This is done partly through reference in dialogue, so that in Act 3, scene 3 several details are given of prodigal behaviour and policing in the city, especially the streets of Holborn. Moll's rich language too, perhaps reflecting Dekker's interest in such matters, is the language of London's streets, both helping to realise her as a character and embedding her in the somewhat roguish and even dangerous urban jungle that the play implies London to be. But the most clear-cut evocation of London life on the streets comes in Act 2, scene 1, which is set among three shops that are to some extent physically realised on stage. Here too colloquial language and plentiful reference to parts of the local geography come into play, but it is essentially the basis of a subplot that focuses on a narrative strand that repeatedly forms part of the city comedy formula – the suggestion of the sexual availability of city wives, especially as an extension of their commercial role as shopkeepers. As in *Westward Ho*, the potential transgressions do not ultimately occur, but the writers engage in an inventive tweaking of the formula by showing a one-sided though ultimately fruitless sexual pursuit by one of the women, Mistress Gallipot. Not only does this strand provide an evocation of a city in which sexual and other misdemeanours are rife, catering perhaps to prurient audience interest, but the potentially shocking female proactiveness of Mistress Gallipot provides a low-level parallel to the roistering figure of Moll herself.

Several aspects of this play typify Dekker's writing and modes of theatre, and the man himself is in many ways a typical representative of the new breed of professional theatre writer of his time. Both in the practical arrangements of his career and the way in which his writing evolves, he helps to define the patterns of early modern playwriting, and manages to exemplify both Elizabethan and Jacobean modes of theatrical authorship. The pity is that the loss of much of his work, together with the fact that many of the surviving plays are collaborations, result in his having a lower profile among his contemporaries than he merits.

NOTES

1 *The Three Parnassus Plays*, ed. J. B. Leishman (London: Ivor Nicholson and Watson, 1949), 986–7.

2 *Poetaster*, ed. Tom Cain (Manchester University Press, 1995), 3.4.321–2.

3 See *Sir Thomas More. Original text by Anthony Munday and Henry Chettle. Censored by Edmund Tilney. Revisions co-ordinated by Hand C. Revised by Henry Chettle, Thomas Dekker, Thomas Heywood, and William Shakespeare*, ed. John Jowett (London: Methuen Drama, 2011), 22–3. Given the nature of their contributions to *Sir Thomas More*, they may have collaborated on the same play without communicating about it with each other.

4 Examples are Robert Wilson's *The Three Ladies of London* (c. 1581) and *The Three Lords and Three Ladies of London* (1588–90), Robert Greene and Thomas Lodge's *A Looking Glass for London and England* (1588), Thomas Heywood's *The Four Prentices of London* (1599) and the anonymous *A Larum for London* (1599).

5 *The Shoemakers' Holiday* in *The Dramatic Works of Thomas Dekker*, ed. Fredson Bowers, 4 vols. (1953–61, rpt Cambridge University Press, 2009), I, 4.2.28. Further references to the play derive from this edition.

6 See, for example, Anthony Munday *et al.*, *The Play of Sir Thomas More* (c. 1595), William Haughton *Englishmen for My Money* (1598), the anonymous *Jack Straw* (c. 1591), and the plays listed in note 4 above.

7 See *Lanthorne and Candlelight* (1609), *The Belman of London* (1610), *Villainies Discovered by Candlelight* (1616), *English Villainies* (1632).

8 *Westward Ho* in *The Dramatic Works of Thomas Dekker*, ed. Bowers, II, 2.1.169–71. Further references to the play are to this edition.

9 See Paul Franssen, 'George Chapman's Learned Drama', Chapter 9 in this volume, pp. 134–48.

10 For these and other quotations from *Northward Ho* see *The Dramatic Works of Thomas Dekker*, ed. Bowers, II.

11 The editor of the Revels Plays edition of *The Roaring Girl*, Paul Mulholland, has observed, that, 'As *The Roaring Girl* was apparently the last joint venture of the two writers, a less formal, freer division of responsibilities may have developed', and '[f]ew scenes point conclusively to either dramatist as the main writer'. See

The Roaring Girl, ed. Paul Mulholland (Manchester University Press, 1987), 8–9, 11.
12 *The Roaring Girl* in *The Dramatic Works of Thomas Dekker*, ed. Bowers, III, 1.1.94–6. All quotations from the play derive from this edition.

Further reading

Adler, Doris Ray, *Thomas Dekker: A Reference Guide*. Boston: G. K. Hall, 1983.

Champion, Larry S., *Thomas Dekker and the Traditions of the English Drama*. New York: Lang, 1985.

Conover, J. H., *Thomas Dekker: An Analysis of Dramatic Structure*. The Hague: Mouton, 1969.

Gasper, Julia, *The Dragon and the Dove: The Plays of Thomas Dekker*. Oxford: Oxford University Press, 1990.

Gibbons, Brian, *Jacobean City Comedy*, 2nd edn. London and New York: Methuen, 1980.

Grantley, Darryll, *London in Early Modern English Drama: Representing the Built Environment*. Basingstoke and New York: Palgrave Macmillan, 2008.

Jones-Davies, Marie-Thérèse, *Un peintre de la vie londonienne: Thomas Dekker*, 2 vols. Paris: Marcel Didier, 1958.

Leggatt, Alexander, *Citizen Comedy in the Age of Shakespeare*. Toronto: University of Toronto Press, 1973.

McLuskie, Kate, *Dekker and Heywood: Professional Dramatists*. London: Macmillan, 1994.

Pierce, F. E., *The Collaboration of Webster and Dekker*. 1909, rpt Hamden, CT: Archon, 1972.

Price, G. R., *Thomas Dekker*. New York: Twayne, 1969.

Wells, Stanley, *Shakespeare & Co.: Christopher Marlowe, Thomas Dekker, Ben Jonson, Thomas Middleton, John Fletcher, and Other Players in his Story*. London: Penguin, 2006.

7

TON HOENSELAARS

Shakespeare: colleagues, collaborators, co-authors

With Shakespeare so firmly established on the Parnassian heights of world literature, some readers of his work still find it difficult to imagine that the dramatist's plays were realised as part of a concentrated process of inter-action with others, in a profession that was and remains 'radically collabora-tive'.[1] However, Shakespeare was never fully autonomous, the sole regulator or manager of the text's meaning. Studying him we must not fail to acknow-ledge a broad range of contemporary cultural and historical determinants that together impacted on the creation and signification of that text, more or less beyond the reach of the author's quill. As the plays were being written, but also as they were being performed, each time they negotiated realities including generic decorum, the specific material conditions of the stage and of the age, as government regulations and a series of conceptions of class, gender, race and religion were being redefined as part of a complex creative process. However, even if the early modern author, as Stephen Orgel put it, was 'by no means at the center of the collaboration', a reading of theatre history and culture can never entirely exclude the individuals, dramatists and collaborative playwrights who were continually redefining notions of dramatic authorship and engaged in realising these on the stages around the nation's capital.[2] As Jeffrey Knapp has argued more forcefully, 'an insti-tutional analysis of Renaissance drama can and indeed must keep authors squarely in the picture'.[3]

Shakespeare had scores of colleagues and collaborated with many in the theatre and its periphery. Some of them contributed to bringing his plays to life at the Globe, the Blackfriars playhouse, or at court – includ-ing the actors on stage, the backstage crew and the audience in the audi-torium, and occasionally also on the stage. Others, too, including the scribes, bookkeepers, censors and printers, have contributed to shaping the appearance of the Shakespearean texts we read and see performed today. Their impact may be different in kind and consequence, but it must not be ignored.[4]

Shakespeare's contemporaries – colleagues or collaborators – left their mark on the shaping of the text of the plays as we know them, even though this is not always clear to see in every edition that appears on the market. The familiar phenomenon of the all-male cast on the early modern popular stage accounts for the relatively limited number of female parts. It explains why kisses in Shakespeare's love plots are rare, but it equally shows how, when they are exchanged, such a professional constraint could also spur the author's creativity and turn kissing into an elaborate ritual, couched in moral, Christian terms that both convey the impression of the lovers' purity and pepper their foreplay, as in *Romeo and Juliet*:

ROMEO: If I profane with my unworthiest hand
         This holy shrine, the gentle sin is this:
         My lips, two blushing pilgrims, ready stand
         To smooth that rough touch with a tender kiss.
JULIET: Good pilgrim, you do wrong your hand too much,
         Which mannerly devotion shows in this;
         For saints have hands that pilgrims' hands do touch,
         And palm to palm is holy palmer's kiss.[5]

Just as the all-male cast conditioned the representation of the physical intimacy of Shakespeare's stage characters, it led to the development of the breeches part for Rosalind in *As You Like It*, Viola in *Twelfth Night* and Innogen in *Cymbeline* – with each play's heroine temporarily in male disguise, for plot reasons, certainly, but also to save the boy actor's voice. The availability of a young actor with French language skills might also explain the doubling in *Henry V* of the Princess of France and the Boy who interprets the French that Pistol fails to understand. And there were numerous instances of what Alan Dessen has called 'conceptual casting', where clever doubling could establish (as it still may) a degree of continuity of the same actor's identity between the various parts he performs in a single play, and, possibly, of course, also across plays.[6]

But the material circumstances of the playhouse itself, too, inevitably conditioned the writing, thus further contributing to a dispersal of factors conditioning the nature of the stage product. The Chorus in *Henry V* deplores the limitations of the 'Wooden O' and invites its audience to eke out the stage's imperfections in their minds. Conversely, the new opportunities of the indoor and small-scale Blackfriars playhouse, which the King's Men leased in 1608, are likely to have suggested the intimate bedroom scene with candle lighting in *Cymbeline*.

As a shareholder in the Lord Chamberlain's Men (later the King's Men), Shakespeare wrote songs with potential singers in view, or stage characters with the actors in mind who were to play them. These may still be identified in the text, as in *Much ado about Nothing*, presumably set from Shakespeare's own manuscript of the play, which would explain why in Act 4, scene 2, the comedy's first quarto (1600) and the First Folio version (1623) give speech prefixes for Verges's lines as '*Couley*' (referring explicitly to the actor William Cowley), and expected the words that Dogberry speaks to be delivered by the comedian Will Kempe, here alluded to as '*Ke.*', '*Kee.*', '*Kem.*', and '*Kemp.*'

Beyond such phenomena that emerge on the editorial level, one also finds larger fingerprints in Shakespeare's work that reveal the playwright's own creativity in social, collaborative terms, and which tell us never to underestimate Shakespeare's management of human resources, being 'not "sources" per se', as Claire McEachern puts it, but 'the personnel of his company, their talents and reputations, and the need to make use of them'.[7] A closer look at Shakespeare's creative personnel administration reveals how, around the turn of the sixteenth century, Will Kempe – the great comic actor with a native skill for improvisation who, besides playing Dogberry, is also thought to have played Lance in *The Two Gentlemen of Verona*, Bottom in *A Midsummer Night's Dream*, Lancelot in *The Merchant of Venice* and Falstaff both in *Henry IV* and *The Merry Wives of Windsor* – changed his engagement with the Lord Chamberlain's Men, soon to disappear from the records altogether. Notably, at around this time, we also witness how Shakespeare begins to write a different type of comic lead, not a buffoonish, clown-like character but more of an intellectual, licensed fool – like Touchstone in *As You Like It*, Feste in *Twelfth Night*, the Fool in *King Lear* or Lavatch in *All's Well that Ends Well* – and that this changing persona of the clown from the comic bumpkin to the fool-as-philosopher coincided with the emergence of a new actor in Shakespeare's company, a gifted dramatist in his own right, Robert Armin.[8] The playwright's creativity here is inseparable from his interaction with colleagues on the workfloor, and we would remain unaware of a dimension of interactive collaboration if we did not consider Shakespeare's plays in their proper social and historical contexts.

Another group of collaborators in the London theatre world to leave their vital mark on the Shakespearean text, ghosting it in various ways, was that of the contemporary prose writers, dramatists and poets, whom Shakespeare is likely to have known and read, and also appropriated (like Thomas Lodge, whose prose romance *Rosalynde, Euphues Golden Legacy* [1578–80], became a direct source for *As You Like It* [1599]), and quoted (like John Lyly in *Henry IV*, where Falstaff nearly quotes Lyly verbatim [2.5.403–14]), and, in much more subtle terms, also Christopher Marlowe.[9] Initially, though, Robert Greene and Henry Chettle stand out. Greene's

Groatsworth of Wit (in which Chettle may have had a hand) famously branded Shakespeare as 'an upstart Crow, beautified with our [= his established colleagues'] feathers', and described the young man from Stratford as one who 'with his Tygers heart wrapt in a Players hide, supposes he is as well able to bumbast out a blanke verse as the best of you: and being an absolute Johannes fac totum, is in his owne conceit the onely Shake-scene in a countrie'.[10] This accusation of Shakespeare as a plagiarist, as someone who reworked the output of other dramatists – a practice which should not be confused with the habit of imitation that Shakespeare practised as much as other contemporary dramatists[11] – may explain why a phrase from Greene's *Menaphon* (or his *Penelope's Web*) occurring in the quarto text of *Henry VI Part Two* ('Abradas the great Masadonian Pyrate') was removed and replaced in the First Folio by 'Bargalus the strong Illyrian pirate', a phrase of Ciceronian origin.[12] Sonnets 110–12 also seem to draw part of their inspiration from the encounter with the ghost of Greene, as is the case, in a more light-hearted vein, when Polonius condemns Hamlet's description of the old man's daughter as 'the most beautified Ophelia'. Did Polonius's dismissive comment – 'that's an ill phrase, a vile phrase' – serve to allude to the infamous use of the word 'beautified' in Greene's *Groatsworth of Wit*?[13] That Greene was still haunting the mind of Shakespeare years after his arrival in London is borne out by the fact that he returned to Greene and his *Pandosto* for *The Winter's Tale*. In addition to rearranging the materials of its prose source, Shakespeare's late play also mimicked the style of Greene's *James IV*, notably in the Bohemia sequence of Act 4.

Not only Greene was to ghost Shakespeare's career as a dramatist. The paths of Chettle and Shakespeare were to cross several times again after the first incident. As a business partner to the stationers William Hoskins and John Danter, Chettle may have been involved in the preparation for the press of the first quarto edition of *Romeo and Juliet*, and in that capacity may be responsible for some dialogue and for the unusually vivid and predominantly descriptive (rather than prescriptive or imperative) stage directions that suggest the personal experience of a spectator at an early performance of Shakespeare's tragedy:

> *Enter Juliet somewhat fast, and embraceth Romeo.*
> *Tibalt under Romeos arme thrusts Mercutio in and flyes.*
> *She goeth downe from the window.*
> *She falls upon her bed within the Curtaines.*
> *All at once cry out and wring their hands.*
> *She stabs herselfe and falles.*[14]

By 1603 Chettle openly took issue with Shakespeare again, though not for stealing but for what he had not written. Following the death of Queen Elizabeth, Chettle, in his *England's Mourning Garment*, criticised Shakespeare for not contributing any verse to commemorate the Queen. Overall, it is a reassuring fact, however, that Chettle's attack was directed also against George Chapman, Samuel Daniel, Thomas Dekker and Michael Drayton, as well as Ben Jonson. This attack reveals more about the querulous nature of the plaintiff than the host of those publicly accused by name, including Shakespeare, on the occasion of the Queen's decease.

Greene's *Groatsworth of Wit* and Chettle's *Mourning Garment* provide what is really only a minor glimpse of the spirit of rivalry that energised the London theatre scene for many decades and significantly affected the drama written and performed in this climate. Another perspective, no doubt, is provided by the association between Shakespeare and Christopher Marlowe. The most important theatrical controversy of the late Elizabethan stage, however, was the 'War of the Theatres' (as it has been known), or the 'Poets' War', as James Bednarz (Englishing Thomas Dekker's term, *Poetomachia*) has recently dubbed the controversy that surfaces in a considerable number of topical plays written during the late 1590s and early 1600s.[15] Countering the influential though much contested interpretation of Alfred Harbage, who interpreted the War as a struggle for the supremacy or commercial success of three prominent repertory companies (the private companies of the Children at Blackfriars and the Children of Paul's vs the Chamberlain's Men), Bednarz has advanced the more flexible and convincing argument that Ben Jonson and Shakespeare (flanked by John Marston and Thomas Dekker) were in actual fact engaged in a struggle over issues of early modern poetics.[16] With reference to the exchanges of hostility between the relevant plays, it is possible to demonstrate how both Jonson (breaking the peace in *Every Man in His Humour* with a satirical attack on *Julius Caesar* and *Henry V*) and Shakespeare (returning fire in *As You Like It*, *Twelfth Night*, *Hamlet* and *Troilus and Cressida*) sought to assert a personal definition of the 'author' writing for the commercial stage, be it the popular stage of the Globe (for which Shakespeare worked) or the stage of the more elite, child companies at Blackfriars and St Paul's (with which Jonson was engaged at the time).

One catches a rare glimpse of the Poets' War in *Hamlet*, when the prince discusses with Rosencrantz and Guildenstern the players announced at the court of Elsinore, and the reason why they should be on the road. 'How chances it they travel?' (2.2.330). Neither their skills not their art have declined, Rosencrantz explains, but their reputation has suffered due to the immense popularity of a company of child actors whose plays are openly critical of the productions of the adults seen at the public theatres:

> But there is, sir, an eyrie of children, little eyases, that cry out on the top of question and are most tyrannically clapped for 't. These are now the fashion, and so berattle the common stages – so they call them – that many wearing rapiers are afraid of goose-quills, and dare scarce come thither. (*Hamlet*, 2.2.339–44)

Since the aggression in this fight has been known to come from both the boys' companies and the adult players, it has been impossible, Rosencrantz explains, to criticise either party more than the other: 'there has been much to-do on both sides, and the nation holds it no sin to tarre them [= the children] to controversy' (2.2.352–4). Besides, plays that engaged in the conflict were crowd-pullers: 'There was for a while no money bid for argument unless the poet and the player went to cuffs in the question' (2.2.354–6). From Rosencrantz's vantage point, however, the children were the more successful, thus also explaining the impending arrival of the travelling players with whom Hamlet, a budding playwright himself, is to collaborate on the script of *The Mousetrap*:

HAMLET: Do the boys carry it away?
ROSENCRANTZ: Ay, that they do, my lord, Hercules and his load too.
                                    (2.2.360–2)

It is difficult not to read a note of personal anxiety into this combined reference to the boys' success and their abduction of what must be the Globe's distinctive logo-image of Hercules shouldering the world's orb.

The Poets' War, the plays involved and the fierce debate that raged between them, may well represent 'the fullest theatrical context currently available for understanding the interactive development of Shakespeare's work'.[17] However, we must not forget that his plays and poems only rarely comment on the contemporary theatre in such explicit terms as one finds in *Hamlet*. As a consequence, the plays cannot be said to convey a very accurate sense of the playwright's active engagement to the general reader. Recognising how rich the textual and paratextual materials of early modern English drama tend to be, and how pervasive the Poets' War really is, we must conclude that when it comes to weaving either his own life or the lives of his contemporaries into his plays and poems, Shakespeare excels at discretion.

By contrast, the complete works of Ben Jonson contain much (often anecdotal) information about the life and work of his rival playwright from Stratford. They include Jonson's satirical treatment, via the character of Sogliardo in *Every Man out of His Humour*, of Shakespeare's application for a family coat of arms. In addition, they include his valuable if not always appreciative remarks in *Every Man in His Humour* and *Bartholomew Fair* about *Titus Andronicus*, *The Tempest* and *The Winter's Tale*, whereas his *Sejanus* may rightly be read as an attack on *Julius Caesar*. They also contain the famous reference to Shakespeare's alleged ease of writing, and Jonson's alleged response:

> I *remember*, the Players have often mentioned it as an honour to *Shakespeare*, that in his writing, (whatsoever he penn'd), hee never blotted out line. My answer hath beene, Would he had blotted a thousand. Which they thought a malevolent speech.[18]

And it is not without glee that Jonson – a man 'sharply impressed and irked' by his Stratford rival, as Park Honan puts it in his sound survey of the relationship[19] – continues to account for the mistakes that dexterous Shakespeare is supposed to have made:

> Many times hee fell into those things, could not escape laughter: As when hee said in the person of *Cæsar*, one speaking to him; *Cæsar, thou dost me wrong.* Hee replyed *Cæsar did never wrong, but with just cause*: and such like; which were ridiculous. But hee redeemed his vices, with his vertues. There was ever more in him to be praised then to be pardoned.[20]

Easily the best known utterance of Jonson's about his nearest and dearest rival, his best of enemies, is that most influential of dedicatory poems, Jonson's 'To the memory of my beloued, / The Avthor / Mr. William Shakespeare: / And what he hath left vs', published in the First Folio of 1623.

Given the astonishing range of Jonsonian allusions to Shakespeare – to be explained 'as malice, obsession, friendly rivalry, or as a neo-classical hangover'[21] – it is remarkable to find nothing as direct about Jonson in Shakespeare. The dearth of explicit allusions to the contemporary theatre or Elizabethan society and politics at large in Shakespeare's work may explain the plays' easy accessibility to later generations of readers and audiences and also their lasting appeal. However, the plays' oblique reference to their contemporary contexts is also likely, for later generations, to have created an imaginary divide between 'Shakespeare' and his own world, nurturing what on closer inspection turn out to be mistaken notions about the man as a retiring personality.[22]

Shakespeare's collaboration with theatre colleagues did not stop at the practicalities of putting on a play, at revising each other's plays for subsequent performance or publication, or even at engaging in serious warfare with paper bullets occasionally aimed at those very same colleagues. Collaboration also included what for post-Romantic readers and audiences has been the sacrosanct act of writing. For a proper appreciation of

Shakespeare and 'his' plays, it is vital to acknowledge what Gerald Bentley has argued in *The Profession of Dramatist in Shakespeare's Time*, namely that collaborative writing was the rule rather than the exception in the London theatre, for Shakespeare as well as Greene, Marlowe, Peele, Dekker, Webster, Middleton, Heywood, and Beaumont and Fletcher.[23] Exceptions to this rule are remarkably rare, and include John Lyly and Thomas Kyd, although one could argue that the literary output that Kyd produced is too small to be representative.

This is not the place to elaborate on the complex practice of collaborative writing in the early modern theatre, or its more or less self-evident place in an increasingly commercial environment that continued to acknowledge the merits of eroding medieval guild structures. Nor is this the place to elaborate on the fascinating patterns that developed during the period, showing who worked for whom, in which capacity, with how many others, intermittently or in the shape of syndicates that could last for years. However, it is important to remember that even as the demand for new plays increased, and as the efficiency and speed of collaborative writing were called for, one also witnesses, even among playwrights who collaborated with others, the idealisation of a certain alternative, of a more individual mode of writing as the product of disinterested self-reflection and retirement, as we witness in the writings of John Webster or, more prominently, in the life and work of Ben Jonson.[24]

Jonson's notion of the dramatic poet as the sole author of a work seems to come into focus as we look at his comments or recognise the occasional silence he observed where it concerned the issue of collaborative writing. Henslowe's diary, for example, speaks of several plays that Jonson collaborated on as a dramatist – like the lost *Hot Anger Soon Cold* (with Henry Chettle and Henry Porter, 1598), and *Robert II, or the Scot's Tragedy* (with Thomas Dekker and Henry Chettle, 1599) – but Jonson himself never mentioned these. Conversely, the address 'To the Readers' prepared for the first quarto of *Sejanus* stated that the entire play was of his own making, and every word his own: the quarto text was 'not the same with that which was acted on the publike Stage, wherein a second Pen had a good share' because Jonson, unwilling to 'defraud' his collaborator with such 'lothed vsurpation', had replaced the other's original text.[25] Not merely the act of replacing the other's words, but also Jonson's charged metaphors here ('defraud', 'usurpation') indicate the urgency driving this emergent sense of individual identity and ownership. In the Prologue to *Volpone*, Jonson famously raised the issue of co-authorship in order to disown the very practice on this instance, taking pride in the sole authorship of the comedy:

> 'Tis knowne, fiue weekes fully pen'd it:
> From his owne hand, without a co-adiutor,
> Nouice, iourney-man, or tutor.[26]

Together the comments that we hear about authorship and collaboration during the early modern period itself may be seen to mark the beginning of a perception of Shakespeare distinguished as one who did not engage in collaborative writing, or whose writing represents a single hand. This perception of Shakespeare as a philosophical poet rather than an industrious professional playwright writing together with colleagues – a perception no doubt nurtured by the fact that there is little explicit documentation of Shakespeare as a collaborative playwright and that the First Folio does not invite us to think of him as other than a sole author – has been justly challenged since the end of the nineteenth century, and we have come to recognise his instances of collaborative writing no longer as 'oddities' but as a common occurrence in his career as a professional dramatist during the early modern period.[27] During the early twentieth century the venerable E. K. Chambers denounced as 'disintegrators' those scholars who searched for hands other than Shakespeare's in the canon. W. W. Greg, by contrast, denounced as 'fundamentalists' (aka 'conservators') those who affirmed Shakespeare's sole authorship of *Titus Andronicus*.[28] Stanley Wells has long supported the view that Shakespeare 'collaborated with other writers at times, especially early and late in his career'.[29] Since the 1970s, however, a wave of new attribution studies by Ward Elliott and Robert Valenza, Jonathan Hope, MacDonald P. Jackson, John Jowett, David Lake, Gary Taylor, Brian Vickers and many others, has revolutionised the field. Vastly improved and more reliable scientific methods combined with computer-supported research have significantly increased the acknowledged proportion of collaborative material in the canon.[30] One just measure of the stage of research in this specialised corner of Shakespeare studies is Arthur Kinney's recent allegation in *Shakespeare, Computers and the Mystery of Authorship* that the man from Stratford 'wrote collaboratively throughout his lifetime'.[31]

Based on the distinctive marks of *collaborative writing* (two or more dramatists simultaneously producing an original, new playtext) and/or *revision* (one or more playwrights working on an existing text to make it meet certain requirements, be it for the stage or the page), the authorship attribution of the plays in the First Folio looks rather different from what the innocent reader might suspect. Besides material by Shakespeare, the first part of *Henry VI* (1592; rev. 1594?) also contains the hand of Thomas Nashe as co-author or reviser (and perhaps of others too). *Titus Andronicus* (1592–3) was written by Shakespeare and George Peele.[32] *All Is True* (1613), which

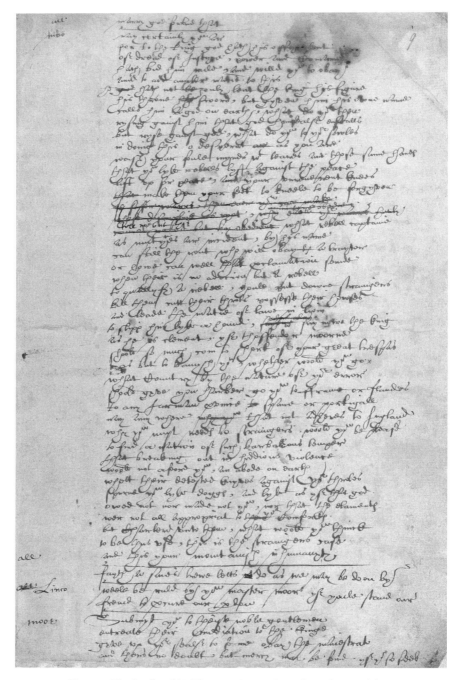

Figure 1 *The Booke of Sir Thomas Moore*, BL Harley MS 7368, fol. 9.
© The British Library Board.

was included in the First Folio as *The Life of Henry the Eight* (sic), is now generally attributed to Shakespeare and John Fletcher. When *The Two Noble Kinsmen* first appeared in the quarto edition of 1634, it was explicitly attributed to 'Mr. John Fletcher, and Mr. William Shakspeare. Gent.'[33] In various plays, the hand of Thomas Middleton has been detected. It is now recognised by many that Middleton worked on *Timon of Athens* (1606) with Shakespeare, even though, ironically, establishing co-authorship still does not seem to make the play more satisfying to theatre audiences. Middleton also revised Shakespeare's *Macbeth* (1606; rev. 1616), and the Oxford edition of Middleton's *Collected Works* (2007) aptly conveys by typographical means how much more substantial his intervention was, beyond the addition of the two songs from *The Witch* in the Hecate episodes of Shakespeare's tragedy. Middleton's altering hand in *Measure for Measure* (1604–5; rev. 1621) – largely applied to adjust the play to a new political climate – is no less pervasive, although it seems right to stress that not all critics have found the arguments that have been advanced equally persuasive, so the discussion is bound to continue.[34] This also applies to the recent claim, advanced by Laurie Maguire and Emma Smith, that the (Folio) text of *All's Well that Ends Well* bears the fingerprints of both Shakespeare and Middleton.[35] *Pericles* (1607), which did not appear in the First Folio, and was to be associated with Shakespeare in the Third Folio of 1664, is now generally attributed to both Shakespeare and George Wilkins. Of other plays not in the First Folio, *Arden of Faversham* (1587–92) is sometimes partly attributed to Shakespeare. *Edward III* now tends to be attributed to Shakespeare and others, and though not included in the First Folio, it has gained a place in the New Cambridge Shakespeare series. Many accept and few challenge the possibility that Hand D in the manuscript of *Sir Thomas More* is Shakespeare's, and the lost play *Cardenio* was written with John Fletcher.

Further attempts have been made to add other plays to the canon, especially those also associated with Shakespeare in the Third Folio of 1664, like *The London Prodigal*, *The History of Thomas Lord Cromwell*, *Sir John Oldcastle*, *The Puritan Widow*, *A Yorkshire Tragedy* and *The Tragedy of Locrine*. Other so-called apocryphal plays include *Edmund Ironside*, *Woodstock* (aka *Richard II, Part One*), and *The Birth of Merlin*.[36] Evidence to achieve consensus has not been conclusive, but one of the benefits of such efforts to extend the range of Shakespeare's complete works has certainly been that these neglected and forgotten chronicles are occasionally staged again.

Another major benefit of the attribution efforts is that, when successful, they grant the reader a rare chance to see Shakespeare at work. When

Shakespeare is not the sole author of a particular play, we are in a unique position to set off his contribution against the rest of the text, thus paradoxically learning to appreciate the playwright's style even better. A case in point is *Sir Thomas More*, which was never printed and probably never performed during Shakespeare's own lifetime, but which has survived in the form of a complex manuscript to which Shakespeare contributed a minor share, known as Hand D. It shows us Shakespeare at work as a true professional, but also as someone who, like any other Renaissance dramatist, would have discovered that the art of collaboration is an interactive one, with action ever inviting and inspiring a rejoinder (Figure 1).

In this biographical history play, set in London during the reign of Henry VIII, the local population rises up against the authorities because of complaints against the aliens in the city. The play's censor, Edmund Tilney, disliked the insurrection, and Shakespeare wrote a special scene in which Thomas More seeks to restore order by reminding the population of their civic duties and appealing to their common humanity towards the foreigners.

The first instance of Shakespeare's interactive writing here simply concerns the speech prefixes that occur in the Hand D fragment. The second speech prefix in this hand, which occurs at line 5, is 'other' because, apparently unfamiliar with the rest of the play, Shakespeare does not know which character will be speaking here. Hand C – whom John Jowett in his very reliable edition of the play identifies as the scribe or the annotator[37] – does know the answer. He deletes Shakespeare's speech prefix 'other' and replaces it with 'Geo bett', represented in the Arden edition as 'GEORGE BETTS'.

Naturally, later speech prefixes presented problems of a similar kind, and on each of these occasions it is fascinating to see how Shakespeare manages the problem. At line 9, Shakespeare repeats his earlier 'other' as a speech prefix (which Hand C then deletes and, in this instance, replaces with 'betts clow', before John Jowett changes it to 'CLOWN BETTS'). The next speech prefix occurs no more than five lines on and the dramatist, Shakespeare in this instance, does not repeat the term 'other'. Routinely, it would appear, he assumes that the abbreviated form 'oth' will suffice, which Hand C then deletes and replaces with 'willian', and which Jowett edits as 'WILLIAM-SON'). At line 21, Hand D is again (or still) in doubt as to which character from the play should speak. In a fashion that John Jowett recognises from *Hamlet*, Shakespeare reverts neither to 'other', nor to its abbreviated form 'oth', but to a mere 'o' (which is subsequently deleted and replaced with 'Clown. betts' by Hand C, and edited to read 'CLOWN BETTS' by Jowett). Tracing Jowett's remarkable journey through the manuscript of *Sir Thomas*

More here, one obtains both a sense of the pace at which Shakespeare worked (progressively abbreviating rather than repeating a standard term), and an insight into the way in which another collaborator (Hand C in this case) could improve on Shakespeare's manuscript with the mere stroke of a quill.

Later in the same Hand D sequence, however, the intervention of Hand C into the work of Shakespeare is less of a practical kind, and more of a personal and aesthetic nature. The situation brings into focus the problem that it is not always easy to establish whether we are dealing with collaborative writing or revision, and, once again, with the quantity of information that the author possessed about the rest of the play in which his contribution needed to fit, more or less seamlessly. Here are the lines of Hand D, with Thomas More seeking to quell the insurrection:

> What do you to your souls
> In doing this? O, desperate as you are,
> Wash your foul minds with tears, and those same hands
> That you, like rebels, lift against the peace,
> Lift up for peace; and your unreverent knees,
> Make them your feet. To kneel to be forgiven
> Is safer wars than ever you can make
> Whose discipline is riot.
> In, in, to your obedience! Why, even your hurly
> Cannot proceed but by obedience. What rebel captain,
> As mutinies are incident, by his name
> Can still the rout? Who will obey a traitor?

With the revisions of Hand C, this becomes:

> What do you to your souls
> In doing this? O, desperate as you are,
> Wash your foul minds with tears, and those same hands
> That you, like rebels, lift against the peace,
> Lift up for peace; and your unreverent knees,
> Make them your feet. To kneel to be forgiven
> ‚C‚*Is safer wars than ever you can make*
> *Whose discipline is riot.*
> *In, in, to your obedience!* Why, even your hurly
> *Cannot proceed but by obedience* ‚C‚
> ‚C‚**Tell me but this:**‚C‚ What rebel captain,
> As mutinies are incident, by his name
> Can still the rout? Who will obey a traitor?[38]

Here, four lines (underlined in Jowett's Arden edition and given here in italics between subscript Cs) are marked for omission by Hand C, who, now also turning author, overwrites Shakespeare, and adds a stop-gap half line ('Tell me but this' – marked between superscript Cs and printed in bold; the Arden edition uses Arial font) for the sake of continuity. Notably, the (italicised) Shakespearean verse, marked for omission in the manuscript here, would never have been heard on stage or have appeared in print. It has been assumed that these lines may have been marked for omission because they seem addressed to the thoughtless apprentices whom Anthony Munday (one of the original two playwrights) had already (without Shakespeare knowing it) removed from the insurrection scene, leaving the better-situated citizens of whom it could not really be said that their 'discipline' was 'riot'.

Scholars are not in agreement about the various inconsistencies that become apparent between the text that Shakespeare writes and the rest of the play to which the scene belongs. Some have interpreted the inconsistencies ironed out by Hand C here as a sign that Shakespeare took part in the original composition of the play when it was not yet possible to know what the scenes being written by others would contain. Others have preferred to read the scene as part of a revision attempt by Shakespeare, with himself possessing little detailed knowledge of the rest of the play, or of the revisions already undertaken or still to be undertaken elsewhere in the text.[39] Whatever the case may be, this intervention of Hand C in *Sir Thomas More* completes a cameo of Shakespeare writing to pacify the citizens, with a colleague who, finding the words too strong and out of character, suggests what appears to be a more diplomatic solution. In the only manuscript writing that we have of Shakespeare, he is actually seen not only to blot his own lines, but, in turn, also to find his own lines blotted by a collaborator, and replaced by a connecting verse.

Detecting collaborative writing and identifying individual authorship in early modern English drama are demanding tasks, fraught with hazards, as the paucity of external evidence demands a need for reliable internal evidence established and presented with sound scientific methods. Such objective methods and the appertaining tests are difficult to define, just as it seems impossible always to avoid the thought – aptly signalled in the 1980s by Maurice Charney, Anthony Dawson, and others[40] – that bad writing cannot be Shakespeare's and that good writing must be his. Attempts at attribution may generate fierce debates that go to the very heart of the entire discipline, like the dispute between those who, for a proper analysis of early modern culture, favour Michel Foucault's notion of the author as a function of discourse, a social function rather than an identifiable individual, and those who, to establish the material text and its genesis, prefer to maintain their focus on the traditional notion of the author as its producer

Figure 2 Tony Lopes, 'Do you have anything new by Shakespeare?'
Reproduced by permission.

(collaborative or not).[41] Witnessing such (often misguided) disagreement between armies of attribution specialists, one is inclined to agree with John Jowett, who has noted that, 'Outside observers could be forgiven for thinking that there is so much tortuous and impenetrable disagreement in this field that it should be left well alone.'[42] Yet, as Jowett also recognises, the field's merits are undeniable, and the achievements of recent years should not be underestimated.

Attribution studies have come a long way since the late nineteenth century, but as Brian Vickers has convincingly demonstrated in *Shakespeare, Co-Author*, some of the earliest assumptions and calculations should not be rejected out of hand, as they may prove a valuable source of inspiration or a valid guide to present-day researchers. Conversely, new attributions should be studied with due caution, as has been shown by Donald Foster's allegation that the 'Funeral Elegy for Master William Peter' was Shakespeare's, and the French scholar Gilles Monsarrat's demonstration that the verse was John Ford's.[43] It is fascinating to discover or witness the discovery of a new text by Shakespeare, and this explains why the theme persists in popular fiction like Arthur Phillips's *Tragedy of Arthur*, a deft novel woven around a 'Shakespeare' play that may have been forged, or Robert Winder's *Final Act of Mr. William Shakespeare*, which captures the process of writing and presents the full text of *Henry VII* as the missing link between the two tetralogies of histories and the collaborative *Henry VIII*.[44] Such fiction fascinates many, and indicates that we would all like to read more new Shakespeare (Figure 2).

As authorial identities have been established with ever greater accuracy over the last forty years, a gulf has been opening up between the field of attribution studies and the criticism of early modern English drama. How does the critic, assuming a fair degree of textual coherence, work with collaborative drama if it is often inconsistent, either because different contributors left their own linguistic fingerprints on the style of the play, or because (as we witnessed in the case of Hand D in *Sir Thomas More*) the collaborators' different contributions in terms of plot or character are often not seamlessly welded, despite the apparent efforts involved?[45] It has been argued that certain inconsistencies might go unnoticed in performance, but would the same have applied when the text was read by one of the collaborators or revisers? If, as we now know, George Peele wrote a large share of *Titus Andronicus*, how would Shakespeare have enjoyed those sections by Peele, the general characteristic of whose style in *Titus Andronicus* is, as Brian Vickers puts it, one of

> verbal expansiveness vitiated by two failings: an inadequate sense of economy, and an inability to vary utterance according to character or context ... Judging by the standards of Renaissance rhetoric, it must be admitted that Peele's use of the figures is often dysfunctional, simply piling up words for emphasis, not doing anything with them.[46]

The distinct styles and their apparent inequality in *Titus Andronicus* may have gone unnoticed in early modern performance, or may have been accepted because modes of listening differed from ours. But how would Peele's handiwork have been evaluated by Vickers's Shakespeare, 'whose use of rhetoric in *Titus Andronicus*, by contrast, is precise, economic, [and] witty' (233)?

Speaking of early modern English drama, Heather Hirschfeld has noted that the 'cooperative sensibility of the stage ... demands a rethinking of the roles and meanings of the dramatist and his work', and that 'no practice demands this rethinking more than the fact of collaborative writing'.[47] This process has only just begun, and it is likely that we may look forward to accounts of the period more sophisticated than the following from *Shakespeare in Love*, although the movie industry here does acknowledge a joint process of creation that Shakespeareans have long been unwilling to recognise:

WILL: I hear you have a new play for the Curtain.
MARLOWE: Not new – my *Doctor Faustus*.
WILL: I love your early work. 'Was this the face that launched a thousand ships and burnt the topless towers of Ilium?'
MARLOWE: I have a new one nearly done, and better. *The Massacre at Paris*.
WILL: Good title.
MARLOWE: And yours?
WILL: *Romeo and Ethel the Pirate's Daughter.* (*beat; sighs despondently*) Yes, I know.
MARLOWE: What is the story?
WILL: Well, there's a pirate ... (*confesses*) In truth, I have not written a word.
MARLOWE: Romeo is ... Italian. Always in and out of love.

WILL: Yes, that's good. Until he meets …
MARLOWE: Ethel.
WILL: Do you think?
MARLOWE: The daughter of his enemy.
WILL: (*thoughtfully*): The daughter of his enemy.
MARLOWE: His best friend is killed in a duel by Ethel's brother or something.
    His name is Mercutio.
WILL: Mercutio … good name.[48]

Tom Stoppard and Marc Norman's interpretation of what it might be like to collaborate wants to be ridiculous, but it also introduces a serious issue that current attribution studies have not yet defined as one of their objectives. If attribution studies want to understand the nature of a collaborative play and the differences it displays between the writers involved, are they not overlooking the phenomenon, more or less acknowledged by Jeffrey Masten, that the collaborative effort between playwright A and playwright B should not simply be represented as a sum in linear terms as A + B, but as the new, previously unknown entity, C?[49] In the process of identifying individual shares and the relations between them, are current attributionists not concentrating their efforts on what is perhaps the most predictable and prosaic, and certainly the least poetic aspect of all collaboration? If any type of writing involves the search for a brand of synthesis, what merger may the simultaneous work of two or more dramatists bring into being? We may be unable (as yet) theoretically to define and capture the added value that represents the product of collaborative writing in a particular text, but we can rest assured that this *terra incognita* is never going to be charted properly if we continue to pursue divisive strategies devised to identify individuals rather than the product of bonding, the supra-individual fallout of collaborative crossover or fusion. Of course, the paradox of the exercise is that, once we are prepared to do so, it will be to find 'Shakespeare' and at the same time to resign our claim to 'Shakespeare'. Arguably, attributionists could derive inspiration not only from each others' distinguished efforts, but also from present-day experiments in collaborative writing as these may have a bearing on Shakespeare, like the decision of Stephen Greenblatt and the leading American playwright Charles L. Mee in 2003 to write and to experience writing a version of the lost *Cardenio* together, or Gary Taylor's 'creative reconstruction' of the same lost play over the years, which also became the subject of an international conference devoted to the play a year later.[50] Such experiments in collaborative recreation, and research that challenges the status of creative writing within an academic context, should teach us ever more about the chemistry of joint writing, and about ways to identify new traces of a collaborative dynamic in texts that may already seem familiar to us. As the notion of 'author' continues to evolve in this way, there will be further challenges to the ways in which we edit and read Shakespeare – the Reader's Guide that Jowett adds to his edition of *Sir Thomas More*[51] is only a practical matter – and perform his work.[52]

In *Shakespeare's Modern Collaborators*, Lukas Erne, with playful seriousness, extends the definition of the term 'collaborator' as it has been employed in this chapter, where it has included Shakespeare's colleagues in the theatre world (including actors and musicians), as well as those who sought to gain an income as well as realise their ambitions as dramatists or poets. Erne really demonstrates how the editors of Shakespeare's work over the past four centuries may also be looked upon as collaborators, since, like his contemporaries, these editors have contributed to shaping the meaning of the text and of 'Shakespeare' himself.[53] By stretching the limits of the term, Erne really agrees that there is no reason to exclude ourselves as collaborators.[54] When we engage with Shakespeare, as readers, audiences, scholars or creative writers, we too collaborate with Shakespeare, 'meaning by Shakespeare' in the very act. Ideally, our awareness of the nature of this activity should continually sharpen our sense also of the interactive and collaborative world which the plays themselves represent. Shakespeare is not only our contemporary, still; we are also his collaborators.

NOTES

1 *A New History of Early English Drama*, ed. John D. Cox and David Scott Kastan, with a foreword by Stephen J. Greenblatt (New York: Columbia University Press, 1997), 2.

2 Stephen Orgel, 'What Is a Text?' in his *The Authentic Shakespeare and Other Problems of the Early Modern Stage* (New York and London: Routledge, 2002), 1. For a lucid discussion of the changing definition of the 'author' in early modern culture and contemporary academe, see also Heather Hirschfeld, '"For the Author's Credit": Issues of Authorship in English Renaissance Drama', in *The Oxford Handbook of Early Modern Theatre*, ed. Richard Dutton (Oxford University Press, 2009), 441–55.

3 Jeffrey Knapp, *Shakespeare Only* (Chicago and London: University of Chicago Press, 2009), 3.

4 This newly theorised recognition on the intra- and interactivity of the London theatre companies has generated a series of fascinating company histories. See Andrew Gurr, *The Shakespeare Company, 1594–1642* (Cambridge University Press, 2004), and *Shakespeare's Opposites: The Admirals Company, 1595–1625* (Cambridge University Press, 2009); Roslyn Lander Knutson, *Playing Companies and Commerce in Shakespeare's Time* (Cambridge University Press, 2001); and Lucy Monro, *Children of the Queen's Revels: A Jacobean Theatre Repertory* (Cambridge University Press, 2005).

5 *Romeo and Juliet*, ed. Brian Gibbons, The Arden Shakespeare (London and New York: Methuen, 1980), 1.5.92–9.

6 Alan C. Dessen, 'Conceptual Casting in the Age of Shakespeare: Evidence from *Mucedorus*', *Shakespeare Quarterly* 43:1 (Spring, 1992), 67–70. See also Thomas L. Berger, 'Casting *Henry V*', *Shakespeare Studies* 20 (1988), 89–104 and Thomas L. Berger, 'Double Casting of Shakespeare's Plays: A Select Bibliography', *Shakespeare Bulletin* 7:6 (1989), 30–1.

7 *Much Ado About Nothing*, ed. Claire McEachern, Arden Third Series (London: Thomson Learning, 2006), 26.

8 David Wiles, *Shakespeare's Clown: Actor and Text in the Elizabethan Playhouse* (Cambridge University Press, 1987). On the playwrighting ambitions of these actors see Nora Johnson, *The Actor as Playwright in Early Modern Drama* (Cambridge University Press, 2003).

9 See Richard Wilson, 'The Words of Mercury: Shakespeare and Marlowe', Chapter 3 in this volume, pp. 34–53.

10 *The Complete Works*, ed. Stanley Wells and Gary Taylor (Oxford University Press, 1986), 12.144.

11 Martin Wiggins, *Shakespeare and the Drama of His Time* (Oxford University Press, 2000), 1–2.

12 *King Henry VI, Part 2*, ed. Ronald Knowles, Arden Third Series (London: Thomas Nelson and Sons, 1999), 4.1.108 and Longer Notes (370).

13 *Hamlet* in *The Complete Works*, ed. Wells and Taylor, 2.2.110–12.

14 *Romeo and Juliet*, ed. Gibbons, 11. See also John Jowett, 'Henry Chettle: Your Old Compositor', *Text* 15 (2003), 141–61.

15 James P. Bednarz, *Shakespeare and the Poets' War* (New York: Columbia University Press, 2001).

16 Charles Cathcart, however, profitably concentrates on Marston and Jonson in *Marston, Rivalry, Rapprochement, and Jonson* (Aldershot: Ashgate, 2008).

17 Bednarz, *Shakespeare and the Poets' War*, 2.

18 *Discoveries* in *Ben Jonson*, ed. C. H. Herford, and Percy and Evelyn Simpson, 11 vols. (Oxford University Press, 1925–52), VIII (1947), 583, lines 647–50. See also Park Honan, *Shakespeare: A Biography* (Oxford University Press, 1998), 253.

19 Honan, *Shakespeare*, 257.

20 *Ben Jonson*, ed. Herford *et al.*, VIII, 584, lines 661–8.

21 E. A. J. Honigmann, *Shakespeare's Impact on His Contemporaries* (London and Basingstoke: Macmillan Press, 1982), 108.

22 In his recent biography of Jonson, Ian Donaldson convincingly demonstrates how '[i]n the small and intensely competitive arena of late Elizabethan theatre Jonson and Shakespeare were clearly observing each other's practice with a sharp eye'. See *Ben Jonson: A Life* (Oxford University Press, 2011), 150. See also Donaldson's discussion of both dramatists' social ambitions (159–64), and of the nature of Jonson's contribution to the First Folio of 1623 (370–6).

23 Gerald Eades Bentley, *The Profession of Dramatist in Shakespeare's Time, 1590–1642* (Princeton University Press, 1971), 197–34. For an attractive reassessment see Philip C. McGuire, 'Collaboration', in *A Companion to Renaissance Drama*, ed. Arthur F. Kinney (Oxford: Blackwell, 2002), 540–52.

24 See Robert Henke, 'John Webster: Collaboration and Solitude', Chapter 12 in this volume, pp. 181–96.

25 *Sejanus* ('To the Readers'), in *Ben Jonson*, ed. Herford *et al.*, IV (1932), 351, lines 44–8.

26 *Volpone*, in *Ben Jonson*, ed. Herford *et al.*, V (1937), 'Prologve', lines 16–18.

27 Bentley, *The Profession of Dramatist*, 234.

28 Brian Vickers, *Shakespeare, Co-Author: A Historical Study of Five Collaborative Plays* (Oxford University Press, 2004), 201.

29 Stanley Wells, *Shakespeare & Co.: Christopher Marlowe, Thomas Dekker, Ben Jonson, Thomas Middleton, John Fletcher, and the Other Players in His Story* (London: Penguin, 2006), 25–6.

30 See Brian Boyd, ed., *Words That Count: Essays on Early Modern Authorship in Honor of MacDonald P. Jackson* (Newark, DE, and London: University of Delaware Press, 2004); Jonathan Hope, *The Authorship of Shakespeare's Plays: A Socio-Linguistic Study* (Cambridge University Press, 1994); MacDonald P. Jackson, *Defining Shakespeare: 'Pericles' as Test Case* (Oxford University Press, 2003); D. J. Lake, *The Canon of Middleton's Plays* (Cambridge University Press, 1975); Gary Taylor and John Jowett, *Shakespeare Reshaped, 1603–1623* (Oxford University Press, 1997); Vickers, *Shakespeare, Co-Author*.

31 Arthur F. Kinney, 'Conclusion', in *Shakespeare, Computers and the Mystery of Authorship*, ed. Hugh Craig and Arthur F. Kinney (Cambridge University Press, 2009), 202–11 at 207.

32 George Peele is also thought to be the author of *The Troublesome Reign of King John*, which Shakespeare drew on for *King John*. Shakespeare might have learnt the use of chronicle material – involving the selection of events and the telescoping of time – from Peele. See George Peele, *The Troublesome Reign of King John, King of England*, ed. Charles R. Forker (Manchester University Press, 2011).

33 John Fletcher's *The Tamer Tamed* is a rare, near-contemporary adaptation of Shakespeare's *The Taming of the Shrew*. See *Adaptations of Shakespeare: A Critical Anthology of Plays from the Seventeenth Century to the Present*, ed. Daniel Fischlin and Mark Fortier (London and New York: Routledge, 2000); and *The Tamer Tamed*, ed. Gary Taylor and Celia R. Daileader (Manchester University Press, 2006).

34 The seminal work on Shakespeare and Middleton by Gary Taylor and John Jowett is reassessed by James P. Bednarz in 'Collaboration: The Shadow of Shakespeare'; Heather Hirschfeld in 'Collaboration: Sustained Partnerships'; and Eric Rasmussen in 'Collaboration: The Determination of Authorship', all in *Thomas Middleton in Context*, ed. Suzanne Gossett (Cambridge University Press, 2011), respectively 218–18, 219–28 and 229–34.

35 Laurie Maguire and Emma Smith, 'Many Hands: A New Shakespeare Collaboration?', *Times Literary Supplement*, 20 April 2012, 13–15.

36 Philip Palmer arrives at a negative conclusion in '*Edmond Ironside* and the Question of Shakespearean Authorship', in Craig and Kinney, *Shakespeare, Computers*, 100–15.

37 *Sir Thomas More, original text by Anthony Munday and Henry Chettle, censored by Edmund Tilney, revisions co-ordinated by Hand C, revised by Henry Chettle, Thomas Dekker, Thomas Heywood and William Shakespeare*, ed. John Jowett, Arden Third Series (London: Methuen Drama, 2011), 28.

38 *Sir Thomas More*, ed. Jowett, 6.119–32. The line 'To kneel to be forgiven' (6.125) is erroneously marked for deletion in the official text of the 2011 Arden edition. The textual commentary for 6.126–8 in the Arden edition correctly excludes this phrase from the passage marked for deletion in the manuscript. The commentary at 6.126–8 corresponds with John Jowett's transcript of the Hand D section (410).

39 On the problems of interpretation here see Vickers, *Shakespeare, Co-Author*, 438–9.

40 Maurice Charney, ed., *'Bad' Shakespeare: Revaluations of the Shakespeare Canon* (London and Toronto: Associated University Presses, 1988). Anthony B. Dawson includes a playful sketch (allegedly discovered among John Payne Collier's papers, but in reality co-authored by Joel Kaplan and Dawson himself) in which Shakespeare (whose heart is not in his writing anymore) allows John Fletcher to doctor his *Henry VIII*. See '*Tempest* in a Teapot: Critics, Evaluation, Ideology', in *'Bad' Shakespeare*, ed. Charney, 61–73 at 63–4. See also Horace Howard Furness, Jr, *The Gloss of Youth: An Imaginary Episode in the Lives of William Shakespeare and John Fletcher* (Philadelphia, PA, and London: J. B. Lippincott Company, 1920), where a young John Milton and Oliver Cromwell soothe an elderly Shakespeare with writer's block by praising the eternal worth of *Hamlet* and *Macbeth*.

41 Extreme positions on the definition of the 'author', the 'co-author', and the (ab) use of Michel Foucault are adopted by Jeffrey Masten, *Textual Intercourse: Collaboration, Authorship, and Sexualities in Renaissance Drama* (Cambridge University Press, 1997); Gordon McMullan in his edition of Shakespeare and Fletcher's *King Henry VIII*, Arden Third Series (London: Cengage Learning, 2000); Jeffrey Knapp, 'What Is a Co-Author?' *Representations* 89:1 (Winter 2005), 1–29, or his *Shakespeare Only* (Chicago and London: University of Chicago Press, 2009); and Brian Vickers, 'Abolishing the Author? Theory *versus* History', in his *Shakespeare, Co-Author*, 506–41.

42 John Jowett, *Shakespeare and Text* (Oxford University Press, 2007), 19.

43 For an extensive discussion of each of these issues, see Brian Vickers, *'Counterfeiting' Shakespeare: Evidence, Authorship and John Ford's 'Funerall Elegye'* (Cambridge University Press, 2002).

44 Arthur Phillips, *The Tragedy of Arthur* (New York: Random House, 2011); Robert Winder, *The Final Act of Mr Shakespeare* (London: Little, Brown, 2010).

45 Brian Vickers, 'Plot and Character in Co-Authored Plays: Problems of Co-ordination', in *Shakespeare, Co-Author*, 433–500.

46 Vickers, *Shakespeare, Co-Author*, 230.

47 Heather Hirschfeld, '"For the Author's Credit": Issues of Authorship in English Renaissance Drama', in *The Oxford Handbook to Early Modern Theatre*, ed. Richard Dutton (Oxford University Press, 2010), 441–55 at 451.

48 Marc Norman and Tom Stoppard, *Shakespeare in Love: A Screenplay* (New York: Miramax Books, 1998), 29–30. The movie also introduces John Webster, who represents the collaborative nature of the theatre to a tee: 'I was in a play. They cut my head off in *Titus Andronicus*. When I write plays, they will be like *Titus*' (53).

49 Jeffrey Masten, 'Playwrighting: Authorship and Collaboration', in *A New History of Early English Drama*, ed. John D. Cox and David Scott Kastan (New York: Columbia University Press, 1977), 357–82; and *Textual Intercourse*.

50 Stephen Greenblatt, 'Theatrical Mobility', in Stephen Greenblatt *et al.*, *Cultural Mobility: A Manifesto* (Cambridge University Press, 2010), 75–95. On Gary Taylor's *Cardenio*, see SHAKSPER, SHK 20.0215 (6 May 2009), available online at http://shaksper.net. Roger Chartier has written an international history of the phenomenon in his *Cardenio entre Cervantès et Shakespeare: Histoire d'une pièce perdue* (Paris: Éditions Gallimard, 2011). Of special interest here is the Epilogue, 'La fièvre Cardenio' (Cardenio fever), 265–84.

51 *Sir Thomas More*, ed. Jowett, 121–9.

52 The winds of change have been most conspicuous in the struggle with the 'text'. See Gordon McMullan, '"Our Whole Life Is Like a Play": Collaboration and the Problem of Editing', *Textus* 9 (1996), 437–60; and Gabriel Egan, 'The Future: Cutting, Collaboration, Literary Authorship and the Legacy of New Bibliography', in his *The Struggle for Shakespeare's Text: Twentieth-Century Editorial Theory and Practice* (Cambridge University Press, 2010), 222–30.

53 Lukas Erne, *Shakespeare's Modern Collaborators* (London: Continuum, 2008).

54 This is also the idea behind Pavel Drábek, Klára Kolinská and Matthew Nicholls, eds., *Shakespeare and His Collaborators over the Centuries* (Newcastle upon Tyne: Cambridge Scholars Publishing, 2008).

Further reading

Elliott, Ward E. Y., and Robert J. Valenza, 'Shakespeare's Vocabulary: Did It Dwarf All Others?' in *Stylistics and Shakespeare's Language – Transdisciplinary Approaches*, ed. Mireille Ravassat and Jonathan Culpepper. London: Continuum, 2011, 34–57.

Foster, Donald W., *Elegy by W.S.: A Study in Attribution*. Newark, DE: University of Delaware Press, 1989.

Hirschfeld, Heather Anne, *Joint Enterprises: Collaborative Drama and the Institutionalization of English Renaissance Theatre*. Boston: University of Massachusetts Press, 2004.

Hoy, Cyrus, 'Critical and Aesthetic Problems of Collaboration.' *Research Opportunities in Renaissance Drama* 19 (1976), 3–6.

Knapp, Jeffrey, 'What Is a Co-Author?'. *Representations* 89:1 (Winter 2005), 1–29.

Koestenbaum, Wayne, *Double Talk: The Erotics of Male Literary Collaboration*. London and New York: Routledge, 1989.

Masten, Jeffrey, 'Beaumont and/or Fletcher: Collaboration and the Interpretation of Renaissance Drama.' *English Literary History* 59 (1992): 337–56.

'Playwrighting: Authorship and Collaboration', in *A New History of Early English Drama*, ed. John D. Cox and David Scott Kastan. New York: Columbia University Press, 1997, 357–82.

Textual Intercourse: Collaboration, Authorship, and Sexualities in Renaissance Drama. Cambridge University Press, 1997.

McLuskie, Kathleen, 'Collaboration', in *The Revels History of Drama in English*. IV, *1613–1660*, ed. Philip Edwards, Gerald Eades Bentley, Kathleen McLuskie and Lois Potter. London and New York: Methuen, 1981, 169–82.

Muir, Kenneth, *Shakespeare as Collaborator*. London: Methuen, 1960.

Schoenbaum, Samuel, *Internal Evidence and Elizabethan Dramatic Authorship: An Essay in Literary History and Method*. Evanston, IL: Northwestern University Press, 1966.

Taylor, Gary, 'Shakespeare and Others: The Authorship of *Henry the Sixth, Part I*.' *Medieval and Renaissance Drama in England* 7 (1995), 145–205.

'What Is an Author [not]?' *Critical Survey* 7 (1995), 241–55.

Vickers, Brian, *Shakespeare, 'A Lover's Complaint', and John Davies of Hereford*. Cambridge University Press, 2007.

8

JEAN E. HOWARD

Thomas Heywood: dramatist of London and playwright of the passions

The one thing most scholars know about Thomas Heywood is his claim, included in his 1633 preface to *The English Traveller*, to have had 'an entire hand, or at the least a maine finger' in 220 plays.[1] We don't know if this is true, but it seems probable, given the length of Heywood's career (he started writing in the 1590s and continued until his death in 1641), his productivity in many genres and his apparent penchant for collaboration. He was, for example, a probable collaborator in *The Book of Sir Thomas More* (1592–3) and a certain collaborator in plays such as *The Witch of Edmonton* (1621). A man of modest origins, Heywood was the son of a country parson, and his studies at Cambridge were cut short when his father died in 1593. Settling in London, he spent most of the rest of his life in the city, becoming in every way a man of London and of the London theatre world.

While the majority of Heywood's writing was done for the theatre, he also wrote a number of works of poetry, including the early 'Oenone and Paris' (1594), a narrative poem resembling Shakespeare's 'Venus and Adonis', and *Troia Britannica* (1609), a history of the world to the present; a defence of the theatre entitled *An Apology for Actors* (1607); two collections of prose stories about women, *Gunaikeion* (1624) and *Nine the Most Worthy Women of the World* (1640); and a rambling philosophical compendium entitled *The Hierarchy of the Blessed Angels* (1635). In the 1590s Heywood was associated with the theatrical enterprises of Philip Henslowe and wrote plays for the Lord Admiral's Men at the Rose. In 1599 the Earl of Derby's Men staged his two-part play, *Edward IV*, and soon thereafter he joined the Earl of Worcester's Company, which metamorphosed into the Queen Anne's Men after King James ascended the English throne in 1603. With the Queen's Men, playing primarily at the Red Bull theatre in Clerkenwell, Heywood had a long and fruitful relationship.

Fully attuned to the theatrical world of which he was a part, Heywood was a notable dramatic innovator, turning received genres to new purposes and inventing new theatrical devices to heighten the emotional impact of his dramas. His *The Four Prentices of London* (c. 1592), for example, rewrites the chivalric romance to accommodate the interests of London guild culture; his *1* and *2 Edward IV* (1599) transform the monarchical history play by intertwining a story of ordinary London citizens with the story of King Edward; and his *A Woman Killed with Kindness* (1603) is now considered the finest example of the emerging genre of domestic tragedy, which probed the tragic potential in the lives of middling sort and gentry people, rather than of the aristocracy. While Heywood has sometimes been seen as a conservative and sentimental writer, interested in preserving the status quo, his plays often challenge that status quo in subtle ways, sometimes through their ambivalent celebration of emerging commercial interests and often through their innovative representations of women who, used to enhance the affective dimensions of performance, also often complicate the overt moral or homiletic thrust of the plays.

Heywood's special brand of dramaturgy can be seen in his experimental play, *The Four Prentices of London*, probably written and performed about 1594 though only published in 1615. Owing a debt to Christopher Marlowe's *Tamburlaine* (1587–8), which created a vogue for plays about Eastern rulers and Eastern lands, *The Four Prentices of London* draws on the story of Godfrey of Bouillon, famous for his leadership of the first crusade to win back Jerusalem from Saracen forces and often named as one of the Nine Worthies. These Worthies exemplified the military and moral virtues found in great leaders and included three classical figures (Hector, Alexander the Great and Julius Caesar), three biblical figures (David, Joshua and Judas Maccabeus) and three Christian figures (Arthur, Charlemagne and Godfrey of Bouillon).

Heywood significantly transformed the Godfrey material while retaining its deep investment in military conquest and Christian solidarity against Islamic foes. As the play opens, the Earl of Bouillon has lost his throne, and he takes his sons to England where, to save them from poverty, he apprentices them in the London guilds. Godfrey, the eldest, becomes a member of the mercers' guild; the other three are apprenticed to a haberdasher, a grocer and a goldsmith. The first notable thing about the play, then, is the way Heywood chauvinistically transposes the story of Godfrey of Bouillon to London and appropriates a tale of aristocratic chivalry to celebrate the city's guilds. After the old earl departs for Jerusalem to die near Christ's tomb, the four sons throw over their actual apprentice duties and enter the service of Robert, Duke of Normandy, son of William the Conqueror, as he sets out on a crusade to the Holy Land. Apprentices turned knights, the brothers brandish the insignia of the London guilds on their shields as they head to Jerusalem. This gesture invites ordinary

London theatregoers to feel that the brothers' crusade is their own, that even middling-sort adventurers can aspire to do chivalric deeds and win glory for their country in foreign lands. The city and the city's guildsmen lie, then, at the heart of the fantasy structure that Heywood's play represents as the four brothers undergo shipwreck, encounter pirates, travel in France, Ireland and Italy, have amorous adventures with various women, one their sister in disguise (!), and finally win victory against the Soldan of Babylon and the Sophy of Persia before the walls of Jerusalem. For their efforts three of the brothers receive the crowns, respectively, of Cyprus, Sicily and Jerusalem, while Godfrey insists on wearing a crown of thorns in imitation of Christ's suffering.

The Four Prentices' improbabilities and rhetorical excesses have elicited some critical scorn. Francis Beaumont in *The Knight of the Burning Pestle* (1607) made fun of a grocer's apprentice who longs to be a wandering knight and who adopts a flaming pestle as his chivalric insignia (the pestle being both a sign of the grocer's trade and also a sly suggestion of a diseased penis). Beaumont even has a citizen refer to Heywood's *Four Prentices* by name, recalling an incident when two of the brothers, Guy and Eustace, toss their pikes in the air to show their strength.[2] Nonetheless, *The Four Prentices* has an exuberant theatrical energy that clearly captured the imagination of London spectators; otherwise, Beaumont would have had no popular reference point against which to launch his satire. Many must have found memorable the play's mixture of the chivalric and the civic, the exotic and the homely.

The energy with which Heywood adapted the story of Godfrey of Bouillon for the early modern stage reveals a love of the theatrical enterprise that undergirds his spirited defence of the stage, *An Apology for Actors* (composed *c.* 1607 and published 1612). In this treatise Heywood details the long and honourable lineage of the theatrical profession and argues for theatre's importance to great cities. Rather than responding at length to contemporary attacks on the theatre as scurrilous or idolatrous, Heywood simply asserts from the opening moments of his treatise that theatre is a force for social good: it provides instruction to princes; it warns audiences against vice and distracts them from political mischief; it helps to improve a nation's language; it teaches the unlettered the history of their country; and it provides necessary recreation for weary minds. Heywood has no hesitation in banishing from his protection all those who promulgate 'lascivious shows, scurrilous jests, or scandalous invectives'.[3] His defence does not extend to them, but only to the many actors and dramatists who from classical times to the present had made of theatre an honourable and profitable profession.

Two things in particular stand out in Heywood's defence. The first is his repeated assertion that all great cities have been the home of great theatres, especially the city of Rome to which he often compares contemporary London. 'Rome was a Metropolis, a place whither all the nations known under the Sun, resorted: so is London, and being to receive all Estates, all Princes, all nations, therefore to afford them all choice of pastimes, sports, and recreations: yet were there Theatres in all the greatest Cities of the world' (sig. C2). For Heywood, London's status as the nation's capital and England's pre-eminent commercial centre seems to demand that it also be a great entertainment centre. Implicit in his argument is the view that, due to the westward movement of civilisation (*translatio imperii*), London is the inevitable inheritor of the distinguished theatrical traditions once so central to Roman cultural life, and he delights in naming the actors and playwrights of the contemporary London scene as inheritors of the classical tradition. The mixture of civic and national pride that informs all of *An Apology for Actors* is apparent, as well, in the content of many of Heywood's plays, as in his honouring of the city's guilds in *The Four Prentices of London*.

Another striking feature of Heywood's defence of the theatre is his focus on its power to play on the emotions and the conscience of the audience. In Heywood's vision of theatre, plays *do things* to spectators. Famously, he attested to the emotional force of what he calls 'our domestic histories', that is, plays based on English history:

> What English blood seeing the person of any bold Englishman presented and does not hug his fame and hunny at his valor, pursuing him in his enterprise with his best wishes, and as being wrapt in contemplation, offers to him in his hart all prosperous performance, as if the Performer were the man Personated, so bewitching a thing is lively and well spirited action, that it hath power to new mold the harts of the spectators and fashion them to the shape of any noble and notable attempt. (sig. C3)

Elsewhere in the *Apology for Actors* Heywood describes how guilty audience members, watching a representation of crimes similar to those they themselves have secretly performed, are impelled to confess their transgressions (sigs. GV–G2). Reading Heywood's account of theatre's effects on audiences, one can understand why anti-theatricalists feared its power. It is imagined as seizing the mind and emotions of spectators, 'new molding' them, and causing them to confess to long-hidden crimes. Of course, in Heywood's account, the theatre always 'new molds' people in beneficial directions, and its power is a force for good. It impels spectators to perform heroic deeds, creates aversion to vice and leads to soul-cleansing confessions. Heywood never considers, however, whether the theatre's power to move the spectator might cause that spectator to emulate vice rather than be repelled by it, nor does he ask if the power of the actor to command the audience's sympathy might not at times contradict or disrupt the moral lesson the play is to teach. While *An Apology for Actors* offers a robust defence of theatre's social value and its ancient lineage, it dodges some of the questions that might trouble Heywood's strategic optimism about the uniformly beneficent effects of the institution to which he was so deeply wedded.

Some of the contradictions that arise from theatre's ability to rouse strong emotions become apparent if we consider one of Heywood's most interesting undertakings, the two-part *King Edward IV, Containing his merry pastime with the Tanner of Tamworth; as also his love to fair Mistress Shore, her great promotion, fall, and misery, and lastly, the lamentable death of both her and her husband.* The lengthy subtitle calls in question the title character's prominence in the action and also suggests the range of emotions the play is imagined to evoke and express, including merriment, love, misery and lamentation. As a history play bearing a king's name in its main title, the play joins many others from the 1590s that represent England's past by highlighting the successive monarchs who held the throne in the late medieval and early modern periods, plays such as Marlowe's *Edward II* (1592–3) and Shakespeare's *Richard II* (1595) or *Henry IV* (1597–9). While some of these plays had subplots and clown figures, as, for example, Shakespeare's *Henry IV* in which the Falstaff episodes have considerable prominence, *Edward IV* is unusual for the degree to which the middle-class story of Jane and Matthew Shore is put in the foreground, throwing into the shadows those parts of Edward's story having to do with his struggles for the throne and his battles in France.

Heywood begins the play with the citizens of London defending the city against invaders in the king's absence. Matthew Shore is a leader in this endeavour, but the king rewards him by determining to seduce his wife, Mistress Shore, legendary for her beauty. To add insult to injury, he does so in Matthew's own shop where Jane sits to watch over the servants and attract customers. Much of the action in both plays involves Jane's piercing remorse over her seduction, her husband's suffering, her saint-like actions in the service of the poor, her eventual fall into abject poverty when Edward dies and her martyr's death on London's outskirts, abandoned by nearly everyone except her husband.

In *An Apology for Actors*, Heywood included Mistress Shore among those unchaste women who serve to warn spectators from vice, just as Lucrece and Diana are instanced as examples of chastity to be emulated (sig. GV). But in dramatising Jane's saintly behaviour and cruel suffering, Heywood makes her much more than a static emblem of vice. She becomes the emotional centre around which the play pivots, a woman as sinned against as sinning. The play elicits tears for the martyrdom of this saintly and beautiful woman whose responsibility for her loss of chastity is mitigated by the power of the King who demanded that loss. Jane is punished by the guilt she feels for her infidelity to Matthew Shore and also by King Richard, who succeeds Edward on the throne and determines to isolate and mortify the former King's mistress. Not even the merry clowning of the Tanner of Tamworth can eclipse the dominantly sombre mood created by the two Shores' bitter fate. Implicitly, *Edward IV* casts the King in a negative light for creating such suffering and for spoiling the domestic harmony of his subjects' household. As a theatrical event, Heywood's play complicates the easy moralism that *An Apology* assigns the stage, in this case making 'the criminal' an object of pity and veneration and creating powerful currents of sympathy for the spectacle of her suffering.

Through its focus on the Shores, Heywood in effect transforms the genre of the English history play from one centred on the monarch and his problems of rule to one equally centred on a couple from the middling ranks of society and on their domestic debacle. In effect, *Edward IV* embeds a sentimental domestic tragedy inside a chronicle history, thereby transforming the genre which Shakespeare had made so prominent throughout the 1590s in the direction of the concerns of ordinary people. This transformation also involved setting the action of the play in a recognisable London landscape. In 1599 when Heywood wrote *Edward IV*, the first stirrings of London city comedy were just being felt. Jonson was writing his humours plays which increasingly took a particularised London for their setting, and in 1599 William Haughton penned *Englishmen for My Money*, a comedy set in part in London's Royal Exchange and making extensive use of London geography in its plot and its jokes.

It was at exactly the same time that Heywood was rooting his citizen story of Jane and Matthew Shore deep in London soil. The play is place rich. When rebels are about to invade the city, they name the particular sites they will loot and despoil: Leadenhall, Cheapside, the Mint, the Tower, Lombard Street, St Paul's, Westminster. The city's defenders vow to defend the city's gates, especially Aldgate and Bishopsgate, and they gather for consultation at the Guildhall. The Mayor of London, John Crosby, is steeped in the city's history, often evoking former mayors such as William Walworth, who during Richard II's reign stabbed a rebel leader in Smithfield. As a result of Walworth's deed, a red dagger was incorporated in the arms of London. Crosby himself is a product of the city. Abandoned as a baby by Cow Cross in Islington, he was given the name Crosby (by the Cross) by the shoemaker who found him. Later, as a prosperous member of the grocers' guild, Crosby endowed a poorhouse in Bishopsgate Street and called it Crosby House. The play links the mayor with the geography and the charitable edifices of the city, and when Jane Shore finally dies in a ditch at the edge of London, the citizens in the play give it the name Shoreditch in memory of her many charitable deeds. The cumulative effect of all these references to London places and people is to make *Edward IV* as much a London history as a monarchical history and to memorialise the heroism of London citizens and the streets, buildings and institutions in which they lived their lives.

The impulse to dramatise events from London history and myth is carried even further in Heywood's remarkable two-part play published in 1605, *If You Know Not Me You Know Nobody*. *Part I* was one of the most popular plays of the period, with editions appearing in 1606, 1608, 1610, 1613, 1623, 1632 and 1639. Only 1,600 lines long, *Part I* depicts the suffering of Elizabeth I before her ascension to the throne when she was held captive, part of the time in the Tower of London, by Queen Mary. Heywood's Princess Elizabeth is exemplary for both her virginity and her virtue, a Protestant martyr holding fast to a prayer book or an English Bible and refusing to give over her faith in the face of the Catholic Mary's persecution. The play ends with her triumphantly ascending the throne of England. In her patient virtue and the pathos caused by her imprisonment, she resembles Heywood's portrait of Jane Shore. Both women exemplify virtue besieged, and while one dies in a ditch and the other becomes Queen of England, the plays in which they appear both invite audiences to empathise with their suffering.

Part II is quite different. In it Heywood focuses, not on one of the classical Nine Worthies but on a local London worthy, Sir Thomas Gresham, a member of London's Mercers' Company who served as royal agent handling financial affairs on the Continent for Edward, Mary and Elizabeth, and who returned from service abroad to build Gresham's Exchange (later renamed the Royal Exchange by Elizabeth I) at the corner of Cornhill and Threadneedle Street. This building, modelled on the Antwerp bourse, had a classical façade, a shopping arcade on the second level and a large inner courtyard where those involved in long-distance trade, many of them foreign merchants, gathered to do business at set hours. Dedicated as it was to the needs of the international merchant community, this imposing edifice signalled London's emergence as one of the great commercial centres of Europe, especially after the collapse of the Antwerp bourse in the 1570s left many merchants seeking a new base of operations.

In *If You Know Not Me, Part II*, Heywood celebrates both the building and the man who built it and in doing so continued to dramatise, as he had in *Edward IV*, the history of London, here the very recent past, since the Exchange was erected in the 1560s. Queen Elizabeth, who comes to the official opening of Gresham's building, has only a minor role within the play's unfolding story. Heywood is not writing monarchical history or even the hybrid version he produced in *Edward IV*, but a kind of mythologised London history with an ambitious London merchant as his protagonist. The details of Heywood's portrait of Gresham, however, point to contradictions and ambivalences in his representation of this merchant and of the emerging world of international, high-risk commerce that he comes to represent. On the one hand, Heywood's Gresham displays breathtaking ambition and capacity for risk. Not only has he built the Exchange, a building to rival the grandest buildings of Europe, but as the play opens he is negotiating to secure a monopoly on Moroccan sugar during the King of Morocco's lifetime in exchange for the staggeringly large sum of £60,000. When the King almost immediately dies, leaving Gresham without his £60,000 or his monopoly, the merchant refuses to be cast down, but dances a dance in the slippers that the Moroccans have insultingly sent to him. Later, in a bravura gesture of conspicuous consumption, he purchases a pearl for £1,500, grinds it up, puts it in wine, and then drinks it down in a toast to Elizabeth.

Gresham has charisma and daring. He dominates the stage. And yet, he fits strangely into the model of city worthy made popular by John Stow's *Survey of London* (1598) and evoked in the play by the Dean of St Paul's, Dr Nowell. Nowell has a gallery in his house containing portraits of many of the prominent men of London's past, all of whom were famous for their charitable acts in founding colleges, poorhouses, libraries and civic buildings. Gresham aspires to their ranks, and yet his great building is as much for his own profit as for public good; he is cantankerously involved in a land dispute with Sir Thomas Ramsey; and his extravagance seems an affront to more sober standards of behaviour. He is juxtaposed throughout the play to old Hobson, a haberdasher of modest means who nonetheless gives charitable aid to some of the city's most impoverished members. Attempting to reconcile Ramsey and Gresham, Hobson rails against spending good money on lawyers when it could be spent to help the poor. The old haberdasher represents London's traditional craft guilds and their values; Gresham in this play represents an emerging group of international merchants who specialise in big money and big risk. From the juxtaposition of these worlds, Heywood creates a play that looks both backward and forward, commemorating what London worthies have created in the past and dramatising with some ambivalence the new breed of men who promise fair to replace them.

Unlike the plays discussed so far, what has come to be recognised as Heywood's most famous play, *A Woman Killed with Kindness*, has no scenes set in London. Rather, it takes place in the countryside of northern

England, near York, though it continues to focus on people of the middle ranks of society, clearly Heywood's preferred locus of attention. *Woman Killed* is part of a subgenre of Renaissance tragedy, the domestic tragedy, that had developed in the 1590s with plays such as *Arden of Faversham* (1592), *A Warning for Fair Women* (1599) and the Jane Shore plot in Heywood's own *Edward IV*. Other domestic tragedies include *Two Lamentable Tragedies* (1601), *The Yorkshire Tragedy* (1608), *The Witch of Edmonton* (1621) and *The English Traveller* (1633); some critics consider Shakespeare's *Othello* (1603–4) as part of the subgenre because of its focus on a husband's murder of his wife. As a group, domestic tragedies typically deal with non-noble figures – those of society's middle ranks – and depict crimes that take place in the household or the neighbourhood such as adultery, bigamy, domestic violence, murder of a spouse or neighbour and witchcraft. As Frances E. Dolan has argued, these plays deal with crimes of 'familiars', that is, people who are known to their victims and often live in intimate relations with them. Hence the peculiar horror of domestic tragedies: they reveal the violence and betrayals that lie just beneath the surface of daily life.[4]

In the main plot of *A Woman Killed with Kindness*, adultery is the worm in the apple. The play opens as a prosperous country gentleman, John Frankford, weds Anne Acton, a woman slightly above him in rank, who is the sister of Sir Francis Acton, a knight. Anne is extolled as a pattern of virtuous womanhood (1.16–24), and the couple seems headed for marital bliss. In soliloquy Frankford speaks about the contentment he feels in his 'mean estate', commenting that

> the chief
> Of all the sweet felicities on earth,
> I have a fair, a chaste, and loving wife,
> Perfection all, all truth, all ornament.[5]

His happiness does not last. The married couple turns into a triad when Frankford invites Wendoll, an out-of-pocket gentleman, to share his household and be his companion, giving Wendoll a servant, a horse and access to his wife's friendship. Wendoll takes advantage of these kindnesses to seduce Anne in Frankford's absence. Only the sharp eyes of a servant, Nick, bring their adultery to light. Alerted by Nick, Frankford finds wife and friend in bed. Wendoll flees, and Frankford then punishes Anne with kindness in that he does not kill or disfigure her (both within his rights as a cuckolded husband), but allows her to live in a distant farmhouse with the proviso that she never communicate with him or their children again. Repentant, Anne refuses food and only on her deathbed is reunited with her family.

This main plot is juxtaposed to a second plot involving the more aristocratic members of the community, Sir Francis Acton and Sir Charles Mountford. They quarrel over whose falcon is the better hunting bird, and in a rage Sir Charles slays two of Sir Francis's servants. In the ensuing legal battles Sir Charles is stripped of most of his wealth. With his sister Susan he is reduced to living in a small manor house and working the few acres that surround it with his own hands. But as more creditors pile on, Charles is imprisoned and only released when Sir Francis Acton, who has fallen in love with Susan, pays all Charles's debts in an act of 'kindness' aimed at overcoming Susan's aversion to him (9.66). Charles, obsessed with maintaining his honour, offers to prostitute Susan to Sir Francis to redress his generosity. Sir Francis, in his turn, declares he wants to marry Susan, and she acquiesces.

This plot demonstrates the profligacy and recklessness of the aristocratic class of which these two knights are members. Only when Charles turns to husbandry and manual labour does he find true contentment (7.1–8). What most directly links subplot and main plot, however, are the issues of kindness and male honour. How kind is Sir Francis's generosity, aimed as it is at winning Susan, not liberating Charles, and, in effect, putting Charles under another heavy obligation which his honour demands he repay? To modern ears the most startling moment in the play may be when Sir Charles offers his sister to Sir Francis in order to save *his* honour, a priority that paradoxically means the eclipse of *her* honour since sex outside of marriage would effectively turn Susan into a whore. This tragedy is averted by the fact that Sir Francis actually wants to marry Susan, though whether she wants to marry him is never asked. Rescued from sexual violation, she simply says: 'I will yield to fate / And learn to love where I till now did hate' (14.147–8). The lack of attention to Susan's wishes and Charles's willingness to sacrifice a sister's virginity and honour to preserve his own honour remain stark reminders of the patriarchal framework within which the play's action unfolds.

In the main plot, Anne, unlike Susan, is guilty of a crime, but Heywood creates sympathy for her plight by making her a remarkably reluctant adulteress. Although she agrees to sleep with Wendoll, she expresses her choice in terms that suggest both confusion and deep ambivalence. Hearing Wendoll's protestations of love, she is moved to 'passion and to pity' (6.140) and speaks of his tongue as having 'enchanted' her (160). Yet from the first she knows that the act she is about to commit leads to 'the labyrinth of sin' (161), and exclaims: 'I blush and am asham'd' (158). She is, then, a divided subject, stirred by passionate and enchanting words, yet knowing that giving in to Wendoll will cause her to lose her soul, her social place and her peace of mind.

Yet Frankford is also to blame, and a concern for male honour figures largely in Anne's fate. Frankford shows bad judgement in bringing Wendoll, a new acquaintance, into his household and putting him in a position of authority in his absence. While friendship was a highly prized relationship in early modern England, Frankford gives a relatively untested friendship a primacy that puts his wife's chastity and his entire household in danger. Nick, his servant, is both more intuitive and more observant than Frankford when it comes to assessing Wendoll. After Frankford invites Wendoll into his house, Nick exclaims: 'I do not like this fellow by no means; / I never see him but my heart still earns' (4.85–6). Later, Nick observes Wendoll kissing Anne (6.164) and swears that he will 'henceforth turn a spy, / And watch them in their close conveyances' (175–6).

Nick's watchfulness, which may be sparked by jealousy over Wendoll's pre-eminence in the household and his hold on Frankford's affections, none-theless is a quality that Frankford, as a householder, should himself display. He fails both to assess Wendoll accurately and to pick up on his growing intimacy with his wife. To that degree he shares in the blame for the catastrophe that overtakes him, though he never acknowledges that this is so. While the play depicts a household in which a wife's adultery is in part occasioned by her husband's bad choice of companions and his inattention to the state of his household, nonetheless, it is Anne alone who is punished.

The mode of her punishment is the play's critical hotspot. How 'kind' is what Frankford does to his wife? Immediately after her discovery in bed with Wendoll, Anne is wracked with guilt and desires death. She is utterly humbled and penitent, but Frankford's honour will not let him re-embrace and forgive her, even though doing so would restore his family and, per-haps, his contentment. Instead, he shows his 'kindness' by declining to kill or to disfigure her but separating her forever from her children, from himself and from her home. His is a cruel kind of kindness, and though it has been argued that he behaves in this way to save Anne's soul, her repentance is immediate and heartfelt, hardly requiring banishment to be effected. What his kindness does bring about is Anne's death. In scenes that recall the suf-ferings of Jane Shore, another guilty wife, Anne weeps her way towards the manor where she is to live, and as she does, she vows to eat and drink no more.

Anne's choice to starve herself to death has been much discussed. Though self-destructive, it has been interpreted as a conscious or unconscious way for Anne to regain control over her fate. In the play's final scene, Anne, in her bed, is once again at the centre of a community of servants, friends and family, orchestrating both her own death and her reunion with her husband. By mortifying her sinful flesh, which had been the source of her husband's displeasure, she emerges as pure spirit, and on those terms, Frankford can again be reunited with her. Yet she pays a high price. Not only is she about to die, but by in effect committing suicide, Anne again puts her soul in danger. Critics have pointed out that even though Anne appears saint-like in her self-mortification, Christian thought condemns suicide as a mortal sin. While penitent for adultery, Anne may risk damnation for taking her own life. Seen in this light, her husband's 'kindness' looks even more ironic.

One thing is very certain – only after Anne has destroyed her body can Frankford again embrace her, saying, 'Though thy rash offence / Divorc'd our bodies, thy repentant tears / Unite our souls' (17.107–9). Frankford's sense of honour would not let him live again in marriage with his repentant wife. Their reunion is premised on her eminent death, as was Jane Shore's reunion with her husband Matthew. Both men can forgive and embrace their wives only when these wives are a few short breaths away from becoming corpses.

A *Woman Killed with Kindness* thus plays in a complex way with the paradoxes of this family tragedy. Heywood's handling of Anne's death and her deathbed reconciliation with Frankford draw out all the pathos of the situation. Those on stage weep as they watch the reunion, and the audience is invited to do so as well. But the sympathy one feels for Anne, who embraces her guilt with masochistic intensity, cannot help but raise questions about the danger in which she has placed her soul by her actions and about the 'kindness' of the husband who exacerbated her suffering and yet seems unaware of any guilt he might himself bear for the debacle that has overtaken his household. The play has a clear moral message, encapsulated in Anne's direct address to the women of the audience:

> O women, women, you that have yet kept
> Your holy matrimonial vow unstain'd,
> Make me your instance: when you tread awry,
> Your sins like mine will on your conscience lie. (13.141–4)

It is a measure of the power of Heywood's dramaturgy and theatrical skill that the play itself seems so much more emotionally and morally complex than Anne's tidy sentiments acknowledge. Yes, adultery is a sin and to be avoided. The play is clear on that point, but in generating sympathy for the sinner, it raises other questions about the sacrifices demanded to punish sin in a way that upholds male honour and about the many ways in which 'kindness' can be unkind.

Heywood went on to write many more plays, often in collaboration with other dramatists, though A *Woman Killed with Kindness* is widely acknowledged as his masterpiece. His most vibrant contributions to the theatre culture of early modern London, however, were notably consistent. He often employed a clear and unadorned dramatic style suited, in terms of rhetorical decorum, to the lives of the common and middling sort characters he often represented; and he helped to create a particular vision of everyday life centred on the activities of London merchants and guildsmen, the households of rural gentry and the crimes and compelling actions of unfaithful wives, village cunning women and those accused of witchcraft. For him, as he made clear in *An Apology for Actors*, theatre moves the emotions of spectators, and nothing is more moving than the suffering of women, whether those women are an imprisoned Princess Elizabeth, an impoverished and saint-like Jane Shore, or a repentant Anne Frankford. Through these representations Heywood had an impact, I would argue, on the creation of many early modern tragic heroines who suffer for real or imagined crimes; and he constructed plays evincing a moral and emotional complexity that scuppers the idea that he was ever a naïve creator of homiletic fictions rather than a skilled dramatist who knew first hand the thrilling contradictions of theatrical performance and the ways in which the aroused emotions can baffle sweet reason.

NOTES

1 *The English Traveller* in *The Dramatic Works of Thomas Heywood, now first collected with illustrative notes and a memoir of the author in six volumes* (1874, rpt, New York: Russell & Russell, 1964), IV, 'To the Reader', 5.
2 Francis Beaumont, *The Knight of the Burning Pestle*, ed. Michael Hattaway (New York: W.W. Norton, 1996), 4.1.49–50.
3 Thomas Heywood, *An Apology for Actors* (London, 1612), sig. F4.
4 Frances E. Dolan, *Dangerous Familiars: Representations of Domestic Crime in England, 1550–1700* (Ithaca, NY: Cornell University Press, 1994).
5 R. W. Van Fossen, *A Woman Killed with Kindness* (London: Methuen, 1961), 4.9–12.

Further reading

Bach, Rebecca Ann, 'The Homosocial Imaginary of *A Woman Killed with Kindness*.' *Textual Practice* 12:3 (1998), 503–24.
Frey, Christopher, and Leanore Lieblein, '"My breasts sear'd": The Self-Starved Female Body in *A Woman Killed with Kindness*.' *Early Theatre* 7:1 (2004), 45–66.
Gasior, Mary Ann Weber, ed., *The Four Prentices of London: A Critical, Old Spelling Edition*. New York: Garland, 1980.
Heywood, Thomas, *If You Know Not Me You Know Nobody, Parts I and II*, Malone Society Reprints. Oxford University Press, 1934–5.
Howard, Jean E., 'Other Englands: The View from the Non-Shakespearean History Play', in *Other Voices, Other Views: Expanding the Canon in English*

Renaissance Studies, ed. Helen Ostovich, Mary V. Silcox and Graham Roebuck. Newark, DE: University of Delaware Press, 1999, 135–53.

'Staging Commercial London: The Royal Exchange', in her *Theater of a City: The Places of London Comedy, 1598–1642*. Philadelphia, PA: University of Pennsylvania Press, 2007, 29–67.

Macfarlane, Fenella, 'To "Try What London Prentices Can Do": Merchant Chivalry as Representational Strategy in Thomas Heywood's *The Four Prentices of London*.' *Medieval and Renaissance Drama in England* 13 (2001), 136–64.

McLuskie, Kathleen, *Dekker and Heywood*. New York: St Martin's Press, 1994.

Orlin, Lena Cowen, *Private Matters and Public Culture in Post-Reformation England*. Ithaca, NY: Cornell University Press, 1994.

Panek, Jennifer, 'Punishing Adultery in *A Woman Killed with Kindness*.' *Studies in English Literature, 1500–1900* 34:2 (1994), 357–78.

Richardson, Catherine, *Domestic Life and Domestic Tragedy in Early Modern England: The Material Life of the Household*. Manchester University Press, 2006.

Rowland, Richard, *Thomas Heywood's Theatre, 1599–1639*. Aldershot and Burlington, VT: Ashgate, 2010.

Rowland, Richard, ed., *The First and Second Parts of King Edward IV*. Manchester University Press, 2005.

Sherman, Anita, 'The Status of Charity in Thomas Heywood's *If You Know Not Me You Know Nobody, Part II*.' *Medieval and Renaissance Drama in England* 11 (1999), 99–120.

Ziegler, Georgianna, 'England's Savior: Elizabeth I in the Writings of Thomas Heywood.' *Renaissance Papers* (1980), 29–37.

9

PAUL FRANSSEN

George Chapman's learned drama

George Chapman (1559/60–1634) was born in Hitchin, Hertfordshire, the younger son of a well-to-do farmer. His elder brother inherited the bulk of the estate, leaving George in financial trouble for much of his life. Little is known for certain about his youth. According to Anthony Wood, the Oxford antiquary, Chapman studied some years at Oxford University, excelled at the classics, but did not take a degree. The influence of classical literature is clear throughout his work, which is erudite and abounds with allusions to ancient culture and history. After university, Chapman seems to have spent some time in the service of a knight, Sir Ralph Sadler, probably in the early 1580s, before fighting the Spaniards in the Low Countries.

By 1594, Chapman had embarked on his literary career, with the publication of his poem *The Shadow of Night*, followed a year later by *Ovid's Banquet of Sense*. His sequel to Marlowe's *Hero and Leander* (1598) is one of his best-known poems. Chapman's learned classical allusions, often ambiguous grammatical constructions and far-fetched conceits ally him with the Metaphysical style of wilful obscurity. His poetry, Chapman boasts, is written for 'serching spirits, whom learning hath made noble, and nobilitie sacred', not for 'the prophane multitude'.[1] Learning, to Chapman, is more than bookish knowledge: it implies an urbanity that ultimately serves a moral function, allowing the scholar to learn from the great classical philosophers. Some of this elitist attitude also permeates his dramatic work, in particular the tragedies. Even the comedies for the public theatres are often based on classical sources (*All Fools* reworks two comedies by Terence, and *The Widow's Tears* dramatises Petronius' *Satyricon*), contain Latin proverbs ('*Sine periculo friget lusus*' in *All Fools*), allusions to classical mythology, and unusual Latin stage directions such as '*Abscondit se*' (he hides himself), '*Amplectitur eam*' (he embraces her), and '*Bibit Ancilla*' (the servant girl drinks).[2]

By 1595, Chapman began working as a dramatist for Henslowe's Lord Admiral's Men, producing first a series of comedies, including *A Humorous*

Day's Mirth (1597), which antedates the fashion for the 'humours' play, usually associated with Ben Jonson, by a year. Many of these plays turn on cuckoldry and gulling, which in *The Widow's Tears* (1604–5?; printed 1612) become so serious that one might speak of a tragicomedy. Chapman's main success in the comic genre, written in collaboration with Ben Jonson and John Marston, was *Eastward Ho* (1605), which will be discussed below.

In the early seventeenth century, Chapman turned to tragedy in a series of plays based on recent French history, as well as one Roman play. The best known of these was *Bussy D'Ambois* (1604?; published 1607), followed by a sequel, *The Revenge of Bussy D'Ambois*, written in about 1610 (published 1613). The other French tragedies are the two-part play *The Conspiracy and Tragedy of Byron* (1608) and *The Tragedy of Chabot, Admiral of France*, which was published posthumously in 1639, but cannot have been written before 1611. The Roman *Tragedy of Caesar and Pompey* (published 1631) is also difficult to date, but shares the French plays' concern with Stoicism and with the conflict between the individual and the powerful ruler.

As well as being a poet and a dramatist, Chapman was a prolific translator, most notably of Homer, which earned him the praise of Keats's famous sonnet, 'On First Looking into Chapman's Homer' (1816). Between his *Seven Books of the Iliads* of 1598 and the *Whole Works of Homer* of 1616, he rendered the *Odyssey* and *Iliad* in English verse. In his poem *The Tears of Peace* (1609), Chapman even suggested that he communed with Homer's spirit:

> what may I reckon thee?
> Whose heauenly look showes not; nor voice sounds man?
> I am (sayd hee) that spirit *Elysian*,
> That (in thy natiue ayre ...) did thy bosome fill,
> With such a flood of soule; that thou wert faine
> (With acclamations of her Rapture then)
> To vent it, to the Echoes of the vale;
> When (meditating of me) a sweet gale
> Brought me vpon thee; and thou didst inherit
> My true sense (for the time then) in my spirit;
> And I, inuisiblie, went prompting thee,
> To those fayre Greenes, where thou didst english me.[3]

Chapman died a poor man on 12 May 1634, and was buried in the Church of St Giles, London.

As an impecunious younger son, Chapman had problems with money during most of his adult life. These were aggravated when, in 1585, he fell into the clutches of the moneylender John Wolfall, who had him thrown in jail for debt in 1600. As late as 1622, Chapman was still fighting legal battles over his debts. Biographical readings of drama are always hazardous, but in Chapman's case it is perhaps more than a coincidence that many of his plays feature poor but ambitious heroes, such as Bussy D'Ambois and younger brother Tharsalio in *The Widow's Tears*.

To escape from poverty, Chapman attempted to win patronage throughout his life, but he was singularly unlucky in this. At first, he was associated with the circle of Sir Walter Raleigh, and wrote *De Guiana, Carmen Epicum*, which celebrated Raleigh's voyage to South America, to coincide with the publication of Raleigh's own *Discovery of Guiana* (1596). By 1598, Chapman was courting Raleigh's rival, the Earl of Essex, dedicating his first instalment of the *Iliad* to him, but Essex fell from favour in 1599 and was executed after his rebellion in 1601. Chapman's next hope was King James's martial son, Prince Henry, but the latter died prematurely at the age of eighteen, in 1612. Chapman never received the £300 he had been promised by the prince, in spite of letters complaining of royal neglect. He then turned to Robert Carr, Earl of Somerset, a royal favourite. In a thinly veiled allegory, *Andromeda Liberata* (1614), Chapman defended Carr's scandalous marriage to Lady Frances Howard, who had divorced her husband, the Earl of Oxford. But then Somerset and his wife fell from grace, due to their involvement in the murder of Sir Thomas Overbury.

For someone so dependent on patronage, Chapman seems to have been prone to run into trouble with the authorities over his writings. Many of his Jacobean plays, in particular, mock at James's creating knights in return for cash, and bringing Scottish favourites down to London. A scene, afterwards cancelled, in *The Conspiracy and Tragedy of Byron*, which depicted a row between the French queen and the king's mistress, led to protests by the French ambassador, resulting in the imprisonment of some of the actors. The play also suggested parallels between Byron's rebellion in France and Essex's in England, and in its original form seems to have represented Queen Elizabeth and Robert Cecil on stage. Chapman often reflected on domestic politics through the mirror of French affairs, which was not without its risks.

Chapman's search for a patron may have resulted in rivalry between him and Shakespeare, who are both mentioned in one breath by Francis Meres as eminent poets and playwrights in 1598. Chapman's first patron, Walter Raleigh, was a well-known free-thinker, and leader of a group of like-minded young men including Christopher Marlowe and Thomas Hariot. This group seems to have been at odds with the circle around Essex to which Shakespeare's patron, the Earl of Southampton, belonged. There has been speculation that Shakespeare's cryptic reference (possibly a textual corruption) to the 'School of Night' in *Love's Labour's Lost* – 'Black is the badge

of hell, / The hue of dungeons and the school of night' – alluded to the eso-
teric interests of Raleigh's circle as well as to Chapman's title *The Shadow of
Night* (1594).[4] *Love's Labour's Lost* (1594–5) deals with a group of young
men who decide to dedicate their lives to study. Chapman, in turn, seems
to have provoked Shakespeare's response by writing, in *The Shadow of
Night*:

> Presume not then ye flesh confounded soules,
> That cannot beare the full Castalian bowles,
> Which seuer mounting spirits from the sences,
> To looke in this deepe fount for thy pretenses.[5]

Chapman alludes to the epigraph of Shakespeare's *Venus and Adonis* (1593)
being Ovid's '*Vilia miretur vulgus; mihi flavus Apollo / Pocula Castalia plena
ministret aqua*', meaning: 'Let common people gawp at common things:
may golden-haired Apollo serve me with his goblets filled from the Castalian
waters [water from the well of the muses]'.[6] Chapman's remark suggests
that Shakespeare's erotic poem had been too obsessed with fleshly delights,
whereas his own far more philosophical work was more worthy of divine inspiration. According to other speculations, Chapman was the real-life
model for the rival poet in Shakespeare's sonnets. In Sonnet 86, Shakespeare
speaks of an unnamed rival, who was 'by spirits taught to write / Above a
mortal pitch', and received nightly visits from an 'affable familiar ghost',
which perhaps glances at Chapman's boast that he had been inspired by
Homer's spirit.[7] The sonnet's opening line, which speaks of 'the proud full
sail of his great verse', may allude to Chapman's use of fourteeners in his
Iliad translation. Accordingly, Anthony Burgess cast Chapman as the rival
poet in his 1964 novel about Shakespeare, *Nothing Like the Sun*.

As a writer of comedies, Chapman's main claim to fame is his share in
Eastward Ho (1605), co-authored with Ben Jonson and John Marston –
there is no scholarly consensus on who wrote what. As the play's title indicates, this was a reaction to an earlier citizen comedy by Thomas Dekker
and John Webster, *Westward Ho* (acted in 1604). Dekker and Webster's
play turns on cuckoldry and chastity. Its plot revolves around an Italian
(and therefore proverbially jealous) merchant living in London, who sus-
pects his wife of infidelity. Through his unreasonable treatment of her, he
almost drives her to commit adultery with an old earl. The merchant, meanwhile, disguises himself as a writing master, and tests the faithfulness of his
fellow citizens' wives, to find out whether he is the only cuckold in town.
It turns out that these women do respond to his charms as well as to those
of other men. They are lured into an expedition to Brainford, a village of
ill repute on the Thames west of London – hence the title, referring to the

cry of the river boatmen indicating their direction – for a rendezvous with some gallants. When it comes to the point, however, they refuse to have sex with the men, for fear of their reputation. Their husbands, who have been warned by the merchant, pursue their wives to Brainford, only to find themselves caught out when it emerges that they themselves were regular customers of a certain prostitute. The play ends in reconciliation, with all partners forgiving each other's frailty; but the moral seems to be that both sexes, given an opportunity, will be adulterous and hypocritical towards their partners.

In its prologue, *Eastward Ho* is explicitly presented as a response to *Westward Ho*. It echoes the plot element of a boat trip on the Thames as a release from traditional morality; yet it also reacts against the satirical thrust of Dekker and Webster's play by taking the side of the citizens. Whereas Dekker and Webster stressed the dubious morality and hypocrisy of the middle classes, *Eastward Ho* portrays them as basically decent, though liable to be corrupted when trying to emulate the higher orders.

Apart from sexual fidelity, the play foregrounds the theme of social climbing, recommending thrift, hard work and other bourgeois values, as opposed to snobbery. Its moral centre is a goldsmith, Touchstone, who has two daughters and two apprentices. The good apprentice, Golding, marries the sensible daughter, Mildred. The foolish daughter, Gertrude, however, insists on marrying a knight, Sir Petronel, who turns out to be penniless and only after his bride's money: he is in debt, and wishes to escape to Virginia to get rich there, leaving his wife behind. To get her out of the way, he sends her ahead to his non-existent castle. The bad apprentice, Quicksilver, also has social ambitions, and behaves like a decadent gentleman, gambling, drinking, keeping a mistress and sporting fine clothes. He pawns his possessions, steals from his master, and loses his apprenticeship after scandalous behaviour when drunk. Now that he is without a job, he decides to join Sir Petronel on his expedition to Virginia, hoping for a quick fix for his money problems. The journey is to be financed by a usurer, Security, in exchange for Gertrude's marriage portion which she has foolishly signed away. The Virginia expedition is an utter disaster before it even begins. The would-be adventurers never even reach their ship, but are overturned in a storm in a small boat on the Thames. They are themselves to blame for this, because they had got drunk in a tavern, and lost the right moment to sail before the storm began. As a consequence of their scheming and weakness, they end up in jail. Thus the play contrasts social ambitions and living beyond one's means with the middle-class values of modesty, thrift and hard work. The latter lead to real advancement, as in the case of Golding, who for his virtues is first accepted by Touchstone as his son-in-law and successor, and then elected as the alderman's deputy. Sinful pride, as in the cases of Gertrude and Quicksilver, just leads to disillusionment and ruin.

The other theme, that of cuckoldry, is the focus of the subplot, which involves the moneylender, Security, and his beautiful young wife. Too well aware of the age difference, Security treats her with jealous tyranny, and this in turn makes her eager to escape from him, so his jealousy is a self-fulfilling prophecy. She has arranged to join the expedition to Virginia along with Sir Petronel, her lover. The shipwreck, tellingly, takes place at a real location on the bank of the Thames called Cuckold's Haven. Quicksilver, who has robbed his mistress of her innocence, is another example of how looseness in social and financial ways and sexual irregularities go together.

The play's final act, which introduces the theme of mercy, has something of a biblical parable, with Touchstone cast in the role of God the Father, who stands for Justice, and his son-in-law Golding as Christ, personifying Mercy. Petronel, Quicksilver and Security are in prison. Golding, the good apprentice who has risen to alderman's deputy, tries to persuade his father-in-law to drop the charges against them by tricking him into visiting the jail. There Touchstone is moved by the repentance of the culprits, and relents. He also forgives his foolish daughter, now penniless and deserted. Thus, in an elaborate parallel with the story of the prodigal child, explicitly activated by the play, the happy ending comes about through repentance and forgiveness.[8]

The play includes some parodical allusions to *Hamlet*, as in a footman called Hamlet being asked whether he is mad (*Eastward Ho*, 3.2.7). More remarkably, it also contains some satirical remarks about the Scots and about King James. There is an ironic passage on Scots as great friends to the English (3.3.44–52), which was omitted in the printed version, probably due to censorship, but which survives in two known copies. In another passage, the castaways ask help from two gentlemen, one of whom speaks in the Scottish accent of King James. He says of Sir Petronel: 'I ken the man weel; he's one of my thirty-pound knights' (4.1.197–8). Obviously, James's habit of creating knights in return for money is being satirised here, as elsewhere in the play, but, surprisingly enough, even the representation of James himself on stage was either overlooked or deemed innocent by the censor, for this passage survived.

Apart from censorship of the text, the authors also suffered personal consequences for their daring, for Chapman and Jonson were jailed, in danger of having their ears cut off and their noses slit, for writing 'something against the Scots' in their *Eastward Ho*, as Jonson later told William Drummond of Hawthornden.[9] Marston, however, seems to have escaped this fate. Chapman wrote letters from prison to noblemen, complaining that it was only two sentences that were offensive, and those had not been written by him and Jonson to begin with, implying they were Marston's.

Another response to *Eastward Ho* was Dekker and Webster's play *Northward Ho* (published 1607). The play again focuses on the theme of cuckoldry, though, like *Eastward Ho*, it also contains a prodigal child, here a son who has to be rescued from the clutches of a prostitute. Compared to *Westward Ho*, the play is less cynical, as it centres on positive role models, the poet and playwright Bellamont, and Mayberry and his wife Mabel. The plot hinges on the honest characters' comical revenge on calumniators, tricksters, lechers and whores. Two knaves, who have tried in vain to seduce Mayberry's chaste wife Mabel, avenge themselves by telling her husband that they have slept with her in his absence. He, however, believes in his wife's innocence, and determines to punish the knaves for their calumny by ensuring they become cuckolds themselves. The subplot involves Mayberry's friend, Bellamont, whose prodigal son is besotted with a whore, Doll. Doll also attempts to seduce Bellamont himself, but finds herself rejected, which makes her genuinely attracted to him. Bellamont manages to cure his son as well as Doll's other suitors of their infatuation, and Doll is married off to one of the knaves of the calumny plot.

Though the play returns to an emphasis on sexual irregularity, in its plot it seems not to be so clear-cut a reply to *Eastward Ho* as that had been a response to *Westward Ho*. Yet the figure of Bellamont, the poet and dramatist, has often been taken as an oblique portrait of Chapman, with his knowledge of Latin comedies and French politics, his tragedies about Caesar and Pompey, which Chapman really did write, and about the Trojan Astianax, which is unknown, but sounds plausible enough for the translator of the *Iliad*. Bellamont also alludes to the 'Duke of *Biron*', about whom Chapman wrote a tragedy in two parts, and to a 'spirit' he has conjured up: Chapman claimed to be inspired by Homer's ghost. If Bellamont really is meant to represent Chapman, it is a good-natured portrait rather than a vicious caricature.[10]

Although some of Chapman's early tragedies may have been lost, his earliest surviving work in that genre has remained the best known. *Bussy D'Ambois* was performed by the children of St Paul's, the up-market boys' company catering to the elite. The hero is one of Chapman's larger-than-life Marlovian individualists, upwardly mobile and proud, whom Eugene Waith, in his classic study of 1962, has appropriately dubbed his 'Herculean' heroes. Chapman depicts Bussy's rise from penniless soldier to courtier and royal favourite, and his subsequent fall through the murder plot of his enemies. Many characters in the play praise his virtues, including King Henry III of

France, who even suggests that, if all men were like Bussy, we would still live in the Golden Age, and kingship and laws would be unnecessary:

> Kings had never borne
> Such boundless eminence over other men,
> Had all maintain'd the spirit and state of D'Ambois.[11]

At the outset of the play, Bussy complains of the neglect of his virtue in a fallen world, which is ruled by Machiavels. Nevertheless he allows himself to be recruited by the play's principal Machiavel, the king's brother, who is known as Monsieur. Once arrived at court, Bussy offends many of the powerful nobles by his arrogant, outspoken and truculent behaviour. He openly flirts with the wife of Guise, a powerful courtier, and secretly begins an affair with Tamyra, the wife of Montsurry. He fights a duel with some courtiers, and kills two of them in his anger. Although he retains the king's favour, eventually he estranges Monsieur, his patron, who brings matters to a head by taunting Bussy and daring him to tell him his true opinion of himself. Rather than flatter, Bussy insults him. Some courtiers admire this flamboyant upstart, and the king is remarkably mild towards him, but he also makes many enemies, who decide to avenge the insults to their honour. Monsieur teams up with Guise and, later, the cuckold Montsurry, to lay a trap for Bussy. Here Chapman adopts the conventions of the Italianate revenge plot popular in the period, in which the most devious, scheming and extreme measures are deemed justifiable, so that the avengers, however just their cause may be, become tainted by their actions. Bussy's enemies not only recruit the maids-in-waiting of the court ladies to spy on Bussy's affairs, but Montsurry even tortures his unfaithful wife to force her to lure Bussy to her, and ultimately Bussy, an expert swordsman, is ignominiously shot from off stage rather than engaged in a man-to-man duel. Bussy, Tamyra and the friar who acts as their go-between take no less extreme counter-measures in raising a devil to learn of their enemies' plans.

Bussy's life at court often falls short of the high ideals he professes at the outset of the play. His energy and courage may be of Marlovian proportions, but he lacks a suitable cause, apart from his own self-enhancement. Rather than ridding the country of its enemies or rooting out the corruption of the court, he becomes a callous killer and an adulterer whose demise is largely his own doing. Once he is mortally wounded, however, he rises to his true Herculean stature, and insists on dying standing up:

> I'll ... (like a man) look upwards even in death.
> And if Vespasian thought in majesty
> An Emperor might die standing, why not I?
> > *She [Tamyra] offers to help him.*

> Nay without help, in which I will exceed him;
> For he died splinted with his chamber-grooms.
> Prop me, true sword, as thou hast ever done:
> The equal thought I bear of life and death,
> Shall make me faint on no side; I am up
> Here like a Roman statue; I will stand
> Till death hath made me marble: O my fame
> Live in despite of murder. (5.3.135–46)

The heroism and Stoic dignity of his agony, in which he also forgives his murderers (5.3.159), contrast with his enemies' cowardly Machiavellian revenge. Bussy's death more than his life deserves the comparison with Hercules made by the friar's ghost in his choric epilogue:

> Farewell brave relics of a complete man:
> Look up and see thy spirit made a star,
> Join flames with Hercules: and when thou set'st
> Thy radiant forehead in the firmament,
> Make the vast continent, crack'd with thy receipt,
> Spread to a world of fire. (5.3.268–73)

Chapman's next tragedy, *The Conspiracy and Tragedy of Byron* (1608), was conceived as a double play from the outset. Again loosely based on a historical French theme, it featured another Herculean hero, but without setting him up for our admiration. The eponymous hero twice mentions himself in one breath with Hercules, once in the *Conspiracy*:

> Happiness
> Denies comparison of less or more,
> And not at most, is nothing: like the shaft
> Shot at the sun by angry Hercules,
> And into shivers by the thunder broken,
> Will I be if I burst; and in my heart
> This shall be written: 'yet 'twas high and right'.[12]

And again, in the *Tragedy*:

> I have Alcides-like [like Hercules] gone under th' earth,
> And on these shoulders borne the weight of France. (*Tragedy*, 3.1.151–2)

Stubborn, over-confident in his own deserts, Byron looms larger than life. Unlike Bussy, he has an impressive track record of patriotic duty. Many monologues, by himself and others, are devoted to his military prowess. There is a Marlovian echo in the catalogues of cities and regions, the sites of his own feats or of those of his classical heroes, like Pompey, with whom he identifies. Pompey, to whom Byron likes to compare himself, had conquered

> Armenia, Pontus, and Arabia,
> Syria, Albania, and Iberia,
> Conquer'd th'Hyrcanians, and to Caucasus
> His arm extended; the Numidians
> And Afric to the shores meridional
> His power subjected. (*Tragedy of Byron*, 5.2.236–41)

Byron's deeds all lie in the past, however, before the end of the civil wars, so that his prowess has to be taken on trust by the audience. Byron complains that it is the peace that corrupts the court. His heroic ethos makes him unsuitable for a new role, as ambassador or councillor to his king. Gradually he is lured into a conspiracy by the Duke of Savoy, a Machiavellian politician in league with the arch-enemy of the French nation, the King of Spain. Byron's own objectives in this remain unclear. Although he sometimes speaks of becoming a king himself, the more insistent theme of his monologues is his injured self-worth. In rhetorical speeches full of learned allusions to the classics, he gives vent to his inflated self-image, which comes to appear increasingly unrealistic to the audience. Even when, the audience knows, he has in fact been condemned to death for treason, he is still confident that his eloquence and his past desert have persuaded the judges of his innocence. His sense of self-worth is exacerbated by his short temper. If there is one thing this giant lacks, it is self-knowledge. Although he behaves like a Machiavel himself, he sees Machiavellian behaviour anywhere but in himself. He is not aware of his own treason, and does not notice that he himself is being manipulated by Savoy as well as by La Fin, a discontented French nobleman who acts on behalf of Savoy to draw him into rebellion, but then informs on Byron to the French king. After his arrest, Byron behaves with the utmost indignity, being by turns furious, self-confident and desperate.

The king, by contrast, is represented as a wise ruler who is concerned for the fair treatment of his subjects, and repeatedly gives Byron a chance to repent. Much of the dramatic interest in the double play comes from the confrontations between the king, who knows of Byron's treason, yet gives him a chance to own up, and an unrepentant Byron. Much as there is to admire in this great man, his undauntedness and independent spirit, one must agree with Chapman's valuation of Byron as a man who is 'great, not good' (*The Conspiracy*, Prologue, 24).

Ironically, Byron, who is himself the victim of his Machiavellian allies, accuses the king of Machiavellianism (*Tragedy of Byron*, 3.1.1–48). Here a topical religious angle comes into play, as Byron criticises kings for 'playing both ways with religion', which will lead to 'afflictions imminent' (3.1.46–7). Byron poses as the champion of Catholicism, while seeing King Henry IV, who only converted to Catholicism to obtain the French throne, as a

Protestant in sheep's clothing. However, when Henry asks his councillors whether Byron's treason was motivated by his 'purely Catholic zeal', his desire to 'be call'd the Scourge of Huguenots' (*Tragedy of Byron*, 1.3.1–3), he is told that Byron is 'of no religion' and had mocked at both Catholicism and Protestantism (1.3.4–6); and indeed, shortly before his execution, Byron mocks the archbishop who is trying to make him repent (*Tragedy of Byron*, 5.4.171–5). After Byron's arrest, one courtier reports on public reactions abroad representing the forthcoming trial of Byron as an anti-Catholic plot (*Tragedy of Byron*, 5.1.75–9). The suggestion is that Byron is just using religion as a pretext to betray Henry. Here, the Herculean hero is portrayed with far less understanding and sympathy than had been the case with Bussy; Byron is a self-deluded fool, without self-control or dignity.

If Byron makes a spectacle of himself before his execution, his foil is his fellow conspirator, the Count of Auvergne, who stoically resigns to his fate. The Stoic ethos was to be a prominent aspect of Chapman's later tragedies, most clearly in *Caesar and Pompey*, which is hard to date as it was only published in 1631, but seems to be alluded to in *Northward Ho* (1607). The play's philosophy is embodied in the figure of Cato, who stands for Roman republican values, and sides with Pompey in the Roman civil wars, regarding him as the lesser of two evils. When Pompey has been defeated by Caesar, Cato takes his own life, the Stoic's ultimate escape from intolerable circumstances, after lecturing his household about the vanity of life under tyranny, which makes suicide not just allowable but almost obligatory. The Stoic concept of the virtuous individual's freedom, irrespective of outward circumstances, underlies his dying words: 'Just men are only free, the rest are slaves' (5.2.177). In accordance with Stoic ideas, he counsels his son Portillius to shun public office (5.2.106–13), for the times are too corrupt to be honest in politics. Anachronistically, however, he also expresses his confidence in an afterlife, which rings more Christian than Stoic (4.5.119–36). Pompey, the play's other protagonist, begins as an ambitious politician who uses slanderous arguments against Caesar in the Senate and worries enough about his reputation for courage to engage in battle against his intuition; but after his defeat, he, too, embraces the Stoic creed, and 'submit[s] himself cheerfully to his fortune' (5.1.152).

Although Stoicism is never mentioned explicitly there, the Stoic dilemma about the public duty of the honest individual in corrupt times also features in *The Tragedy of Chabot, Admiral of France* (published 1639; written no earlier than 1611).[13] The noble hero's public spirit is such that he pays no heed to his father-in-law's warnings that the court is a cesspool of corruption where it is hard to retain one's integrity (1.2.1–84); he relies on his 'innocence, which is a conquering justice / And wears a shield that both defends and fights' (2.2.56–7). Yet, by the machinations of his rivals at court, he is subjected to a trial connived at by the king; and even though his innocence emerges in the end, he dies soon after from a broken heart.

Stoicism also plays a central role in Chapman's sequel to his great success, *The Revenge of Bussy D'Ambois*. Its hero, Bussy's brother Clermont, is a Stoic, and a foil to his impetuous and ambitious brother. Where Bussy had soon lost his temper when taunted by Monsieur, Clermont reacts with remarkable restraint in a parallel situation, showing he is in control of his passions (1.1.190–277); and he summarises the arguments of the Stoic philosopher Epictetus about the vanity of human ambitions (1.1.333–42). Full of learning, he illustrates the Stoic notion that virtue should be its own reward with classical examples (3.2.29–60); and accepts his arrest on false accusations of treason with remarkable equanimity (4.5.2–25). Even the news that his mistress has gone blind with weeping only moves him to say, 'All must be borne', followed by a disquisition on Platonic love (5.1.150).

Yet this Stoic philosopher is made into the unlikely protagonist of a revenge plot: he is visited by his brother Bussy's ghost who singles him out as the only man allowed to avenge him. This is ironical, partly because Clermont's best friend is Guise, who was one of the conspirators who killed his brother, yet is here portrayed as a moral paragon; but chiefly because Seneca, the Stoic philosopher with the greatest impact in the early modern period, had objected to revenge specifically, and had even written revenge tragedies to dissuade people from becoming the slaves of their passions by showing them the disastrous results. Yet in Chapman's tragedy the hero, who is called a 'Senecal' man by his friend Guise (4.4.42), is both the epitome of Stoicism, and the designated avenger. Clermont has reluctantly agreed to his brother's demands, and will only carry out the revenge in an open duel, not by dishonest means. Never roused to 'vicious fury' (3.2.109), he even regrets he ever accepted the task of avenging his brother, as 'never private cause / Should take on it the part of public laws' (3.2.115–16). The difficulty of honourable dealing in a dishonourable world is constantly foregrounded: the intended victim, Montsurry, cowardly refuses to see anyone, so that no challenge can be delivered to him. Even when some of Clermont's associates have managed to do so, by bribing one of Montsurry's guards, Montsurry refuses to answer the challenge. Much of the plot sketches Clermont's efforts to get access to Montsurry, and to force him to defend himself in an honest fight. Even the completion of the revenge is devoid of that excess that is the hallmark of Italianate revenge tragedies: Clermont restrains his fury, and praises the dying Montsurry for at last finding the courage to stand to him and fight, which makes up for his cowardly life before (5.5.116–19).

Thus Clermont has achieved his goal of avenging his brother without falling prey to excessive passions himself. The play's ending is all the more surprising: Clermont takes his own life on being told that Guise, his best friend, has been killed at the king's orders. The hero who was barely touched by the blindness of the woman he loved, and bore all injustice to himself with equanimity, finds himself incapable of living on without his bosom friend, Guise. Nor is action against the guilty monarch an option for him: 'There's no disputing with the acts of kings, / Revenge is impious on their sacred persons' (5.5.151–2). The religious implications of these words do not, however, remind him of what Hamlet calls the 'canon' of 'the Everlasting … 'gainst self-slaughter'.[14] For a Stoic, suicide was an option under extreme circumstances; but although the friendship between Guise and Clermont is shown as very deep, Clermont's Stoic 'apathy' elsewhere in the play suggested a different outcome.

The high principles and honourable life of Clermont stand in stark contrast with the corruption that has the court in its grip. King Henry III, sympathetically portrayed in *Bussy*, here is weak, and allows himself to be swayed by the play's chief Machiavel, Baligny, who seeks to improve his own fortunes by slandering Clermont and his powerful friend Guise. Baligny shamelessly reveals his moral principles to the king, telling him:

> I will be honest, and betray for you
> Brother and father: for, I know, my lord,
> Treachery for kings is truest loyalty;
> Nor is to bear the name of treachery,
> But grave, deep policy. (2.1.30–4)

In his erastianism, Baligny even equates the king to God:

> Nor is comparison a flatterer
> To liken you here to the King of kings. (2.1.45–6)

Henry agrees that 'the simile at all parts holds, / As all good subjects hold that love our favour' (2.1.57–8).

In dealing with fellow courtiers, Baligny fosters their discontent, to inform on them later, while remaining safely in the background himself. He is successful in having Clermont, his own brother-in-law, arrested, and in having Guise murdered by the king's orders. That Baligny escapes punishment for his crimes bears out the countess's choric words after Clermont's death: 'In heaven's course comfort seek, in earth is none' (5.5.215).

Admirable as Chapman's Stoic characters such as Clermont, Chabot and Cato may be, their passivity, which also bedevils Jonson's Stoics in plays like *Sejanus*, does not make for exciting drama. In that light, it is not surprising that Chapman's tragedy of Bussy, with its sword fights, rousing rhetoric, ghosts and devils, should have remained his most successful play ever since the early seventeenth century.

NOTES

1 George Chapman, *Ovid's Banquet of Sense*, quoted in Eugene M. Waith, *The Herculean Hero in Marlowe, Chapman, Shakespeare and Dryden* (London: Chatto and Windus, 1962), 98.

2 *All Fools* in *The Plays of George Chapman: The Comedies*, ed. T. M. Parrott (New York: Russell and Russell, 1910), respectively 3.1.302; 1.1.240; and 1.1.141. The final example comes from *The Widow's Tears*, in Parrott, 4.2.135. Unless stated otherwise, all references to George Chapman's comedies will be to this edition.

3 George Chapman, *Euthymiæ Raptus; or the Tears of Peace* in *The Poems of George Chapman*, ed. Phyllis Brooks Bartlett (New York: Russell and Russell, 1962), 'Induction', lines 73–85.

4 *Love's Labour's Lost*, ed. H. R. Woudhuysen, Arden Third Series (Walton-on-Thames: Thomas Nelson and Sons, 1998), 4.3.250–1.

5 George Chapman, *The Shadow of Night*, in *Poems of George Chapman*, ed. Brooks Bartlett, 'Hymnus in Cynthiam', lines 162–5.

6 *Shakespeare's Poems: 'Venus and Adonis', 'The Rape of Lucrece' and the Shorter Poems*, ed. Katherine Duncan-Jones and H. R. Woudhuysen (London: Thomson Learning, 2007), 127.

7 *Shakespeare's Sonnets*, ed. Katherine Duncan-Jones (London: Thomas Nelson and Sons, 1997), respectively lines 5–6 and 9. For a full discussion of the putative rivalry between Chapman and Shakespeare, see Katherine Duncan-Jones, *Shakespeare: Upstart Crow to Sweet Swan, 1592–1623*, The Arden Shakespeare Library (London: A. & C. Black, 2011), Chapter 4.

8 For the allusion to the prodigal child, see George Chapman, Ben Jonson and John Marston, *Eastward Ho*, ed. R. W. Van Fossen (Manchester University Press, 1979), 5.5.223. Further quotations from *Eastward Ho* are keyed to this edition.

9 *Eastward Ho!*, ed. Van Fossen, 4.

10 *Northward Ho!*, in *The Dramatic Works of Thomas Dekker*, ed. Fredson Bowers, 4 vols. (1953, rpt Cambridge University Press, 2009), II (1955), 4.1.7–10, 4.1.36–37, 4.1.53 and 4.1.126–27 respectively. Further references to the work of Thomas Dekker in the text will be to this edition.

11 *Bussy D'Ambois [by] George Chapman*, ed. Nicholas Brooke, The Revels Plays (London: Methuen, 1964), 3.2.95–7. Further references to Chapman's *Bussy* in the text will be to this edition.

12 *The Conspiracy and Tragedy of Byron* in *The Plays of George Chapman: The Tragedies*, ed. T. M. Parrott (New York: Russell and Russell, 1910), *The Conspiracy*, 1.2.38–44. All subsequent references to this and other tragedies by Chapman (except for *Bussy D'Ambois*) are to this edition.

13 The play was co-written with James Shirley, but again, it is unclear who wrote what. T. M. Parrott conjectures that this was a case of posthumous collaboration,

with Shirley revising Chapman's original after his death (*Chapman: The Tragedies*, 632–3).

14 *Hamlet, Prince of Denmark*, ed. Philip Edwards, updated edition (Cambridge University Press, 2003), 1.2.131–2.

Further reading

Braunmuller, A. R., *Natural Fictions: George Chapman's Major Tragedies*. Newark, DE: University of Delaware Press, 1992.

Beach, Vincent W., Jr, *George Chapman: An Annotated Bibliography of Commentary and Criticism*. Boston: G. K. Hall, 1995.

Crawley, Derek, *Character in Relation to Action in the Tragedies of George Chapman*. Salzburg: Institut für Englische Sprache und Literatur, Universität Salzburg, 1974.

Duncan-Jones, Katherine, *Shakespeare: Upstart Crow to Sweet Swan, 1592–1623*, The Arden Shakespeare Library. London: A. & C. Black, 2011.

Hillman, Richard, *French Origins of English Tragedy*. Manchester University Press, 2010.

'The Tragic Channel-Crossings of George Chapman, Part I.' *Cahiers Élisabéthains* 65 (Spring 2004), 25–43.

'The Tragic Channel-Crossings of George Chapman, Part II.' *Cahiers Élisabéthains* 67 (Spring 2005), 23–31.

Jackson, MacDonald P., 'Francis Meres and the Cultural Contexts of Shakespeare's Rival Poet Sonnets.' *Review of English Studies* 56 (2005), 224–46.

Kennedy, Edward D., 'James I and Chapman's Byron Plays.' *Journal of English and Germanic Philology* 54 (1965), 677–90.

Leech, Clifford, 'Three Times *Ho* and a Brace of Widows: Some Plays for the Private Theatre', in *The Elizabethan Theatre III*, ed. David Galloway. Toronto: Macmillan of Canada, 1973, 14–32.

MacLure, Millar, *George Chapman: A Critical Study*. Toronto: University of Toronto Press, 1966.

Nicoll, Allardyce, 'The Dramatic Portrait of George Chapman.' *Philological Quarterly* 41:1 (1962), 215–28.

Ribner, Irvin, *Jacobean Tragedy: The Quest for Moral Order*. London: Methuen, 1962.

Tricomini, Albert H., 'The Revised Version of Chapman's *Bussy D'Ambois*: A Shift in Point of View.' *Studies in Philology* 70 (1973), 288–305.

10

CATHERINE HENZE

Francis Beaumont and John Fletcher's tragicomedy as musical melodrama

> Their Plays are now the most pleasant and frequent entertainments of the Stage;
> two of theirs being acted through the year for one of *Shakespeare's* or *Johnson's*.
> (John Dryden)[1]

Shakespeare's contemporaries Francis Beaumont (*c.* 1584–1616) and John Fletcher (1579–1625) dominated the English stage for much of the seventeenth century. Dryden's affirmations notwithstanding, their popularity quickly faded thereafter, and Beaumont and Fletcher have been in near oblivion for centuries. Generations of critics would probably agree with T. S. Eliot's harsh assessment: 'The blossoms of Beaumont and Fletcher's imagination draw no substance from the soil, but are cut and slightly withered flowers stuck into sand'.[2] After individual experimental plays – Beaumont's *The Knight of the Burning* Pestle (1607) and Fletcher's *The Faithful Shepherdess* (1608–10) – the playwrights achieved spectacular collaborative success. They are best known for developing English tragicomedy, the new, hybrid genre that dominated the English stage for nearly a century and substantively influenced future English drama.

Even though the collaborators did not technically invent tragicomedy, which was an outgrowth of the English tradition (Marston's earlier *Malcontent* [1603] was registered as a 'tragicomedia'), they perfected and disseminated it. Sir Philip Sidney disparages mingling 'Kings & Clownes' and 'Horne-pypes and Funeralls' in 'mungrell Tragy-comedie'[3] and Shakespeare's Hamlet, joining the quarrel, asserts that in serious scenes clowns should 'speak no more than is set down for them' (3.2.32) – that is, not add lines with improvisation. In response to these opinions, in his address 'To the Reader' published with *The Faithful Shepherdess* in 1609 Fletcher writes, 'A tragie-comedie is not so called in respect of mirth and killing, but in respect it wants deaths, which is inough to make it no tragedie, yet brings some neere it, which is inough to make it no comedie: which must be a representation of familiar people'.[4] The genre is not a mechanical joining of two forms, but a seamless, new whole. Tragicomedy's distinguishing characteristics are (1) an imitation of the familiar world's manners, yet remoteness from that world; (2) an intricate plot; (3) a hypothesis that is improbable; (4) a pervading atmosphere of evil; (5) unpredictable characters; and (6) vivid passion, depicted with 'the language of emotion'.[5]

Borrowing heavily from other playwrights (including Shakespeare, Jonson and themselves), Beaumont and Fletcher created dramas – not only tragicomedies – that were 'artificial', so deliberately not realistic, but which also called attention to their dramatic form. For example, in their collaborative *The Captain* (*c.* 1609–12), upon hearing of his friend's sudden marriage, a courtier states,

> If a marriage should be thus slubberd up in a play, er'e
> almost any body had taken notice you were in love,
> the Spectators would take it to be but ridiculous. (*The Captain*, 5.5.32–4)

Moreover, in *The Woman Hater* (1606), Oriana's brother tells her to 'keep on the foreside oth' Curtaine' if she attends the theatre (1.3.51). Whereas in the Jacobean period 'artificial' meant skilled, the term's connotation subsequently became negative – not coincidentally, along with Beaumont and Fletcher's reputation.

An important and enlightening aspect of artificiality is the music that infuses many of the plays. Illustratively, in *The Captain*, Franck asks,

> These are your eyes;
> Where were they *Clora*, when you fell in love
> With the old foot-man, for singing of Queen *Dido*? (3.3.31–3)

These lines illustrate the power of music to destabilise the soul to the point of dulling judgement, and Renaissance playwrights believed in the transformative power of songs to profoundly impact all who hear them. The fifteenth-century philosopher Marsilio Ficino explains that music, 'more than anything else perceived by the senses, conveys … the emotions and thoughts of the singer's or player's soul to the listeners' souls'.[6] Not understanding the seminal role of music can lead to critical misunderstanding, as will later be seen in the analysis of *The Knight of the Burning Pestle*. It can also allow dramatists to criticise a ruler without risking censorship. For example, the words for 'Care Charming Sleep' (5.2.13–22) from Fletcher's *Valentinian* (*c.* 1610–14) convey a message of somnolent peacefulness. Sleep, the 'easer of all woes' should 'give nothing that is lowd, / Or painfull' and should 'kisse' the recipient, Emperor Valentinian, 'into slumbers like a Bride'. Yet, the music is filled with harsh dissonances and melodic leaps, seemingly intended to keep the emperor awake. Whereas the song on its own is confusing, it makes perfect sense in the context of the play because Valentinian is a vicious rapist and murderer, for whom a song of veiled torment is appropriate.

Valentinian is one of many plays in which Beaumont and/or Fletcher are critical of a monarch, particularly of the doctrine of the divine right of kings. England's King James I, who wrote *The True Law of Free Monarchies* (1598), was a staunch supporter of this doctrine, which was also a Protestant response to the Pope's authority. It is hardly surprising that Beaumont would oppose it, because his family suffered for its faith: as Catholic recusants, they lost most of their land and income, and his brother lived imprisoned on his own property. The dramatists, however, go a step further, and in *The Maid's Tragedy* (c. 1608–11) support justified regicide. Yet, King James is known to have attended Beaumont and Fletcher's plays and presumably enjoyed them. In addition, Beaumont wrote a wedding masque in honour of the king's daughter. The playwrights may have escaped censorship because the theatrical kings and emperors they created as villains fitted King James's criteria for unjust rulers: coming to power unlawfully, and breaking the laws of nature.

Moreover, the dramatists, often criticised for focusing on art at the expense of meaning, may have blinded the censors with their skilful artistry. Beaumont and Fletcher's work has been termed a series of stunning, extravagantly emotional, sensationalistic scenes, combined with dazzling rhetorical display. Their art is compared to scenes in a ballet or opera with characters who more frequently suggest or attempt suicide than ponder alternative solutions to conflicts. Furthermore, their plays are known for improbable endings. For example, *A King and No King* (1611) concludes with the revelation that distraught incestuous sibling lovers are not siblings after all – nor is, therefore, the protagonist a king. Criticism seems to be more directed towards Beaumont and Fletcher's chosen dramatic form than towards how well they created art within their own newly established, highly popular set of dramatic conventions.

Beaumont, Fletcher, and Beaumont and Fletcher

Beaumont came from an aristocratic line of highly successful judges and lawyers. He went to Oxford, and followed his family into the Inns of Court. After a relatively brief literary career he married, retired and died a few years later. He is buried in the Poets' Corner of Westminster Abbey. In addition to *The Knight of the Burning Pestle* and a masque, Beaumont's solo creative output included poetry (particularly his narrative *Salmacis and*

Hermaphroditus of 1602, and occasional verse – primarily elegies) and a satiric 'Grammar Lecture' (*c.* 1600–5).

Fletcher originated from a slightly less aristocratic family. Although his father had been Bishop of London, as a result of his unfortunate marriage Bishop Fletcher lost his position for a year, during which time he died, leaving his family in debt. John, his orphaned son who had spent his early childhood in elegant bishops' palaces, then grew up with his literary cousins, Giles and Phineas Fletcher, both of whom were steeped in Spenserian pastoral tradition.[7] The playwright may have attended Cambridge. After Beaumont retired, Fletcher, who succeeded Shakespeare as the primary writer for the King's Men, wrote steadily for over another decade. He died in 1625, probably of the plague. Fletcher was frequently a collaborator, and in addition to the plays with Beaumont, wrote with many others, including Shakespeare for *The Two Noble Kinsmen* (1613) and *Henry VIII* (1613).[8]

Although Beaumont and Fletcher collaborated on only thirteen plays, beginning in 1606–7, the entire fifty-plus collection of their dramas is commonly known as the 'Beaumont and Fletcher plays'. In spite of the statements that Beaumont and Fletcher are 'both so knit / That no man knowes where to divide [their] wit'[9] and that the bachelors shared a 'Wench … clothes and cloake',[10] twentieth- and twenty-first-century scholars, beyond a traditional 'Saint Beaumont, Sinner Fletcher' division, have attempted to divide the authors, particularly in the light of the well-accepted, linguistic-based work of Cyrus Hoy in *Studies in Bibliography*.[11] In addition, recent studies have shown that the writers can be distinguished by their distinctive use of music; Robert Johnson, the King's Men's lutenist who wrote music for their plays as well as for those of Shakespeare and others, was a favoured collaborator.[12] Although Fletcher is traditionally termed the musical intelligence of the pair, the two used music almost equally in the plays of collaboration. Moreover, Beaumont provided most of the masque sequences. In sections calling for music, Fletcher more typically provided scenes with drinking songs, while Beaumont wrote complicated love songs.[13] The earliest collection of their plays is *Comedies and Tragedies Written by Francis Beaumont and John Fletcher, Gentlemen* (London, 1647).[14] For a proper appreciation of Beaumont and Fletcher's dramaturgy, what follows is an examination of their four most famous plays: *The Knight of the Burning Pestle*, *The Faithful Shepherdess*, *Philaster* and *The Maid's Tragedy*.

The Knight of the Burning Pestle

Beaumont's solo *The Knight of the Burning Pestle* was performed *c.* 1607 by the children's company of Blackfriars. The author wrote in the preface to the 1613 edition that its first audiences, misunderstanding its 'privy marke of *Ironie*', utterly rejected it. Yet, it has become the most popular of the collaborators' plays, one in which Beaumont boldly and experimentally combines three different dramas.

As the Prologue begins, a 'Citizen' and his 'Wife' (also actors) dash forward and join the gallants on stage, where a prodigal son play is beginning. George and Nell, however, demand – primarily by bullying interruptions – that their grocer's apprentice, Rafe, instead star in a chivalric romance. Hence, the three plays are *The London Merchant* (well rehearsed by professional boy actors), *The Knight of the Burning Pestle* (scripted, but seemingly impromptu, staged by the 'audience' and an enthusiastic but decidedly amateur actor[15]), and the un-named story of the incessantly interrupting Citizens. Scenes from the two named dramas appear in unordered succession, with characters from one occasionally participating in the other, as the professional players and the Citizens fight for possession of the stage.[16] The Citizens' takeover highlights the conflict between artistic values and the tastes of the public. However, since the values of the takeover plot of Rafe's adventures (sacrifice, magnanimity and romantic love) are preferable to those showcased in *The London Merchant* (middle-class greed, social ambition and hostility to romantic love), the play is more than simple derogatory satire of citizen tastes.[17]

There are numerous similarities between *The Knight of the Burning Pestle*'s chivalric plot and *Don Quixote*, and many believe Cervantes's story was its source. However, it is not known which work came first. A citizen comedy, Beaumont's experiment is a satire of the popular Heywoodian adventure play, most notably Thomas Heywood's *The Four Prentices of London* (c. 1592). It makes direct reference to Thomas Dekker's *The Shoemakers' Holiday* (1600), particularly its main character, Rafe, and is similar in tone and materials to *Eastward Ho* (1605), which also begins with a dismissed apprentice. Moreover, the format is reminiscent of John Day's *The Isle of Gulls* (1605), a drama beginning with three gentlemen interrupting the Prologue, each one requesting a different play. *The Knight of the Burning Pestle* obviously satirises popular chivalric romances such as the *Palmerín de Oliva* (Salamanca, 1511). In the character of Merry-thought, Beaumont parodies Heywood's *The Rape of Lucrece* (1607), with its 'merry lord', the singing Valerius. Even Shakespeare does not escape parody: Rafe misquotes one of Hotspur's speeches, and Hamlet's ghost is invoked comically when Jasper's face is covered in flour.

The messy, intrusive 'frame' involving the Citizens permeates virtually every part of the drama. George and Nell are arguably its most well-rounded characters, and Beaumont is often complimented for knowing them so well – including the detail that Nell carries liquorice in her purse. Nell talks to the gallants who share the stage with her and, at the end, invites them to her home. In spite of her generosity, it is highly unlikely that they would transcend class barriers and come. The Citizens are also naïve about the fact that they are watching a play. For example, Nell believes that *Palmerin of England*, an Iberian romance read aloud by Rafe, is a presentation of actual historical events, and the Citizens repeatedly provide money that is needed by the chivalric character Rafe portrays. Oddly interspersed with this confusion of theatrical worlds is Nell's motherly concern for the offstage lives of the boy actors.

What the Citizens demand is not really a play, with theatrical conventions such as plot, but a series of chivalric adventures by their very own apprentice. Typically, Rafe rescues syphilis patients ('prisoners') from the barber-surgeon caring for them (the giant, Barbarossa) and takes them to an inn, believing it to be a castle. Not to be outdone by *The London Merchant*, the Citizens demand a dramatic concluding death scene for Rafe. The boy actor opposing the Citizens allows it, but states, ''Twill be very unfit he should die, sir, upon no occasion, / and in a Comedy too' (5.273–4). This incident again foregrounds the conflict of taste, and the battle for control of the stage.

Notwithstanding the interruptions, the professional actors put on *The London Merchant*, a parody of popular prodigal son plays, with the serious theme of marriage for love versus marriage for money. The apprentice Jasper falls in love with his master's daughter, Luce, who is about to marry her father's wealthy friend. Ironically, the prodigal son is not Jasper, but his father. Merry-thought believes that worries are overrated, and so he sings, and sings, and sings – more than three dozen times throughout the play, including over thirty song fragments and a half dozen longer songs.[18] He consistently stands in direct opposition to the materialistic values of London's rising middle class.

Equally important is the singing of Jasper and Luce. Alone in the woods together, prior to chaste sleep they sing 'Tell Me (Deerest) What is Love?', a duet composed by Robert Johnson specifically for this play. The honourable Jasper suggests a song, to see how it 'will worke upon our sences', and invites Luce to 'rob' him of his heart 'with that inchanting voyce' (3.25–8). Although both Jasper and the audience might expect the song to deepen the pair's love, instead, Luce slumbers while Jasper works himself into an emotional frenzy of doubt about Luce's chastity and, as a test, attempts to stab her. An analysis of the music reveals that

TELL ME (DEEREST)

Figure 3 Historical reconstruction of 'Tell Me (Deerest) What is Love?' by Lawrence Lipnik and Catherine Henze based on Drexel MS 4175, No. 44. Treble and bass lines are transcriptions of Drexel 4175. Exception: bar 7, the first note of the bass line is D.

it is the song that so radically changes Jasper from devoted lover to enraged doubter.

'Tell Me (Deerest)' is a parody of a love song set among the historical debates about women (Figure 3). Before it even begins, the possibility for misunderstanding is established by the Renaissance belief that if a woman were heated up sufficiently to be able to sing she would also be too heated to control her sexual appetite. In the song, Jasper's questions about women's faithfulness are in minor harmony, denoting their seriousness. Luce answers – in major harmony, with light, lilting notes – that women are basically not true, and are full of sexual desire. Particularly problematic for Jasper is the way Luce sings the word 'desire' in bar 9, drawing it out longer than most of the song's other words. Luce continues that love is a smile that 'doth beguile'. Between the words 'smile' and 'doth beguile' the music rises by an interval of a minor sixth. In the Renaissance, this construction denoted lasciviousness – something that would not have been lost on either Jasper or the Blackfriars audience. We might imagine a stage direction here for Luce's eyes slowly to close as she innocently sings her part and drifts towards sleep while Jasper's eyes widen with rage as he interprets Luce's words.

After Luce sings 'doth beguile', Jasper angrily interrupts her musical line, on the very same note, to assert that what is beguiled – or tricked – is 'the poore hearts of men' – that is, himself. He is so upset that he changes the topic from love to women, and asks if they are true. Instead of the expected answer that they are (perhaps citing historical examples), Luce responds, with music that is again in major harmony, that women 'love change', followed by her accusation to Jasper, 'so do you'. Three times Jasper begs to know if women are virtuous, and Luce consistently answers that they are not, followed by attacks on the constancy of males in general, and Jasper in particular. Finally, when asked if women are forward, she says that they are, 'ever toward those that love, to love anew' – that is, they are forward with men who want new lovers. The song then ends, and Luce falls asleep. Jasper, practically seething, tells her, 'dissemble it no more'. He then ponders women's chastity during a twenty-eight-line monologue, concludes that he has ample evidence to doubt Luce and determines to test her with an attempted stabbing. Presumably, were she guilty, his false attack would reveal the truth: she would beg forgiveness for crimes either committed or desired.

Critics have long misunderstood this scene, believing Jasper's action to be unmotivated. However, when the actual song is heard with its original music – as we have here – the scene makes perfect sense. Just as the Citizens take everything they hear on stage literally, Jasper mistakes Luce's play-acting in the song for her sincere sentiments. These nuances are, however, lost on the Citizens, who want to call the police. Full appreciation of *The Knight of the Burning Pestle* requires delighting in Beaumont's parody of a kaleidoscopic whirl of dramatic forms, musical and literary traditions, and societal values – more than was possible for Beaumont's first audience. Although not a tragicomedy, the play includes many of its elements, including the imitation of manners, an intricate plot, and an improbable hypothesis.

The Faithful Shepherdess

Like Beaumont's solo play, Fletcher's *The Faithful Shepherdess* (*c.* 1608) was experimental. It was also a stage failure, probably because its slow-moving plot focused on chastity rather than a more exciting theme. The pastoral tragicomedy, a subset of tragicomedy infused with the pastoral tradition, was no doubt influenced by the author's cousins Giles and Phineas Fletcher. Its primary source is not Giovanni Guarini's *Il Pastor Fido*, the source for its title, but the English pastoral tradition, particularly the third book of Spenser's *Faerie Queene*, 'Of Chastitie'. Other sources include Shakespeare's *A Midsummer Night's Dream* (1595–6) and Longus's *Daphnis and Cloe*. Moreover, Fletcher's main character Clorin may be a theatrical homage to Elizabeth I, England's virgin queen (1533–1603).

The play's plot is tightly unified. All characters are judged by their relationship to chastity, exemplified by Clorin, who is devoted to her dead paramour and lives alone in the woods, tending his grave. Characters, illustrative of the spectrum of love, range from the ideal lovers Amoret and Perigot to the promiscuous Cloe (with her suitors, the bashful Daphnis and passionate Alexis) to the lustful Sullen Shepherd. The major complication occurs when Amaryllis, who also loves Perigot, changes into the shape of his beloved Amoret, and then comes to Perigot, beckoning him to her bed. When the real Amoret appears, Perigot, believing her to be unchaste, attempts murder. In the end, all of the characters except Sullen Shepherd embrace chastity.

These characters are regularly criticised for being more hypothetical than real, mere allegorical abstractions. Not only are they remote, but so is the setting, filled with supernatural beings, such as the god Pan. The play is also called overly artificial, especially for its stilted language. For example, when Amaryllis, magically appearing as Amoret, tries to seduce Perigot, she says, 'Still thinkst thou such a thinge as Chastitie, / Is amongst women?' (3.1.296–7). Overall, the language is more poetic than dramatic, with frequent rhymed couplets and rich pastoral imagery.

Music further contributes to the play's otherworldly artificiality. Containing four songs, it begins and ends with ritual singing in Pan's honour. The most notable singing, however, is by the flirtatious Cloe. She laments that she is unable to find a lover, and, having a lovely face and large flock of sheep, wonders why. Then she sings 'Come Shepherds Come', which ends:

> Come and have it,
> Thinke not I,
> Dare deny,
> If you crave it. (1.3.83–6)

Cloe blatantly offers herself, and the music (unfortunately lost) would surely reinforce her invitation. After her song, shepherds come running, seemingly out of the woodwork. According to Renaissance ideology, the music would have physiologically changed all who heard it to desire Cloe's love. Once again, we have a scene from a Beaumont–Fletcher play that seems to lack motivation until the music is taken into account.

Throughout, the play establishes the genre of tragicomedy. Although it contains comic scenes, it is not a comedy, and characters do face life-threatening situations. Yet, no one dies, and the ending is a happy one.

Philaster, or Love Lies a-Bleeding

The collaborative *Philaster, or Love Lies a-Bleeding* (1610) is the first Beaumont and Fletcher play performed by the adult actors of the King's Men. Very much a stage success, it is known as the flowering of mature Beaumont–Fletcher tragicomedy, and is unequivocally one of the pair's best dramas. In it, the rightful heir to Sicily, Philaster, who has been robbed of his kingdom by the current ruler, is enamoured of the king's daughter, Arethusa, who loves him in return. However, she is betrothed to marry the Spanish prince Pharamond, who, unable to persuade Arethusa to bed him before their wedding, has an affair with the lascivious Megra. The subsequent discovery of the illicit lovers contributes to the later dissolution of the planned wedding. The plot is additionally complicated by Bellario (a boy who wants only to be Philaster's page) because Megra, when caught with Pharamond, accuses Arethusa of intimacy with the youth. The tragicomedy is resolved by the revelation that Bellario is a woman, and therefore Arethusa must be innocent. Pharamond and Megra are sent to Spain, and the rest are to live somewhat improbably happily ever after.

Several Shakespearean plays are likely sources. Often termed a shallow Hamlet, Philaster is also compared to Othello for his jealous rage. Although the most obvious similarities are between *Philaster* and Shakespeare's *Cymbeline* (1609–10), it is unclear which play came first. As well as thematically borrowing from Sidney's *Arcadia*, the dramatists take from their own plays, especially *Cupid's Revenge* (1607–8) and *The Faithful Shepherdess* (1608–10).

More relevant than source hunting, however, are the topical political issues that *Philaster* invokes, particularly foreign marriages (in a country with extensive anti-Spanish sentiment) and antipathy towards the divine right of kings. The play's king insists on being obeyed, even though he acknowledges that he came to the throne unlawfully. Both his desperate desire for divine right and his subjects' willingness to confront him are shown below:

KING: the King
        Will have it so! whose breath can still the Winds,
        Unclowd the Sunne, charme down the swelling Sea,
        And stop the flouds of heaven: speak, can it not?
DION: No.
KING: No! Cannot the breath of Kings doe this?
DION: No, nor smell sweete itself, if once the lungs
        Be but corrupted. (4.4.38–44)

A few lines later, the king, acknowledging his limited powers, laments:
'when we come to try the power we have, / There's not a leafe shakes at our
threatenings' (4.4.50–1). More importantly, Dion is not punished – here, or
later – for his direct affront to the king's authority.

Other salient thematic elements in *Philaster* are misogyny and jealousy, both not atypical as themes for Beaumont and Fletcher plays. For
example, when Megra and Pharamond are caught together, the king says
to the prince, 'Sir, I must dearely chide you for this looseness, / You have
wrong'd a worthy Lady; but no more' (2.4.124–5). However, to Megra,
he rails:

        Thou troubled sea of lust: thou wildernesse,
        Inhabited by wild thoughts: thou swolne clowd
        Of Infection: thou ripe mine of all diseases:
        Thou all sinne, all hell, and last, all Divells. (2.4.138–41)

Moreover, when Philaster rants against his beloved Arethusa for her perceived dishonesty, he chastises not just her, but all women. He readily believes
Megra's accusations, and hears Dion's confirmation without requesting
details. Although the jealous husband is a common trope in Jacobean drama,
Philaster is extreme.

As we should expect, Philaster dominates the play. Known for rhetorical
tirades and wild mood swings, he is more interested in love than in regaining
his kingdom. While contemporary playgoers might see his erratic emotional
outbursts as comic (he offers to commit suicide five times), he is meant to
be taken seriously; the devotion of virtually all who know him allows the
audience to suspend judgement.

Philaster's harsh interaction with his beloved most clearly shows his
extremes. When he finds Arethusa together with Bellario in the woods
(innocently, although Philaster does not know this), he wounds them both
in a rage. Arethusa's death is prevented by the Country Fellow, who accidentally comes upon them as Philaster is about to stab the princess. Amazingly,
Arethusa rebuffs her protector for intruding on her and Philaster's 'private
sports, our recreations' (4.5.90). The Country Fellow is so shocked that he

vows never again to have anything to do with city or court. Not dissuaded from rescuing the innocent woman, he states, 'I know not your rethoricke, but I can lay it on if / you touch the woman' (4.5.96–7), and proceeds to attack Philaster. This bizarre scene may be an implicit critique of King James's scandal-ridden court.

Only more unbelievable than the wounding scene, however, is the play's dizzying final act, where Philaster secretly marries Arethusa, is pardoned by the king, subdues a revolt of the populace and comes to power as a ruler. Just over 100 lines from the end of the play, Bellario reveals that he is really Dion's daughter Euphrasia, who simply wants to be near Philaster; she knows that her social class forbids marriage to him, and desires no other match. Euphrasia delays her revelation simply because of a private vow, which she breaks only when she is about to be tortured and, hence, her womanhood discovered.

This tragicomedy (which, oddly, contains no music, in spite of the fact that Bellario's name means 'beautiful singing') is well suited to Jacobean taste. *Philaster* also perfectly fits Fletcher's description of a tragicomedy, most simplistically because no one dies, yet some come close. Its tragicomic elements of otherworldliness, swiftly changing characters, improbable hypothesis and vivid passion set the standard for the new genre.

The Maid's Tragedy

Like *Philaster*, the collaborators' *The Maid's Tragedy* (c. 1608–11) was a stage success. In it, Amintor is to wed the fair Aspatia; however, we immediately find out that the king has ordered him instead to wed Evadne. After a first act dominated by an atypically long, complicated wedding masque, the eager groom discovers that he cannot bed his bride because she is the king's mistress, and the entire wedding was a sham to protect the ruler. The rest of the play deals with the eventual murder of the king by Evadne, and, secondarily, the accidental death of the disguised Aspatia by Amintor, who then commits suicide.

The most important element of the play is its theme: again, the politically dangerous one of opposition to the divine right of kings, but now carried to the next step, justified regicide. The wronged Amintor refuses to kill his king, and even Evadne is opposed, stating 'All the gods forbid it', only to be answered by her brother Melantius, 'No all the gods require it, / They are dishonored in him' (4.1.144–6). In the end, Evadne, Amintor and Aspatia are dead, and the king's brother is the new king. His final statement summarises the play's moral:

> May this a faire example be to me,
> To rule with temper, for on lustfull Kings
> Unlookt for suddaine deaths from God are sent,
> But curst is he that is their instrument. (5.3.292–5)

Though the play is known as a 'revenge tragedy' both terms are problematic. First, the one most in need of revenge, Amintor, is unable to act because he deeply believes in the divine right of kings. Moreover, unlike most who seek revenge, Melantius wants to, and does, survive. The other question is the identity of the 'maid' in the play's title – certainly Aspatia (not the primary focus of the play) but also Evadne, who expects to have a loving husband after she has killed their king. However, Amintor so objects to regicide that he scorns her, to which she responds with suicide.

The characterisation in *The Maid's Tragedy* is unusually complex for all major characters except the king, and an examination of three crucial scenes (none involving the king) helps us to understand the collaborators' dramatic art. First, in 2.1 Aspatia sings 'Lay a Garland on My Hearse', and the music intensifies the heart-breaking pathos of the scene. Then, another maid, Dula, follows with the surely raucous and decidedly bawdy 'I could Never Have the Power to Love One above an Houre'. Aspatia's and Dula's singing brings to mind Desdemona and her worldly maid Emilia, who says she *would* cheat on her husband 'for all the world' (*Othello*, 4.3.65). In *The Maid's Tragedy* the worldly maid is Evadne, and the pair of songs implicitly contrasts Aspatia and her nemesis.

A second illustrative scene immediately follows, that of Amintor and Evadne's wedding night. Amintor is naturally shocked when his bride reveals that she will not bed him – that night, or ever. When asked why, the sexually knowledgeable and confident Evadne responds, 'A maidenhead *Amintor* / At my years?' (2.1.193–4), implying that virginity is old-fashioned. This is one of the dramatists' most-quoted lines, and the entire scene, of Evadne's swaggering worldliness and Amintor's emotional shifts – from joyful anticipation, to incredulity, to anger, to Stoic acceptance as he faces the reality of life not as Aspatia's true husband but as Evadne's cuckolded one – is considered to be among Beaumont and Fletcher's best.

The scene where Amintor discloses his sorrow is also particularly noteworthy for what it reveals about Melantius. Amintor is both too ashamed and too protective of his king to confess his torment, and his façade deceives all but this best of friends. At length, Melantius discovers the truth and must face his horror that both his king and his sister are involved in such perversity. If the collaborators are to justify regicide successfully, then its instigator,

Melantius, must be shown to be honourable, intelligent and perceptive. This scene illustrates that he is all that and more.

Beyond the sensational scenes and the theme of regicide, however, *The Maid's Tragedy* is noted for its lengthy masque (probably by Beaumont), which takes up a full third of the first act. Even longer than Beaumont's *Masque of the Inner Temple and Gray's Inn* (1613), it is virtually undistinguishable from the court entertainment. There is a tight association between the rest of the play and the masque, which contains songs that are atypically dark and focus more on secret love-making than joyful pleasure. More importantly, the masque ends with the character of Boreas, the god of the north wind, having broken his chains and freed himself. This unusual loose end is appropriate for *The Maid's Tragedy*, however, because the wedding has already been blasted by the north wind of the king's duplicity, leaving the groom with a very cold marriage. The tragedy contains many characters who break the chains of obedience to the king, resulting not in post-masque serenity, but in the ragged aftermath of a storm.

Although not a tragicomedy, *The Maid's Tragedy*, another often-praised culmination of Beaumont and Fletcher's collaboration, succeeds on the basis of its tragicomic elements. The play's premise of protecting the king's mistress is both evil and improbable, one that brings out varied passionate responses in all the characters it affects.

Conclusion

Beaumont and Fletcher owe much to Shakespeare, but they also contributed to his works. In *The Winter's Tale* (1611) Shakespeare benefited from the collaborators' sense of tragicomic form, and in *The Tempest* (1611) from their music-filled otherworldliness. It was not only Shakespeare, however, who was influenced by Beaumont and Fletcher. Milton appropriated a speech from *The Faithful Shepherdess* for his masque *Comus* (1634), and the entire seventeenth century and after continued to build on the dramatists' tragicomic form. The four most famous Beaumont and Fletcher plays examined here, music-filled and sensationalistic, have much to recommend them, not only as highly crafted entertainments, but also in terms of addressing the important political issue of challenging the divine right of kings. The playwrights' intentionally unrealistic dramas, so valued on the Jacobean stage, are much more dynamic, instructive and entertaining than mere 'withered flowers'.

NOTES

1 John Dryden, *Of Dramatick Poesie, An Essay* (London, 1684), 34.
2 T. S. Eliot, 'Ben Jonson', in *The Sacred Wood: Essays on Poetry and Criticism* (London: Methuen, 1920), 116.

3 Sir Philip Sidney, *A Defence of Poesie* (London, 1595), sig. K2r.

4 'To the Reader', *The Faithful Shepherdess*, in *The Dramatic Works in the Beaumont and Fletcher Canon*, ed. Fredson Bowers, 9 vols. (Cambridge University Press, 1966–94), III, 497. All references to Beaumont and Fletcher are from this edition.

5 Eugene M. Waith, *The Pattern of Tragicomedy in Beaumont and Fletcher* (New Haven, CT: Yale University Press, 1952), 36–40.

6 Marsilio Ficino, quoted in D. P. Walker, *Spiritual and Demonic Magic* (London: Warburg Institute, University of London, 1958), 9.

7 See A. B. Langdale, *Phineas Fletcher: Man of Letters, Science, and Divinity* (New York: Columbia University Press, 1937).

8 Fletcher's affiliation with Shakespeare is not only brought into focus by the plays on which the two dramatists worked together. Fletcher's *The Woman's Prize, or The Tamer Tamed* (1611) is a deft sequel to *The Taming of the Shrew* and may also be read as a comment on Shakespeare's earlier comedy. Fletcher also draws on Shakespeare in plays like *Bonduca* and *The Island Princess*.

9 Jasper Maine, *Comedies and Tragedies Written by Francis Beaumont and John Fletcher, Gentlemen,* (London, 1647), sig. D1r.

10 *Aubrey's Brief Lives*, ed. Oliver Dick (Ann Arbor, MI: University of Michigan Press, 1957), 21.

11 Cyrus Hoy, 'The Shares of Fletcher and His Collaborators in the Beaumont and Fletcher Canon', *Studies in Bibliography* 8 (1956), 129–46; 9 (1957), 143–62; 11 (1958), 55–106; 12 (1959), 91–116; 13 (1960), 77–108; 14 (1961), 45–67; and 15 (1962), 71–90.

12 Catherine Henze, 'How Music Matters: Some Songs of Robert Johnson in the Plays of Beaumont and Fletcher', *Comparative Drama* 34 (2000), 1–32 at 6.

13 Catherine Henze, 'Unraveling Beaumont from Fletcher with Music, Misogyny, and Masques', *Studies in English Literature* 44 (2004), 379–404 at 382–91.

14 For a complete listing of the dramas, see Cyrus Hoy, 'Francis Beaumont and John Fletcher', *Dictionary of Literary Biography*, vol. LVIII, *Jacobean and Caroline Dramatists*, ed. Fredson Bowers (Detroit: Gale, 1987), 3–6.

15 Lee Bliss, *Francis Beaumont* (Boston: Hall, 1987), 47–8.

16 Philip Finkelpearl, *Court and Country Politics in the Plays of Beaumont and Fletcher* (Princeton, NJ: Princeton University Press, 1990), 83.

17 Francis Beaumont, *The Knight of the Burning Pestle*, ed. John Doebler (Lincoln, NE: University of Nebraska Press, 1967), xix–xx.

18 See Francis Beaumont, *The Knight of the Burning Pestle*, ed. Sheldon Zitner (Manchester University Press, 2004), 'Appendix D: The Songs'; and *The Knight of the Burning Pestle*, ed. Doebler, 'Appendix A: Music for the Songs'.

Further reading

Beaumont, Francis, *The Knight of the Burning Pestle*, ed. Michael Hattaway. London: Methuen, 2002.

Bliss, Lee, 'Tragicomic Romance for the King's Men, 1609–1611: Shakespeare and Beaumont and Fletcher', in *Comedy from Shakespeare to Sheridan: Change and Continuity in the English and European Dramatic Tradition*, ed. A. R. Braunmuller and J. C. Bulman. Newark, DE: University of Delaware Press, 1986, 148–64.

Foakes, R. A., 'Tragicomedy and Comic Form', in *Comedy from Shakespeare to Sheridan*, ed. A. R. Braunmuller and J. C. Bulman. Newark, DE: University of Delaware Press, 1986, 74–88.

Kinney, Arthur F., ed., *Renaissance Drama: An Anthology of Plays and Entertainments*. Oxford: Blackwell, 1999.

Kirsch, Arthur C., *Jacobean Dramatic Perspectives*. Charlottesville, VA: University Press of Virginia, 1972.

Miller, Ronald F., 'Dramatic Form and Dramatic Imagination in Beaumont's *The Knight of the Burning Pestle*.' *English Literary Renaissance* 8 (1978), 67–84.

Mincoff, Marco, '*The Faithful Shepherdess*: A Fletcherian Experiment.' *Renaissance Drama* 9 (1966), 163–77.

Munro, Lucy. '*The Knight of the Burning Pestle* and Generic Experimentation', in *Early Modern English Drama: A Critical Companion,* ed. Garrett Sullivan, Patrick Cheney and Andrew Hadfield. New York: Oxford University Press, 2006, 189–99.

Taylor, Gary, and Andrew J. Sabol, 'Middleton, Music, and Dance', in *Thomas Middleton and Early Modern Textual Culture: A Companion to the Collected Works*, ed. Gary Taylor and John Lavagnino. Oxford: Clarendon Press, 2007, 119–81.

MICHELLE O'CALLAGHAN

Thomas Middleton and the early modern theatre

The *Oxford Middleton* assigns thirty-two plays to Thomas Middleton either as sole author or co-writer or reviser. Middleton was a versatile playwright, who moved between different acting companies throughout his career, experimenting with the latest fashions in plays, from sharp comedies set in Jacobean London to baroque revenge tragedies. From James I's accession to 1606, he wrote a series of comedies for the Children of Paul's, tailoring his plays to an all-boy acting company performing in an indoor playhouse, and to the audiences that congregated in the fashionable theatre district. He was also selling plays to the King's Men at this time, including *A Yorkshire Tragedy* (c. 1605), *The Revenger's Tragedy* (1606), and *Timon of Athens* (c. 1606), co-written with William Shakespeare, whose *Macbeth* (1606) and *Measure for Measure* (1604–5) he also substantially revised, in 1616 and 1621 respectively.[1] Middleton consolidated his reputation in the 1610s with *The Roaring Girl* (1611), co-written with Thomas Dekker, and *A Chaste Maid in Cheapside* (1613). The early 1620s were the high-point of his career: he wrote his major tragedies, *Women Beware Women* (c. 1621) and *The Changeling* (1622), the latter co-written with William Rowley, and he regularly produced mayoral pageants for the City of London. His last play, *A Game at Chess*, was his most sensational play, and its popularity, coupled with its political topicality, meant that it was Middleton's last play performed on the public stage.

What is most notable about Middleton when surveying the range of his works is his versatility. Middleton, jestingly, likened the playwright to the tailor who works with an eye to the fashion. His own preference for 'neater inventions' – voiced in 'To the Comic Play-readers, Venery and Laughter'[2] – expresses something of the ingenuity of Middleton's plots. Middleton is the master of multiple plots, rivalled only by Jonson, and brilliantly exemplified by his *tour de force*, *A Chaste Maid in Cheapside*. His architectural skills in plotting extend to his stagecraft, making him one of the most innovative of the Jacobean dramatists. He has a highly sophisticated and symbolic approach to the architecture of the stage, frequently setting in motion a complex interplay between dramatic and metaphorical spaces, whose full resonance is revealed in the course of the plot. This holistic approach to the theatre reaches its peak in *The Changeling*, but it is evident in his early plays, particularly for the boy companies, which typify the way Middleton exploits the theatrical opportunities offered to him.

Middleton's London

Middleton is a London playwright. His sharp urban comedies dramatise the transformation of London into a crowded and busy metropolis and satirise the various cultural practices encoded within urban spaces.[3] London's private households and public meeting-places are evoked on stage through the complex interplay between stage properties, action and narration. The opening scenes of *The Roaring Girl*, for example, are set in the fashionable household of Sir Alexander Wengrave, a locale signified on stage through characters, including the thoroughly urbanised servingman, Neatfoot. Differentiated spaces within the household, like the 'inner room' (scene 2, line 6), are metonymically figured by the objects within it, the 'Chairs, stools, and cushions' (scene 2, line 45) brought on stage by servants for Wengrave's guests.[4] From the household, the play moves to the street. The third scene of the play opens with '*three shops … in a rank*' (stage direction) which provide visual realisation of the commerce of the city, while the cry of the citizen wives, 'Gentlemen, what is't you lack?' (scene 3, line 1) and subsequent exchanges with the predatory gallants, serve symbolically to equate sex with shopping. The interplay between character types, objects, action and dialogue both draws on the audience's local knowledge of London, and defines and satirises the social values attributed to such places within the city. Middleton's plays do not imagine a homogeneous London, but have a highly sophisticated sense of the socioeconomic differentiation of space within the city that, in turn, is encoded with different ethical, cultural and political meanings.[5]

His comedies written for Paul's Boys were performed at an indoor playhouse in the churchyard, surrounded by the traffic of those either passing through on their way from the Strand to Cheapside or transacting business in the shops which had sprouted up in the courtyard, and even inside the cathedral itself. The immediate environs of the playhouse are worked into the temporal and spatial fabric of the opening scenes of *Michaelmas Term* (1604). The allegorical figure of Michaelmas Term presides over the Induction and ritualistically sets out temporal schema of the play. *Michaelmas Term* is a very modern morality play, artfully recoding an old structure with novel meanings. The Induction allegorises a new socioeconomic phenomenon: the season beginning in autumn with Michaelmas term, when the gentry came from their country estates to 'town' to pursue cases through the law courts, to socialise and to spend. Michaelmas Term's opening speech describes how the natural generative rhythm of the year, symbolised by harvest, has been consumed by a new way of organising time based on an alignment of the legal system with this culture of consumption. The summer harvest, drawn 'by sweat from the rough earth', in autumn 'enrich[es] this silver harvest, Law' (Induction, 9–10). The names of the two characters who open the following scene, Salewood (sold estate) and Rearage (arrears), signify the rapacious appetite of a city economy dominated by Michaelmas term in which men consume themselves, their estates and their fellows through the law. Middleton insistently aligns this new season with the dimensions of the play itself. *Michaelmas Term* ends with a detailed analogy between theatrical time and space and the law year: instead of his legal fees, the audience need only pay 'sixpenny fees', the price of a seat, and imagine these 'two hours' (Induction, 65) within the theatre are 'the circumference of those six weeks whereof Michaelmas Term is lord' (Induction, 73–4).

St Paul's, the hub of the new London season, offered Middleton a very rich dramatic and metaphoric store. The first scene brings the area just outside the theatre's doors right onto the stage. Many of the playgoers would have arrived at the playhouse through Paul's Walk, the middle aisle of the cathedral, and one of the fashionable meeting-places in the city where gallants walked and talked, and observed other 'Paul's walkers'. Middleton makes extensive use of the doors on each side of the stage to represent Paul's Walk. Rearage enters the stage from '*one door*' (1.2, opening stage direction) meeting Salewood presumably coming from the other door, and this pattern is again followed when Cockstone enters '*meeting Master Easy*' (1.2, stage direction at 41–2). The rhythm of the entry and exit of characters mimics the traffic of Paul's Walk, and gives particular symbolic and dramatic freight to the door as a permeable threshold between the onstage action of the play and the offstage world of St Paul's. The proximity of these two worlds is foregrounded when characters stop, presumably in front of one of the onstage doors, and discuss the notices or '*siquisses*' posted on the great west door of St Paul's.

The locale of *A Chaste Maid in Cheapside*, Middleton's definitive London play, extends to the east of St Paul's, to Cheapside. The opening scene is set in Yellowhammer's shop on Goldsmith's Row, a wealthy centre of commerce renowned for its magnificent houses and shops. The locale associates the Yellowhammers with the social aspirations of the wealthy citizen classes.[6] The domestic world of Yellowhammer's household is coterminous with his goldsmith's shop. This is not a dramatic contrivance on Middleton's part, since early modern shops and residences frequently occupied the same building. The opening scene exploits this social fact of everyday mercantile life, relying heavily on the continuity between domestic and commercial worlds for its drama and symbolism. The Yellowhammers' conversation about their children's prospects is interrupted by a customer wanting his gold chain valued. This onstage action gives material definition to the language of the goldsmith's trade used to describe the marriage negotiations between the Yellowhammers and Sir Walter Whorehound, both his own marriage to the wealthy citizen's daughter, Moll, and the marriage of his whore, the Welsh Gentlewoman to Yellowhammer's heir, Tim. *A Chaste Maid in Cheapside* is structured by a sexual economy of circulation and exchange that ultimately, in the case of the Welsh Gentlewoman, can turn a whore into a wife. Both men and women profitably trade off their sexuality in this play: the fecundity of Mistress Allwit, who is pimped by her husband to another man, Whorehound, is mirrored in the virility of Touchwood Senior, who pimps himself, and is paid by Sir Oliver to inseminate his wife, Lady Kix.

A Chaste Maid in Cheapside is an elaborately plotted play. The four lines of action move between three houses, those of the Yellowhammers, the Allwits and the Kixes, which are distinguished by different socioeconomic imperatives, often figured in the material goods that are displayed on stage and make their way into the dialogue through metaphor and metonymy.[7] The Allwit household is most closely linked with the burgeoning market for luxury goods. In the play's eroticised economy, Mistress Allwit's maternal appetites are largely material. Her swelling maternal body is satirically mirrored in the copious variety of luxuries she possesses and consumes: 'embossings, / Embroid'rings', 'As if she lay with all the gaudy-shops / In Gresham's Burse about her', the stock of 'a drug-shop', as well as 'whole loaves' of sugar and 'wines by runlets' (1.2.32–8). Gresham's Burse, or the Royal Exchange, was located to the east of Cheapside; its shopping arcade was famous for the expensive mercery described by Allwit.[8] The depiction of Mistress Allwit's coalescing maternal and material appetites arises out of the ubiquitous cultural equation of women's bodies with household goods, and provides a clear illustration of how consumption is frequently feminised within satiric accounts of the city. The Allwits end the play moving house westward from Cheapside to 'take a house in the Strand' (5.1.161). The Strand epitomised the fashionable West End of London, and it is here that the Allwits will establish their high-class brothel 'richly furnished ... with household stuff' (5.1.159) from the thoroughly decayed nobleman Sir Walter Whorehound. Their profit at his expense, evident in the passage of material goods, is a sharply witty satire on the decline of the old nobility and the rise of the entrepreneurial classes in early modern London.

The action of *A Chaste Maid in Cheapside* takes place in Lent. The play imagines a city driven by carnal appetite, in which the sacred has been profaned, and Lent reduced to a commercial opportunity for exploiting restrictions against eating meat. The promoters, employed by the City to enforce Lenten restrictions, are instead confiscating meat from their fellow citizens for their own profit. Like the creditors in Middleton's earlier city comedy, *A Trick to Catch the Old One*, who demand either 'money or carcass' (*Trick* 4.3.51), the promoters embody the city's predatory energies and are likened to crows pecking on the 'dead corpses of poor calves and sheep, / Like ravenous creditors' (*Chaste Maid*, 2.2.62–3). Underlying this series of analogies between promoters, creditors and crows is the early modern condemnation of usury. Since money was understood to be a communal resource, the restriction of its circulation, by confining lending to those able to pay and redeeming loans whatever the effect on the debtor, was likened to cannibalism. Merchants in Middleton's city comedies, from Quomodo in *Michaelmas Term* to Pecunius Lucre in *A Trick to Catch the Old One*, have very similar appetites, happily feeding off others, even their own kin.

Plots in Middleton's London plays often revolve around religious and social rituals that ideally should function to reaffirm the bonds and values of the community, but instead are subject to the disruptive forces of parody and burlesque. The lying-in scene in *A Chaste Maid in Cheapside* (3.2) has at least six female characters on stage at the same time. Middleton is once again exploiting the available resources. The play was performed by the Lady Elizabeth's Men, whose recent merger with the Children of the Queen's Revels meant that there were a large number of boy actors able to play women's parts.[9] It enabled Middleton to create a fantastic and grotesque female world, imagined in terms of an 'endlessly consuming female appetite'.[10] Allwit's misogynist choric commentary renders this scene a patriarchal nightmare of incontinent women.[11] And yet, Allwit is a very faulty observer, and is not granted the moral detachment from proceedings that would confer trust in his judgement. Instead, luxuriating in his own cuckolding, he is heavily implicated in the fallen world he describes.

Patriarchy is highly unstable in this play populated by either sexually unruly (Touchwood Senior, Sir Walter Whorehound) or deficient men (Allwit, Sir Oliver Kix). *A Chaste Maid in Cheapside* repeatedly invokes the hereditary principles of primogeniture that lie at the basis of early modern patriarchy, but inserts carnivalesque instability into its very foundations. The children who will secure Sir Oliver Kix's title and land for posterity will all be bastards; moreover, given that Kix is reliant on the sexual services of

Touchwood Senior for his heirs, he occupies a comparable position in the play to the cuckold Allwit. If patriarchy is endorsed in *A Chaste Maid in Cheapside*, then it is left in a self-consciously bastardised form.[12]

A Chaste Maid in Cheapside is an example of urban tragicomedy. Tragicomedy was characterised by a miraculous reversal, typically achieved through the intervention of a sacred authority in human affairs. There are several 'miracles' in the last act: the young lovers, Tim and Moll, believed dead, are 'resurrected' at their funeral; and the barren Lady Kix is 'miraculously' pregnant. Yet, Middleton's interests are not in sustaining the dramatic illusion, but in parodying the form. The *deus ex machina* is replaced with the trickster, Touchwood Senior, who has stage-managed these sudden reversals.[13] Middleton's London plays are generically eclectic. The result is stylistic discord, a deliberate tonal and ideological dissonance that reverberates throughout the plays, and signifies both Middleton's virtuosity and the particular pressures that the new metropolis placed on the forms through which it was imagined.[14]

Early tragedies: *A Yorkshire Tragedy* and *The Revenger's Tragedy*

Middleton's tragedies for the King's Men, *A Yorkshire Tragedy* and *The Revenger's Tragedy*, in different ways, focus on the patriarchal household. *A Yorkshire Tragedy* is a domestic tragedy centred on the gentry household, and considers the tragic consequences of the dangers posed by unruly men. The play is based on a 'true story', that of Walter Calverley who murdered his two young sons, and attempted to murder the third in 1605, at his family estate in Yorkshire, which inspired a number of pamphlets and plays.[15] The locale of *The Revenger's Tragedy* is Italy, the favoured landscape for revenge tragedy. Like *A Yorkshire Tragedy*, it dramatises quite sensational cruelty, but it does so in the service of revenge, and the patriarchal household is given political rather than domestic expression. Unruly men in these tragedies, from the murderous Husband to the lusty Duke, figure a disorderly masculinity that, in associating violence with manhood, undermines patriarchal ends. The further complication in revenge tragedies is that the revenger uses violence against violence, recalling the personal combats of an older honour culture that is itself now under suspicion.[16] The forms of masculinity that constitute early modern society, both patriarchal and anti-patriarchal, are held up for scrutiny in these plays, thus complicating their representation of manhood.

The Husband in *A Yorkshire Tragedy* is a type of prodigal gentleman familiar from Middleton's city comedies, who has 'consume[d] his credit and his house' (scene 2, line 3) through gaming. Whereas in the comedy

A Trick to Catch the Old One, the prodigal gentleman Witgood is on the path to reform, throughout this tragedy the Husband remains hell-bent on a life of excess and beggaring his heirs. If *A Chaste Maid in Cheapside* celebrates a bastardised patriarchy, then *A Yorkshire Tragedy* dramatises its self-destruction. The heading of a household was equated with manhood itself in the early modern period. But the Husband hates the role of husband and the responsibilities it brings. The community is assembled in various guises – the Wife, the Gentlemen, the college Master – to remind the Husband of his obligations as a gentleman to govern himself by subordinating his own desires to patriarchal interests. The Husband's murder of his children is an extension of his prodigality, since a gentleman who destroys himself necessarily destroys the source of his social identity, the household.[17] The Husband has no affective bond with his sons. With self-conscious irony, their murder is his way of taking responsibility for his actions since they embody his debts. On his way to murder his youngest child, he puns that he 'want[s] one small part to make up the sum' (scene 5, line 47) to redeem his brother from debtor's prison. Infanticide is unnatural in the play and condemned, but it has some logic within Roman patriarchalism, which gave fathers the right to dispose of their children.[18] *A Yorkshire Tragedy* produces an uncomfortable view of early modern patriarchy, not only in its study of domestic violence, but in the depiction of the Wife's forgiveness of her children's murderer because 'Dearer than all is my poor husband's life' (scene 8, line 65). This may define her wifely virtue, but it is a poor defence of the household.

The Revenger's Tragedy is also a play concerned with families and honour. Of the two central families in the play, the ducal family epitomises the corruption of factional intrigue. The Duke's stepsons, Ambitioso and Supervacuo, conspire to murder his heir, Lussurioso, and so take his place, but instead are unwittingly responsible for the execution of their younger brother, the rapist, Junior. The Duke's bastard, Spurio, cuckolds his father with his wife, the Duchess, because he 'was begot in impudent wine and lust' (1.2.190), thus 'Adultery is my nature' (1.2.177). Vindice's family offers an alternative to the court, and is governed by the memory of his dead father, a Tacitean good man destroyed by a corrupt court. Yet, the play refuses any simple distinction between a virtuous past and contemporary corruption, since the threat to Vindice's household comes as much from within as from without. It is Vindice, disguised as the malcontent Piato, who is employed by Lussurioso to corrupt his sister, Castiza, and when this fails, he turns to his mother, Gratiana, who proves less resilient.

The honour of the patriarchal household is invested in the chastity of women's bodies. When Antonio's wife is raped by the Duchess's son, Junior, she is only able to redeem her husband's honour through her suicide. Her dead body, like that of Gloriana, becomes the site of a power struggle between men as well as the 'altar' on which male alliances are forged.[19] The chaste, enclosed female body is accorded a transcendent value. Yet such a valuation arises out of a deep misogyny that views the woman's body as the gateway to hell, hence the need to keep it enclosed. This double view of women's nature makes it possible for Vindice to put Gloriana's skull to a variety of uses. In the opening scene, Gloriana's skull is used as a *memento mori*, both a reminder of the idealised, chaste female body and a troubling emblem of the interdependence of lust and death, identified with the earthly beauty of women that seduces men, leading to their spiritual destruction. Thus, later in the play, the skull, now painted and '*dressed up in tires*' (stage direction at 3.5.44), figures the 'false forms' (3.5.97) of women that will take the Duke straight to hell with a poisoned kiss.

The murder of the Duke is accomplished with a particularly witty cruelty that renders it disturbingly and grotesquely humorous. When the Duke cries in agony that his 'teeth are eaten out' (3.5.159), and then his tongue (3.5.162), Vindice jests that it 'will teach you to kiss closer, / Not like a slobbering Dutchman' (3.5.163–4). The Jacobean revenge tragedy is defined by such 'horrid laughter', which is intensified by a heightened and self-conscious theatricality.[20] A dramatic interest in cruelty does not appear to be confined to the revenge plot of tragedies, since it also features in *A Yorkshire Tragedy*. The Husband's murder of his eldest son is particularly cruel. Grabbing the son when he is playing a child's game, the Husband strikes him, quipping on the boy's plea that he is his 'white boy' (scene 4, line 99), or favourite, that now he 'shalt be my red boy' (scene 4, line 100), before callously stabbing him. When confronted by the horrified and incredulous Master whether this is how he has repaid his brother's debts, the Husband again quips 'Why, he can have no more on's than our skins, / And some of 'em want but flaying' (scene 6, lines 23–4). Although 'flaying' is an image of the famished state he has been reduced to, presumably it also refers to his children's bloodied bodies seen on stage in the previous scene.

A Yorkshire Tragedy is a strange play at many levels. Criticism has been levelled at the first scene since it sits strangely with the subsequent tragedy, and is more in keeping with Middleton's city comedies.[21] The servant, Sam, newly come from London, having undergone a typical city sartorial transformation, promises to show his fellows a London drinking game. Such low humour provides an uncomfortable frame for the tragic story the servants tell of an abandoned mistress and an abusive husband. Middleton's plays are characterised by such disturbing hybridity. *The Revenger's Tragedy* delights in the grotesque disjunctions of its dark humour and celebrates the neatness of Vindice's inventions, apparent in the wit of his plot to poison the Duke with the skull of the woman he poisoned, and then entertain him with a dumb show in which his wife cuckolds him with his bastard. *The Revenger's Tragedy* is a type of morality play, but it critiques and subverts moral orthodoxies, just as it flouts generic conventions.[22]

Later tragedies: *Women Beware Women* and *The Changeling*

Women Beware Women and *The Changeling*, co-written with William Rowley, first returned to the stage in the 1960s, and since that time have been the playwright's most admired and most performed plays. *Women Beware Women* can usefully be described as a domestic tragedy or a 'city tragedy', a term which draws attention to its many affinities with Middleton's early city comedies. Unlike *The Revenger's Tragedy*, the play's focus is on the private household rather than dynastic politics, and this is evident in the way domestic interiors are realised on stage through attention to material goods.[23] *The Changeling*, with its double plot, is a generically hybrid play. There is a seemingly neat division between the tragic castle plot centred on Beatrice-Joanna and the comic asylum plot headed by Isabella, except that the two plots quite self-consciously mirror each other, resulting in both shocking juxtapositions and a grotesque hybridity which refuses to keep separate the world of madhouse and that of the castle.[24]

Both tragedies have women at their centre. The situation of the young wife, Bianca, in the opening scenes of *Women Beware Women*, is an extended and highly stylised exploration of the lapidary metaphor, deriving from the biblical proverb, 'the price of a good woman is above rubies'.[25] Leantio, the young factor, has 'stolen' Bianca from her wealthy parents, and now must keep this 'jewel … cased up from all men's eyes' (1.1.170). This proprietorial attitude towards women's bodies is given architectural expression in *The Changeling*. The analogy between Beatrice-Joanna and her father's castle is established from the opening scene. Just as her father, Vermandero, grants access to his castle, so too he determines who will have his daughter in marriage. The problem is that the servant, De Flores, is the keeper of the keys and knows all the castle's secret places, and it is De Flores who ultimately takes possession of Beatrice-Joanna, both sexually and spiritually.[26] Leantio is unable to keep possession of Bianca, and she is 'stolen' by the Duke, her rape signifying the right of possession he claims due to his higher social status. Leantio, in turn, will himself be bought by Livia, the wealthy widow. The patriarchal household required the submission not only of women, but also of the young. It is this more complex interplay between gender and age that structures the patriarchal economy of *Women Beware Women*. The younger generation is bought and sold by their elders: the two young lovers, Bianca and Leantio, and the dependants, Isabella and the Ward. Middleton more than once turns to the theme of intergenerational conflict, pitting grandson against grandfather in *A Mad World My Masters* (1605) and sons against fathers in *The Old Law* (c. 1614–18).

Both *Women Beware Women* and *The Changeling* engage in a sustained study of seeing in relation to women both as the object of the male gaze and as independent desiring subjects. Middleton's Calvinism is most pronounced in his attitudes towards looking. His earliest work, *The Wisdom of Solomon Paraphrased* (1597), described how 'our heart is blinded with our eyes, / Our eyes are blinded with our blinded heart' and 'Our bodies on both parts defilèd lies' (ch. 2, lines 175–7). It is a cycle of infection in which the human eye cannot detach itself from the world of sin, and therefore is incapable of resisting temptation. This doctrine sees danger in seeing but also in being seen, and finds in women a particular vulnerability because they are governed by carnal appetites. Alibius imprisons his wife in order to keep her from the 'quick enticing eyes' (*The Changeling*, 1.2.55) of handsome gallants, since once she is seen, she will return their gaze and succumb to temptation. Similarly Harebrain in *A Mad World My Masters* carefully watches his wife to observe the 'slippery revolutions of her eye' (3.1.11). The problem is that women are not passive objects of the male gaze, but actively look back, which endows seeing with a potent carnality. Bianca's initial seduction is visual; to 'prepare her stomach' Guardiano 'showed her naked pictures by the way' (*Women Beware Women*, 2.2.400–2). Her sexual fallenness following her rape is signified by her desire to see and be seen, 'To stand in a bay window and see gallants'.[27]

Men's ability not only to keep watch over but to see into 'women's secret places' is explored in *The Changeling*. Both Beatrice-Joanna and Alsemero begin the play voicing a very positive account of the ability of judgement to 'check the eyes' (1.1.76). Yet, even though it is Beatrice-Joanna who issues warnings about the dangers of seeing, tellingly it is her eyes that have already wandered. If the secrets of Beatrice-Joanna's body and self remain hidden from those men putatively in control, she is also denied self-knowledge until her 'true nature' is revealed by De Flores. From a Calvinist perspective, her confidence in the judgement of her eyes and heart is folly and, ironically, is the product of her spiritual blindness, signified by her giddy, turning will.[28] John Stachniewski points out that, from the play's beginning, Beatrice-Joanna bears the signs of the damned since her actions are governed by the flesh. Hence, she assumes that her birth and beauty carry moral and spiritual privileges that will defend her against the servant, De Flores.[29] She ends the play turned into a spectacle that illustrates the fate of the adultress, her polluted blood cast out from the patriarchal body into the 'common sewer'.[30] A different fate is reserved for her virtuous counterpart in the play, Isabella. Unlike Beatrice-Joanna, she is accorded a clear-sightedness that allows her to identify folly in its many forms, both in her husband and in the importuning lovers she resists. Her ability to govern herself and preserve her chastity in the face of temptation is seemingly rewarded in the play, since she is given command over the inner resources of language and hence the self, but her agency is dependent on her willingness to keep her body enclosed.[31]

The dramatisation of secret, interior spaces is so powerful in *The Changeling* because Middleton makes highly inventive use of stage machinery. The famous claustrophobia of the play owes much to the more intimate space of the indoor playhouse, which allowed lighting to be manipulated for dramatic effect. But *The Changeling* also makes extensive and unparalleled metaphorical, architectural and dramatic use of the discovery space, the curtained-off area at the back of the stage that is in full view of the audience, yet hides action from view. The discovery space in *The Changeling* is a dark place of secrets and the domain of the illicit. This is the likely place where De Flores conceals the murdered Alonzo, and it becomes the space of Alsemero's closet, which is transformed from a type of scientific cabinet, where he keeps the 'virginity test', in Act 4 into the 'hell' (5.3.163) that receives De Flores and Beatrice-Joanna in the final scene. The symbolic association between these two uses of the closet speaks to the desire to reveal 'women's secret places' that runs through the play.[32] With *Women Beware Women*, Middleton turned his attention to the upper stage in a similarly striking and innovative way. The upper stage is used at the end of the first act to represent the window to Leantio's house. Here, Bianca and the Mother appear, while below the Duke and his court process in state. Bianca stands framed in the window/upper stage, thus accentuating her situation of looking and being looked at and her objectification in the erotic economy of the play. The aesthetic and sexual dynamics of this interplay between the upper and main stage are recast in Act 2, scene 2. The upper stage now represents the gallery of paintings and statues in Livia's house that Bianca is shown before her rape. Below, on the main stage, are Livia and the Mother playing chess. This split-level action enables the audience to recognise that the chess moves played below are a coded commentary on the action above, and part of the dangerous games of sexual intrigue dramatised in the play as a whole.

Middleton reuses the dramatic device of the chess game in a much more ambitious way in *A Game at Chess*. Chess provides the allegorical and dramatic structure of this play about political conspiracy. *A Game at Chess* also shares a sexualised language of court corruption with his earlier tragedies. From the early 1610s into the 1620s, this language had coalesced around the figure of Frances Howard, who had scandalously divorced her first husband to marry the royal favourite, Robert Carr, and then, even more scandalously, was found guilty of complicity in the murder of Sir Thomas Overbury, who had spoken against the marriage. Middleton's *The Changeling* alludes to the scandal, most notably in the virginity test, which recalls the examination Howard was subjected to during her divorce trial. *A Game at Chess* goes much further in its political satire by openly impersonating contemporary and high-ranking members of the English and Spanish courts on stage. This daring play marks the high-point of Middleton's theatrical innovation *and* the end of his dramatic career. He was briefly imprisoned, and seems to have stopped writing plays either as a condition of his release or because he could no longer sell his plays to wary playing companies.

Middleton is a dramatist who takes risks. His plays unsettle decorum and are suffused by a wit that frequently mixes venery and piety to disturbing effect. The aesthetics of trickery that structure his multivalent plotting disrupts conventions through artful play and operates at stylistic, social and political levels. While his major plays have long enjoyed critical attention, lesser-known plays, like *A Yorkshire Tragedy* and his early city comedies, deserve fuller study.

Middleton on the contemporary stage

Middleton's major tragedies have been regularly performed on the British stage since the 1960s. This decade, which witnessed Middleton's stage revival, was rocked by sexual scandals within the political establishment. Donald Cammell's and Nic Roeg's anarchic *Performance*, filmed in 1968, portrayed a London in which a hedonistic urban elite cohabited with a violent criminal underworld. This was the time when theatre producers excitedly discovered their own society's reflection in the violently unstable amalgam of sex and power in Middleton's plays and their decadent, criminalised elites. The theatre critic, Ronald Bryden, equated Trevor Nunn's 1966 revival of *The Revenger's Tragedy* with Fellini's savage satire on 1950s Italian high society in *La Dolce Vita*: 'The Revenger's Tragedy is much the same kind of circus of viciousness, delighting in each exposure of degeneracy in high places, in the grotesque distortions to which lust drives humanity.'[33] Mary Ure, who had recently played Alison in John Osborne's *Look Back in Anger*, took the role of Beatrice-Joanna in Tony Richardson's 1961 revival of *The*

Changeling.[34] When *Women Beware Women* returned to the stage in 1962, Kenneth Tynan discovered a sexually liberated Middleton, in contrast with the more staid, socially conservative Shakespeare.[35]

The stage success of *Women Beware Women* is, in part, due to the opportunities it offers actresses of a certain age. As Jonathan Bate has noted, 'older women's parts' were Middleton's 'speciality'.[36] When Penelope Wilton played Livia in Laurence Boswell's 2006 Royal Shakespeare Company production, she added pathos to the stereotypical 'lusty widow' in her portrayal of a middle-aged woman besotted with a younger man. Harriet Walter's widely acclaimed Livia dominated Marianne Elliott's 2010 production at the National Theatre; for Susannah Clapp, Walter's Livia was 'a woman whose ability has no … outlet', other than her sexual scheming.[37] Elliott's production, updated to 1950s Italy, once again drew comparisons with Fellini, but a Fellini for the current times; the programme essay insisted on the play's continuing relevance in a world of predatory capitalism where greed is 'an epidemic'.[38]

While Middleton's comedies are less frequently performed, there are a number of notable exceptions. Perry Mills's recent productions with a boys' company from King Edward VI School, Stratford-upon-Avon, reflected very productively on Middleton's work with the Paul's Boys, for whom he wrote the majority of his city comedies.[39] An all-boy company, with an age range from early to late teens, provides a fascinating illustration of the inflections a boy's age gives to the woman's part. This was particularly notable in the lying-in scene in *Chaste Maid* in which those boys playing women ranged from the delicate prettiness of the pre-pubescent boy to the lusty stature of the youth. A boys' company adds a certain frisson to the licentious sexual play of Middleton's city comedies. The bed scene with Penitent Brothel and Mistress Harebrain in Act 3, scene 2 was highly stylised, with its sexual energies relayed through the comic timing of noise and verbal wit. Laurie Maguire and Emma Smith noted that this production 'may have achieved something akin to the early modern boys' companies' disconcerting investment in bawdy suggestion'.[40]

King Edward VI School is, of course, Shakespeare's school. Gary Taylor's fashioning of Middleton as 'our other Shakespeare' has informed stage performances of Middleton's work. Declan Donnellan staged *The Changeling* alongside *Twelfth Night* as its dark mirror in 2006, while Celia Daileader called *The Revenger's Tragedy* a 'feminist *Hamlet*' in her programme essay for Melly Still's 2008 production. Yet, it is interesting to reflect that when Middleton was fêted on the stage in the 1960s it was precisely because, as Tynan and others noted, he was not Shakespeare.

NOTES

1 The attribution of these plays is still open to debate, although critical consensus assigns *A Yorkshire Tragedy* and *The Revenger's Tragedy* to Middleton, and recognises his hand in *Timon of Athens*. See *Thomas Middleton: The Collected Works*, ed. Gary Taylor and John Lavagnino (Oxford: Clarendon Press, 2007). All references to Middleton's plays and poems will be to this edition.

2 *The Collected Works*, 726.

3 Darryll Grantley, 'Middleton's Comedy and the Geography of London', in *Thomas Middleton in Context*, ed. Suzanne Gossett (Cambridge University Press, 2011), 28–36.

4 Catherine Richardson, 'Domestic Life in Jacobean London', in *Thomas Middleton in Context*, ed. Suzanne Gossett (Cambridge University Press, 2011) 59–60 and Michelle O'Callaghan, *Thomas Middleton, Renaissance Dramatist* (Edinburgh University Press, 2009), 60–3.

5 Andrew Gordon, '*The Puritan Widow* and the Spatial Arts of Middleton's Urban Drama', *Thomas Middleton in Context*, ed. Suzanne Gossett (Cambridge University Press, 2011), 37–8.

6 Jean E. Howard, *Theater of a City: The Places of London City Comedy, 1598–1642* (Philadelphia, PA: University of Pennsylvania Press, 2007), 136–7.

7 Richard Levin, *The Multiple Plot in English Renaissance Drama* (University of Chicago Press, 1971), 94–5; and Catherine Richardson, 'Domestic Life in Jacobean London', in *Thomas Middleton in Context*, ed. Suzanne Gossett (Cambridge University Press, 2011), 52–60.

8 Howard, *Theater of a City*, 29–32.

9 Lucy Munro, *Children of the Queen's Revels: A Jacobean Theatre Repertory* (Cambridge University Press, 2005), 23–4.

10 Matthew R. Martin, *Between Theater and Philosophy: Skepticism in the Major City Comedies of Ben Jonson and Thomas Middleton* (Newark, DE: University of Delaware Press, 2001), 118.

11 Gail Kern Paster, *The Body Embarrassed: Drama and the Disciplines of Shame in Early Modern England* (Ithaca, NY: Cornell University Press, 1993), 53–7.

12 See also Joanne Altieri, 'Against Moralizing Jacobean Comedy: Middleton's *Chaste Maid*', *Criticism* 30 (1988), 171–87 at 181–4; and Karen Newman, '*A Chaste Maid in Cheapside* and London', in *Early Modern English Drama: A Critical Companion*, ed. Garrett A. Sullivan, Patrick Cheney and Andrew Hadfield (Oxford University Press, 2006), 237–40 at 243–5.

13 Altieri, 'Against Moralizing Jacobean Comedy', 175.

14 P. K. Ayers, 'Plot, Subplot, and the Uses of Dramatic Discord in *A Mad World My Masters* and *A Trick to Catch an Old One*', *Modern Language Quarterly* 47 (1986), 3–18 at 9–10.

15 Lena Cowen Orlin, *Private Matters and Public Culture in Post-Reformation England* (Ithaca, NY: Cornell University Press, 1994), 235.

16 *Four Revenge Tragedies*, ed. Katharine Eisaman Maus (Oxford University Press, 1995), ix–xi.

17 Frances E. Dolan, *Dangerous Familiars: Representations of Domestic Crime in England, 1550–1700* (Ithaca, NY: Cornell University Press, 1994), 153–9.

18 Orlin, *Private Matters and Public Culture*, 236.

19 Jonathan Dollimore, *Radical Tragedy: Religion, Ideology and Power in the Drama of Shakespeare and his Contemporaries* (Brighton: Harvester Press, 1984), 141–2.

20 Nicholas Brooke, *Horrid Laughter in Jacobean Tragedy* (New York: Barnes & Noble, 1979), 10–27.

21 *A Yorkshire Tragedy*, ed. A. C. Cawley and Barry Gaines (Manchester University Press, 1986), 13–15.

22 Brooke, *Horrid Laughter*, 14; Dollimore, *Radical Tragedy*, 138–43.

23 Margot Heinemann, *Puritanism and Theatre: Thomas Middleton and Opposition Drama under the Early Stuarts* (Cambridge University Press, 1980), 180–8.

24 Swapan Chakravorty, *Society and Politics in the Plays of Thomas Middleton* (Oxford: Clarendon Press, 1996), 165; Suzanne Gossett, 'Middleton and Dramatic Genre', in *Thomas Middleton in Context*, 235–42.

25 Kathleen McLuskie, *Renaissance Dramatists: Feminist Readings* (Hemel Hempstead: Harvester Wheatsheaf, 1989), 127–8.

26 Cristina Malcolmson, '"As Tame as the Ladies": Politics and Gender in *The Changeling*', *English Literary Renaissance* 20 (1990), 320–39 at 330–1, 336–8.

27 *Women Beware Women*, 3.1.131. See Marcus Nordlund, *The Dark Lantern: A Historical Study of Sight in Shakespeare, Webster, and Middleton* (Göteborg: Acta Universitatis Gothoburgensis, 1999), 437–9, 455–61.

28 Nordlund, *The Dark Lantern*, 442–3.

29 John Stachniewski, 'Calvinist Psychology in Middleton's Tragedies', in *Three Jacobean Revenge Tragedies, A Casebook*, ed. R. V. Holdsworth (Basingstoke: Macmillan, 1990), 226–47 at 236.

30 *The Changeling*, 5.3.153. See also Paster, *Body Embarrassed*, 88–90.

31 Bruce Boehrer, 'Alsemero's Closet: Privacy and Interiority in *The Changeling*', *Journal of English and Germanic Philology* 96 (1997), 349–68 at 365–6; Caroline Bicks, 'Gender and Sexuality', in *Thomas Middleton in Context*, ed. Gossett, 263–70.

32 Mark Hutchings, 'De Flores between the Acts', *Studies in Theatre and Performance* 31:1 (2011), 95–112; Boehrer, 'Alsemero's Closet', 349–53.

33 *The Observer*, 9 October 1966.

34 On the stage history of *The Changeling*, see Roberta Barker and David Nicol, 'Does Beatrice-Joanna Have a Subtext? *The Changeling* on the London Stage', *Early Modern Literary Studies* 10:1 (May, 2004), 1–43.

35 McLuskie, *Renaissance Dramatists*, 19.

36 Jonathan Bate, 'Dampit and Moll: Sexing the Language, Languaging the Sex, Doubting All Truth, Mastering All Dramatic Modes: Enough of a Case for Thomas Middleton?', *Times Literary Supplement*, 25 April 2008, 5.

37 *The Observer*, 2 May 2010.

38 Juliet Fleming, 'Male Hysteria', *Times Literary Supplement*, 25 June 2010, 10.

39 John Jowett, '*A Chaste Maid in Cheapside*, performed by Edward's Boys, 2–6 March 2010, King's College London, Somerville College Oxford, and Levi Fox Hall, K.E.S. [King Edward's School]', *Stratfordian*, 2010, 64–5.

40 '"Time's Comic Sparks": The Dramaturgy of *A Mad World, My Masters* and *Timon of Athens*', in *The Oxford Handbook to Middleton*, ed. Gary Taylor and Trish Henley (Oxford University Press, 2012), 181–95 at 186.

Further reading

Dollimore, Jonathan, *Radical Tragedy: Religion, Ideology and Power in the Drama of Shakespeare and his Contemporaries*. Brighton: Harvester Press, 1984.

Friedenreich, Kenneth, ed., *'Accompaninge the Players': Essays Celebrating Thomas Middleton, 1580–1980*. New York: AMS Press, 1983.

Gossett, Suzanne, ed., *Thomas Middleton in Context*. Cambridge University Press, 2011.

Heinemann, Margot, *Puritanism and Theatre: Thomas Middleton and Opposition Drama under the Early Stuarts*, 2nd edn. Cambridge University Press, 1982.

Leinwand, Theodore, *The City Staged: Jacobean City Comedy, 1603–1613*. Madison, WI: University of Wisconsin Press, 1986.

McLuskie, Kathleen E., and David Bevington, eds., *Plays on Women*. Manchester University Press, 1999.

Schoenbaum, S., *Middleton's Tragedies: A Critical Study*. New York: Columbia University Press, 1955.

Stallybrass, Peter, 'Reading the Body and the Jacobean Theater of Consumption: *The Revenger's Tragedy* (1606)', in *Staging the Renaissance: Reinterpretations of Elizabethan and Jacobean Drama*, ed. David Scott Kastan and Peter Stallybrass. London and New York: Routledge, 1991, 210–20.

Thomson, Leslie, '"*Enter Above*": The Staging of *Women Beware Women*.' *Studies in English Literature* 26 (1986), 331–43.

12

ROBERT HENKE

John Webster: collaboration and solitude

The life and work of John Webster suggest a fundamental and probably generative paradox. On the one hand, he was deeply and continuously conditioned by urban networks generated from his father's business, his education and his collaborative work in the theatre. On the other hand, his erudition, literary ambition and individualised poetic achievement seem to reflect some measure of independence and solitude.

Especially after Mary Edmond's identification of Webster's father as a wealthy coach-maker in London, it has become possible to trace certain social networks that generated collaborative relationships and even shaped ideological proclivities throughout the playwright's life: Webster's involvement with his father's coach-making business and the guild that was associated with it, the Merchant Taylors' Company; the dramatist's probable attendance first at Richard Mulcaster's Merchant Taylors' School and later at the Middle Temple; his early playwriting apprenticeship as one of 'Henslowe's hacks' with citizen-dramatists such as Thomas Dekker and Thomas Middleton, with whom he would continue to write collaborative plays his entire career; an identification with city-based Protestant values opposed to the court of James I; and a corresponding sympathy with the fifth column of militant Protestants galvanised in James' court around the figure of William Herbert, Earl of Pembroke.[1] Webster may have worked for his father's coach-making enterprise, taking care of the business side of things as M. C. Bradbrook has speculated, becoming a full member of the Merchant Taylors' Company in 1615.[2] In 1624, he was honoured to serve as official poet for the company, designing the festivities for the investiture of Sir John Gore, a merchant taylor, as Lord Mayor of London.

Although we possess a smaller number of documents pertaining to Webster's life than we do for Shakespeare, they are more revealing precisely because of the ways in which they point to urban and citizen networks: contexts that can frame Webster's work in illuminating ways. Seeing these networks, it need hardly come as a surprise that Webster's collaborative work outnumbered his single-authored plays by about three to one (thus even superseding the roughly one-to-one ratio of collaborative to single-authored playwriting that Gerald Eades Bentley ascribes to the period).[3]

Still, a habit of slow and laboured composition, a tendency to write in an opaque style not dissimilar to that of the metaphysical poets, a bookish penchant for intertextual allusion, and a demonstrable aversion to the public stages favoured by his citizen colleagues Dekker and Heywood bespeak an impulse towards a literary approach to playwriting, and by extension perhaps also an inclination to some privacy. The brooding sense of interiority detectable in characters such as Bosola and the Duchess herself in the *The Duchess of Malfi* might be seen as cognate with this. The revealing note 'To the Reader' that Webster prefaced to the 1612 quarto edition of *The White Devil* – published soon after, and apparently as a kind of literary antidote to the failure of the play at the popular Red Bull amphitheatre – refers to a habit of laboured composition that must have been quite at odds with the temporal exigencies of collaborative writing, often contracted to individual playwrights by single acts and doubtlessly constrained by strict deadlines.[4] So Webster:

> To those who report I was a long time in finishing this tragedy, I confess I do not write with a goose-quill, winged with two feathers, and if they will needs make it my fault, I must answer them with that of Euripides to Alcestides, a tragic writer: Alcestides objecting that Euripides had only in three days composed three verses, whereas himself had written three hundred: 'Thou tell'st truth', (quoth he) 'but here's the difference, – thine shall only be read for three days, whereas mine shall continue three ages'.[5]

Webster's habit of slow composition, which appears to reflect a Jonsonian attention to his work's literary integrity as a kind of 'monument' independent of the social vicissitudes of the theatre crowd, is corroborated by Henry Fitzjeffery's pillory of Webster in a poem he wrote satirising various character-types in the audience of the Blackfriars theatre, where the King's Men had performed *The Duchess of Malfi* in 1614:

> Was ever man so mangl'd with a *Poem*?
> See how he draws his mouth awry of late,
> How he scrubs: wrings his wrests: scratches his *Pate*.
> A *Midwife*! helpe! By his *Braines coitus*,
> Some *Centaure* strange: some huge *Bucephalus*,
> Or *Pallas* (sure) ingendred in his *Braine*,
> Strike, *Vulcan*, with thy hammer once again.[6]

Bosola's riddling assertion, in *The Duchess of Malfi*, that 'a kind of geometry' is the last support for the veteran soldier because he must swing his crutches as a geometrician manipulates his twin compasses is as tortured as John Donne's very different use of the same metaphorical vehicle in 'A Valediction Forbidding Mourning'.[7] Bosola's befuddled interlocutor Delio ('Geometry?' he asks [1.1.63]) might possibly evoke the auditors at the Red Bull, whom Webster condescendingly maligns (via two cryptic allusions to Horace) as like those whose breath reeks of garlic or who feast on pig slop. Such an 'uncapable multitude', Webster decries, could not appreciate the conceits, allusions, sententiae and complex stage synchronisation of verbal and visual images over which he must have significantly laboured before birthing his first single-authored play.[8] Fitzjeffery's satiric perspective suggests an author who, at least at times, may have preferred books to people: no other dramatist of his time cites, plagiarises, appropriates and parodies so many other authors, even in ways that now suggest the concept of intertextuality.

Generally, in *The White Devil* preface 'To the Reader', we may discern two rather different strains: on the one hand, the affable Merchant Taylors' Company member and collaborating dramatist, and, on the other hand, the proud and prickly 'author':

> Detraction is the sworn friend to ignorance: for mine own part I have ever truly cherish'd my good opinion of other men's worthy labours, especially of that full and height'ned style of Master Chapman, the labour'd and understanding works of Master Jonson: the no less worthy composures of the both worthily excellent Master Beaumont, and Master Fletcher: and lastly (without wrong last to be named) the right happy and copious industry of Master Shakespeare, Master Dekker, and Master Heywood. (To the Reader)

Webster argues that the learned person is precisely one who is not impervious to collaborative influence, declaring himself fully open to working in London's environment of social dramatic production. What initially impresses is the list's sheer inclusiveness, which includes the popular playwrights Thomas Dekker and Thomas Heywood, with whom his working relationship spanned twenty-two and twenty-five years, respectively.[9] Indeed, Dekker appears to have served as a kind of mentor for the young Webster at the start of his career up to the successful city comedies *Westward Ho* and *Northward Ho* (first performed in 1604–5), and in this connection it is interesting to note that whatever antipathy Webster directed at the Red Bull (Dekker and Heywood's preferred venue) and its patrons in the preface to *The White Devil*, in 1624 he was to co-write with Dekker, John Ford and William Rowley a play entitled *A Late Murder of the Son upon the Mother, or, Keep the Widow Waking* that would return to the Red Bull.

But if this inclusive, eclectic list of Webster's debts does reflect a generous and wide collaborative reach, it is also quite possible to interpret the list's order to indicate a hierarchical ranking arguably in keeping with the overall thrust of the note, which is to defend the high art of the laboured dramatist against the cruder tastes of Red Bull theatregoers. It is only to the first two figures, George Chapman (a dramatist with whom Webster has sometimes been compared) and Jonson (the dramatist best known for his antipathy to the public theatres) that genuinely specific praise is accorded – and praise that matches Webster's self-defence for the gravitas, labour and learning consecrated to *The White Devil*. The rhetorical compensation ('no less worthy … without wrong last to be named') accorded to Francis Beaumont, John Fletcher, Shakespeare, Dekker and Heywood smacks of their subordination in Webster's esteem. Interestingly, Chapman and Jonson are among the few English dramatists with whom Webster did *not* collaborate; additionally, they make up the team, along with John Marston, who wrote the more successful *Eastward Ho* in response to Dekker and Webster's citizen comedies. Given that the popular writers Dekker and Heywood prospered at venues like the Red Bull, it may be possible to read in the three-year period of Webster's great tragedies and tragic elegy written at the death of Prince Henry (1612–14) – and critics have noticed the transfer of conceits from the elegy for the dead prince to the tragedy of the dead duchess[10] – a certain yearning to escape his apprentice roots, supplanted by a final phase in the 1620s that was characterised by a return to collaborative work again with Dekker, Heywood and others.

Webster's dramaturgical reflections also reveal a tension between the respective claims of theatre and literature. In his note 'To the Judicious Reader' prefacing *The Devil's Law-Case* (printed 1623), Webster refers to his play as a 'poem'.[11] In this way he stakes out a claim for literary merit for its own sake, and argues for literary excellence as a *sine qua non* for theatrical effectiveness: 'A great part of the grace of this (I confess) lay in action; yet can no action ever be gracious, where the decency of the language, and ingenious structure of the scene, arrive not to make up a perfect harmony.'[12] Webster's tribute in the *White Devil* preface to Jonson's 'labour'd and understanding works' reflects his self-defence of the time and labour bestowed on his own ill-received play, and his praise for Chapman's 'full and height'ned style' coheres with the prescriptions for ideal tragedy enumerated in the preface to *The Devil's Law-Case*: 'height of style', 'gravity of person' and the use of a 'sententious Chorus' and 'passionate and weighty Nuntius'.

But such dramatic 'laws' – common assumptions in a time increasingly well acquainted with neo-Aristotelian, continental dramatic theory and probably lifted from Jonson's preface to *Sejanus* (1605) – conform more to the perfect *literary* tragedy than one that actually works on the stage. Not unlike Lope de Vega in his *El arte nuovo de hacer comedias* Webster takes care to assure his reader of his thorough familiarity with the rules, even as he demonstrates the willingness to flaunt them.[13] Pitched to the exigencies of the stage, as Webster somewhat defensively admits in the preface to *The Devil's Law-Case*, *The White Devil* and *The Duchess of Malfi* surely complicate these neo-classical dicta with their tragicomic fluctuations of style; characters of high station such as Duke Bracciano and Duke Ferdinand who are simultaneously capable of grandeur, grandiosity and bathos; the placement of choric sententiousness not in a single organ but dispersed throughout the dramatis personae, often refracted by irony and parody; and a penchant for anti-classical, onstage violence probably unmatched by any other English early modern dramatist.

Furthermore, Webster throughout his career went out of his way to praise and valorise the art of the actor. He supplied commendatory verses to his friend Thomas Heywood's 1612 *Apology for Actors*, and probably contributed the character 'An Excellent Actor' along with thirty-one other entries to the sixth edition of Thomas Overbury's *Characters* (1615). He specially commended Richard Perkins, the actor in the Queen's Men who played Flamineo and Bosola, in an epilogue to *The White Devil*, and either he or the printer Nicholas Okes (or both of them) had the actors' names and roles printed in the 1623 quarto of *The Duchess of Malfi*. Written early in his career, the Induction that Webster wrote for the King's Men's version of John Marston's *The Malcontent* bespeaks a thorough familiarity with the five actors from the company represented in it: Will Sly, John Sincler, Richard Burbage, Henry Condell and John Lowin; and surely the fact that Webster was awarded the writing of the Induction must be taken as indicating some measure of insider status.

In fact the plays, especially the three extant sole-authored works, are resolutely theatrical (sometimes, in fact, in extreme ways faulted by critics, like George Bernard Shaw, who referred to Webster as a 'Tussaud laureate').[14] As a poet who himself juxtaposed realism and convention in striking and unsettling ways, T. S. Eliot defends what he calls the 'impurity' generated by Webster and other Elizabethan and Jacobean dramatists, who strove 'to attain complete realism without surrendering any of the advantages which as artists they observed in unrealistic conventions'.[15] Eliot notes 'their artistic greediness, their desire for every sort of effect together, their unwillingness to accept any limitation and abide by it'.[16] To critics censoring Webster for either lapses in realism or departures from dramaturgical consistencies of plot, character and structure, defenders of Webster's 'impure art' such as Inga-Stina Ekeblad have noted his resonant staging, often refracted or parodic, of theatrical conventions, such as the masque in the madmen scene from

The Duchess of Malfi – still Webster's most popular play with an impressive track record of stage productions stretching across 400 years, to the present day.[17] Typological (if also individually nuanced) 'characters', severed hands, wax figures, ghosts, dumb shows, a parade of madmen, poisoned bibles or helmets, and theatrically ostentatious religious rituals strikingly counterpoint moments of equally striking realism in the plays: the references to the Duchess's sleeping habits (3.2.13), the Duchess herself noting the tangling (3.2.52) and then the greying (3.2.57–9) of her hair or asking, just before she dies, that syrup be given to her son for his cold (4.2.196–8). Feminist critics might also note a mixture of realism and convention in Webster's use of character typologies resonant with social and political contexts, such as Ferdinand's distilled, exaggerated, but no less disturbing misogyny in *The Duchess of Malfi*. Defences of Webster's art tend to stress patterns of echo and resonance that work at a different level of integration from the prime dramaturgical co-ordinates, like the plot: structures of verbal and visual imagery, repetition, parallelism and refraction that reward sustained reading and performance of *The Duchess of Malfi* and *The White Devil*.[18]

Like dramatists dating back to Marlowe, Webster codes the Catholic Italy of his tragedies as persistently corrupt and morally baseless, but he is less ideologically blatant than his fellow citizen playwright and mentor Thomas Dekker and clearly interested in exploiting the inherent theatricality of Catholic ritual, which in his work carries a certain inherent power despite Webster's satirical perspective. In the meticulously researched representation of the papal conclave in *The White Devil* – based, among other things, on Hierome Bignon's *A Briefe, but an Effectuall Treatise of the Election of Popes* (1605) – Webster comes close to representing Catholic ritual per se, with the sustained and resonant intonation of Latin formulae providing uncanny theatrical power. Contrastingly, in *The Duchess of Malfi*, the Cardinal's divestiture as a churchman and installation as a soldier, replete with the requisite military objects, parodically reverses the Catholic ritual of investiture.[19] After a solemn, private prayer, Isabella in *The White Devil* dies by kissing, relic-like, the poisoned portrait of Duke Bracciano (2.2), so that something like the Catholic veneration of objects is both satirised and lent potent theatrical power. Just moments before his brother Flamineo murders him, Marcello recounts how his brother tore off a piece of a crucifix as an infant, as if this desecration continued to hold strange potency (5.2). Disguised as Capuchin friars, Lodovico and Gasparo administer last rites to the dying Bracciano, in a grisly but effective deployment of the sacrament (5.3).

To be sure, Webster's theatricality is of a particular sort. Although Webster's work was performed in a wide range of venues, his allusive, satiric, ironic, perspectivally unstable and sceptical plays tended to thrive more in the indoor, private theatres, with an educated, ambitious audience of young male lawyers and intellectuals who would have enjoyed the complex webs of intertextual allusion. The Queen's Men, the company for which Webster wrote *The White Devil* and *The Devil's Law-Case*, relocated sometime between 1617–19 (the probable date of Webster's tragicomedy) from the Red Bull to Christopher Beeston's indoor Cockpit (or Phoenix), where the latter play was probably first performed.[20] Webster might have even had his first experience of indoor theatre at the Merchant Taylors' School, whose founder Richard Mulcaster believed in the educational value of staging plays. The Middle Temple, where Webster was probably admitted in 1598, would have exposed him to indoor ritual and pageantry, the kind of arch saturnalian festivity celebrated in the famous Christmas-time Revels; and a legal habit of mind facile with entertaining alternative points of view. Crucially, at the Middle Temple, Webster would have also begun his friendship with the older John Marston, who probably began his attendance there in 1595, and with whom Webster would in 1604 collaborate in a revision of Marston's satiric, ironic and highly theatrical tragicomedy *The Malcontent*, produced for the King's Men.[21] It appears that this so-called 'Inns of Court' style was particularly congenial for the new genre of tragicomedy, which (*unlike* Shakespeare and *like* other London dramatists) Webster divested of the pastoral mode that Italian playwrights such as Tasso and Guarini had conjoined with it, making it a courtly and urban form characterised by a complex plot, quick shifts of perspective, satire and rhetorical virtuosity.

Webster's involvement with Marston and *The Malcontent*, entered as a 'Tragiecomedia' in the Stationers' Register – and which, G. K. Hunter has argued, reflects a systematic attempt to introduce the form in England – bespeaks Webster's fine attunement to the arts of genre, and a willingness to work in a wide range of forms and modes, juxtaposing and cross-pollinating them to a greater degree than Chapman and Jonson (the two playwrights whom, as we have seen, Webster ranks highest in regard to erudition and labour).[22] Two early collaboratively produced tragedies – *Caesar's Fall* (1602, with Thomas Dekker, Michael Drayton, Thomas Middleton and Anthony Munday); and *Lady Jane* (performed in 1602, followed by a sequel, with both plays amalgamated and published in condensed form as *Sir Thomas Wyatt* in 1607) – indicate a taste for *de casibus* tragedy, which with its propensity for sceptical and Stoic reflection might have appealed more to Webster than pure revenge tragedy. If *Caesar's Fall* might have been prompted by Shakespeare's *Julius Caesar*, the Lady Jane plays (co-written with fellow citizens Dekker and Heywood) reflect Protestant homiletic subjects recently dramatised in plays such as *Thomas of Woodstock* and *Sir*

John Oldcastle, and also present Webster's first dramatisation of powerful women.[23] In addition to writing the important Induction to the 1604
Malcontent, Webster made five comic-satiric additions to the play, all but
one centred on the new character of Passarello, the fool to Bilioso, and
almost certainly played by the clown of the King's Men, Robert Armin.[24]

Westward Ho and *Northward Ho*, first performed in 1604–5 by the
Children of St Paul's boys' theatre do not usher in a period of comedy for
Webster, which may at least partially be explained by the declining fortunes
of the boys' companies beginning around 1605–6. After the 1607 printing
of *Northward Ho*, *Westward Ho* and *Sir Thomas Wyatt*, there is a significant hiatus up until the 1612 *White Devil*. The five-year interval, plausibly
characterised by a greater degree of solitude and labour, may partially be
explained by the 'long time in finishing this tragedy' mentioned by Webster
in his preface 'To the Reader'. Charles Forker notes that most of Webster's
borrowings in the tragedy come from books published in 1608 or earlier, and speculates that he could have been during this time assembling his
materials, thus slowing the writing of the play.[25] If there is a distinctive
Websterian 'voice' to the two great tragedies, notwithstanding their pervasive borrowing, he would have been developing it during this period. An
additional explanation for the hiatus is Webster's marriage in March 1606,
and the birth of his first child two months later. The period 1612–14 marks
Webster's most productive period, formally dominated by tragedy and tragic
elegy.[26] Another hiatus after 1615 may be explained by Webster's full entry
into the Merchant Taylors' Company in that year. Then, beginning in 1621,
Webster re-embraced collaborative writing, engaging in five collaborative
projects between then and 1627: one comedy (*Anything for a Quiet Life*,
c. 1621, with Middleton); two tragedies (*A Late Murder of the Son upon the
Mother, or, Keep the Widow Waking*, 1624, with Dekker, Ford and Rowley;
and *Appius and Virginia*, *c.*1627, with Heywood); and two tragicomedies
(*The Fair Maid of the Inn*, 1625–6, with Fletcher, Ford and Massinger; and
A Cure for a Cuckold, 1624–5, with Rowley).[27]

A genre-based overview of the overall oeuvre is revealing. Webster wrote
or co-wrote seven tragedies, of which three were single-authored (the lost
tragedy *Guise*, in addition to *The White Devil* and *The Duchess of Malfi*);
four comedies, all of which were collaborative works; and four tragicomedies, of which only *The Devil's Law-Case* was single-authored. The following generalisations can be made: (1) In regard to single-authored works,
Webster seems to have had a preference for tragedy. (2) He seems to have
preferred the mixed genre of tragicomedy to comedy, especially when the arc
of his complete career is considered. After 1605, he only returns to comedy
once (*Anything for a Quiet Life*, with Middleton, *c.* 1621) but repeatedly

returns to tragicomedy, either inflected by the 'Inns of Court' style developed by Marston or, in the collaborative work of the 1620s, influenced by the Beaumont and Fletcher model.

Webster's restless intertextual imagination renders him particularly congenial to the present critical imagination, especially cognisant of the ways in which texts cite, parody, contextualise, appropriate, transform, echo and refract each other. Webster's extensive borrowings from William Alexander, George Chapman, John Donne, Stefano Guazzo (trans. George Pettie), Joseph Hall, Ben Jonson, Montaigne (trans. John Florio), Nicholas de Montreux (trans. Robert Tofte), Sidney and Shakespeare (to cite the most frequent appropriations in the *Duchess of Malfi* and *The White Devil*) have generated critiques such as that of R. W. Dent, in the course of his meticulous cataloguing of the borrowings: 'The man worked strangely, his creativity receiving some written stimulus at almost every turn. Sometimes he appears strikingly original, occasionally merely commonplace, but almost always – unless our present evidence is very misleading – he worked from sources.'[28] As Leah Marcus has argued, critique like Dent's draws on and perpetuates the Romantic notion of original, non-derivative creativity, a notion that is as unsatisfactory for Shakespeare as it is for Webster.[29] Marcus points out the free and often contestatory ways in which Webster deploys the borrowings, such as when Delio, at the end of *The Duchess of Malfi*, alludes to part of Horace's famous *Integer vitae* ode. If the Horatian text claims that the upright person need not fear the wolf, the recent fact of Ferdinand's lycanthropy ironically subverts the citation.[30] More subtly, Antonio's uncontestable but cold *sententia* to the Duchess, after their banishment from Ancona, that 'Man, like to cassia, is prov'd best being bruis'd' evinces her proud retort: 'Must I like to a slave-born Russian / Account it praise to suffer tyranny' – in an exchange of 'speech genres' not unlike that theorised by Mikhail Bakhtin (3.5.72).[31] And Webster's characters often contest each other with argumentative, duelling sententiae. To be sure, often Webster does not ironise or transform his citations; borrowings from Montaigne, Guazzo, Sidney and Chapman lend the kind of 'sententious gravity' that all Renaissance dramatists thought decorously appropriate to tragedy, however willing they also were to counterpoint the high style with comic and tragicomic modalities.

In particular, Webster's borrowings from Shakespeare have been pointed out, sometimes with the ulterior motive of demonstrating the former's inferiority. When Bosola maliciously asks the Duchess whether her children can yet speak, she echoes Shakespeare's Caliban in retorting: 'But I intend, since they were born accursed, / Curses shall be their first language' (3.5.113–14). In *The White Devil*, just after her son Marcello has been murdered by his brother Flamineo, Cornelia desperately asks an attendant 'fetch a looking glass, see if his breath will not stain it' (5.2.37–8) – an obvious borrowing from the end of *King Lear*. But Webster seldom borrows slavishly. Instead, he often reverses or problematises the original Shakespeare citation, as in the psychologising and debunking of Francisco's perception of Isabella's ghost. Unlike Hamlet, Francesco both conjures and dismisses the ghost by psychological will:

> To fashion my revenge more seriously,
> Let me remember my dead sister's face:
> Call for her picture: no; I'll close my eyes,
> And in a melancholic thought I'll frame
> Her figure t'fore me.
>   *Enter* ISABELLA'S *Ghost.*
>   Now I ha't – how strong
> Imagination works! how she can frame
> Things which are not! methinks she stands afore me;
> And by the quick idea of my mind,
> Were my skill pregnant, I could draw her picture.
> Thought, as a subtle juggler, makes us deem
> Things supernatural, which have cause
> Common as sickness. 'Tis my melancholy, –
> How cam'st thou by thy death? – how idle am I
> To question mine own idleness? – did ever
> Man dream awake till now? – remove this object –
> Out of my brain with't: what have I to do
> With tombs or death beds, funerals, or tears,
> That have to meditate upon revenge? (4.1.98–115)

It should not be forgotten that other Renaissance dramatists, especially Chapman and Jonson, are cited almost as often as Shakespeare.

If some degree of tension between the public and the private realms might have characterised and even structured Webster's life and work, *The Duchess of Malfi* might be seen as the dramatisation of a heroic, though doomed, attempt on the part of the Duchess and her secret husband Antonio ('crypto-Protestants', as they have been called by William Empson)[32] to carve out private life and private space in the midst of a corrupt, inexorably public court. When, during their private marriage *per verba de presenti*, apparently designed by the Duchess as an alternative to a church ceremony, Antonio raises the spectre of her brothers, she constitutes the private space by speech-act fiat:

> Do not think of them.
> All discord without this circumference
> Is only to be pitied and not feared. (1.2.377–9)

Bosola construes her body and the supposed (and true) pregnancy as a mystery, wishing to undress her down to a 'loose-bodied gown' (2.1.153–6) so that he can 'pluck out the heart of [her] mystery' – to quote Hamlet, another character deeply conflicted between private and public life. Of course, the 'fantastical scholar' Bosola himself, like Flamineo a former student from the University of Padua and arguably the character type in the corpus most congruent with Webster himself, employs an obscure style that is itself perceived to hide a mysterious secret: after a particularly knotty conceit used by the malcontent, Antonio professes 'I do understand your inside' (2.1.88). On the other side of the moral equation, Ferdinand's evil is construed to reside in some kind of mysterious interiority, both by others (3.1.21–3) and by himself:

> He that can compass me and know my drifts
> May say he hath put a girdle 'bout the world
> And sounded all her quicksands. (3.1.84–6)

The quixotic attempt to measure the depth of quicksand imagistically aligns itself with other forms of knowledge sceptically discredited in the play: physiognomy (1.2.152–5), popular superstition (2.2.69–73), mountebank remedies (3.1.70–7), and both astrology and Galilean astronomy (3.1.59–62). Still, Ferdinand appears confident that he can penetrate the Duchess's mystery, threatening that her 'darkest actions' and her 'privatest thoughts, will come to light' (1.2.231–2), and of course her marriage does become discovered.

This is not to erect a critical *cordon sanitaire* around the Duchess's virtue (hypostatising the Duchess's goodness into an abstract ideal so as to efface its vital cultural resonance), and Ferdinand's vice, the latter nicely traced into its misogynist cultural texts and contexts by feminist critics such as Leah S. Marcus and Dympna Callaghan,[33] but to see how the play itself thematises the divide between private and public consciousness – so important in this period of religious controversy. The Duchess's 'heroic marriage' to Antonio and her brave death, which if not averting her tragic end surely has a transformative effect on Bosola, surely does constitute an exemplary act of Stoic virtue – a generative type of virtuous act congruent with other exempla of virtue in the play[34] – but it also intervenes in crucial historical and social contexts, as the work of Marcus, Callaghan and others has demonstrated.

Notwithstanding the fact that the stylistic and generic variety of Webster's work, especially in its vital collaborative dimension, has been underappreciated, it is undeniable that his reputation has rested, and probably will continue to rest, on his two extant single-authored tragedies (if

Webster clearly admired the author of *Bussy D'Ambois*, his lost *Guise* provokes speculation as a Chapman-like foray into contemporary French political events). And at the centre of these two great tragedies, written at the height of both his literary and theatrical powers, lie two of the most compelling female protagonists in all of English early modern drama: Vittoria Corombona in *The White Devil* and the Duchess of Malfi. The title of Webster's first tragedy resonates ironically, not describing Vittoria but satirising the exaggerated responses to her by her accusers: first Montecelso and Francisco in the famous trial scene, and then her lover Bracciano, who has been credulously deceived by Francisco's amorous letter to her. Bracciano's violent exclamation 'How long have I beheld the devil in crystal?' (4.2.88) anticipates the clearly deranged responses of the equally choleric Ferdinand to his twin sister's marriage in *The Duchess of Malfi* (which many critics see as the return of repressed incestuous desire), which the cooler Cardinal attempts to check. After Montecelso 'expounds' the 'perfect character' of the whore to Vittoria in the trial scene (3.2.79–101), she convincingly refutes his typological portrait ('This character scapes me' [3.2.101]), suggesting the ways in which Webster employs his Theophrastan 'characters' added to Overbury's 1615 collection in particularising and critically challenging ways.

Webster deliberately represents Vittoria's role in the murders of Camillo and Isabella as indirect, resting on Flamineo's and Bracciano's interpretation of her enigmatic 'yew tree' dream. Before Vittoria says anything explicit, the scene is suddenly interrupted by the sudden entry of Vittoria's mother, whose stiff rebuke of her daughter's confirmed adultery resonates as valid, yet somehow uncompelling. Vittoria is magnificently 'virtuous' in the Machiavellian sense: a 'brave spirit', according to the English ambassador at her trial (3.2.140), a force of nature largely amoral, yet also keenly revealing the contradictions and corruptions of the misogynist court. What the Conjurer says of Bracciano might be even better applied to Vittoria as a trans-moral tragic principle: 'Both flowers and weeds spring when the sun is warm, / And great men do great good, or else great harm' (2.2.56–7).

It is surprising to note how many 'virtues' (in both the older and contemporary sense of the word) are transferred from Vittoria, the misnamed 'white devil', to the Duchess. In this respect true to her historical model, Vittoria protests that her love of 'beauty and gay clothes, a merry heart, / And a good stomach to a feast, are all, / All the poor crimes' that she can be charged of (3.2.208–10). Just as, with good reason, Vittoria argues that her attackers distort her festivity into the 'character' of a whore, so Ferdinand and the

Cardinal – examples of the choleric and the phlegmatic man, respectively – wilfully misread the Duchess. Says Ferdinand to her,

> I would have you to give over these changeable revels;
> A visor and a masque are whispering rooms
> That were ne'er built for goodness. (1.2.248–50)

In one respect the 'humorous' brothers are right: the Duchess's active, festive nature is indeed linked to her desire to remarry, and subversively so. The scenes between her, Antonio and Cariola, located within the private 'circumference' of the only court over which she (ephemerally) prevails, are full of wit, banter, festivity and even a bawdiness that, because linked to marriage, a Protestant citizen could celebrate. Negatively, the Duchess's clandestine marriage might evoke Lady Arabella Stuart, a cousin of James I who married secretly against his will, was imprisoned in the Tower, went mad and died in 1615. Positively, as Leah Marcus has noted, the Duchess counterpoints the barren Elizabeth I, providing 'a vision, albeit fleeting, of a radiant female ruler who has used her sexuality productively'[35] – and at the end of the play the eldest son of the Duchess and Antonio is ready to succeed her.

Not unlike Vittoria, the Duchess is theatrically virtuous, as she demonstrates with her 'magnanima mensogna' ('magnificent lie' [3.2.179]): the staged fiction that Antonio has stolen her jewels, thus allowing him to escape. But rather than ratcheting such theatricality up to the rapid pace of the revenger, as with Malevole of Marston and Webster's *The Malcontent*, or staging the flamboyant diva persona as he does with Vittoria, Webster fashions out of the Duchess's Stoic heroism what might be called the theatricality of immobility or stasis, epitomised in the famous line 'I am the Duchess of Malfi still' (4.2.137) and particularly arresting because of its contrast with the frenetic plotting of intriguers such as Bosola.[36] The two-dimensional virtue of the good characters Cornelia, Isabella and Marcello in *The White Devil*, structurally but somewhat flatly conceived as a *Gestus* contrasting the more numerous evil characters, becomes in the Duchess both fleshed out (even in the sexual sense) and interiorised, with language and conceit often interchangeable with Webster's 'monumental' tribute for Prince Henry. The life and death of the Duchess is sufficient to move the play's malcontent Bosola, also more fully interiorised than his counterpart Flamineo in the earlier tragedy. If Bosola might reflect the somewhat 'fantastical scholar' Webster himself, his tragic fate in the fiction of the play might also be seen to reflect the tension he suffers between public constraint and private interiority, which, in Webster's own life, seems to have been worked out more successfully.

NOTES

1 Mary Edmond, 'In Search of John Webster', *Times Literary Supplement*, 24 December 1976.

2 M. C. Bradbrook, *John Webster: Citizen and Dramatist* (London: Weidenfeld and Nicolson, 1980), 4.

3 Gerald Eades Bentley, *The Profession of Dramatist in Shakespeare's Time* (Princeton University Press, 1971), 199.

4 Bentley, *Profession of Dramatist*, 228–34.

5 John Webster, *The White Devil*, ed. John Russell Brown (London: Methuen 1960). Further references in the text derive from this edition.

6 'Notes from Black-Fryers' (1620), in *The Works of John Webster: An Old-Spelling Critical Edition*, ed. David Gunby, David Carnegie, Antony Hammond, Doreen DelVecchio and MacDonald P. Jackson, 3 vols. (Cambridge University Press, 1995–2007), 1 (1995), 15. Hereafter referred to as *Works* in the text.

7 John Webster, *The Duchess of Malfi*, ed. Leah S. Marcus (London: A. & C. Black, 2009), 1.1.60–6. Further references in the text derive from this edition.

8 Charles Forker, *The Skull Beneath the Skin: The Achievement of John Webster* (Carbondale and Edwardsville, IL: Southern Illinois University Press, 1986), 104.

9 Webster first collaborated with Dekker in the lost play *Caesar's Fall* in 1602, and well after writing *Westward Ho* and *Northward Ho* with him in 1604 and 1605, once more collaborated with him in 1624 in the lost play *A Late Murder of the Son upon the Mother, or, Keep the Widow Waking*. With Heywood, Webster's collaboration spans from 1602, when he probably wrote the first Lady Jane play with Heywood and several other dramatists (lost, but in a different form later published as *Sir Thomas Wyatt* in 1607), to 1627, when Webster and Heywood co-wrote *Appius and Virginia*. For the dates of Webster's single-authored and collaborative plays, see the chronological listing in Gunby, *et al.*, *The Works of John Webster*, 1, xxxii–xxxiii.

10 *Duchess of Malfi*, ed. Marcus, 9.

11 Also in a preface to the first edition of *The Duchess of Malfi* (1623) does Webster call the play a 'poem'. For a discussion of the tension between literary and theatrical impulses in Webster, see *Duchess of Malfi*, ed. Marcus, 7–8; and Lukas Erne, *Shakespeare as Literary Dramatist* (Cambridge University Press, 2003).

12 John Webster, *The Devil's Law-Case*, ed. Frances A. Shirley (Lincoln, NE: University of Nebraska Press, 1972), 4.

13 'The New Art of Making Comedies', available in English in Allan H. Gilbert, *Literary Criticism: Plato to Dryden* (Detroit: Wayne State University Press, 1962), 540–8.

14 Forker, *Skull Beneath the Skin*, 480.

15 'Four Elizabethan Dramatists', in *Selected Essays of T. S. Eliot* (London: Harcourt Brace Jovanovich, 1936), 96–7.

16 Eliot, 'Four Elizabethan Dramatists', 18.

17 Inga-Stina Ekeblad, 'The "Impure Art" of John Webster', in *Twentieth-Century Interpretations of 'The Duchess of Malfi'*, ed. Norman Rabkin (Englewood Cliffs, NJ: Prentice Hall, 1968), 49–64. For a critical discussion of the rich stage history of *The Duchess of Malfi* see Elizabeth Schafer, 'Troublesome Histories: Performance and Early Modern Drama', Chapter 16 in this volume, pp. 244–68.

18 *Works* I, 18–29.
19 *Duchess of Malfi*, ed. Marcus, note to 3.4.6.
20 *Works* II, 46.
21 Bradbrook, *John Webster*, 28–46.
22 G. K. Hunter, 'Italian Tragicomedy on the English Stage', *Renaissance Drama*, n.s. 6 (1973), 123–46.
23 Forker, *Skull Beneath the Skin*, 66–7.
24 *Works* III, 306.
25 Forker, *Skull Beneath the Skin*, 104.
26 The lost tragedy *Guise*, based on recent political events in France, was probably composed between 1614 and 1618, and so falls roughly within this period.
27 All dates, which refer to the first appearance of the play whether on stage or in print, are based on *Works* I, xxxii–xxxiii.
28 R. W. Dent, *John Webster's Borrowing* (Berkeley and Los Angeles, CA: University of California Press, 1960), 11–12.
29 *Duchess of Malfi*, ed. Marcus, 49.
30 *Duchess of Malfi*, ed. Marcus, 51.
31 Richard Allen Cave, *'The White Devil' and 'The Duchess of Malfi': Text and Performance* (London: Macmillan, 1988), 13; M. M. Bakhtin, 'The Problem of Speech Genres', in *Speech Genres and other Essays*, ed. Caryl Emerson and Michael Holquist, trans. Vern W. McGee (Austin, TX: University of Texas Press, 1986), 60–102.
32 *Duchess of Malfi*, ed. Marcus, 36.
33 *The Duchess of Malfi: Contemporary Critical Essays*, ed. Dympna Callaghan (London: Macmillan, 2000).
34 See the paradigm of the virtuous French court evoked by Antonio at the beginning of the play, or even fleeting references, usually counterpointing the more pervasive acts of evil, such as 'the primitive decency of the church' (1.2.82).
35 *Duchess of Malfi*, ed. Marcus, 14.
36 For a discussion of the theatrical power of stasis and silence in ancient Greek tragedy, see Kostas Valakas, 'The Use of the Body by Actors in Tragedy and Satyr Play', in *Greek and Roman Actors: Aspects of an Ancient Practice*, ed. Pat Easterling and Edith Hall (Cambridge University Press, 2002), 78–80.

Further reading

Callaghan, Dympna, ed., *The Duchess of Malfi: Contemporary Critical Essays*. London: Macmillan, 2000.

Cave, Richard Allen, *'The White Devil' and 'The Duchess of Malfi': Text and Performance*. London: Macmillan, 1988.

Dent, R. W., *John Webster's Borrowing*. Berkeley and Los Angeles, CA: University of California Press, 1960.

Dollimore, Jonathan, *Radical Tragedy: Religion, Ideology, and Power in the Drama of Shakespeare and his Contemporaries*, 3rd edn. Basingstoke: Palgrave Macmillan, 2004.

Luckyj, Christina, *A Winter's Snake: Dramatic Form in the Tragedies of John Webster*. Athens, GA, and London: University of Georgia Press, 1989.

McLuskie, Kathleen, and Jennifer Uglow, eds., *The Duchess of Malfi*. Bristol Classical Press, 1989.

Morris, Brian, *John Webster*. London: Ernest Benn, 1970.

Rabkin, Norman, ed., *Twentieth-Century Interpretations of 'The Duchess of Malfi': A Collection of Critical Essays*. Englewood Cliffs, NJ: Prentice Hall, 1968.

Webster, John, *The Duchess of Malfi*, ed. John Russell Brown, 2nd edn. Manchester University Press, 2009.

13

LISA HOPKINS

John Ford: suffering and silence in *Perkin Warbeck* and *'Tis Pity She's a Whore*

Almost every aspect of the life and career of John Ford (1586–c. 1637) presents us with a puzzle. We can be confident that he was the second son of Thomas Ford of Ilsington in Devon and his wife Elizabeth Popham, who was the niece of Sir John Popham, the Lord Chief Justice, and was related through her mother to the important South Welsh family of Stradling. One of the many important trials over which Popham presided was that of Sir Walter Raleigh, which Ford mentions in *The Golden Mean*, and the Stradling family included, among other interesting members, the Sir John Stradling who translated Justus Lipsius' *De Constantia*, whose Stoic outlook is very much in tune with Ford's own work. However, the name John Ford is such a common one (the dramatist shared it with at least one of his own cousins, John Ford of Gray's Inn, to whom he dedicated his play *Love's Sacrifice*) that we can never hope for absolute certainty when dealing with any of the later aspects of his career, and even when we can feel reasonably confident that we are dealing with the right man, the story tends to present oddities. The dramatist is probably the John Ford who attended Exeter College, Oxford, and went from there to the Middle Temple; however, he was never called to the bar, and his principal occupation and the source of his income remain a mystery, which is intensified by the fact that after the publication of his last known play, *The Lady's Trial*, in 1639 he disappears without trace.

The course of his writing career is no clearer than that of his adult life. In 1606, at the age of twenty, he published a poem, *Fame's Memorial*, mourning the death of Charles Blount, Earl of Devonshire, and a prose piece, *Honour Triumphant*, associated with the chivalric entertainments provided in connection with the visit of Christian IV of Denmark, brother-in-law of James I. Ford is also now usually accepted as the author of another elegy, on the Devon-born William Peter, which appeared in 1612; this was briefly and controversially attributed to Shakespeare, but the question of its authorship seems to have been settled by the publication of Brian Vickers's exhaustive study *'Counterfeiting' Shakespeare*.[1] In 1613 came the long religious poem *Christ's Bloody Sweat* and the moralising prose tract *A Line of Life*, whose title may perhaps glance punningly at the *Lignum Vitae* of St Bonaventure, whose name returns as that of the Friar in *'Tis Pity She's a Whore*. In 1619 another prose tract, *The Golden Mean*, brought to a close Ford's career of non-dramatic writing so far as we know it, and two years later came the first known collaborative play, *The Witch of Edmonton*, written together with Thomas Dekker and William Rowley. It is generally supposed that Ford contributed the Frank Thorney subplot of this, and certainly the emphasis on disturbed food rituals – it is the knife he uses to cut his chicken that reveals Frank's guilt of his wife's murder – is very much of a piece with the imagery of this kind later found in his single-authored plays. This was followed in 1623 by *The Welsh Ambassador*, a pseudo-historical tragicomedy, and a moral masque, *The Sun's Darling* in 1624, both also co-written with Dekker. There seem also to have been other plays, known now only by their titles: *An Ill Beginning has a Good End* (1613?); *Beauty in a Trance*, which was acted at court by the King's Men in 1630; *The London Merchant*;[2] some further collaborative works with Dekker, including *The Bristow Merchant*, *The Fairy Knight* and *A Late Murer of the Son Upon the Mother* (on the last of which John Webster also worked); and perhaps some involvement in the writing of *The Spanish Gipsy* (1623), *The Laws of Candy* (1619–23), *The Fair Maid of the Inn* (1626), and *The Great Favourite: Or, The Duke of Lerma*, which was published in 1668 as having been written by Sir Robert Howard but which seems to incorporate remnants of an older play.[3]

This chapter focuses chiefly on two of Ford's most distinctive works, *'Tis Pity She's a Whore*, his great tragedy of incest, and *Perkin Warbeck*, his belated, elegiac contribution to the proud tradition of the English history play, which begins by noting that

> Studies have, of this nature, been of late
> So out of fashion, so unfollowed, that
> It is become more justice to revive
> The antic follies of the times than strive
> To countenance wise industry.[4]

Ford, however, did not care that he was working in a genre which had fallen out of favour, for he was not a follower of fashion; in prologue after prologue he notes his disdain for popular opinion and current trends. His plays pursue an aesthetic agenda all his own, offering an eerie mixture of violence and bloodshed with a passive, Stoic sensibility. This can first be seen sketched out in his early non-dramatic work. The prose tract *The Golden Mean*, for instance, begins:

> Men, as they are all the Sonnes of their Mothers, are all the subjects of miserie
> … If men could as well frame their mindes to their change of fortunes, as their
> change of misfortunes doth corrupt their mindes, greatnesse would as truly
> welcome calamitie, as the base doe rejoyce in being great.[5]

This sense that the only true nobility lies in lofty disdain of earthly acci-
dents is a keynote in all Ford's work, and though he dedicated most of
his plays to members of the nobility ('Tis Pity She's a Whore to the Earl
of Peterborough, Perkin Warbeck to the Earl of Newcastle), he does so in
terms which habitually distinguish between the mere accident of title and
true merit of character, as when he writes in his dedication to the Earl of
Peterborough that 'Greatness cannot often claim virtue by inheritance', or in
that to Newcastle that 'Eminent titles may indeed inform who their owners
are, not often what'.

The earlier of the two plays I shall be discussing, though it is impossible
to know by how much, is 'Tis Pity She's a Whore. The dating of this is
almost as difficult to determine as the dramatist's attitude towards his err-
ing but hugely vibrant characters. It was published in 1631, along with The
Broken Heart and Love's Sacrifice, but many critics have suggested that it
'feels' earlier, and indeed some have proposed that it may have been written up to twenty years previously. This strange and troubling play is set in
Parma and tells the story of an incestuous brother and sister, Giovanni and
Annabella. It opens with Giovanni confessing his love to his confidant Friar
Bonaventura, who immediately reproves him in terms which might recall
the religiously motivated execrations which a generation earlier had been
raised against both Christopher Marlowe himself and his characters Doctor
Faustus and Tamburlaine:

> wits that presumed
> On wit too much, by striving how to prove
> There was no God, with foolish grounds of art,
> Discovered first the nearest way to hell,
> And filled the world with devilish atheism.[6]

Giovanni, however, is unmoved. It is not clear how far he initially tries
to follow the Friar's advice to 'Cry to thy heart, wash every word thou
utter'st / In tears and, if't be possible, of blood' (1.1.72–3) (in Giuseppe
Patroni Griffi's 1971 film of the play, entitled Addio, fratello crudele, which
took the idea of incest as a metaphor for the director's own homosexuality, Oliver Tobias's Giovanni jumps down a well at this point, which
might suggest a particularly radical form of washing) but soon enough
he is revealing his love to Annabella, who admits that she reciprocates it
and is not hindered by her amoral guardian Putana. The affair continues

for some time while Annabella fends off her various suitors: the foolish ward Bergetto, the unsavoury but well-connected Grimaldi, and Soranzo, a local nobleman who is engaged in hostilities with both his rival Grimaldi and his cast-off mistress Hippolita. Hippolita in turn provides the main structural link to a subplot in which her husband Richardetto, supposed dead but actually disguised as a doctor, hatches two separate plans, one to marry his niece Philotis to Bergetto and the other to have Grimaldi kill his own rival Soranzo. These become fatally entangled, leading to Grimaldi mistakenly killing Bergetto but being shielded from justice by the all-powerful Cardinal, and the bereaved Philotis entering a convent. Annabella meanwhile has discovered that she is pregnant and on the advice of the Friar agrees to marry Soranzo. Hippolita thinks she has suborned Soranzo's servant Vasques to help her poison Soranzo at the wedding feast, but Vasques double-crosses her and she inadvertently poisons herself instead, leading the Friar to observe 'that marriage seldom's good / Where the bride-banquet so begins in blood' (4.2.110–11). Annabella and Soranzo are no sooner married than her pregnancy becomes apparent and the outraged Soranzo threatens to kill her unless she confesses the identity of the father, but Vasques persuades him to dissemble and pretend to forgive her while he himself extracts the information from Annabella's terrified guardian Putana, whom he then blinds. Soranzo invites Giovanni to what he says is a feast for his birthday while Annabella, weeping alone on her balcony, is seen by the Friar, who persuades her to repent. She asks him to convey a letter of penitence and warning to Giovanni, but Giovanni will have none of it. The Friar, despairing of him, leaves Parma while Giovanni heads to Soranzo's house where he kills Annabella and appears at the banquet with her heart impaled on his dagger. After revealing the whole story, upon which his father Florio dies of shock, Giovanni stabs Soranzo and is himself stabbed by Vasques. The Cardinal confiscates everyone's goods for the church, banishes Vasques (who reveals that he is a Spaniard) from Italy, and orders the blinded Putana to be burnt.

Like *Perkin Warbeck*, *'Tis Pity She's a Whore* both draws on and inverts a tradition. The idea of incest had been flirted with by a number of dramatists, including Francis Beaumont and John Fletcher in *A King and No King* and Middleton in *Women Beware Women*, but actual incest had usually been averted at the last moment when the pair who are attracted to each other are revealed not to be biologically related to each other after all. *Women Beware Women* had challenged this pattern by having Livia pretend that her niece Isabella is not a biological relative of her supposed uncle but then reveal that she actually is, and Ford remembers this, for the Bergetto and

Poggio subplot of *'Tis Pity She's a Whore* draws on the Ward and Sordido episodes in *Women Beware Women*. However, Hippolito and Isabella are only uncle and niece, which was indeed a degree of relationship already tolerated by the Habsburgs, with Philip II of Spain having married his niece Anna of Austria in 1570. Annabella and Giovanni are full brother and sister, which is surely more shocking.

What has really shocked many of Ford's critics, though, is that Ford himself does not appear to be shocked at all. His tone throughout is cool and dispassionate; indeed he approaches the dissection of the incestuous lovers' relationship almost as clinically as Giovanni does the dissection of his sister's body, as when he ludicrously demands:

> 'tis a heart,
> A heart my lords, in which is mine entombed.
> Look well upon't; d'ee know't? (5.6.26–8)

Ford also sprinkles the play liberally with signposts to intellectual issues which might well seem to take precedence over emotional response. The fact that Giovanni has studied at Bologna, for instance, seems designed to invite us to read his actions in terms of the culture's growing obsesssion with anatomy and the interior of the body, especially in the wake of Gabriel Harvey's announcement in *De Motu Cordis* (1628) of his discovery of the circulation of the blood, for Bologna was a centre for such studies.[7] Equally, when the Cardinal challenges the townspeople over their attempted arrest of Grimaldi and asserts that they have now entered his jurisdiction, we are surely invited to contemplate the uncertain boundary between political and ecclesiastical authority:

> Why, how now, friends! what saucy mates are you
> That know nor duty nor civility? (3.9.30–1)

The attention paid to the contrast between the Friar and the Cardinal might well focus the mind on issues of faith and confession, as might Giovanni's musing on the afterlife, the fact that Annabella is first seen on the balcony and reascends to it when she repents, and the obvious parody of the Annunciation when she tells Soranzo that

> This noble creature was in every part
> So angel-like, so glorious, that a woman,
> Who had not been but human as was I,
> Would have kneeled to him, and have begged for love. (4.3.36–9)

So too might the fact that the play, like much of Ford's work, was dedicated to someone whose family was strongly associated with Catholicism (in 1625 the head of the English mission was operating out of the home of the Earl of Peterborough's mother).

Other aspects of the play seem similarly calculated to prompt a measured rather than a gut reaction. Giovanni's reference to Juno ('Juno for her forehead did exceed / All other goddesses' [1.2.193–4]) might prompt the audience to remember that incest had traditionally been tolerated fictionally in creation myths and factually in ruling families, not least by the Habsburgs, of whom a scion was currently ruling Parma, which Ford chooses as the setting for his play; it is though rather different for someone like Annabella, to whom Hippolita cuttingly refers as 'Your goodly Madam Merchant' (2.2.49).[8] At the same time as the audience was registering such ideas, moreover, they might well feel further induced to respond intellectually rather than emotionally by the clear invitations to spot the deliberate inversion of Shakespeare's *Romeo and Juliet* (both plays feature young lovers attended by a nurse and a friar, but this time the marriage is too much within the family rather than too far outside it) as well as the obvious borrowings from *Women Beware Women*, just as Soranzo, contemplating the beauty of Annabella, reaches mentally for the literary tradition represented by Jacopo Sannazaro (2.2.1–17) rather than falling back on personal experience. The whole experience might indeed seem to be the polar opposite of the Muse's exhortation to Astrophel, in Sir Philip Sidney's *Astrophel and Stella*, to 'look in thy heart and write'.[9] Ford, we might think, looks in his head and writes, and encourages us to respond in the same way, just as in *The Lover's Melancholy* the emotional effect of music is described rather than staged and experienced in Menaphon's description of the singing contest between the supposed Parthenophil and a nightingale.[10]

And yet it is inside his sister's heart that Giovanni so famously looks, when he cuts it out and enters the stage with it impaled on a dagger in a stage picture which surely cries out for an emotional rather than an intellectual response, and this is supplemented by the way in which the very mention of incest speaks to the visceral, irrational power of the taboo. 'Her own brother? O horrible!' (4.3.236–7) exclaims Vasques, who ought to be concerned solely with the blemish on his master's honour, which is equally grave no matter who has inflicted it, but who nevertheless pauses to register a moment of pure revulsion which has nothing to do with his plans for revenge.

Something similar is achieved by the play's handling of the Bergetto subplot, which has a very different tonality from its original in *Women Beware Women*: there the Ward is simply brutish, but Bergetto is more than that, and it would be a very insensitive reader or audience member who failed to register and respond to the genuine affection which links him to both Poggio and Philotis, as when he asks Poggio 'didst see the codpiece-point she gave me, and the box of marmalade?' (3.1.11–12), which touches his story with pathos even if not with tragedy. In the end, perhaps the play's title is not as flippant and dismissive as it seems: it is, in fact, a pity that Annabella cannot fulfil the place that her society has allocated to her, and that as a direct result of that so much of that society collapses.

Perkin Warbeck works very differently. Weaving together elements from two principal sources, Francis Bacon's *History of the Reign of King Henry VII* (1622) and Thomas Gainsford's *The True and Wonderful History of Perkin Warbeck* (1618), Ford focuses on the elusive and contested figure of the fifteenth-century pretender to the throne Perkin Warbeck, arguably the most important of several actual or self-proclaimed survivors from the previous Yorkist regime to trouble the newly established Tudor king Henry VII, who had killed Richard III, the last king of the house of York, at the Battle of Bosworth in 1485. According to the received narrative, not least as told in Shakespeare's play about him, Richard III had not only usurped the throne from his young nephew Edward IV but had imprisoned both little Edward and his younger brother Richard, Duke of York in the Tower, where both were secretly murdered. Perkin Warbeck, however, claims that he himself is the younger prince, Richard of York, and had survived by some miracle which he is coy about specifying.

The first part of Ford's play is set in Scotland, where Perkin Warbeck is received with honour by the young and headstrong James IV, who not only recognises Perkin as his kinsman and peer but arranges a marriage for him with his cousin Lady Katherine Gordon despite the fact that she is already courted by the noble but impoverished Daliell. Katherine and Perkin form a loving relationship but Perkin is less successful in the field, and James becomes disillusioned when various forays into northern England fail to elicit any local support. When Henry VII sends an ambassador to offer James a marriage with his daughter Margaret Tudor if he will dismiss Perkin from his court, James agrees. Perkin and Katherine head south, accompanied by the devoted Daliell, Katherine's faithful maid Jane and Perkin's ragbag train of disreputable Irish hangers-on. They try to capitalise on local economic discontent in Cornwall, but Perkin suddenly leaves the camp – it is not clear whether he simply runs away or learns that he is about to be betrayed – and is captured by Henry's forces. At this point Ford telescopes events so that we learn in rather rapid retrospect that Perkin is initially imprisoned and offered the same sort of clemency as had already been shown to Lambert Simnel, a previous pretender now working in Henry's kitchens (where he famously invented Simnel cake), whom we see taunting Perkin. However, after Perkin escapes from the Tower and is recaptured Henry finally decides to execute him. He takes a dignified farewell of Katherine, who has been treated well by Henry but who vows to refuse any offer of a better second marriage, and resolves to die nobly.

In *'Tis Pity She's a Whore*, we know that Giovanni and Annabella are brother and sister, and we are overwhelmingly likely to share the general assumption that incest is wrong. In *Perkin Warbeck* we cannot be sure who the hero really is and we therefore have no idea what we should think about him. Is he really, as he says, the younger of the two Princes in the Tower, nephews of Richard III – and if so how on earth did he escape? – or is he, as Lambert Simnel claims and as historians have generally concluded, a Flemish-born pretender:

> Your pedigree is published; you are known
> For Osbeck's son of Tournai, a loose runagate,
> A landloper. Your father was a Jew,
> Turned Christian merely to repair his miseries. (5.3.21–5)

And if so what on earth motivates his sustained and determined imposture, and what accounts for the fact that, as Miles Taylor observes, 'the playwright avoids including the public confession he found in his sources and neglects to invent a private confession'?[11] This radical uncertainty represents a significant departure from the well-established tradition of the English history play, where part of the point had been that the audience could be expected to be in full possession of the major facts of the story from the outset.

Ford shows himself very well aware of this tradition through a number of significant debts to Marlowe's *Edward II* and Shakespeare's *Richard II* in particular, as well as *Richard III*, which is remembered when Daliell says that Perkin has fled because 'by some secret friend he had intelligence / Of being bought and sold by his base followers' (5.1.67–8), echoing the earlier play's 'Jockey of Norfolk, be not so bold, / For Dickon thy master is bought and sold'.[12] Indeed, towards the beginning of Ford's play, Durham offers what can effectively stand as a summing-up of the events previously chronicled by the genre so far:

> For ninety years ten English kings and princes,
> Threescore great dukes and earls, a thousand lords
> And valiant knights, two hundred fifty thousand
> Of English subjects have in civil wars
> Been sacrificed to an uncivil thirst
> Of discord and ambition. (1.1.16–21)

In the traditional history play, however, the weight of a great public past presses heavily on characters who are radically constituted not as individuals but as products and conduits of their heritage, their social rank and the acts of their ancestors, which the audience will in many cases already have seen dramatised. *Perkin Warbeck* is completely different from this. Insofar as it has a chronological relationship with any existing history play, it could as equally be one of direct contradiction rather than continuation, since the story which Perkin Warbeck tells would imply that much of what we are told in Shakespeare's *Richard III* was not true, for if he is telling the truth at least one of the Princes in the Tower must have survived, and we are told in *Richard III* that both have been killed.

Another way in which *Perkin Warbeck* differs from previous examples of the English history play is that it does not confine its interests and actions to England. Although the action in Shakespeare's history plays frequently moves to France, it only occasionally ventures into Wales and never into Ireland or Scotland. *Perkin Warbeck*, though, announces its setting as 'The Continent of Great Britain'. Ford knew this was a contested term: the commissioners appointed to look into the question of the protection of fishing rights, something at which, as we shall see, *Perkin Warbeck* glances, asked Charles 'to style himself in all documents "King of England, Scotland, France and Ireland," so that Scotland might no longer be confounded "under the name of Great Britaine, altho there be no unioun as yitt with England nor the style of Great Britane received there"'.[13] The play also declares in its prologue that

> We cannot limit scenes, for the whole land
> Itself, appeared too narrow to withstand
> Competitors for kingdoms. (Prologue, 21–3)

This is a play which insistently registers the impact of foreign affairs, as when a Spanish ambassador, with whom the King of England has already discussed Ferdinand and Isabella (3.3.3–4), discusses the current international scene with a politically minded English bishop:

HIALAS: France, Spain, and Germany combine a league
          Of amity with England; nothing wants
          For setting peace through Christendom but love
          Between the British monarchs, James and Henry.
DURHAM: The English merchants, sir, have been received
          With general procession into Antwerp;
          The Emperor confirms the combination.
HIALAS: The King of Spain resolves a marriage
          For Catherine his daughter with Prince Arthur.
DURHAM: France courts this holy contract.
HIALAS: What can hinder
          A quietness in England? (4.3.1–11)

The Welsh magnate Sir Rhys ap Thomas is also mentioned (5.2.20), and we hear of how

> Ten thousand Cornish,
> Grudging to pay your subsidies, have gathered
> A head, led by a blacksmith and a lawyer;
> They make for London. (1.3.129–32)

We also see a masque of *'four Scotch Antics, accordingly habited'* and *'four wild Irish in trouses, long-haired, and accordingly habited'* (3.2.112–14), in one of a number of scenes set in Scotland. Willy Maley suggests that this 'seems both to recall and parody Ben Jonson's *Irish Masque at Court* (1613)', so that *Perkin Warbeck* is thus positioning itself not only within the tradition of the history play but also within the tradition of writing about the court.[14] This is particularly pertinent given the play's dedication to William Cavendish, Earl of Newcastle, who was one of the principal advocates of the idea that the king should always take care to consult the views of his nobility (as Henry in *Perkin Warbeck* pointedly does and as James IV equally pointedly does not).[15]

Nevertheless, *Perkin Warbeck* presents itself as the last English history play – indeed Miles Taylor terms it 'a history play about the end of history plays'[16] – as Warbeck himself makes clear when he says:

> Our ends, and Warwick's head,
> Innocent Warwick's head – for we are prologue
> But to his tragedy – concludes the wonder
> Of Henry's fears; and then the glorious race
> Of fourteen kings, Plantagenets, determines
> In this last issue male. (5.3.189–94)

Perkin is clearly including himself among the last male issue of the Plantagenets, but even if we do not concur, Warwick undoubtedly is the last male scion of the house, and during the course of the play we have been privy to the conversations and machinations that will ensure his execution. In the decade before the execution of Charles I, Ford might well seem to be prescient in thus staging the end of a dynasty, but it is important to remember that he is simultaneously staging the birth of one, for the marriage between Margaret Tudor and James IV which is envisaged at the end of the play will be that through which the Stuarts will eventually claim the throne of England.

Perhaps because of its sense of belatedness, the play feels at liberty to set its own aesthetic agenda. In the Prologue, it sets out its stall as

> a history couched in a play.
> A history of noble mention, known,
> Famous and true: most noble 'cause our own;
> Not forged from Italy, from France, from Spain,
> But chronicled at home. (Prologue, 14–18)

Declaring an unequivocal allegiance to what is 'true' and 'chronicled' rather than what is 'forged' (and implicitly equating 'truth' with what is domestic and 'forgery' with what is foreign), Ford also uses the Prologue to proclaim the seriousness of the play:

> Nor is here
> Unnecessary mirth forced, to endear
> A multitude. On these two rests the fate
> Of worthy expectation: Truth and State. (Prologue, 23–6)

There is no Falstaff here, there are no grotesquely comic moments of Richard III demanding the death of yet another enemy; instead there is misunderstood nobility and a profound sense of loss and waste.

Another aspect of its historical belatedness is its notably secularising perspective. In *Richard III*, ghosts appear, and in *1 Henry VI*, Joan receives diabolical assistance from her fiends. In *Perkin Warbeck*, however, the idea of the supernatural is introduced only to be revealed as a metaphor rather than an actuality. The play opens with Henry's lines:

> Still to be haunted, still to be pursued,
> Still to be frighted with false apparitions
> Of pageant majesty and new-coined greatness,
> As if we were a mockery king in state,
> Only ordained to lavish sweat and blood
> In scorn and laughter to the ghosts of York. (1.1.1–6)

There is also repeated imagery of witchcraft, but the overall effect, as in *The Witch of Edmonton*, is essentially secularising, with human action seen as socially rather than supernaturally produced, as we see when Urswick dismisses Perkin's continued claims of royal birth with:

> Thus witches,
> Possessed, even to their deaths deluded, say
> They have been wolves, and dogs, and sailed in egg-shells
> Over the sea, and rid on fiery dragons. (5.3.103–6)

While the role of the supernatural in Shakespeare's history plays is too complex and subtle for proper discussion here, destabilising the idea of an overarching supernatural order in this way clearly contrasts with practice in history plays in general, since it effectively forecloses on any possibility of the strongly teleological orientation of earlier, cruder history plays such as *The Troublesome Reign of King John*, *The Famous Victories of Henry V* and *The Famous History of Sir Thomas Wyatt*, which presented events firmly within a framework of England's Protestant destiny.[17] In *Perkin Warbeck*, not only can we not be sure who the hero is, but we also cannot feel sure that what happens to him is divinely ordained for the ultimate good of the realm (something further complicated by the fact that in this case we are so pointedly dealing with realms in the plural, whose interests are clearly not identical).

In one respect, however, *Perkin Warbeck* does indeed channel the spirit of its predecessors, for like them it proves to be using the past as a safe veneer for the discussion of the dangerous politics of the present. There is a very pointed reference to a contemporary political issue when the Scottish herald, Marchmount, tells the Earl of Surrey that James IV of Scotland is offering him single combat,

> fairly
> Proposing these conditions only, that
> If victory conclude our master's right,
> The earl shall deliver for his ransom
> The town of Berwick to him, with the fishgarths. (4.1.28–32)

The question of fisheries in Scottish waters was one of acute political interest. In his history of the royal fisheries of the seventeenth century, John R. Elder notes that Charles I 'set himself, almost immediately on his accession, to devise some means of establishing the British fisheries as a national industry worthy of the name', in the wake of the Dutch having asked for permission to fish in Scottish waters in 1594.[18] One of the problems the king faced was the different Scottish and English understandings of the scope and extent of territorial waters, so that fishgarths in a town like Berwick, which was located on the actual border, would be subject to two different interpretations of where they began and ended, in ways which were of acute political interest at the time Ford was writing.

Ford was on even more pointedly political and in this case dangerous ground when Daliell makes the apparently innocuous observation that

> I could add more; and in the rightest line
> Derive my pedigree from Adam Mure,
> A Scottish knight, whose daughter was the mother
> To him that first begot the race of Jameses
> That sway the sceptre to this very day.
> But kindreds are not ours when once the date

> Of many years have swallowed up the memory
> Of their originals; so pasture fields,
> Neighbouring too near the ocean, are supped up
> And known no more. (1.2.29–38)

Peter Ure has shown that in 1633–4, when the play was first performed and published, this seemingly innocent comment actually packed a huge political punch, for it glances at an incident which embarrassed Charles I and, in the year of his Scottish coronation, had the potential to strike at the very heart of the Stuart claim to the throne of Scotland by reminding the audience that there was doubt about the legitimacy of Robert II's marriage to Elizabeth Mure, from which the Stuart kings were descended.[19] Moreover, Daliell's observation that the force of ancestry is diluted by the passage of time is surely equally applicable not only to the scions of kings but also to kings themselves, while his image of the contours of the land diminishing and changing over the course of time carries an eerie and unnerving force.

In the end, however, Daliell, like Perkin, can only register a protest against the march of history rather than make any real attempt to change it. The characters of the play are acutely aware of the processes and protocols of their own inscription in history. Katherine says to Daliell,

> It shall be my delight that worthy love
> Leads you to worthy actions, and these guide ye
> Richly to wed an honourable name,
> So every virtuous praise in after ages
> Shall be your heir, and I, in your brave mention,
> Be chronicled the mother of that issue,
> That glorious issue. (1.2.151–7)

Perkin too has an eye to posterity:

> But let the world, as all to whom I am
> This day a spectacle, to time deliver,
> And by tradition fix posterity,
> Without another chronicle than truth,
> How constantly my resolution suffered
> A martyrdom of majesty! (5.3.69–74)

Ford here echoes the Stoicism of his cousin Sir John Stradling, translator of Lipsius, and once again reminds us of the core value of his work: that the only true nobility lies in dignified surrender to indignity and suffering, and that posthumous reputation is the thing most worth caring about. This sensitivity to the opinion of posterity is found in 'Tis Pity She's a Whore too: immediately before Giovanni stabs Annabella he assures her that

> If ever after-times should hear
> Of our fast-knit affections, though perhaps
> The laws of conscience and of civil use
> May justly blame us, yet when they but know
> Our loves, that love will wipe away the rigour
> Which would in other incests be abhorred. (5.5.68–73)

In both *Perkin Warbeck* and *'Tis Pity She's a Whore*, then, Ford may not be willing to offer his audience much guidance on what their response should be or even to confirm the real identity of one of the key characters to whom they are responding, but he leaves the audience in no doubt that it is their responses, engagement and opinions which make his plays truly come alive.

NOTES

1 Brian Vickers, *'Counterfeiting' Shakespeare: Evidence, Authorship and John Ford's 'Funerall Elegye'* (Cambridge University Press, 2002).

2 I have argued elsewhere that some traces of this may survive; see Lisa Hopkins, 'Lillo's *The London Merchant*: An Elizabethan Palimpsest?', *English Language Notes* 36:2 (December, 1998), 4–11.

3 See Alfred Harbage, 'Elizabethan-Restoration Palimpsest', *Modern Language Review* 35 (1940), 287–319.

4 John Ford, *Perkin Warbeck*, in *'Tis Pity She's a Whore and Other Plays*, ed. Marion Lomax (Oxford University Press, 1995), Prologue, 1–5. All further quotations from the play are taken from this edition and reference is given in the text.

5 John Ford, *The Golden Mean*, in *The Nondramatic Works of John Ford*, ed. L. E. Stock, Gilles D. Monsarrat, Judith M. Kennedy and Dennis Danielson (Binghamton, NY: Medieval and Renaissance Texts and Studies, 1991), 241.

6 John Ford, *'Tis Pity She's a Whore*, ed. Derek Roper (London: Methuen, 1975), 1.1.4–8. All further quotations from the play are taken from this edition and reference is given in the text.

7 On the Renaissance interest in anatomy in general, see Jonathan Sawday, *The Body Emblazoned: Dissection and the Human Body in Renaissance Culture* (London: Routledge, 1995); on its pertinence for *'Tis Pity She's a Whore*, see for instance Christian Billing, 'Modelling the Anatomy Theatre and the Indoor Hall Theatre: Dissection on the Stages of Early Modern London', *Early Modern Literary Studies* special edition 13 (2004), available online at http://extra.shu.ac.uk/emls/si-13/billing/index.htm; Catherine Silverstone, 'Fatal Attraction: Desire, Anatomy and Death in *'Tis Pity She's a Whore*'; and Mark Houlahan, 'The Deconstructing *'Tis Pity*?: Derrida, Barthes and Ford', both in *'Tis Pity She's a Whore: A Critical Guide*, ed. Lisa Hopkins, Continuum Renaissance Drama Guides (London: Continuum, 2010), respectively 77–93 and 136–51.

8 On the choice of setting, see for instance my 'Incest and Class: *'Tis Pity She's a Whore* and the Borgias', in *Incest and the Literary Imagination,* ed. Elizabeth Barnes (Gainesville, FL: University Press of Florida, 2002), 94–113.

9 Sir Philip Sidney, *Sir Philip Sidney: Selected Poems*, ed. Katherine Duncan-Jones (Oxford: Clarendon Press, 1973), 117.

10 John Ford, *The Lover's Melancholy*, ed. R. F. Hill (Manchester University Press, 1985), 1.1.98–153.

11 Miles Taylor, 'The End of the English History Play in *Perkin Warbeck*', *Studies in English Literature* 48:2 (spring 2009), 395–418 at 404.

12 *Richard III*, ed. James R. Siemon, Arden Third Series (London: A. & C. Black, 2009), 5.3.304–5. On the ways in which *Perkin Warbeck* echoes Shakespearean history plays, see also Willy Maley, *Nation, State and Empire in English Renaissance Literature* (Basingstoke: Palgrave, 2003), 130–1.

13 John R. Elder, *The Royal Fishery Companies of the Seventeenth Century* (Glasgow: James Maclehose and Sons, 1912), 41.

14 Maley, *Nation, State and Empire in English Renaissance Literature*, 127.

15 For comment on this, see Irving Ribner, *The English History Play in the Age of Shakespeare* (Princeton University Press, 1957), 302.

16 Taylor, 'The End of the English History Play in *Perkin Warbeck*', 395.

17 See Judith Doolin Spikes, 'The Jacobean History Play and the Myth of the Elect Nation', *Renaissance Drama* n.s. 8 (1977), 117–49.

18 Elder, *The Royal Fishery Companies of the Seventeenth Century*, 38.

19 Peter Ure, 'A Pointer to the Date of Ford's *Perkin Warbeck*', *Notes and Queries* 17:6 (1970), 215–17.

Further reading

Anderson, Donald K., Jr, *'Concord in Discord': The Plays of John Ford, 1586–1986*. New York: AMS Press, 1986.

Hopkins, Lisa, *Drama and the Succession to the Crown*. Aldershot: Ashgate, 2011.
    John Ford's Political Theatre. Manchester University Press, 1994.

Lomax, Marion, *Stage Images and Traditions: Shakespeare to Ford*. Cambridge University Press, 1987.

Neill, Michael, ed., *John Ford: Critical Re-Visions*. Cambridge University Press, 1988.

Randall, Dale, B. J., *'Theatres of Greatness': A Revisionary View of Ford's Perkin Warbeck*. Victoria, BC: English Literary Studies, 1986.

14

RUI CARVALHO HOMEM

Philip Massinger: drama, reputation and the dynamics of social history

Philip Massinger (1583–1640) has long been a challenging subject for criticism. For many, he was definitively put to rest by T. S. Eliot's notorious 1920 essay, which in no uncertain terms declared his work 'inferior' and accused him of having 'initiated' the historical split between emotion and intellect that Eliot was famously to dub 'dissociation of sensibility'. Eliot's description of a dramatist swayed by conventions while lacking emotions or imagination, whose verse suffered from 'cerebral anaemia' and whose dramatic skills revealed a lack of awareness of people, still resonates nearly a century later as a disincentive to encounter Massinger (especially on the page).[1] However, this indictment was only one late but influential example of the alternating reactions that have accompanied Massinger's work since his own time, revealing not only the instability of his reputation, but also his remarkable capacity to remain on the critical record.

The sheer facts of Massinger's career show that he was unquestionably successful in his lifetime. He began, in the 1610s, by writing collaborative work (with John Fletcher and others), but went on to write independently and indeed became chief playwright for the King's Men after Fletcher's death in 1625. He is believed to have authored or co-authored over fifty plays, of which thirty-three have survived (fifteen of single authorship). He enjoyed significant stage triumphs, and may in fact have been 'the most commercially successful dramatist of his day'.[2] However, the reactions of his contemporaries set the tone for both the admiration and the opprobrium that he would later receive. Thomas Jay, in commendatory verses to *The Roman Actor* (1629; first performed 1626), praised Massinger's elevated diction or 'loftie straine', and the performative qualities of his dramatic language, which 'can / Giue Swords, and legions to DOMITIAN'; while the rival playwright William Davenant (in the context of theatrical quarrels of the 1630s) had no qualms in damning the supposedly 'flat / dull dialogues' of 'this Mechanicke play-wright' who offered 'no Character entire'.[3]

Assessments of Massinger's work and of his place in literary and dramatic history in the period after the heyday of Shakespeare and Jonson have largely oscillated between praise for his theatrical sense and rhetorical sophistication, and denigration of his weak and inconstant characterisation and unadventurous language. The vagaries of his reputation reflect trends in intellectual and cultural history, but also elements of accident – the contentiousness of the literary-theatrical scene and the effects of fashion as much as faction. In unknown measure, such factors probably contributed to the crucial omission of any reference to Massinger in the folios containing what was to become known as the works of 'Beaumont and Fletcher', published in 1647 and 1679, which thus failed to relay to literary and theatrical posterity any notion of his role in co-authoring that canon. Further, personal taste could run counter to dominant opinion, causing contemporaries to differ. Massinger enjoyed a significant vogue in the late eighteenth and early nineteenth centuries (largely reflecting, on page and stage, the respective efforts of William Gifford as editor, and Edmund Kean as actor of some of his plays). However, William Hazlitt made no secret of the fact that he found Massinger 'harsh and crabbed', offering 'not exactly what we look for in poetry', whereas Coleridge, at around the same time, was praising his skills with regard to plot and 'dramatic versification'.[4] The latter part of the century was to bring Leslie Stephen's memorable dictum of 1877 on the perception of a loss of emotional vigour 'when we turn to Massinger' after reading Shakespeare or Jonson: 'The blood has grown cool.'[5] And this diagnosis in fact pointed forward to Eliot's denunciation, which would prove crucial for the ensuing currency of 'a recognisably modernist view of Massinger', based on formally exigent critical expectations that were to prevail in mid-twentieth-century Anglo-American criticism – in the light of which Massinger was found wanting.[6]

The recovery of an interest in Massinger since the last quarter of the twentieth century can likewise be seen to reflect current concerns, which in this case have involved revaluing aspects of his career and reputation that had previously been liabilities. Indeed, the counter-canonical tendencies that have pervaded criticism in recent decades, involving a sceptical approach to the hierarchies that underlie literary fame, can bring renewed attention to a playwright who, despite his substantial oeuvre and stage successes in different contexts, has so often been the object of negative comparisons. Aspects that historically caused Massinger to appear as the underdog of late Jacobean and Caroline drama, but may now contribute to a renewed interest in his work, include forms of social prejudice that affected his reputation in his own day and age – when poets and rival playwrights associated with the court scorned this professional dramatist for his relatively modest origins (his father, though a gentleman, was a steward of the Earl of Pembroke).[7] The strong element of collaboration in his early writing, and the sense that literary history has given him less than his due in this regard, gain increased relevance in the light of the current interest in co-authorship in early modern English drama.[8] Recent readings of Massinger's work have also tended to draw on the contradictory nature of his politics, which ranges from the most conservative, static and deferential pronouncements on power and society to forms of characterisation that suggest an under-standing of the socially constructed nature of the self. His representations of gender roles have even led to claims that he espoused an *avant-la-lettre* 'rec-ognition of the rights of women'.[9] Further, Massinger's practices as regards genre can appeal to a readership interested in elements of incoherence or hybridity: he wrote 'a gallimaufry of tragedies, satiric comedies, tragicom-edies, and permutations of these kinds', a generic fluidity that arguably finds a rhetorical correlative in the claim that 'metamorphosis ... becomes one of Massinger's ruling motifs'.[10] This latter trait may in turn be connected to Massinger's fascination with theatricality, as displayed in his frequent use of the play-within-the-play – which a recent critic has hailed as 'the foundation of Massinger's dramaturgy'.[11]

A common element to these critical views, and one that can prove help-ful when dealing with specific aspects of Massinger's plays, is the tension between stasis and dynamics, immobility and change. This tension is argu-ably intrinsic to all drama in the sense that a dramatic plot usually thrives on conflict and on the dislocations undergone by divergent wills as they interact and evolve towards the recomposition brought about by the play's denouement. But the crucial (and often swift) transformations that char-acterised the early modern period – in politics, society, religion, the econ-omy – have accorded particular relevance to critical notions based on the tension between mobility and change: hence, Stephen Greenblatt's view that the period witnessed the rise of a 'mobile sensibility', and the currency of arguments grounded on oppositions such as constraint vs mobility, or con-tainment vs subversion.[12] Massinger's much discussed 'transitional' place in seventeenth-century drama, combined with his preoccupation with social change, expressed in the years of growing instability that preceded the Civil War, certainly brings his work within range of these concerns. Further, an awareness of the tension between stasis and mobility in Massinger's plots may shed some light on his handling of dramatic form, particularly the chal-lenges posed by genre. Massinger has been described as 'a playwright of eth-ical issues'; but it has also been noted that he shows a stronger inclination to represent social and political conflicts rather than strictly personal ones, and that his characters often tend towards a quasi-allegorical neatness of 'complete goodness or thorough villainy', as against the complexities of tragically 'mixed characters'.[13] Consequently, a reading of Massinger which is especially alert to the tension between stasis and mobility is bound to privilege his comedies and some of his tragicomedies.

Massinger's tragedies, nonetheless, are of a piece with the rest of his work in their persistent focus on traditional notions of social and political legitimacy. These are often expressed as denunciations of the decline in respect for the primacy of birth and heredity as sources of power and deference. In *The Roman Actor* (1626), the opening description of the depths to which Rome has fallen includes the lament (which tends to become standard with Massinger), 'to be nobly borne / Is now a crime' (1.1.73–4). And in the earlier *The Duke of Milan* (1621–2) the downfall of Francisco, though made ethically complex by the reasons for his revenge, is nonetheless construed as the politically instructive moral tale of the subaltern who, having been 'rais'd' by Duke Sforza 'and made / The mignion of the time' (5.2.223–4), will perforce end up with desires and ambitions crassly above his state.

In the tragicomedies, the transgressions of aspiring stewards (and hence, the penalties they have to face) may be less damning, but the moralising on birth and power is no less incisive. In *The Maid of Honour* (?1621–2) it is in keeping with Massinger's representations of the links between lineage, ethics and action that the king's hateful 'mignion', who trafficks in influence at court (because he has 'the Kings eare', 26), should be described as 'A Gentleman, yet no lord', who

> hath some drops
> Of the Kings blood running in his veines, deriv'd
> Some ten degrees off. (1.1.23–5)

And in *The Great Duke of Florence* (1627), although Sanazarro's transgression extends no further than concealing Lidia's devastating beauty from Duke Cozimo, the duke nevertheless expresses his sense of betrayal by regretting

> The honors we have hourely heap'd upon him,
> The titles, the rewards, to the envie of
> The old Nobility. (5.1.103–5)

Thus, he gives voice to a standard aristocratic complaint about the increased latitude of preferment (hence, access to the nobility) practised by early modern monarchies.

This pervasive reverential attitude, combined with antipathy towards individual mobility within the social structure and cautionary remarks on the dire consequences of infringing the decorum of social and political status, also affects the love experience, in terms that are often at odds with the lover's characteristic abasement before the lady (a key trait in both Petrarchism and the courtly love tradition). This is especially to be seen in an early dialogue between Giovanni (the duke's heir) and Lidia, in *The Great Duke of Florence*, when Giovanni expresses (with remarkable candour) his awareness that she is not his 'equall' (1.1.227); this sense of his ineluctable superiority is also confirmed in his envy of her lowly 'condition' (219), which allows her to experience the 'golden meane' (216) denied to those that are born into greatness. Symmetrically, dialogues involving Sanazarro and Fiorinda in the same play are also insistent on the former's unfitness (despite the high favour in which the duke holds him, his position at court, and his fame as a general) ever to become the recipient of Fiorinda's romantic interest (1.2.157–61).

This forbidding sense of social and political degree, grounded on birth and heredity, is the bedrock of the satiric design of Massinger's best-known comedies, *A New Way to Pay Old Debts* (1625) and *The City Madam* (1632) – and hence possibly a fundamental condition for the success of these plays. *A New Way to Pay Old Debts*, a favourite with actors and audiences at various points of its stage history, famously centres on the 'monstrosity' of Sir Giles Overreach's social-climbing plans. The rise-and-fall structure of the plot matches the villain's career, from his gloating celebration of his predatory enrichment – in particular at the expense of his 'prodigal' nephew, the revealingly named Wellborn – to his ultimate raving madness at finding himself overreached. This is tantamount to representing the ambitions of lower gentry to enter the ranks of the nobility as fundamentally disruptive and potentially criminal, and Massinger often spells out such social lessons in full. Hence, Lady Allworth's observation to Lord Louell (with whom she shares a normative status within the ethical and social world of the play) that

> 'twill not agree
> With those of eminent blood …
> To study large additions to their fortunes
> And quite neglect their births

as against those

> common men [who]
> Make sordid wealth the obiect, and sole end
> Of their industrious aimes. (4.1.180–7)

The very terms of Lord Louell's abhorrence of a possible marriage below his rank,

> I would not so adulterate my blood
> ... and so leaue my issue
> Made vp of seuerall peeces, one part scarlet
> And the other *London*-blew (4.1.223–6)

reinforces the play's antipathy to that 'exceptional degree of social mobility' that, in early modern England, had found its epitome in wealthy citizens becoming landed or titled through marriage with impoverished nobility.[14]

The City Madam is possibly Massinger's most thorough and explicit satiric treatment of such social dynamics, as indeed suggested by the centrality conferred by the play's title upon the citizen's wife. She and her daughters cherish extravagant 'dreams ... / Of being made Countesses' (1.1.17–18), which Massinger thoroughly exposes. We are shown the socially negative side of the citizen's wife's ambition, when she yearns for the humiliation of her betters and longs to be served by 'Some decay'd Ladie' (2.2.122). However, the most devastating satiric device is probably the overall debasement that derives from the presence, among the play's aspiring characters, of Shavem, the whore, who partakes in the City's acquisitive spirit – 'what's one friend? / I would have a hundred' (3.1.7–8) – and on whose behalf the pimp explicitly equates 'marriage' and 'the other thing' that Shavem has on offer: 'The commoditie is the same' (3.1.80–1). Indeed, the whore's aspirations are phrased at their clearest just two scenes after the citizen's daughters renounce the austere ethos implied by their family name (their father is the merchant Sir John Frugal) and set out their outrageous demands to their suitors. The lengthy list of goods, services and retinue on which (in 2.2) they contractually insist, effectively itemising those 'hopes above their birth and scale' (1.1.17) that define them, rather swiftly leads to their disgrace, to be followed by punishment and reform. The stark terms of these women's claims to 'rule, preeminence, and absolute Sovereigntie' (2.2.88), combined with the play's overall satiric design, are promptly recognisable as self-damning. Their naked materialism and raw vanity are the polar opposite of the ideals underlying courtly love, as a refined model of female enthroning that would otherwise seem to match their yearning for aristocratic status. But neither are these brazen ambitions represented in the terms of popular festive culture, which has yielded alternative memorable images of female power. The households envisaged in *The City Madam*, in which empowered wives tyrannise over abject husbands, are indeed based on a logic of inversion – but not on the merry topsy-turvydom of carnival. Indeed, the rewards for which the Frugal women yearn in their vision of an upside-down world are not laughter, sex, a full belly and the dilution of all conventional distinctions amid riotous misrule, centred on the bounty of the body;[15] but rather money, titles and estates, all to be appropriated by self-styled 'wise *Viragoes*' who mean to engross their future husbands' 'rents' and reduce each of them 'to his pension' (2.2.168–70).

Massinger's exposure of these women's ambition as a 'monstrous Metamorphosis' (4.4.92) is characteristic also of the explicit moralising that defines and energises the satiric impetus. Once brought down from her extravagant yearnings and forced, with her daughters, to revert to their 'naturall forms, and habits', Lady Frugal promptly exclaims:

> I am sick, and meet with
> A rough Physician. O my pride! and scorn!
> How justly am I punish'd! (4.4.149–51)

The normative core, the sense of righteousness that animates satire is here revealed in three concurrent features: firstly, in Massinger's description as 'naturall' of what might otherwise be construed as the effect of culture or nurture; secondly, in Lady Frugal's organic and surgical allusion to a 'Physician', in fact echoing the tropes of extirpation and healing that the self-appointed 'new Satyrist', Luke, had invoked as conventional analogues for the operation of satire: 'I'le cut off / What ever is exorbitant in you, / Or in your Daughters' (4.4.130–2); and thirdly, in the promptness with which Massinger's rogues and fools accept and express the reasonableness of their punishment.[16]

Indeed, Massinger's work is pervaded by an apparent belief that contrite transgressors prove convincing mouthpieces for the values in the name of which they were created. This sometimes becomes evident in connection with minor transgressions, such as those lamented by Sanazarro in a soliloquy that begins by signalling the speaker's exemplary value – ''Tis prov'd in me, the curse of human frailty' – and evolves towards the *ubi sunt* theme in the rhetorical questions:

> Where is now
> My borrowed greatness, or the promised lives
> Of following courtiers echoing my will?
> (*The Great Duke of Florence*, 5.1.1, 12–14)

However (as if to vindicate the fame of Massinger's best-known play), the most memorable and candid admissions may yet be those in *A New Way to Pay Old Debts*. They emerge both in the accepting lines with which petty rascals mark their own downfall – such as Tapwell's 'Vnthankefull knaues are euer so rewarded' (4.2.82) – and in the impenitent brazenness with which the goal-oriented arch-villain, Overreach, dismisses his daughter's refusal to learn 'the strumpetts fashion' for entrapping a suitor, and prescribes instead:

> Learne any thing,
> And from any creature that may make thee great;
> From the Diuell himselfe. (*A New Way to Pay Old Debts*, 3.2.120–2)

Massinger's aptness to render lessons explicit that other playwrights might leave for their audiences to infer, and to associate such lessons with characters that appear predictable in their trajectories and static in their social and moral identities, may be construed as reflecting a wish for satiric clarity. However, it has strongly contributed to his reputation for poor characterisation and for endorsing a reactionary aversion to social mobility. Conversely, these traits of Massinger's dramatic writing have also become a focus for arguments on his behalf, in the context of his recovery in critical esteem. For example, Ira Clark's emphasis on the pervasiveness of theatrical reference in the work of professional Caroline playwrights allows him to suggest that Massinger's characters can owe their apparent fixedness to their constant role-playing within and throughout the plots that they serve, which itself reflects a sociopolitical context haunted by fears of 'disintegration' and intense unease about status and position. Hence, Massinger's apparently simplistic characterisation (an inability to offer convincing representations of human complexity) may in fact reveal a perception of identity as constructed and contingent, rather than essential; concurrently, Massinger is seen as following Jonson's rather than Shakespeare's example in delineating his characters on sociological rather than psychological grounds. In such a reading, even Massinger's insistence on birth and heredity (usually voiced by ethically normative characters) becomes less an entrenchment against any form of social mobility than a reflection of the anxieties of an era torn 'between reaction and revolution', and indeed of a wish to compromise in the face of accelerated change – in Massinger's case, by exalting patronage as a system for cohesion on the basis of 'reciprocal gratitude', under which merit (rather than just birth) can find its rewards.[17]

Clark's argument that Massinger advocates 'gratitude' as a social 'mediating agency', and 'mobility based on merit', may contain an element of critical zeal.[18] Unquestionably, though, plays that feature passages extolling the values of a declining sociopolitical order also show some ambivalence in the way they construe the legitimacy of power, wealth and status in a changing society, specifically with regard to the dichotomy social conservatism vs mobility. In *A New Way to Pay Old Debts*, the opening quarrel between Wellborn (the prodigal decayed gentleman) and Tapwell (his former steward, now a tapster and creditor) has its most vehement moment when Wellborn denounces Tapwell's roguish ingratitude, which seems to epitomise the irreverent greed of the new business ethics; but the argument also includes the tapster's disarming remark, in response to Wellborn's charge that his prosperity derives from the 'whores and canters' among his customers:

> True, but they brought in profit,
> And had a gift to pay for what they call'd for
> And stucke not like your mastership.
> (*A New Way to Pay Old Debts*, 1.1.62–5)

In spite (or even because) of the gentleman's utter inability to honour his debts, the outcome of the plot vindicates Wellborn (and hence, in the light of his name, the primacy of birth as a source of social distinction). However, the denouement also suggests that his former faults as an all-round wastrel, combined with his shadowy recipe for success (which validates the play's title), require some form of penance before Wellborn can be returned to full social dignity. Wellborn's decision to undertake a period of redemptive soldiering abroad is thus presented as a form of acceptable sociopolitical dynamics, for ethical as much as topical reasons: 'It is a time of Action' (5.1.395). Extolling personal redemption through military action is not, per se, proof of Massinger's endorsement of social mobility through merit under the specific conditions of his time (the ideal in question had a long history in a variety of contexts, including the feudal order and the culture of chivalry); but the repeated occurrences in Massinger of a discourse of military self-vindication, combined with transparently topical allusions, certainly suggest its relevance for the sociopolitics of Caroline England.

Martial prowess may appear as a particular and intense form of active virtue, the quality that in *The Great Duke of Florence* Massinger projects onto Giovanni, the ruler's young successor, when he is encouraged to

> arrive unto
> The Theory of those high mysteries
> Which [he] by action, must make plaine in Court.
> (*The Great Duke of Florence*, 1.1.138–40)

However, Massinger is intensely alert to the ethical complexities involved in individual promotion through war, as proved by the debate that opens Act 3 of *The Duke of Milan*, in which soldiers yearn for the failure of 'compositions' so that (in the absence of a truce) they can go on the rampage and loot at will: 'The spoyle, the spoyle, 'tis that the soldier fights for' (3.1.1). Coming from a playwright who has been said to stand for compromise and accommodation in the face of an unstable history, the passage might seem an indictment of warmongering, an exposure of the age-old brutal acquisitiveness of the battlefield. However, the same scene ultimately vindicates the soldiers' ravaging ethics, when Medina presents it as a virtuous scourge of the prosperity of wealthy citizens, who, 'like *Scarabes* in the dung of Peace' (3.1.26), fatten themselves on the commonwealth 'by cozenage, perjury, or sordid thrift' (3.1.30). The final item on this disparaging list is enlightening, since 'thrift' was otherwise the name for a key virtue in the new urban, commercial ethos, and (as pointed out in classic studies of the link between religion and the new economy) was often cited in thoroughly positive contexts: 'thrift, diligence, sobriety, frugality'.[19]

Another paean to mobility through military action occurs in *The Maid of Honour* – '[Massinger's] first independent production, and one that epitomises many of his values'.[20] In this case, it is even more relevant as regards Massinger's position on mobility and acquisitiveness, since England is explicitly cited as a foil to the play's nominal Sicily. In Bertoldo's plea for greater ambition, presented to his reluctant half-brother, the King of Sicily, the fact that their country is 'an Island' (1.1.196), with no wealth of raw materials and a growing population, justifies a more aggressive and expansive policy, while England is extolled for making herself 'The Mistress of the Ocean' (1.1.225), thereby achieving prosperity. Significantly, the venal king decides not to commit himself or his state to war, but merely allows those gallants in his court who are keen to prove 'their boasted valours' (1.1.257) to try their luck 'as Adventurers, and Voluntiers' (1.1.255) without royal support. The non-normative and villainous status of this lethargic and anti-acquisitive king is confirmed, for the early modern audience, when he is described as keeping a 'state Catamite' (1.1.272). In Massinger, yielding to lust always proves disastrous for those in power, as proved by the fate of Sforza in *The Duke of Milan* and Domitian in *The Roman Actor* (and even by Donusa's near-fatal renunciation of chastity in *The Renegado*); but in *The Maid of Honour* its negative import is compounded by taboo practices.

In the person and rule of the monarch in *The Maid of Honour* Massinger thus disparages the option to stay at home and reject action, war and acquisitiveness. Indeed, he does so not just politically, by implying negligence, but also ethically, by associating it with a debased sexuality. Compared to this, the uplifting and dynamic zest displayed by Bertoldo in his praise of England's oceanic triumphs seems to show Massinger (in this play at least) endorsing the argument for an active and ambitious English imperial design, which had been regularly upheld by a variety of commentators since the mid-sixteenth century.[21] This, however, is hardly compatible with his apparent attraction elsewhere to the satiric view of voyagers and colonists as daredevils, rascals or fools, brought together by material ambition and opportunities for mobility (spatial as much as social, in this case). Decayed nobility, ambitious younger sons of gentry and others with few prospects of preferment in their home country proved especially vulnerable to hopes of easy fortunes in the colonies.[22] The type had found an early dramatic embodiment in the venal and foolish Sir Petronel Flash of *Eastward Ho* (the great Chapman, Jonson and Marston *succès de scandale* of 1605), but aspects of it emerged also in the characterisation of some of the gallants-turned-voyagers in Fletcher and Massinger's collaborative *The Sea Voyage* (1622) (in spite of this play's more positive representation of the sea venture). In *The City Madam*, good Sir John Frugal's wealth significantly depends on spatial mobility (through voyaging) and the 'rich fraught' of merchant vessels, as made clear by the play's opening reference to 'the ship', aptly named *Speedwell* (1.1.1–2); but the fullness of its sails appears tainted when replicated in the ambition that 'swells' the merchant's daughters (1.1.2, 16). Indeed, the play hardly endorses a dynamic attitude towards the extended geographic spaces of the early modern economy and imagination. In Act 5, the New World provides a disguise for the characters that are about to unmask and punish Luke – the formerly disgraced and impecunious younger brother who, once given control of his brother's estate, promptly turns into a tyrannical miser. Posing as American Indians and claiming to represent the devil, they parade before the eyes of their dupe the temptations of exchanging the 'felicity' of home for the wealth-cum-damnation of being 'miserable in another world' (5.1.50–1) – an indictment of elsewhere (even when fake, as is the case).

The picture of Massinger that emerges from this reading is complex and potentially contradictory. His tragedies, comedies and tragicomedies seem to authorise, in the voice of characters whose social and dramatic success gives them normative status, a set of attitudes towards power, social salience and wealth that are hardly compatible with one another. They display a prevalent reverence towards the powers that be, often with explicit reference to birthright and heredity – but also a fascination for the potentially disruptive panache of adventurers who take to the battlefield in order to translate their prowess into upward mobility. They appear pervaded by a cavalier attitude towards forms of affluence and social standing that derive from the rising money economy, as against the traditional land-based sources of distinction – but also allow for the arguments of subalterns to be heard (especially when they abide by a code of humility towards their perceived betters). The voices that triumph in Massinger's plots seem to appeal predominantly to the staid values of an organic, sedentary society, often with regressive overtones – but occasionally convey, with rhetorical aplomb, the expansive and acquisitive ethos of the growing early modern world. As suggested above, the cultural paradigm within which we read early modern texts today – dominated as it is by a fascination for the hybrid, the less than coherent, the non-totalising – could hardly be more amenable to a playwright that raises such perplexities.

Annabel Patterson's observation that 'it is not improbable that Massinger will do well in the next cycle', may largely hold true a generation later; but it is cultural congeniality, rather than critical recantation, that has created the conditions for her prescience.[23] Defences of Massinger in the intervening years have often been predicated on a diagnosis of critical insufficiency, suggesting that, if critics were to grasp Massinger's underlying coherence, the rift between 'the artistic Massinger' and 'the moral Massinger' would be healed, yielding a symbiotic writer of 'consistent answer[s]', who indeed combined the talents of 'his collaborator, Fletcher', 'his model, Jonson' and 'his predecessor, Shakespeare'.[24] Massinger's writing, however, stoutly resists this bid for wholeness and totality. If he is to come into his own in our age, Massinger can hardly be read as if he wrote out of a full-fledged social and moral philosophy – rather than out of the constraints proper to a professional theatre, the accommodations imposed by patronage and the disparate traditions of representation and characterisation that defined his skills as a playwright. His characteristic genre may indeed be tragicomedy – again, not as an integrative and totalising device (the expression of a 'moral commitment'), but rather as a perplexed dramatic form. When read along these lines, Massinger emerges indeed as a playwright for our time, the practitioner of an art that, in its very contingency, confirms our sense of the human.

NOTES

1 T. S. Eliot, 'Philip Massinger' (1920), in *Collected Essays*, 3rd edn (London: Faber, 1951), 205–20 at 206, 211–13.

2 'Introduction', *The Renegado*, ed. Michael Neill (London: Methuen Drama, 2010), 1.

3 For these and other responses to Massinger's work until 1900, see Martin Garrett, ed., *Philip Massinger: The Critical Heritage* (London: Routledge, 1991), 56, 62. A very useful overview of Massinger's work and reputation can also be found in the 'General Introduction' to the standard edition: *The Plays and Poems of Philip Massinger*, ed. Philip Edwards and Colin Gibson, 5 vols. (Oxford: Clarendon Press, 1976), I, xv–lxxxii. All quotations from Massinger's work in this chapter refer to this edition.

4 Garrett, *The Critical Heritage*, 126, 143.

5 Garrett, *The Critical Heritage*, 193.

6 See also Annabel Patterson, *Censorship and Interpretation* (Madison, WI: University of Wisconsin Press, 1984), 79. The critical values in question appealed to such notions as the organic coherence of the work of major authors, which supposedly makes it more than the sum of their various writings; the interdependence of word, intellect and emotion as a defining trait of a work of verbal art; and the mutually enlightening rapport between authorial singularity and the history of the writer's medium.

7 Ira Clark, *Professional Playwrights: Massinger, Ford, Shirley, and Brome* (Lexington, KY: University Press of Kentucky, 1992), 3–5, 34.

8 The fundamental scholarly study of collaboration in the Beaumont and Fletcher plays is still the series of articles published by Cyrus Hoy in the 1950s and early 1960s: Cyrus Hoy, 'The Shares of Fletcher and His Collaborators in the Beaumont and Fletcher Canon', *Studies in Bibliography*, vols. 8–9 and 11–15 (1956–62). In view of the vast number of recent publications on authorship and collaboration in sixteenth- and seventeenth-century drama, only one contribution (which focuses on Shakespeare, but also sheds light on other areas of early modern drama) will here be cited: *Shakespeare, Computers, and the Mystery of Authorship*, ed. Hugh Craig and Arthur F. Kinney (Cambridge University Press, 2009).

9 Philip Edwards, 'Massinger's Men and Women', in *Philip Massinger: A Critical Reassessment*, ed. Douglas Howard (Cambridge University Press, 1985), 39–49 at 49.

10 Respectively Russ McDonald, 'High Seriousness and Popular Form: The Case of *The Maid of Honour*', in *Philip Massinger*, ed. Howard, 83–116 at 83; and Michael Neill, '"The Tongues of Angels": Charity and the Social Order in *The City Madam*', in *Philip Massinger*, ed. Howard, 193–220 at 203.

11 Joanne Rochester, *Staging Spectatorship in the Plays of Philip Massinger* (Farnham: Ashgate, 2010), 1.

12 *The Greenblatt Reader*, ed. Michael Payne (Oxford: Blackwell, 2005), 134, 161, 163 and *passim*.

13 Respectively Rochester, *Staging Spectatorship*, 2; and Douglas Howard, 'Massinger's Political Tragedies', in *Philip Massinger*, ed. Howard, 117–37 at 118–20.

14 Margot Heinemann, *Puritanism and Theatre: Thomas Middleton and the Opposition Drama under the Early Stuarts* (Cambridge University Press, 1980), 3 and *passim*.

15 This understanding of the 'carnivalesque' follows Mikhail Bakhtin's disquisition in his influential *Rabelais and His World*, trans. Hélène Iswolsky (Bloomington, IN: Indiana University Press, 1984).

16 This understanding of satire as predicated on a sense of ethical certainty, assisted by 'militant irony', derives from Northrop Frye's classic essay on 'The Mythos of Winter: Irony and Satire' and Alastair Fowler's study of genres and modes: Frye, *Anatomy of Criticism: Four Essays* (Princeton University Press, 1973; first published 1957), 223–4; Fowler, *Kinds of Literature: An Introduction to the Theory of Genres and Modes* (Oxford: Clarendon Press, 1982), 110.

17 Ira Clark, *The Moral Art of Philip Massinger* (Lewisburg, PA: Bucknell University Press, 1993), 95–8 and *passim*; Clark, *Professional Playwrights*, 37, 39.

18 Clark, *Professional Playwrights*, 37, 39.

19 R. H. Tawney, *Religion and the Rise of Capitalism* (London: John Murray, 1926), 110; see also 245, 248.

20 Patterson, *Censorship and Interpretation*, 79.

21 Andrew Hadfield, ed., *Amazons, Savages, and Machiavels: Travel and Colonial Writing in English 1550–1630: An Anthology* (Oxford University Press, 2001), 16ff., 24ff. and *passim*.

22 *Three Renaissance Travel Plays*, ed. Anthony Parr (Manchester University Press, 1995), 20–1.
23 Patterson, *Censorship and Interpretation*, 79.
24 Clark, *The Moral Art*, 16, 31, 97.

Further reading

Adler, Doris, *Philip Massinger*. Boston: Twayne Publishers, 1987.
Butler, Martin, *Theatre and Crisis, 1632–1642*. Cambridge University Press, 1984.
Dunn, T. A., *Philip Massinger: The Man and the Playwright*. London: Thomas Nelson and Sons, 1957.
Garrett, Martin, ed., *Philip Massinger: The Critical Heritage*. London and New York: Routledge, 1991.
Howard, Douglas, ed., *Philip Massinger: A Critical Reassessment*. Cambridge University Press, 1985.
Lawless, Donald S., *Philip Massinger and His Associates*, Ball State Monograph 10. Muncie, IN: Ball State University, 1967.
Maxwell, Baldwin, *Studies in Beaumont, Fletcher, and Massinger*. Chapel Hill, NC: University of North Carolina Press, 1939.
Neill, Michael, '"Wits most accomplished Senate": The Audience of the Caroline Private Theatres.' *Studies in English Literature 1500–1900* 18 (1978), 341–60.
Sanders, Julie, *Caroline Drama: The Plays of Massinger, Ford, Shirley, and Brome*. Plymouth: Northcote House, 1999.

15

HEATHER HIRSCHFELD

Richard Brome and the idea
of a Caroline theatre

At the centre of *The Antipodes*, now his best-known play, Richard Brome (*c.* 1590–1653) stages an elaborate parade of London city types – lawyers, courtiers, statesmen – who present themselves and their preoccupations to one of the play's central figures, Peregrine Joyless. One set of professionals is of particular interest to Peregrine: watermen and carmen, labourers whose courtesy and decorum stand in striking contrast to the unruly, brusque behaviour of the courtiers and gentry. As one of them announces to Peregrine, he is 'humble, yet ambitious / In my devoir to do you best of service'.[1]

Ambitious to be humble – such an ostensibly oxymoronic disposition aptly describes our playwright, who took special care to style himself as eagerly unassuming and deferential. In a commendatory epistle to Beaumont and Fletcher's *Comedies and Tragedies* (1647), for instance, Brome asks to 'retain still [his] wonted modesty' amidst the other poets, the 'large train of Fletchers friends' for whom he wants only to serve as a 'Follower'.[2] In an earlier work, the Prologue to his *Damoiselle* (published 1653), Brome refuses to be considered an 'Author, or Poet', adopting instead the title of 'Playmaker', and admitting that

> though [I] be none
> Of those, whose towring Muses scale the Throne
> Of Kings, yet [my] familiar mirth's as good
> When 'tis by you approv'd and understood. (sig. A2)

Such verses, of course, are part of a deliberate programme of self-construction: they are not a disinterested depiction of a true self but rather an artful creation of a public persona. But the construction is deeply persuasive, and it is perpetuated by his colleagues and reinforced by the facts of Brome's life: his unknown, and therefore probably humble, origins; his lack of university training; and his professional beginnings, pithily remarked in *Bartholomew Fair* (performed 1614), as Ben Jonson's 'man'. This connection between

Jonson and Brome, master and man, was central to Brome's identity as a humble man of the stage. In the Prologue to his *Northern Lasse* (published 1632), Brome declared himself an 'underservant in [Jonson's] Tribe' (sig. A4v), and Jonson famously chronicled the relationship in a commendatory poem to the same play:

> I had you for a Seruant once, *Dick Brome*;
> And you perform'd a Seruants faithfull parts:
> Now, you are got into a nearer roome,
> *Of Fellowship*, professing my old Arts.
> And you doe doe them well, with good applause,
> Which you haue iustly gained from the *Stage*,
> By obseruation of those Comick Lawes
> Which I, your master, first did teach the Age. (sig. A3)

Brome's contemporaries recognised the hierarchical link between the men: a notice at the start of *The Antipodes*, published three years after Jonson's death in 1637, proclaims: 'Jonson's alive! ... He sojourns in his Brome's Antipodes' (21–2). And the connection became particularly resonant for Brome's associates after the closing of the theatres in 1642, when they recalled master and man to memorialise a now silent stage. Thus the compiler of the 1658 *Five New Playes* addressed detractors, 'who think they lessen this *Author's* worth when they speak the relation he had to *Ben. Johnson*', by insisting that

> we very thankfully embrace the Objection, and desire they would name any other Master that could better teach a man to write a good Play. The materials must flow from all parts of the world; but the *Art* and *Composition* come onely from Books and such living masters as that our great *Laureat*. (sig. A4)

Of course, a variety of impulses contributed to the cultivation of Brome's humility, including that perennial motive, political cautiousness, as Brome wrote in the Prologue to *The English Moor*:

> we'le make it good
> To utter nothing may be understood
> Offensive to the state, manners or time,
> We will as well look to our necks as climb. (sig. A2)

But at the heart of the construction was an idealised understanding of the cultural, social and even psychic role of the professional theatre, an understanding for which Brome has become, in a kind of self-fulfilling prophecy, a chief representative. This understanding – of a theatre industry populated by long-term professionals, among them Shakespeare, who shared the goal of delighting, teaching and healing audiences – was believed under threat in the 1630s and early 1640s, the result of an incursion into the playhouses of courtly amateurs (such as William Davenant and Sir John Suckling) with ambitions of playwriting. But their ambitions, Brome complained, were not to please and profit but to 'beguile' with 'gaudy Sceane[s]' and 'Love-toy[s]' (*Court Beggar*, sig. N4v).

The incursion of courtier-dramatists into playhouse precincts was the theatrical counterpart to a broader political trend: the 'autocratic and ineffective interference from Whitehall in local affairs' during the eleven years of Charles I's personal rule. Historians have been careful to insist that these years did not render inevitable the Civil War which rocked the nation in the 1640s, but they have also made it clear that the king's policies – particularly his efforts to raise money through impositions and monopolies as well as his favouring of the distinctly ceremonialist, anti-Calvinist archbishop William Laud – were experienced by many contemporaries as arbitrary, alienating and potentially absolutist.[3] Such policies were themselves dramatic fodder for playwrights such as Brome, as we shall see. But they also symbolised potential risks to the professional theatre, which, although traditionally patronised and monitored by the government, operated at an ideological as well as aesthetic distance from the court it ostensibly served. That distance looked to be compromised, theatre historians have explained, by the drawing of the King's Men 'close to the court's interests' and by the increasingly heavy-handed intervention of Charles I's Master of the Revels, Sir Henry Herbert, into matters of censorship and licensing.[4] Against this backdrop, then, Brome's humility stands as both a rebuke to a new brand of playwright and as a reminder of an older theatre and its artistic and social commitments. It was a political as well as a professional statement by a playwright who wrote, as Martin Butler (radically elaborating on the issues raised by R. J. Kaufmann in his 1961 biography of Brome), put it, 'with a consciousness of his theatre as an institution with a separate and continuous professional history'.[5]

Thanks to Kaufmann and perhaps even more to Butler's catalysing *Theatre and Crisis*, we have learnt to think of Brome, and Caroline drama more generally, as politically active and engaged rather than decadent or escapist. The Caroline stage, Butler writes, 'inherited and continued to develop the rich, varied and essentially independent-minded tradition of the Elizabethan–Jacobean professional theatre'; it also trafficked in highly topical scenes meant to provide its audiences with 'images of themselves in parks, squares, taverns and gaming houses, supplying standards against which forms and codes of behaviour could be established, scrutinised and adjusted'.[6] The result was that this theatre, like Shakespeare's before it, supplied both the artistic substance and the material venue for shaping opposition to court, king and counsel. And the work of Brome, who 'affirmed his debt to English dramatic traditions' by invoking predecessor plays, by ranging widely in comic genres and conventions, and, perhaps most important, by asserting the integrity of the professional stage in elaborate metadramatic scenarios meant to testify to the theatre's curative potential, was central to this agenda.[7] In what follows, then, I look at a representative sampling of Brome's dramatic output, paying special attention to the ways in which he interpreted native traditions of dramatic delight for political as well as psychological ends.

After the 1614 shout-out in Jonson's *Bartholomew Fair*, the next theatrical record for Brome is a 1623 citation in Sir Henry Herbert's account book, in which he is named as one of two composers of 'A new Comedy, a *Fault in Frendship*, by Young Johnson and Broome'.[8] The play, now lost, was licensed for the Prince's Men; in 1628 Brome was listed in a patent for Elizabeth's Men, who were about to go on tour. But by February of the following year he was writing for the theatre's most prestigious playing company, the King's Men, Shakespeare's company, providing them with the *Love-Sick Maid* (lost), a breakout hit whose 'good success' was recorded by the Master of the Revels.[9] Brome's *Northern Lasse* followed a few months later, in July 1629, and it was published in 1632 with several congratulatory poems, including Jonson's verses quoted above. Fellow playwrights Thomas Dekker and John Ford also contributed praise, Dekker referring to Brome as his 'Sonne and Friend', and Ford lauding the play in opposition to the work of courtiers: 'The Court affords / No newer fashion, or for Wit, or Words' (sig. A3v).

The Northern Lasse has been dismissed as 'weak and immature', despite its King's Men's provenance and its success on both of the company's stages (the title page reads 'As it hath been often Acted with good Applause, at the *Globe*, and *Black-Fryers*').[10] Yet more recent critics like Matthew Steggle have found much in it to recommend, particularly its engagement with the social complexities of urban marriage and the niceties of marital law.[11] The play, a romantic comedy with a gritty, urban sensibility, rotates around multiple, and competing, marriage contracts. It begins with the arrival of the northern lass, Constance, in London in search of her beau, Philip Luckless, to whom she mistakenly believes she is betrothed on the basis of a kiss. Ignorant of Constance's attachment and despite the warnings of his friend Tridewell, Luckless has got engaged to the widow Fitchow, whose idea of marriage conforms to the period's stereotypes of the wifely scold: Fitchow intends, she tells the audience, to be singular in [her] will; to raigne, gouerne, ordaine lawes and breake 'hem, make quarrells and maintaine 'hem; professe truthes, deuise falshoods; protest obedience, but study nothing more then to make our husbands so. (sig. c2v)

Tridewell goes to discourage the widow from marrying his friend (during which time he falls in love with her); meanwhile Constance's nurse, Trainwell, goes to accuse Luckless of betraying her young charge. Luckless denies all wrongdoing and proceeds with a hasty marriage to Widow Fitchow, which both regret almost immediately after the ceremony. The newlyweds refuse to sleep together on the bridal night, and they thus pave a path towards annulment. As a friend tells Luckless: 'There's a Canon for it Sir. If both parties agree to divorce after Marriage, so it be before Copulation' (sig. F4). This news has yet to reach Constance, who has sunk into a deep, seemingly irreparable melancholy both from the loss of her Philip and from the threat of an arranged marriage, engineered by her uncle Squelch, to the unattractive Nonsense. But Luckless's clever friends and servants come to the rescue in a final banquet in Act 5: they humiliate Squelch, whose attachment to a whore compromises his authority over Constance, and they prove Luckless and Fitchow's marriage invalid (since it was not performed by a minister). The play comes to a ringing close with the uniting of Luckless and Constance, of Tridewell and Fitchow, and of Squelch and Trainwell.

Much of this is the typical stuff of city comedy: the blocking (and ethically compromised) authority figure, the effeminising widow, the good-natured whore, the wily but helpful servant. But *The Northern Lasse* is significantly inflected by Brome's idiosyncratic concerns: his interest in regional dialects, not unlike Shakespeare's in *Henry V*; his fixation on the asymmetries of wardship, which gave relatives like Squelch undue power over their charges; and his fascination with emotional states like melancholy, understood as a delicate combination of physiological and psychological causes. The drama is also governed by Brome's metadramatic ethic, according to which plays and playing enable both social communion and individual redemption. This ethic, which reaches its height in *The Antipodes*, is pursued here in a series of masques: the first, for Luckless and Fitchow's wedding night, prevents them from consummating the unfortunate marriage; the second, in the play's final scenes, features the central characters 'disguis'd and Masqu'd' (sig. L3v), who slowly reveal and rearrange themselves into desired couplings.

Brome's next play for the King's Men was *The Novella*, a romantic comedy set in Venice; his subsequent and final play for the company was *The Late Lancashire Witches* (1634), a collaborative affair with the dramatist Thomas Heywood. Like their subject – a witchcraft case that began in 1633 in the northern county of Lancashire but, having become the talk of the realm by the following year, was brought to London for royal evaluation – the writing pair was unusual. Heywood, whose first recorded effort for the theatre dates to 1596, was a full theatre generation ahead of Brome, with experience not only as a dramatist but also as an actor and sharer in Worcester's Men (which became the Queen's Company in 1603). Their styles – Heywood was an episodic and earnest writer, Brome lapidary and satiric – were distinct, as was their approach to genre: Heywood wrote across a range of dramatic kinds, and is perhaps best known now for his moving domestic tragedy *A Woman Killed with Kindness*; Brome proclaimed his dedication to the comic. And Heywood, who acknowledged in his *English Traveller* that he 'had either an entire hand, or at the least a maine finger' in approximately 220 plays, offered a counter-example to the model of 'possessive authorship' promoted by Brome's master, Ben Jonson.[12] But if Heywood and Brome were in many ways an 'odd couple', they were both similarly devoted to the educative and therapeutic power of the theatre: Heywood more explicitly, in his *Apology for Actors* (1612) and in writings against William Prynne's attack in *Histriomastix* (1633), and Brome more implicitly, as we have begun to see, in the body of his plays. Whether or not this shared perspective *caused* their joint work on *The Late Lancashire Witches* (or on their other collaborations, the lost *Life and Death of Martin Skink* and *The Apprentice's Prize*), it certainly *informs* the play, a journalistic drama which portrays the witchcraft incident as something festive rather than frightening, a very different approach to the supernatural from Shakespeare's some thirty years earlier, when he staged the 'instruments of darkness' that haunt *Macbeth*. Brome and Heywood's portrayal endorses neither of the reigning approaches to the occult current at Charles's court, where witchcraft was viewed as either a genuine threat or as a matter of superstition. Stepping outside these ideological confines, the playwrights cast Lancastrian witchcraft as a comic affair, a real but unthreatening phenomenon centred on 'sport, not hurt' (*Witches*, 195). In so doing they 'expose[d] the self-interest that motivates *both* superstitious belief in *and* empirical skepticism of witchcraft', preserving their play from an unequivocal alignment with court influences even as they capitalised on the subject's topical appeal to audiences.[13]

There is no explicit evidence to suggest that the peculiar dynamics of *Witches* sullied Brome's relationship with the King's Men (though Freehafer suggests Davenant 'may have displaced him' in the company's good graces).[14] But the play was to be Brome's last for the company. He had already been writing for other companies: Prince Charles' [II] Men and the King's Revels Men. His sole play for the Prince's Men, the politically sharp and aggressive *Weeding of Covent Garden*, was performed around 1632, though not published until 1658. It is a premier example of topographical realism – the detailed presentation of multiple features of the urban landscape which gives a play both immediacy and symbolic resonance – which was current in Caroline drama. Set in and around Covent Garden, at the time a popular meeting-ground under construction for the Earl of Bedford into a fashionable piazza by Inigo Jones (impersonated here in the character of Rooksbill), *The Weeding of Covent Garden* is dominated by the figure of Crosswill, an extraordinary caricature of paternal authority pursued to its extreme. Crosswill insists not only that his children obey his will (indeed, they 'do things that other fathers would rejoyce at'), but that he be 'obeyed in my own way' (*Weeding*, 4). The result is a family dynamic constructed on an abyss of reverse psychology: the children do what they do *not* want to do in order to get Crosswill to insist that they do what they *do* want to do, while Crosswill gives his children all sorts of liberties in order to appear unconstrained by them. Against the customary protocols of parental authority, for instance, he demands that his long-suffering daughter Katherine find her spouse rather than have him dictate her choice: 'I have sworn she shall make her own choice, though it be of one I hate. Make me her match-maker! Must I obey her, or she me?' (*Weeding*, 6). In Butler's precise formulation, Crosswill 'takes obedience to his will to be a device to limit his own freedom of action', imagining any agreement as 'a challenge to his freedom to have his own individual and wholly singular will'.[15] The consequence of such logic, as the play itself notes, is that none of Crosswill's children 'make any conscience of crossing him' (*Weeding*, 51).

Crosswill has come to London from the country with his daughter Katherine and his elder son, Gabriel, in search of his younger son, Mihil, who is supposed to be studying at the Inns of Court but is really leading the profligate life of a gallant city wit. Crosswill's contact in London is Justice of the Peace Cockbrain, a friend of Rooksbill and a direct descendant of Adam Overdo from Jonson's *Bartholomew Fair*.[16] The plots of these befuddled but demanding father figures intersect when Cockbrain goes in pursuit of the Crosswill and Rooksbill brothers at various taverns, where the gallants try to intoxicate Gabriel out of his rigid Puritanism and where Cockbrain is, like Overdo, duped and humiliated by the men he is trying to outwit. After a series of plot twists that exploit the perversities of Crosswill's intransigence, Brome concludes the play by bringing Gabriel out of his Puritan fanatacism (which we learn along the way was precipitated not by a religious awakening but by the mistreatment of his beloved cousin, Dorcas) and by bringing the other children into marriage. Mihil is paired with Lucy, daughter of Rooksbill, Katherine with Anthony, son of Cockbrain, and Dorcas with Nicholas, son of Rooksbill.

The Weeding of Covent Garden is the harbinger of other place-realism plays like *The Sparagus Garden*, written for the King's Revels Men at Salisbury Court. *Sparagus Garden* was an astonishingly lucrative play (in legal documents Brome claimed, with probable exaggeration, that it earned for the company £1,000), a success that likely led to a contract between Brome and Richard Heton, owner of Salisbury Court. The contract itself has not been found, but court depositions from a 1640 suit against Brome invoke its particulars, providing scholars with extraordinarily detailed information about the socioeconomic conditions of the early modern play-wright. According to the agreement, Brome was to work solely for Heton at Salisbury Court, writing three plays a year for three years, for a salary of 15 shillings per week and the benefit of 'one day's profit of playing such new play as he should make'.[17] Brome had not entirely fulfilled these demands (though he claimed that his revisions of and additions to older plays were the equivalent of his missing scripts) when the contract was renewed in 1638, this time for another seven years.

Brome's years under contract with Salisbury Court were by no means serene. Brome wrote *The New Academy* and *The Queen and the Concubine* – the former a charged city comedy designed to make fun of both gallants and merchants, and the latter a version of the Patient Griselda story – for the company before an outbreak of plague shut down the theatres from May 1636 to October 1637. During the long closure, Brome composed his *Antipodes* for surreptitious performance by another company at Christopher Beeston's Cockpit. But the Master of the Revels intervened and when the theatres reopened the play was offered on the Salisbury Court boards (though, according to Brome's remarks in the published edition of 1640, in a version shortened from the original script).

The Antipodes weaves, with great aplomb, the conventions of travel narrative with an extended meditation on the therapeutic efficacy of the stage, themes brought together most memorably in *The Tempest*. Indeed, although his cohorts remarked Jonson's presence in the play, *The Antipodes* is clearly indebted to Shakespeare and his final vision, in *The Tempest*, of an exiled playwright-figure who uses dramatic magic to orchestrate the reconciliation of families and dynasties. It opens on a London just recovering from the plague: 'To me, and to the city, sir, you are welcome', the painter Blaze says to his friend Joyless, a country gentleman,

> And so are all about you: we have long
> Suffered in want of such fair company.
> But now that time's calamity has given way
> (Thanks to high Providence) to your kinder visits. (1.1.1–5)

But Joyless is in no celebratory mood: he is with his son, Peregrine, whose unfulfilled wanderlust has prevented him from consummating his marriage to Martha, who has been plunged into the distractedness of the sexually unsatisfied wife. Meanwhile Joyless himself suffers from that traditional male disease: jealousy of his younger wife, Diana. The family appeals to Doctor Hughball, who promises to cure them by a 'medicine of the mind' which 'begets both wonder and delight' (1.1.26).

That medicine is a dramatic production at the house of Lord Letoy, an 'odd lord' who writes his own plays and keeps his own company of players, including the unpredictable By-Play, whose extemporising recalls the Elizabethan clowns of Shakespeare's day, Will Kempe and Richard Tarlton, and to whom Letoy has granted licence 'to alter or diminish what the writer / With care and skill compos'd' (2.2.42–3). The production, to be watched by Joyless, Diana and the Blazes, is designed around the unwitting Peregrine, who is drugged into thinking that he has truly travelled to the fictional locale of the Antipodes, whose inhabitants are personated by Letoy's players. Peregrine, in other words, is indulged in his malady – an indulgence which reaches its climax when he attacks the props in the tiring house and crowns himself king – in order to be purged of it. The inner play is richly and complexly developed as a utopian satire of the city. In many ways the Antipodes are an anti-London, with social and personal values entirely opposite those of the real city: poets have rights and lawyers refuse payment, gentlemen ask to be arrested and sergeants refuse, old men go to school and youngsters populate the professions. But often the Antipodes's topsy-turviness – wives rule over husbands, servants over masters, courtiers beg money from beggars, victims of theft are punished instead of thieves – seems to be an exaggerated mirror of a feared reality: that lurking just behind an idealisation of London's order and hierarchy is truly a world-turned-upside-down, where, in Shakespeare's words,

> liberty plucks justice by the nose,
> The baby beats the nurse, and quite athwart
> Goes all decorum. (*Measure for Measure*, 1.3.29–31)

Such a vision, Butler reminds us, was meant to disturb not only the play audience but also the play's audience, since 'it demonstrates how upside-down is the real England under Charles'.[18]

Peregrine assumes a mandate to reform the situation – 'reform' is a word he uses over and over – and he embarks on an effort to 'reduce the manners / Of this country to his own' (3.6.25–6). He is diverted from these efforts when Martha, now unrecognisable to him, is presented in an elaborate dumb show as queen of the land and the woman he must take to bed. Peregrine hesitates at first, recalling his wife back in London but really frightened by the greatest threat to a traveller: 'the dangerous passage of a maidenhead' (4.11.44). 'She may be of that serpentine generation', Peregrine worries, 'That stings oft times to death' (4.11.46–7). But Hughball and By-Play insist that they go to the bridal bed for the sake of the nation, and, as Letoy comments to Diana in the audience, he is sure that 'the youth / Will give her royal satisfaction' (4.13.36–7).

Now, with Peregrine and Martha safely stowed, Letoy turns his attention to Joyless, whose jealousy has accelerated into blind, tormented outrage, the kind of 'anguish and insecure tyranny, which rise from [male] pride in the power of patrilineage despite the fact that he can possess only uncertain faith that he perpetuates and governs his own family's traditionally continuous identity'.[19] Letoy plans to help by staging another scene, in effect making the 'outer' play the 'inner' one: he pretends to seduce Diana so that Joyless can, from the wings, witness her unshakeable fidelity. But here the performative cure undermines itself, and Joyless, at first assured of his wife's fidelity but then suspicious of her as simply another actor, 'fall[s] back again' into fits (5.6.23). Only after Diana is revealed as Letoy's daughter – whom he abandoned precisely because he was, like Joyless, doubtful about his wife – can Joyless relax and delight in the final outcome presented to him by Letoy: Peregrine and Martha, returned to their senses. The play closes with yet more inset showpieces, courtly forms that serve not the court but an urban crown of gentry, artisans and wives.

The theory governing the metadrama of *The Antipodes* is that any one beset by a psychological affliction must be

> made a fool, before
> Art can take hold of him to wind him up
> Into his proper center. (4.13.11–13)

In a famous discussion of the play, Jackson Cope has described this logic as part of Brome's long-standing interest in 'dreams, dramatics, and that toward which both in their ways tend, therapeutics for the ruptured or raptured reason'. Here, Brome has organised what Cope calls a 'double illusion by which a man is to receive his own invented world as a reality which engulfs him rather than emanates from him'. When fantasy is developed in such a way, it comes, 'at the extreme point ... back to reality'.[20] *The Antipodes* is Brome's most virtuosic presentation of this logic, full of improvisational energy as well as carefully planned exploits, but its premise, we have seen, had already been a shaping force in his earlier plays. It was to continue to inform his subsequent plays, though in very different shapes and modes.

Brome went on to write for Salisbury Court for nearly two years after the first performance of *The Antipodes*. Included in these works is *The English Moor*, whose depiction of a young wife made to go in blackface by her jealous husband – a jarring rewrite of *Othello* – should be of special interest to contemporary scholarship interested in race and gender. (The play is also noteworthy for the revenge narrative it tucks inside the story of the jealous usurer, in which a young woman, Dionisia, serves as the conflicted revenger.) Brome explicitly draws on Jonson's 1604 masque for Queen Anne, *The Masque of Blackness*, in which female masquers, faces blackened, performed as daughters of Niger who hoped to be transformed white by visiting Britain. Brome's version is far less courtly, but its racial and gender dynamics echo those of the the masque conceit. In his play the jealous usurer Quicksands is so threatened by the thought of cuckoldry that he cannot consummate his marriage, and he decides that if he puts his wife in blackface she will be too unattractive for any man to desire. Millicent, his young wife, agrees, as long as he does not try to sleep with her for a month, which is precisely enough time for the plot to unfold so as to reveal that Quicksands has a bastard son, whom he has abandoned in the country, and to ensure that Millicent is returned, still a virgin, to her true love, Theophilus. Kim Hall, in her seminal *Things of Darkness*, contextualises the play in a socioeconomic landscape in which women's bodies had become 'the site of struggle between, on the one hand, the need for both colonial trade and cultural assimilation through union and, on the other, the desire for well-recognised boundaries between self and other'. Brome's play, she explains, exploits racial values and stereotypes (particularly those of the sexually voracious black woman) as part of its more global vision of the arbitrary, and often fear-fueled, assertion of male power, as 'painting [becomes] an exercise in patriarchal privilege'.[21] But this privilege turns against itself at the play's close, when, in a final masque, Quicksands does not get to reveal his white bride but is instead revealed as the father of a bastard son. The metadrama, in other words, is not so much therapeutic as it is punitive and compensatory.

One may wonder whether Brome's next play, *The Love-Sick Court*, with its aggressive parody of the cult of Platonic love associated with Queen Henrietta Maria, should be interpreted as a resignation letter from Queen Henrietta Maria's Men, the company now installed with Heton.[22] Certainly by late in 1639 Brome had violated his contract, going to work for the Beestons at the Cockpit; he was to claim, in the 1640 suit against him, that Heton and his players had always intended 'covenously or fraudulently to deceive and defraud him'.[23]

It is impossible for us to read his final two plays for the Cockpit, performed in 1641, without the retrospective awareness that the English theatre was to be shut down a year later. But even without this special resonance it is clear that *The Court Beggar* and *The Jovial Crew*, despite their cover of mirth, were deeply concerned with political vice and civil disorder. We recognise *The Court Beggar* as a general indictment of the mendacities of court life as well as a calculatedly *ad hominem* attack on Sir John Suckling and William Davenant, courtiers whom Brome perceived as especially threatening to the theatre. The play's eponymous protagonist, Mendicant the court beggar, sold his estate to come to the city and has lost all his money in failed projects (a series of different projectors haunt him through the play). Now, destitute, he is determined to 'sell' his daughter Charissa to the wealthy, philandering courtier Ferdinando – the Suckling figure – in order to recoup his losses. Charissa, who is in love with the poor but moral Frederick, objects to the match, while Ferdinando, rejected by the object of his affections, the widow Lady Strangelove, appears to be going mad. Allowed into Lady Strangelove's home because of his fits, he tries to rape her, a brutal scene that lays bare the violence lurking underneath court manners. Frederick seizes the opportunity to redress the wrongs Ferdinando has done both to Lady Strangelove and Charissa, but Ferdinand refuses to fight. Instead, he begs forgiveness:

> First for the wrong I did thee, noble youth
> In my designe against *Charissa's* honour,
> It is confess'd, repented; and her selfe
> For satisfaction to be given to thee,
> I'le fall upon my Sword else. (sig. R5)

Then, unaware that Lady Strangelove is eavesdropping, Ferdinand explains the ruse to Frederick: assisted by the doctor, he feigned madness in order to get into the lady's house and attempted to seduce her. Once the story has been fully disclosed, Lady Strangelove enters, threatening to make Ferdinand 'the perpetuall shame of Court', unless he helps to unite Frederick and Charissa. Ferdinando agrees, and in the swirl of inset plays that comprise the final act (and that feature Lady Strangelove's serving woman, Philo, as a player, since 'women-Actors now grow in request' [sig. s2v]), Charissa and Frederick emerge happily married. So do Lady Strangelove and Ferdinando, who bestow £3,000 on the young couple and announce that the Mendicant estate, thanks to the loyal servant Gabriel, has been saved. The play ends with a splendid emblematic display: Mendicant having 'hanged himself' – that is, Mendicant having hung all his patents and papers to his body (sig. s7).

At the beginning of the play, Charissa had offered a stinging indictment of what her father had given up in order to finance his town life. Her condemnation includes an evocative pastoral vision of country landscape and social relations, a highly localised version of John of Gaunt's famous paean to 'this blessed plot', Charissa recalls:

> Large fruitfull Fields, rich Medowes and sweet pastures
> Well cropt with courne and stockd as well with Cattell,
> A parke well stor'd with Deere too, and Fishponds in't,
> And all this for a lodging in the Strand now. (sig. N6)

She goes on to remind her father that on his estate he was beloved: people praised his hospitality, the poor prayed for him, he had a raft of caring servants.

Charissa's description of the father she has lost well describes the father found in the character of Oldrents, the central figure of Brome's final play, *The Jovial Crew*. The play, among the very last on the boards before the Civil War, is highly conscious of the perilous time of its performance, as the Prologue opens:

> The title of our play, A Jovial Crew,
> May seem to promise mirth, which were a new
> And forc'd thing in these sad and tragic days
> For you to find, or we express in plays. (1–4)

Or as Butler puts it more polemically: *The Jovial Crew* 'is a profoundly historical play, giving vigorous expression to the most central preoccupations of its time, and painfully sensitive to the uniqueness of the moment at which it was being performed'.[24]

The scene opens on a fading world of landed hospitality. Oldrents, the kindly owner of a country estate, has been made melancholy by a prophecy that his daughters, Meriel and Rachel, will become beggars. They chafe against their 'father's rule and government', and sneak away with their beaux, Vincent and Hilliard, to meet their fortune head on by joining a group of beggars. They are encouraged and enabled by Oldrents' chief servant, the vibrant Springlove, who annually joins such vagabonds. He tells the foursome that if they become beggars, they 'shall absolve [their] destiny nevertheless, and cure [their] father's grief' (2.1.269–70).

At this point the play begins to chronicle the adventures, some potentially sinister, of the couples and Springlove. In so doing it jests with gender assumptions by making the men far less able to tolerate the discomforts of the begging life; it jests with social assumptions by making all four gentles so dependent on their servant, Springlove; and it jests with aesthetic and ethical assumptions about the viability of the pastoral romance, whose failure to acknowledge the realities of rural life are amply displayed. But the real thrust of the plot is to work through pressing questions about political and personal liberty raised by the existence of 'th' beggars commonwealth' (2.1.48). To Meriel and Rachel, hemmed in by the 'hot hospitality' of their father's estate, the beggars appear to enjoy a charmed independence (2.1.17). They are 'the only free men of a commonwealth', the young women claim,

> Free above scot-free; that observe no law,
> Obey no governor, use no religion,
> But what they draw from their own ancient custom,
> Or constitute themselves, yet are no rebels. (2.1.173–6)

After being threatened with rape and nearly arrested, they – as well as the audience – learn that the beggars' freedom is illusory, the freedom of those who have to laugh raucously in order to disguise the cries of a woman in labour. It is the freedom of the unfree. But the women's idealisation of the 'jovial crew' suggests the powerful appeal of even the most compromised notions of freedom in the face of an intransigent authority, whether father, judge or king. And, as Jeffrey Knapp has argued, Brome was one of several Renaissance playwrights who came to celebrate and privilege vagrancy as a symbolic model of a 'better "rogue" society, one that was more civil and godly than the vagabonds but less strict and intolerant than puritans'.[25]

Jovial Crew is full of references to the stage and its history: there is a play-wright, for instance, amidst the begging crew who, told that he is both poet and actor, comments that 'so have been many famous men' (4.2.171). And it relies on inset performances to carry off a festive ending. By Act 5 the whole group has been gathered at the home of the Justice of the Peace, the implac-able Clack, who talks over everyone, prefers to determine guilt or inno-cence after punishment, and has a particular animus against players: 'I'll pay them above all the rest … Yes, I'll put 'em in stocks, and set 'em up to the whipping-post. They can act justices, can they? I'll act a justice among 'em' (5.1.104–8). But instead of receiving a whipping, the vagabond-players are invited to perform for Oldrents, who is asked to choose from 'a bill of their plays' (5.1.282). The titles include 'The Two Lost Daughters', 'The Vagrant Steward' and 'The Old-Squire and the Fortune-teller' – all titles naming what we have been watching, and what Oldrents has been experiencing, all along. Oldrents settles on the 'The Merry Beggars', believing that it will represent a story unconnected to his world. But he realises almost immedi-ately that the performance is intimately tied to his own biography: it opens with a scene explaining his grandfather's unethical theft of land and then proceeds with scenes that feature Springlove, Meriel and Rachel's departure. Recognising the meaning of the drama, Oldrents interrupts it, anxious to be reunited with his family. But this cannot happen until one of the beggars, the Patrico or minister, explains that he is the grandson of the man 'Whom your grandfather craftily wrought / Out of his estate' (5.1.411–13). The Patrico further reveals that he is the brother of a servant woman with whom Oldrents begot an unacknowledged child (thus Oldrents's line, early in the play, that he wants to make 'expiation of a crime / That's charg'd upon my conscience till't be done' (2.2.142–3). The child, it turns out, is Springlove, who displays an Agnus Dei relic as proof. In a festive triumph, father and children are reunited, and three couples are joined in wedlock.

Earlier criticism considered *The Jovial Crew* to be an example of Caroline escapist drama, a form of entertainment designed to allay the audience's fears and concerns. But as Butler argues, 'Escapism is indeed Brome's theme, but the play is about escapism rather than itself escapist.'[26] Indeed, what *The Jovial Crew* displays so powerfully is the inability of its central character and authority figure to escape the obligations and claims of the past, the sins of the self as well as of the father. Those claims have haunted Oldrents throughout the play; they are put to rest through the play-within-the-play, as Oldrents is made to recognise himself on stage, and his guilts, on stage. There is nothing escapist about this model of theatre, which ultimately had to face, head-on, the breakdown of the English polity, and the English stage, in 1642.

Brome continued to write after the outbreak of the Civil War; his most extensive undertaking, before his death in 1652, was editorship of a collection of elegies, entitled *Lachrymae Musarum*, on the death of Henry Huntingdon, Lord Hastings. Hastings was a royalist, as were some of Brome's former dedicatees, including William Cavendish, Duke of Newcastle, and William Seymour, Earl of Hertford. But it is important not to allow these royalist connections to determine our sense of Brome's own political and aesthetic allegiances in the 1630s and 1640s, especially since Cavendish and Seymour came over to the king's party only after a long history of operating at an ideological distance from the court and sovereign. Certainly the introductory apparatus to Brome's posthumous collected works, the *New Plays* of 1653 and 1658, implicitly aligned Brome with the royalist position, insofar as that position lamented the loss of the professional theatre to the edicts of the Puritan government, and any plays published during the Interregnum would no doubt have served to please the royalists.

But the idea of the theatre that Brome defended with such commitment and concentration was, as we have seen, in no way a royalist one. It was one dedicated, above all, to the exposure and analysis of human humours, grievances, crimes and sins. This is a therapeutic theatre which, in Brome's hands, included all sorts of comic curiosities and sensitivities. Some border on the misogynist, as when the would-be rapist Oliver in *The Jovial Crew* delights in glimpsing Rachel and Meriel's legs under their beggars' outfits: 'There,

there, I saw above the ham as the wind blew' (3.1.304). But more often they display a certain sympathy even to traditionally unlikable characters, like the rejected suitor Tallboy in *The Jovial Crew*, who agrees to bear his loss manfully, 'But what I feel, I feel' (202).

At the start of *The Court Beggar*, a projector appeals to Mendicant with an idea

> For buylding a new Theatre or Play-house
> Upon the *Thames* on Barges or flat boats
> To helpe the watermen out of the losse
> They've suffer'd by Sedans. (sig. o1v)

This passage is usually read as a satiric reference to Davenant's plan to build a theatre in Fleet Street, and thus an idea to be mocked rather than applauded. But there is something genuinely charming about this image of a floating theatre, unbound from the land, rocking in gentle waves. It seems to me fanciful but not unwarranted to see a version of this floating theatre realised in the twenty-first century in the *Richard Brome Online* project, where texts and videos of Brome's dramas are on display in a virtual, rather than watery, space. The stunning website provides quarto and modern editions (viewable side-by-side or individually) of each of the sixteen plays, thorough scholarly introductions, a collection of additional essays, a capacious bibliography, and, most remarkable of all, video clips of scenes of Brome's plays in rehearsal – clips which can be reached through a 'gallery' or by links within the plays themselves. The website is a spectacular achievement that brings the resources of twenty-first-century technology to bear on a dramatist who, offering 'one of the truest records of the economic, social, and moral climate of a people living in a period of transition',[27] might very well have appreciated it.

NOTES

1 Richard Brome, *The Antipodes*, ed. Anne Haaker (Lincoln, NE: University of Nebraska Press, 1966), 4.8.13–14. Unless stated otherwise, references to the other plays by Richard Brome in the text derive from the following sources: *The Court Beggar* and *Weeding of Covent Garden* in *Five New Plays* (London, 1653); *The Damoiselle* (London, 1653); *The Northern Lasse* (London, 1632); and *The English Moor* in *Five New Playes* (London, 1658). The texts are available at *Richard Brome Online*, general editor Richard Cave (www.hrionline.ac.uk/hri-online). See also *The Jovial Crew*, ed. Anne Haaker (Lincoln, NE: University of Nebraska Press, 1968), and Richard Brome and Thomas Heywood, *The Late Lancashire Witches*, ed. Laird H. Barber (New York: Garland Publishers, 1979).

2 Francis Beaumont and John Fletcher, *Comedies and Tragedies* (London, 1647), sig. G1r.

3 Derek Hirst, *Authority and Conflict: Kingdom, Community, Commonwealth* (Cambridge, MA: Harvard University Press, 1986), 31, 146.

4 Andrew Gurr, *The Shakespeare Company, 1594–1642* (Cambridge University Press, 2004), 155.

5 R. J. Kaufmann, *Richard Brome: Caroline Playwright* (New York: Columbia University Press, 1961); and Martin Butler, *Theatre and Crisis, 1632–1642* (Cambridge University Press, 1984), 101.

6 Butler, *Theatre and Crisis*, 4, 111.

7 Ira Clark, *Professional Playwrights: Massinger, Ford, Shirley, and Brome* (Lexington, KY: University of Kentucky Press, 1992), 172.

8 Nigel Bawcutt, *The Control and Censorship of Caroline Drama: The Records of Sir Henry Herbert, Master of the Revels, 1623–73* (Oxford: Clarendon Press, 1996), 145.

9 Bawcutt, *The Control and Censorship of Caroline Drama*, 167. Brome's success with *Love-Sick Maid* is often juxtaposed to the contemporaneous failure of his master Jonson's *The New Inn*.

10 Kaufmann, *Richard Brome*, 16.

11 Matthew Steggle, *Richard Brome: Place and Politics on the Caroline Stage* (Manchester University Press, 2004), 27.

12 Thomas Heywood. *The English Traveller* (London, 1633), sig. A3. See also Joseph Loewenstein, *Ben Jonson and Possessive Authorship* (Cambridge University Press, 2002).

13 Heather Hirschfeld, *Joint Enterprises: Collaborative Drama and the Institutionalization of the English Renaissance Theater* (Amherst, MA: University of Massachusetts Press, 2004), 135.

14 John Freehafer, 'Brome, Suckling, and Davenant's Theater Project of 1639', *Texas Studies in Language and Literature* 10 (1968): 367–83 at 370.

15 Butler, *Theatre and Crisis*, 152, 153.

16 In a lovely nod to *Bartholomew Fair*, Cockbrain explicitly invokes Jonson's character when he embarks on this effort: 'And so as my Reverend Ancestor Justice Adam Overdoe, was wont to say, *In Heavens name and the Kings*, and for the good of the Common-wealth I will go about it' (*Weeding*, 2).

17 Glynne Wickham, Herbert Berry and William Ingram, eds., *English Professional Theatre, 1530–1660* (Cambridge University Press, 2000), 658.

18 Butler, *Theatre and Crisis*, 217.

19 Clark, *Professional Playwrights*, 185.

20 Jackson Cope, *The Theater and the Dream: From Metaphor to Form in Renaissance Drama* (Baltimore, MD: Johns Hopkins University Press, 1973), 140, 148, 152.

21 Kim Hall, *Things of Darkness: Economies of Race and Gender in Early Modern England* (Ithaca, NY: Cornell University Press, 1995), 125, 169.

22 Steggle, *Richard Brome*, 139.

23 Wickham *et al.*, *English Professional Theatre*, 662.

24 Butler, *Theatre and Crisis*, 279.

25 Jeffrey Knapp, *Shakespeare's Tribe: Church, Nation and Theater in Renaissance England* (University of Chicago Press, 2002), 65.

26 Butler, *Theatre and Crisis*, 271.
27 Haaker, *The Jovial Crew*, xx.

Further reading

Andrews, C. E., *Richard Brome: A Study of his Life and Works*. New Haven, CT: Yale University Press, 1913.

Astington, John H., *English Court Theatre, 1558–1647*. Cambridge University Press, 1999.

Atherton, Ian, and Julie Sanders, eds., *The 1630s: Interdisciplinary Essays on Culture and Politics in the Caroline Era*. Manchester University Press, 2006.

Cave, Richard, 'The Playwriting Sons of Ben: Nathan Field and Richard Brome', in *Jonsonians: Living Traditions*, ed. Brian Woolland. Aldershot: Ashgate, 2003, 69–91.

Davis, J. L., *The Sons of Ben: Jonsonian Comedy in Caroline England*. Detroit, MI: Wayne State University Press, 1967.

Donaldson, Ian, *The World Upside-Down: Comedy from Jonson to Fielding*. Oxford: Clarendon Press, 1970.

Hirschfeld, Heather, 'Collaborating across Generations: Thomas Heywood, Richard Brome, and the Production of *The Late Lancashire Witches*.' *Journal of Medieval and Early Modern Studies* 30 (April 2000), 339–74.

McLuskie, Kathleen, 'Caroline Professionals: Brome and Shirley', in *The Revels History of Drama in English, 1613–1660*, ed. Philip Edwards, G. E. Bentley and Lois Potter. London: Methuen, 1981, 237–48.

Sanders, Julie, 'The Politics of Escapism: Fantasies of Travel and Power in Richard Brome's *The Antipodes* and Ben Jonson's *The Alchemist*', in *Writing and Fantasy*, ed. Ceri Sullivan and Barbara White. London: Longman, 1999, 137–50.

Shaw, Catherine M., *Richard Brome*. Boston: Twayne Publishing, 1980.

16

ELIZABETH SCHAFER

Troublesome histories: performance and early modern drama

Performance history has much to contribute to scholarly engagement with, and understanding of, early modern plays, and this chapter is grounded in the belief that performed responses to the dramaturgical challenges posed by any Renaissance play are worth attending to, criticising and learning from. Even the most scrupulous reader or editor will struggle to understand the full theatricality of a play without the insights provided by performance: the real impression a silent character can make on stage; the effect of hearing a song rather than reading it; the comic impact of a skilfully performed chase sequence. In addition, character relationships can become clarified by asking pragmatic staging questions. For example in Richard Brome's rarely performed play, *The City Wit*, Brome characterises the marriage of Sir Andrew and Lady Ticket as loveless. While the tiny, but telling, detail that the Tickets never speak to each other in the entire play is not obvious when reading this fast-moving comedy, the actors playing the Tickets in Kim Durban's 2007 production of *The City Wit* identified this aspect of the Tickets' relationship almost immediately, simply by asking pragmatic acting questions in rehearsals: 'Who is my character speaking to? And who is my character *not* speaking to?'[1]

As very few Renaissance plays apart from the set texts, the canonical plays by Marlowe, Jonson, Webster and Middleton, have had their performance histories attended to, there is still a real need for more performance-centred criticism in relation to most early modern plays.[2] Some performance histories are sketched out in introductions to editions of plays, but provision is very erratic; most editors are not recruited on the grounds of their theatrical intelligence and some produce little more than dutiful, but dull, lists. The most critical question to ask here is 'Why is this performance history being written?'[3] Is it being written because the general editor of the series insists it has to be done? Is it being written to speak to theatre practitioners and/or students and/or the general public and/or the scholarly community? Is it for an English literature or performance studies readership? Is it being assembled by a dramaturge for use by a director, performer or designer? Is it going to be published as a programme note or is it a PhD thesis? Or might it be written because the combination of performance history, bibliography and critical scholarship can produce a stimulating cocktail which reveals much about the potential dramaturgy of a play?

An additional issue is the macro as opposed to the microhistorical approach: macrohistory produces grand narratives that can comfortably sweep from a play's premiere in the 1590s to the latest cutting edge, twenty-first-century production. By contrast microhistory digs down deep, focuses on the particular, and might – in an extreme example – offer an in-depth exploration of a single production of *A Mad World, My Masters* in Tristan da Cunha. This exploration might include political, sociological, economic and aesthetic imperatives in circulation at the time of the production; certainly sociologist Wendy Griswold has demonstrated how useful an analysis of 'sociologically significant actions' can be in shedding light on 'when and why' a society reaches 'into its cultural archive' to 'pull something out'.[4] It might be important to consider what other plays are in the repertoire at the time (*The Tamer Tamed* piggy-backing on yet another revival of *The Taming of the Shrew* at the Royal Shakespeare Company [RSC] in 2003);[5] what world events might affect programming (Margaret Webster reviving *Richard II* on Broadway in 1937 to coincide with a sudden interest in abdication); what centenaries are in the offing (*A New Way to Pay Old Debts* revived by the RSC in 1983, the quatercentenary of Massinger's birth); what local resonances might pertain (revivals of Marlowe in his birthplace of Canterbury; the Salisbury Playhouse revival of *The Picture* in Massinger's home city in 2010). Once the cultural specificity of a production of a Renaissance play has been examined, it is also crucial to ask 'What is the political positioning of the historian?' In order to explore these challenges further, this chapter will *not* be offering a performance history of the plays of Shakespeare and his contemporaries from the early modern period to today; rather it will focus what would otherwise become a completely unwieldy discussion by considering three case studies: John Webster's frequently performed *Duchess of Malfi* (1612–13), Ben Jonson's frequently performed *Alchemist* (1610), and Anon.'s infrequently performed 1592 play, *Arden of Faversham*.

The first case study, *The Duchess of Malfi*, helps illuminate a strategy typical of the macrohistorical approach to the performance of Renaissance drama, the survey of general trends. Here the performance history of a play will largely follow the contours of any mainstream history of theatre – such as those written by, for example, Phyllis Hartnoll or Oscar Brockett.[6] The major problem with the general survey approach is that it fills in background but risks inaccuracy; anyone investigating the detail is likely to find instances that contradict or complicate the generalisations. However, surveys have their uses as maps, especially for newcomers to performance history, and they can help contextualise the journey a play has taken over the centuries.

The Duchess of Malfi is comparatively well served in terms of performance history: John Russell Brown (a theatre scholar and practitioner) has four pages on 'Theatre Productions' in the introduction to his Revels edition;[7] there is an excellent Text and Performance volume by Richard Cave (a theatre scholar) which looks at two productions of *The White Devil* before examining Peter Gill's 1971 and Philip Prowse's 1985 productions of *The Duchess of Malfi*;[8] there is a Plays in Performance volume by Kathleen McLuskie (a literature specialist associated with feminist and cultural materialist criticism), and Jenny Uglow (a writer of biography).[9] McLuskie and Uglow provide impressive annotation about precise stage business as well as offering a more analytical discussion of the play's performance history in general.[10] A recent performance history of Bosola by John Buckingham is readily available online and is written from the perspective of a scholar, teacher and director who has himself directed *The Duchess of Malfi* and who grounds his scholarship in the pragmatics of theatre.[11] The internet publication of Buckingham's performance history is significant as he has more space for words and pictures than in commercial hard copy publishing. Indeed internet publishing is becoming a significant force in constructing more and more performance histories, as practitioners document their own practice on YouTube and elsewhere. And on the internet, commercial considerations might not hinder, as they would with book publishing, the publication of a performance history of, for example, Elizabeth Cary's *The Tragedy of Mariam, Fair Queen of Jewry*, on the grounds that such a history might have a small readership.

Focusing on a single play such as *The Duchess of Malfi* and marching through the centuries leave little space for considering any production in detail or in terms of its specific cultural context. More importantly, equally instructive stage histories might be constructed using different mechanisms for structuring the analysis such as feminisim, Marxism, race politics, post-colonial theory. However, a macro survey might begin with Renaissance playhouse conditions and look at premieres and revivals during the Elizabethan, Jacobean and Caroline periods. Immediately the problem of periodisation arises and whether it is useful to think in terms of categories such as 'Jacobean' or 'Caroline' (answer: 'not if you want nuance'). However, given that the first performances of *The Duchess of Malfi*, around 1614, would have played at both the Blackfriars and the Globe playhouses, there is an opportunity for speculation over the differences this might have produced, especially in relation to the Act 4 display of waxworks in an indoor or outdoor playhouse with different lighting conditions. Indeed *The Duchess of Malfi*'s five-act structure seems marked by indoor, rather than outdoor, playing conditions, with breaks allowing for candle trimming. The original actors in Webster's play included Richard Burbage as Ferdinand, Richard Sharpe as the Duchess and John Lowin as Bosola. John Buckingham is able to take eight pages to explore what John Lowin might have brought to his role, working from what is known about this player and his other theatre work. But a survey will have to gallop straight on into the Interregnum, which in a macrohistory might be characterised by private theatricals plus illegal performances of extracts, and the short comical redactions of a play known as drolls. During this period *The Duchess of Malfi* was available for reading, but there are no records of performance. Restoration audiences, some of whom had been sojourning in France with Charles II for many years and had become accustomed to female performers, would have been the first to see the role of the Duchess played by a woman, Mary Betterton, acting opposite her husband, Thomas Betterton, as Bosola. *The Duchess of Malfi* was popular, and returned Royalist audiences, who would view Charles I as a martyr, might be inclined to view sympathetically the sufferings of an imprisoned ruler being prepared for execution. It is tempting to pause in the survey to speculate over how moving from the Elizabethan open stage playhouse to the Restoration theatre might have affected *The Duchess of Malfi* especially in terms of the shift in the direction of the proscenium arch and away from the use of natural light. Increased opportunities for scenery would certainly alter the three-dimensionality of the play in performance; when *The Duchess of Malfi* played at Lincoln's Inn Fields, it was in a converted tennis court, as opposed to the quasi theatre-in-the-round Globe.

Some Renaissance plays did well in the Restoration period compared with today, simply because Shakespeare had not yet become dominant: he was not yet the Bard of Avon nor the twentieth century's set-text box office attraction. Nevertheless many Renaissance plays were radically and strategically adapted during the late seventeenth century to speak to a contemporary political moment or fashion. As material for cultural history these adaptations are a rich resource, but they also offer very detailed, if occasionally extreme, critiques of the Renaissance plays in question. *The Duchess of Malfi* was adapted in 1707 as *The Unfortunate Duchess of Malfy or the Unnatural Brothers* and the title suggests a commitment to the Duchess as victim rather than, as a late twentieth-century reading might have it, a feminist or an existential hero. The Duchess went on to gain a happy ending in a 1733 rewrite by the editor of Shakespeare, Lewis Theobald; although entitled *The Fatal Secret*, this adaptation was less fatal than Webster's play and the Duchess was reunited with Antonio and her children. Theobald also cut down on the sex and Julia's story line was excised. A macrohistory might emphasise the importance of star performers in the eighteenth century and their importance in promoting certain plays which exhibited their talents. The star actor in *The Fatal Secret* was James Quin but his performance was not enough to make *The Fatal Secret* a success and *The Duchess of Malfi* then has no recorded performance history for the next 150 years. Certainly by the time of the French Revolution, and English reactions to it, the play's interest in the deposition and execution of a ruler might have made its subject matter difficult to navigate on the London stage (which, inevitably, is the focus of a macro survey of performances of this play). While other eighteenth-century theatre fashions include adding songs to Renaissance plays or compressing them into short afterpieces, to play after the main performance of the evening, the most significant macro trend of the time is the rise of overt editing of play texts: during this period many Renaissance plays became more readily available for reading than they had been in a long time. Published collections such as Robert Dodsley's *Old Plays* gave new access to non-Shakespearean drama and when Webster's contemporaries could be read alongside *The Duchess of Malfi*, his dramaturgy might begin to seem less lurid.

When *The Duchess of Malfi* returned to the stage in 1850 it was a vehicle for the intrepid Isabella Glyn, in partnership with Samuel Phelps, at the off West End venue of Sadler's Wells. Glyn used an adaptation by R. H. Horne and became associated with this Duchess-centric rewrite for eighteen years; as Horne's adaptation was published as a performance edition, it is possible to go beyond reviews – with their inevitable political loading – in excavating performance details. However, the Victorian period, in a macrohistorical survey, might also be seen as the moment when a passion for historical accuracy and detail becomes increasingly more fashionable. J. R. Planché's designs and Charles Kean's commitment to historical pageantry helped the development of a pictorial stage in which history plays like Shakespeare's *King John* could flourish. Plays were rearranged, and scenes reordered, to reduce scene changes made cumbersome by large amounts of stage furniture and set. The historical dimension of *The Duchess of Malfi* would offer opportunities for pictorial, well-upholstered stagings that could appeal to Victorian taste. The play's intersection with melodrama might also increase its box office appeal. Glyn's advocacy of *The Duchess of Malfi* was, however, critical in a period when the actor-manager's search for roles that provided a vehicle for his specific talents meant that many ensemble Renaissance plays dropped from the repertoire and were read but not performed.

At the end of the nineteenth century William Poel, following the lead of the much earlier German pioneer Ludwig Tieck, started his campaign to bring back the apron stage for the performance of Renaissance drama in England. As part of this campaign Poel produced Renaissance plays which had not been performed for a very long time. So a macrohistory might be slightly startled to find that, despite the director's commitment to 'original practices', Poel's 1892 staging of *The Duchess of Malfi* used scenery and that, like Theobald and Horne before him, Poel shifted the actual strangling of the Duchess so that it could take place decorously off stage.

Poel's example inspired several student societies, such as the Cambridge-based Marlowe Society, to follow his lead and start producing lesser-known Renaissance plays; the rise of English studies at university level is also important here in the creation of student theatre societies, and student audiences for Renaissance plays.[12] Another significant force was the London-based Phoenix Society, a group of professional performers who experimented with non-commercial plays. The Phoenix Society particularly promoted early modern non-Shakespearean plays and during the period 1919–25 they staged twenty-six Renaissance plays; one of the first, in 1919, was *The Duchess of Malfi*, at the Lyric Theatre, Hammersmith, with a basic set designed by Norman Wilkinson. Three years later Nugent Monck revived *The Duchess of Malfi* at his Elizabethan-style Maddermarket Theatre, the first of several Monck productions of the play.

By the mid-twentieth century, *The Duchess of Malfi* was beginning to appear more frequently in the professional theatre. The question of tone was emerging as a challenge: directors seeking to ban giggles over the play's horrors had an uphill battle on their hands. The role of the Duchess was attracting major twentieth-century actresses – Peggy Ashcroft (1945, 1960), Elisabeth Bergner (1946) – but the play also garnered attention from the theatre left: Brecht did an adaptation and in 1956 Theatre Workshop did a production, directed by John Bury, at Stratford East. As the play gained in popularity, however, the macrohistorical approach risks becoming superficial; there is no space to excavate in detail Canada Lee's whiteface Bosola (New York 1946); or the RSC's choice of the play (showcasing Peggy Ashcroft) to open their London base, the Aldwych, in 1960; or Kate Brooke's superb 1998 production at the Ustinov Studio in Bath, starring Tanya Ronder as a Jackie Kennedy lookalike, paparazzi-hounded Duchess whose 'bravery', 'stubborn sense of self' and 'intense enjoyment of life are beacons of light in a world where nothing is certain or clear'.[13]

Late twentieth-century theatre saw a marked increase in certain kinds of Renaissance production – anything with an opportunity for designer violence or kinky sex to be simulated on stage was popular, and the *Revenger's Tragedy* – which offers both – became a great favourite, particularly with student and fringe theatre groups. In the UK subsidised theatre, production centres such as the RSC or the National Theatre (NT) are now able to throw significant resources at the production of Renaissance drama, not simply in terms of set, costume, acting and directing personnel but also in the form of voice coaching and support for work on text. It is important to acknowledge broader trends and influences in theatre – Antonin Artaud, Rudolf Laban, Jerzy Grotowski, Gardzienice theatrical practices – but again the problem with the macrohistorical approach is scope; if every international exploration of every Renaissance play were to be examined, the sheer scale of the survey would become more than one lifetime's work. Ideally, major political movements should also be taken into account; for example, post-1960s feminism has had an impact on the staging of the default misogyny of many Renaissance plays. Postmodernism has inflected the reception of queer readings, such as Declan Donnellan's 1995–6 *Duchess of Malfi*. Celebrity casting continues to be an important factor: after the release of *The Long Good Friday*, the pairing of the stars of that film, Helen Mirren and Bob Hoskins, in Adrian Noble's 1980–1 Manchester Royal Exchange *Duchess of Malfi* tends to upstage what seems, in retrospect, the intriguing casting of Pete Postlethwaite as Antonio. *The Duchess of Malfi*'s shift to film also needs assessing; for example, in 1972, Cedric Messina's television production gave the play a lovingly realist treatment, an approach in tension with the play's anti-illusionistic aspects, one which decks the action out in English Heritage costumes and a stately-home setting.

Continuities across the macrohistory – such as the desire to make Antonio more of a romantic hero than Webster allows – are revealing, but even though survey-style generalisations are grounded in a macrohistorical truth, they need to be tested out with great care. And, as Edward Hallett Carr advised all aspiring historians in *What is History?*, it is important to 'Study the historian before you study the work'.[14] So it is pertinent to the survey I have produced above that – try as I might to avoid this – my responses to *The Duchess of Malfi* are still haunted by my first encounters with the play which began, in a rather unscholarly way, when I read *Sleeping Murder* by Agatha Christie. In this posthumously published novel, a performance of *The Duchess of Malfi* – the 1945 George Rylands production starring John Gielgud and Peggy Aschcroft – is the setting for a seminal moment in a Miss Marple plot, which has an obsessive and borderline incestuous brother murder his sister. Shortly after reading this novel I had my first encounter with the play in the theatre; this was a soul-scarringly bad school production with an utterly chaste Julia and Cardinal, costumes hired from the RSC (Judi Dench's frock) and a final scene that seemed to last forever; indeed I didn't see the ending as I had to leave in time to catch the last bus home. Thirty years later,

I still cannot sit through the dying moments of *The Duchess of Malfi* without thinking of the 130 bus and its imminent departure from Birmingham New Street. Ironically, although I have subsequently seen the play in the theatre many times, one the most memorable *Duchess of Malfi*s I have ever encountered is a production that never happened: the production satirised in director Michael Blakemore's *roman-à-clef*, *Next Season*.¹⁵ Meanwhile my personal gold standard with *The Duchess of Malfi* is the stunning performance by Harriet Walter – in Bill Alexander's 1989 RSC production (Figure 4) – which included moments of extraordinarily intense emotion, worthy, it seemed to me, of Sarah Siddons. These experiences will undergird any discussion I will ever produce of *The Duchess of Malfi* in performance. And tugging away underneath it all is my feminist distaste for any play that displays the systematic torture and execution of a female character.

A useful counterpoint to the performance history of the high tragedy of *The Duchess of Malfi* is provided by the performance history of Ben Jonson's great farce, *The Alchemist*. My personal encounters with this comedy in the theatre have all been very positive; the first *Alchemist* I saw was Gregory Hersov's excellent 1987 *Alchemist* for the Manchester Royal Exchange;¹⁶ subsequent highlights include two shimmeringly good productions: Sam Mendes's 1991 RSC *Alchemist* and Neil Armfield's 1996 production at the Belvoir St Theatre, Sydney, starring Hugo Weaving as Face and Geoffrey Rush as Subtle. But a historical survey must start by stating that the play was written to be performed by the King's Men at their newly acquired Blackfriars playhouse in 1609–10.¹⁷ Because the playhouses had been closed due to the plague, it is probable that *The Alchemist* was actually first performed in Oxford in September 1610.¹⁸ The play was revived several times before the Interregnum and also played in seventeenth-century Dublin, where the play's Londonness must have carried extra political loading. During the closure of the playhouses *The Alchemist* seems to have survived as a droll and it was popular with several celebrity actors in the eighteenth century, being especially associated with David Garrick who repositioned Drugger as the star of the play. Jonson's bawdy jokes ensured that *The Alchemist* was absent from the stage during the nineteenth century until Poel resurrected it in 1899. From the mid-twentieth century on, it has been revived several times but there has been a (predictable) tendency towards: making *The Alchemist* darker, emphasising the dark undertow (for example, Tim Pigott-Smith's 1996 performance of Subtle as a character who 'really is an alchemist' and who 'has been imprisoned for it');¹⁹ updating language ('harem' for 'seraglio');²⁰ depositing cumbersome scenery in the way of the performers playing Face, Subtle and Doll, as they try to race across the stage. A less predictable recent development has been the rehabilitation

Figure 4 Harriet Walter as the Duchess of Malfi in a rare happy moment at the
Royal Shakespeare Company, directed by Bill Alexander, 1989. Joe Cocks Studio Collection
© Shakespeare Birthplace Trust.

of the notion of the philosopher's stone in the wake of the first Harry Potter
novel and film.

The performance history of *The Alchemist* is particularly marked by an
urge to make the play 'relevant'. Claiming relevance is an ongoing issue for
any production of any Renaissance play and, while scholars are free to conduct theory wars on the universalist fallacy, theatre workers know that a
theoretically elegant production that does not in some way partake in strategic universalism – 'this is about you and me, now' – is likely to be heading
towards box office disaster followed by a period of unemployment. Tyrone
Guthrie was the first director to make the case for the contemporary relevance of *The Alchemist* by putting the play into modern dress, firstly with the
Old Vic company at the Liverpool Playhouse in 1944, and again at the Old

Vic itself in 1962.[21] But in 1962 Guthrie felt he needed to write a programme essay justifying this modernisation, which extended to updating some language: the *Guardian* (29 November 1962) records a reference to 'the spirit of dead Einstein', Kastril and Pliant as 'ton-up motor-cyclists' and Charles Gray's Sir Epicure as 'recognisably a crumbling pillar of the Carlton Club'. Bamber Gascoigne, reviewing the production for the *Spectator* (7 December 1962) argued Guthrie's updating produced 'almost total disaster', and cited examples of unnecessary changes such as 'coach and six' being changed to 'limousine'. Despite Gascoigne's strictures, however, many subsequent directors, performers and designers have followed Guthrie's example in updating the action of *The Alchemist*; in 2002 Joss Bennathan relocated the play to the 'greed is good' 1980s and Thatcher's Britain with Doll as 'a cheerful whore in a Madonna cone-breasted girdle' and a lot of feng shui (*What's On*, 16 January 2002). Subtle was black and 1980s hit records provided a soundtrack to the action. A production by Michael Kahn in 2009 responded 'to the financial bubble-burstings of the previous couple of years, notably the collapse of the Bernie Madoff Ponzi scheme' and was 'aggressively contemporary'.[22] One aspect of the play that is often wittily updated is the depiction of the Anabaptists: Guthrie made Tribulation Wholesome a woman and in Frank Dunlop's 1972 Young Vic production both Puritans became 'Salvation Army lasses' (*The Times*, 9 June 1972). In Peter James's 1968 production for the Everyman, Liverpool, Jonathan Holt played Ananias as a recognisable version of the Reverend Ian Paisley (*Guardian*, 24 April 1968); in 2009 Michael Kahn had Tribulation Wholesome as 'a Jimmy Swaggart-style televangelist in frosted pompadour and white suit'.[23] Despite all this cultural relocation, Barry Edelstein, when he directed the play in 2000, still, like Guthrie, felt the need to defend his use of what he called 'a double lens of 1610 and 2000' in the *New York Times* (13 February 2000); Edelstein's production included a Doll (Johann Carlo) who 'in a blond wig and red leather suit, descends the stair, talking to a toy monkey and singing "Hello, Dolly!" in a baby voice. The lecher, Epicure, is agog. He wants "a taste of her … wit"' (*New York Times*, 25 February 2000). The joke of Doll singing "Hello Dolly" is – whether you laugh or groan at it – a memorable nugget of performance history.

The Alchemist has also time-travelled to other periods. In 1947 John Burrell placed the play in the eighteenth century, with a *Beggar's Opera* look. *The Times* (1 February 1978) thought Richard Eyre's Nottingham Playhouse 'transposition of the play … to Dickensian London does little to open up the play'. Griff Rhys Jones's Victorian *Alchemist* was seen by *The Times* (10 September 1985) as existing in 'one of the darker booths in *Vanity Fair*'. An intriguing ADC (Amateur Dramatic Company) student production took place in Cambridge in 1950 which featured RSC director-to-be John

Barton as Face in an early nineteenth-century setting; the *Times* review (30 November 1950) thought the production shrunk the play 'to the dimensions of the toy theatre'.

Because the process of invoking period on stage is (usually) heavily dependent on visuals, particularly set and costume, any performance history is likely to benefit from the use of illustrations. One image of any of *The Alchemist*s just mentioned could evoke a great deal about the production. However, when images appear, they draw focus and they can argue with as well as complement performance history. Take, for example, the photograph I have reproduced of Geoffrey Rush as Subtle (Figure 5). This illustration vividly evokes the *contemporary* aspect of Neil Armfield's brilliant 1996 *Alchemist*. But this production actually mixed a 1996 Sydney ethos with Jacobean grunge. Elsewhere Rush appeared as a distinctly Jacobean dotty doctor. But the memorable Subtle-in-a-sarong image makes it hard to keep the more Jacobean elements of this production in mind. Of course, using theatre photographs in relation to performance history is always inherently political, something which has been analysed very persuasively by Barbara Hodgdon in her essay 'Photography, Theater, Mnemonics; or, Thirteen Ways of Looking at a Still'.[24] Hodgdon ranges very widely in her analysis of different kinds of visual documentation of theatre production – stills, contact sheets, postcards, rehearsal shots, marketing and the like – and yet she does not take account of the most pragmatic of considerations: cost. Whether that cost is time (chasing photographers for permission or for high-quality originals to reproduce) or money (very different rates charged by different archives) or space (a maximum of five illustrations), this will have an impact on the choice of photograph(s) used. And this chapter is making a very deliberate statement by offering three images relating to the performance history of *Arden of Faversham* but only one each in relation to *The Alchemist* and *The Duchess of Malfi*. The politics of cover photographs are even more dizzying. Books with little or no interest in theatre quite often use engaging theatrical images on their covers as a marketing strategy.[25]

By engaging with details such as the image from Neil Armfield's *Alchemist* I have, of course, shifted from macrohistory, if not to microhistory then at least to something between the two (median history?). And, of course microhistory also brings major challenges in its wake; overwhelmed with detail, the performance historian can struggle to lick the material into shape for consumption by the general interest reader rather than by the performance history anorak. And how many microhistorians of performance really delve into the lighting and sound cues when researching a production? (I don't.) The chronological imperative in history can also become predictable (the Victorians don't do bawdy jokes on

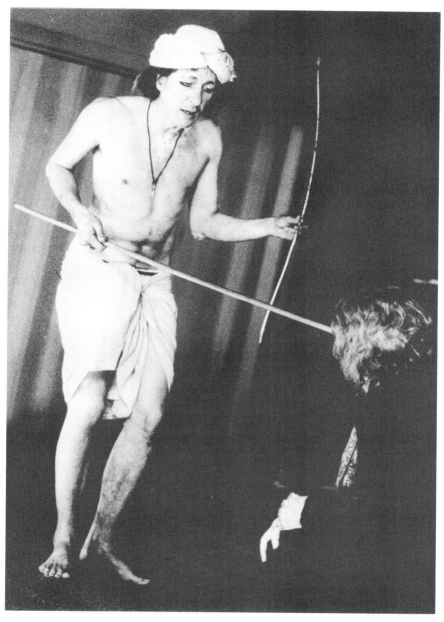

Figure 5 Geoffrey Rush as Subtle in *The Alchemist* at Belvoir St Theatre, Sydney, directed by Neil Armfield, 1996. Photo: Heidrun Löhr. Reproduced by permission.

the legitimate stage), and there might be value in exploring beyond history into other disciplines. One potentially very useful approach might be performance geography.[26] This could address the three-dimensionality of set design, the movement of performers around the stage space, the physical relation of audience to stage. And *The Alchemist* provides a particularly useful example of a performance geography in relation to two productions only ten years apart: Nicholas Hytner's 2006 NT production and Bill Alexander's 1996 production, both of which appeared in the same theatre space: the NT Olivier stage.

Both productions had sets which were much discussed in the reviews and, in a farce-based comedy like *The Alchemist*, the set, and the stage geography it creates, will be of paramount importance. In Alexander's 1996 production, William Dudley's huge, gothic set, slowed everything down painfully; the cast kept running but they had such distances to cover that they could not keep up a fast pace. Some reviewers certainly admired the look of the set; it was 'like a Mad Max world banged together with scrap metal' (*Sunday Express*, 22 September 1996) and 'the impression is that some mad blacksmith made scores of cogs, spanners, pipes, radiators, candlesticks and a few instruments of torture, and then squashed them into a sort of black brutalist Gothic: Gormenghast chic' (*The Times*, 18 September 1996). However, the *Telegraph* (18 September 1996) thought it 'a Heath Robinson-style junkyard of a set which is too elaborate for the play's own good' and the *Daily Express* (20 September 1996) advised 'Someone should torch the set.' Even a reviewer who thought the set 'superb' characterised it as like 'a collaboration between Heath-Robinson and Richard Rogers: grandiose and impractical' (*Sunday Times*, 22 September 1996); the *Spectator* (19 October 1996) condemned it for taking hours to cross; it was 'just awful in every way'. A curtain map of the London Underground with the station names in Latin epitomised some of the problems; the cleverness of the set upstaged, and hindered, the performers even though the production featured a virtuoso display of acting:

> Simon Callow excels himself as the protean Face, brilliantly scrambling in and out of a medley of disguises – including a plummy, moustachioed blimp, a hump-backed Brummie furnace-tender who seems to be alchemy's answer to Mrs Overall in *Acorn Antiques* and a smirkingly smug butler who dispenses falsehoods in sedate Morningside tones. Eerily, even the Sarf London wideboy he 'really' is feels more like a default setting than a true identity, another mask beneath the masks. Delivering the final speech to the audience, Callow emphasises this by shifting around all his preceding accents, a tantalising tease to the end. (*Independent*, 18 September 1996)

And yet even this bravura performance struggled for attention in the context of the dominating set.

Nicholas Hytner's 2006 *Alchemist* was far better received critically but this production was also relatively slow in its pacing. The production opened with Face, Subtle and Dol sitting and glowering resentfully at each other and the build up of energy took time. The opening scene of *The Alchemist* can be tricky as, if the speed at the beginning is too frantic, too explosive, there is no opportunity for the audience to savour the precision of Jonson's insults. Meanwhile performances that are more careful about the words risk being low energy.

As with the Alexander production, the pacing was affected by the set. The *Sunday Times* (17 September 2006) characterised it as

> exceptionally clever, like the solution to a difficult puzzle: an open-sided main room that revolves 360 degrees within a half-square of little terraced houses, with two staircases that only encourage more and more clownish running up and down as the convoluted plot unfolds.

Meanwhile the *Independent* (15 September 2006) complained 'I never properly understood the geography of the set'; the *Evening Standard* (15 September 2006) thought 'Mark Thompson's oddish design ... misses the right claustrophobic sense.' Overall the *Financial Times* (22 September 2006) concluded 'the Olivier Theatre is far too broad and deep a space for this kind of busy intrigue'.

The cultural geography of this production evoked contemporary London even though Subtle's personas included a Californian hippie (for Drugger, with some 'om' meditating); a Scots accountant (for the Anabaptists); a white-robed New Age monk (for Epicure). Drugger became an Indian 'nerdy Asian corner shop owner', which risked becoming 'ridiculously racist' but avoided it (*Morning Star*, 12 October 2006).[27] Kastril was 'given a master-class in African-American trash talk' (*New Statesman*, 25 September 2006). Pliant was black. The production was largely seen as a two-star vehicle for two former Hamlets – Alex Jennings (Subtle) and Simon Russell Beale (Face);[28] it also featured the NT debut of Ian Richardson as Sir Epicure. Richardson put in a very fine performance with impeccable, but slightly historical, speaking of the verse. While, once again, *The Alchemist* seemed uncomfortable on the cavernous Olivier stage, Hytner's *Alchemist* also, by means of the programme, claimed the culturally geographic significance of taking place not far from the location of Jonson's original setting in the Blackfriars.[29]

Two *Alchemist*s on the same stage only ten years apart is unusual, but in the context of cultural geography and its explorations of how people use space, these productions might also encourage an examination of why Renaissance drama has flourished in particular *milieux* (the NT, the Stratfords, Shakespeare's Globe). Other theatrical centres worth analysing in this context might include the Old Vic, the 'home of Shakespeare' under Lilian Baylis but also a home for *The Witch of Edmonton*, *The Knight of the Burning Pestle*, *A New Way to Pay Old Debts*, *The Shoemakers' Holiday*. And in Nottingham, Peter Barnes and Richard Eyre ensured that, while they were based at the Nottingham Playhouse, an impressive range of plays were performed. But specific geographies can make a difference: Faversham, in Kent, has seen a larger than average number of performances of *Arden of Faversham*.

The performance history of *Arden of Faversham* is particularly amenable to a politically engaged analysis of theatre-centred reactions to, and readings of, an early modern play and here I will offer a feminist performance history that is grounded in macrohistory, contains elements of microhistory, but seeks to combine the two in producing new insights into the play's dramaturgy. Macrohistory records that *Arden of Faversham* is usually dated *c.* 1590 and the play was published in 1592, which suggests some degree of popularity.[30] *Arden of Faversham* was adapted in the eighteenth century by George Lillo and John Hoadly; this adaptation premiered, after Lillo's death in 1759, and was the preferred stage version for the next hundred years. In 1897 Poel produced an abridgement entitled *Lilies that Fester*. This was followed by several student-society productions and Poel staged a version much closer to the original play in 1925. In the later twentieth century the play has inspired some radical reimaginings such as Alexander Goehr's 1966 opera *Arden Must Die* and Andrei Serban's 1969 production/adaptation for La MaMa in New York.

A feminist performance history of *Arden of Faversham* might well begin with the representation of the historical woman Alice Arden. *Arden of Faversham* is based on the 1551 murder of Thomas Arden, a murder which resulted in the execution of his wife Alice, her lover, Mosby, and a large number of accomplices. Alice has had her story voiced many times by men: the court chroniclers, the history writers, the anonymous, presumably male, author of the play, followed by the boy actors who played Alice in the early modern playhouse.[31] A significant number of women directors – including Joan Littlewood, Buzz Goodbody and Katie Mitchell – have been drawn to Alice's story, and while nothing can be *proved* from grouping their productions together, what the grouping *can* generate is a trenchant, and feminist, discussion of *Arden of Faversham* and Alice.

Joan Littlewood's 1954 *Arden of Faversham*, at the Theatre Royal, Stratford East, exhibited what were later to be seen as Littlewood's trademarks as a director of Renaissance plays: she would grab them by the scruff of the neck, ransack them for relevance, and foreground class issues.[32] So although Littlewood considered *Arden* one of the finest plays in the English language, her 1954 *Arden* constructed Thomas Arden as a land-grabbing class villain. She also repositioned Alice significantly: as a shocked Kenneth Tynan put it, 'the retribution scene was omitted, so that we did not see what the title-page promised, "the shameful end of all murderers"'.[33] Alice was not *seen* to get her comeuppance and *The Times* (29 September 1954) commented that Littlewood 'omits Dick Reede and the sailor and brings down her final curtain on the arrest of Alice Arden in Act V scene i, leaving to our imagination the apprehension of the other conspirators and the death sentences'.[34] Reviewing the 1955 revival, J. C. Trewin in the *Illustrated London News* (21 May 1955) thought: 'It was no doubt wise of Miss Littlewood to do away with all the straightening-out and clearing-up at the end, even if some people may have wondered what happened next.'

This deep cutting, however, completely changed the audience's final impressions of Alice: she did not weep over her husband's body as it bled, indicating her guilt; she did not repent her affair with Mosby – 'but for thee I had never been strumpet' (scene 18, line 14). She was far less contained, less penitent, and she offered a far more challenging vision of female criminality.

Reviews of Barbara Brown's performance help excavate Littlewood's approach to the murderous heroine. *The Times* (29 September 1954) thought 'Miss Barbara Brown [was] effective as the country Clytemnestra'. Tynan claimed 'the rampant *Bovarysme* of Barbara Brown's Alice could hardly be bettered' and 'Lady Chatterley and Strindberg's Miss Julie must', he felt, 'be looking down with approval on these premonitions of their plight'.[35] Wearing a dress 'of a vivid red sparkling under the spotlights', Brown sent the *Figaro* reviewer into raptures:

> Hardly has one glanced at her than one is only conscious of her violence, her presence and even of the grace of her movement … Miss Barbara Brown is run through by a shiver of lover's fury. She growls with happiness or rage. We can understand the lover who gives in to her, and the husband who lets himself be deluded by the comedy she plays so well.[36]

Equally vivid is the review in the Paris newspaper *Combat* which records Brown as Alice 'whirling around her husband like a serpent which encircles its victim in rapid spirals. She acts with her body, her hair. She is enveloping, provoking, sensual, versatile; perversity itself.' While several papers (including *Combat*) report that, as so often with productions of *Arden*, Black Will

Figure 6 Barbara Brown as Alice and Harry H. Corbett as Mosbie in Joan Littlewood's 1954
Arden of Faversham, Theatre Royal, Stratford East. Reproduced by permission.

and Shakebag occasionally upstaged Alice, Brown clearly made Alice a
forceful and passionate presence (Figure 6).

Alice was also the centre of attention when leading actress Dorothy
Tutin played the role in Buzz Goodbody's 1970 *Arden* for the RSC's
Theatregoround Festival. For Michael Billington (*The Times*, 6 November
1970), Dorothy Tutin gave 'a passionately, richly spoken and impressively
full-blooded performance'.[37] Nicholas de Jongh witnessed acting 'of gor-
geous conviction' with Tutin moving her tongue 'nervously over the lips'
while her 'eyes move everywhere' (*Guardian*, 6 November 1970); and, for de
Jongh, Alice 'is seen as a skittish voluptuary brimming with enormous passion she cannot understand'. The word 'skittish' was also used by Kenneth
Hurren in the *Spectator* (14 November 1970), who detected in Tutin's Alice

Figure 7 Dorothy Tutin as Alice and David Bailie as Mosbie in Buzz Goodbody's 1970
Royal Shakespeare Company *Arden of Faversham*. Photo credit: Reg Wilson © Royal
Shakespeare Company.

'a more skittish humour than is wholly encouraged by the text', and it is
suggested by the *Stage* (12 November 1970), which complained that Tutin
'hops and skips and in a most bizarre manner' and, in a particularly loaded
phrase, expressed disappointment that 'Miss Tutin doesn't suggest, at all,
the raging sexuality of Alice'. Returning to de Jongh's patronising notion
that Tutin's Alice 'cannot understand' her 'enormous passion', it seems reasonable to point out that the play text constructs Alice as a woman who
not only understands what she is doing but is determined to do it; indeed
Alice's motto might be summarised as 'if at first you don't succeed, try, try
again'. De Jongh's reading also appears to work against production photographs where Tutin's mature Alice appears not only to know, but also to
be thrilled at, what she is doing (Figure 7). Indeed the *Sunday Telegraph*
(8 November 1970) thought 'Dorothy Tutin [lent] her unique distinction
to the adulterous Alice, endowing her at times with a delicacy worthy of
Emma Bovary'. John Peter recorded 'a performance of finely controlled
frenzy' (*Sunday Times*, 8 November 1970).

While Alice was a focus of attention for the male reviewers, Michael Billington (*The Times*, 6 November 1970) did praise Goodbody's *Arden of Faversham* as 'a revival that puts its trust in the text' even though it was 'not the full scale, meticulously realistic version one would like to see'.[38] In fact Goodbody's cuts were significant. While early on these cuts generally improved clarity and ease of understanding, later on Black Will and his narrative were far more deeply cut than other narrative lines.[39] So when the *Sunday Times* (8 November 1970) applauded the cast for treading the 'razor-edge between giggles and grand-guignol with awesome skill', it is important to acknowledge that this balance was partly achieved by cutting, which also helped Goodbody and Tutin to increase the focus on Alice.

While both Littlewood and Goodbody had set *Arden of Faversham* in largely unadorned, almost bare boards settings, Katie Mitchell's production of the play at the Old Red Lion Theatre, London, in 1990, adopted a very different approach.[40] This *Arden of Faversham* was the first production by Classics on a Shoestring, the company which established Mitchell's reputation, and the *Independent* (11 August 1990) thought it a 'gripping, vividly-staged revival' which exploited the tiny studio theatre space and heightened 'the atmosphere of claustrophobic intensity by playing many of the scenes in the glow of candlelight'.[41] The *Independent* further records that the 'stage is covered with a thick carpet of earth' creating 'a mood at once homely and sinister' and Mitchell also 'keeps you mindful of religious devotion throughout, with the frescos of haloed saints which glimmer intermittently through the gloom'. *City Limits* (16 August 1990) describes how, 'On a trampled earth floor, overlooked by defaced murals, actors hurl themselves (and their props) around, play entire scenes by candlelight; simple effects, such as drumming on the walls, have real resonance.' In addition music, 'a kind of barbaric, wordless plain chant, is performed on stage by the cast' (*Evening Standard*, 10 August 1990).

Mitchell's production was grounded in Gardzienice practice, characterised as '[a] darkened stage, emphasis on movement, carefully balanced lighting, the use of chanting, resourceful economy of props and controlled ensemble work' (*Time Out*, 15 August 1990). This made a big impact on reviewers, but *What's On* argued that it was the presentation of Susan that 'most comfortably and successfully accommodated the impositions of the Gardzienice technique' (15 August 1990). Susan was important in Mitchell's production: the *Evening Standard* (10 August 1990) detected excess when Susan 'is obliged to pirouette wildly, scattering earth as she whirls', and Jeremy Kingston in *The Times* commented acerbically that Susan 'crouches, keens, throws sand on her hair and crawls under a table. Very Polish' (19 August 1990). The *Independent* also records 'the bursts of liturgical keening which erupt from Susan (Emma Rice), the possessed seeming maid' (11 August 1990). Susan's role was expanded in the play: she was given extra lines;[42] she sang, for example, during the attempt to poison Arden; she mumbled when Greene spoke of his wrongs in scene 1.

Mitchell had researched the play in detail and chose *Arden*

> because of the lively historical setting and because it is set in a kitchen and not a court. Many of the issues tackled remain potent and concrete now. And, in the character of Alice Arden, the difficulties then faced by women are brought into unusually sharp and three dimensional focus.[43]

This sympathetic engagement with Alice's predicament was not something reviewers necessarily detected in Valerie Gogan's performance of the role (Figure 8): the *Guardian* found this Alice 'marvellous in her lust … and in her sweet-voiced dissimulation' (13 August 1990). The *Independent* felt that for both Alice and Mosby '[t]he danger of their position is clearly an erotic turn-on' (11 August 1990). For Maureen Paton in *The Stage*, 'the glittering-eyed Gogan's bold amorality dominates' and Alice is 'an ambitious woman so determined upon having it all that she is 400 years ahead of her time' (30 August 1990).

One important moment in the production was Alice's proto-feminist demand in scene 10: why should Arden 'govern me that am to rule myself'?[44] In addition, Alice's desecration of the prayer book (scene 8) was a key section, and linked up with other moments in the play which explore penance, a concept Alice engages with thoroughly after Arden's murder. Notions of penance and devotion were particularly significant because the production was grounded in the historical moment of Alice Arden's crime, in the period when England changed its official attitude towards penance, devotion 'became protestant over-night' and 'many of the icons and frescoes that used to decorate our parish churches were brutally defaced and folk customs stamped out'.[45]

These three different Alice Ardens, in three different decades, can help create a sustained feminist engagement with *Arden of Faversham*, whatever the individual director's politics. They also help to adjust the imbalance in history whereby Alice Arden has been overly interpreted and represented by men.[46] Joan Littlewood, Buzz Goodbody and Katie Mitchell are not marginalised figures, and yet their productions of *Arden of Faversham* have not received much critical attention, even though all three productions were very successful in their different ways. My performance history of *Arden of Faversham* may have an overt political agenda, but it also points to how much is unexplored in more macrohistorical approaches, and how much scope there still is for doing things differently, when working with detail instead of general trends.

Figure 8 Valerie Gogan as Alice in Katie Mitchell's 1990 *Arden of Faversham*, the Red Lion Theatre. Photo credit: Tristram Kenton. Reproduced by permission.

Performance histories at their best can offer detailed engagement with and insight into Renaissance plays, informed criticism of their dramaturgy and a cultural history of responses to them in the marketplace that is theatre. They can offer creative provocations for future readers and theatre practitioners at the same time as reminding readers of the blind spots of their own historical moment. Twenty-first-century audiences may struggle to understand master–servant relationships; secular audiences may be affronted by productions that are serious about spirituality; middle-class, university-educated, liberal audiences may be offended by illiberal politics in a play or production. But performance histories can challenge current complacencies, whatever they may be, and unsettle twenty-first-century certainties, and that is why we need more of them.

NOTES

1 Post-production discussion with the cast after a performance of Kim Durban's production of *The City Wit*, the Boilerhouse Theatre, Royal Holloway, 2007.

2 For a discussion of Renaissance plays, the UK school syllabuses and the impact of this on performance, see Lucy Munro, 'The Early Modern Repertory and the Performance of Shakespeare's Contemporaries Today', in *Performing Early Modern Drama Today*, ed. Pascale Aebischer and Kathryn Prince (Cambridge University Press, 2012), 17–34. Postgraduate dissertations exist in this area but many remain difficult to access. Web resources which are making it easier to track material include www2.warwick.ac.uk/fac/arts/ren/elizabethan_jacobean_drama/stage_history.

3 I would like to acknowledge many discussions over the years with Richard Cave, Christine Dymkowski and Jacky Bratton around this issue. For me, the crucial arguments are best examined in Bratton's *New Readings in Theatre History* (Cambridge University Press, 2003).

4 Wendy Griswold, *Renaissance Revivals: City Comedy and Revenge Tragedy in the London Theatre, 1570–1980* (University of Chicago Press, 1986), respectively 3 and 7.

5 For the performance history of Fletcher's *The Woman's Prize, or the Tamer Tamed* see Introduction to *The Tamer Tamed*, ed. Lucy Munro (London: Methuen, 2010).

6 Phyllis Hartnoll, *The Theatre: A Concise History* (London: Thames and Hudson, 1968); Oscar Brockett, *History of the Theatre* (Boston, MA: Allyn and Bacon, 1968). Both histories have been much republished, and material added since their original publication. A fine example of the survey approach is Lois Potter's survey essay, 'Tragedy and Performance', in *The Cambridge Companion to Renaissance Tragedy* ed. Emma Smith and Garrett A. Sullivan Jr (Cambridge University Press, 2010), 102–15. However, I was left wishing Potter, with her wealth of knowledge and experience, had been allotted more room to develop her discussion. Munro, 'The Early Modern Repertory', takes a more thematic approach to the challenge of the survey chapter, looking at large British centres of production – the RSC, the NT and Shakespeare's Globe – and the 'Lost Classics'

project at the White Bear, the 'Read not Dead' staged readings at Shakespeare's Globe and the 2002 and 2005 'Jacobethan' seasons at the RSC.

7 John Russell Brown, 'Introduction', *The Duchess of Malfi*, The Revels Plays (Manchester University Press, 1974), lv–lix.

8 Richard Allen Cave, *'The White Devil' and 'The Duchess of Malfi': Text and Performance* (Basingstoke: Macmillan, 1988), 49–70.

9 Kathleen McLuskie and Jennifer Uglow, eds., *Plays in Performance: 'The Duchess of Malfi'* (Bristol Classical Press, 1989). The Plays in Performance series was conceived as ranging widely in its remit and was to include, for example, *The Alchemist* but when the series was taken on by Cambridge University Press it was renamed Shakespeare in Production and published volumes on approximately a third of Shakespeare's plays.

10 There are also several useful lists of productions of *The Duchess of Malfi*, covering British and US performances, compiled by David Carnegie, a New Zealand-based dramaturge as well as an academic, and by Frank Wadsworth, a theatre historian. See Frank Wadsworth, 'Some Nineteenth Century Revivals of *The Duchess of Malfi*', *Theatre Survey* 8 (1967), 67–83; '"Shorn and abated": British Performances of *The Duchess of Malfi*', *Theatre Survey* 10 (1969), 89–104; 'Webster, Horne and Mrs Stowe: American Performances of *The Duchess of Malfi*', *Theatre Survey* 11 (1970), 151–66. David Carnegie's list appears in *Research Opportunities in Renaissance Drama* 26 (1983), 55–63.

11 John Buckingham, '"The Dangerous Edge of Things": John Webster's Bosola in Context and Performance', PhD thesis, Royal Holloway, University of London, 2011, available online at http://pure.rhul.ac.uk/portal/files/4060550/2011BUCK INGHAMJFPHD.pdf. Buckingham also lists professional productions between 1998 and 2011 in an appendix.

12 Michael Dobson's *Shakespeare and Amateur Performance: A Cultural History* (Cambridge University Press, 2011) does not discuss student theatre although its unpaid nature makes it a subsection of amateur theatre. In relation to the performance of Shakespeare's contemporaries, student theatre is critically important.

13 Director's Notes, programme.

14 Edward Hallett Carr, *What Is History?* (London: Macmillan, 1961), 15.

15 Michel Blakemore, *Next Season* (New York and London: Applause Books, 1995). The central character is appearing in *The Duchess of Malfi*; the theatre company involved intersects with the RSC *c.* 1960.

16 For more on this production, as well the productions of Mendes and Armfield, see Elizabeth Schafer and Emma Cox, '*The Alchemist* on the Stage: Performance, Collaboration and Deviation', in *The Alchemist*, Continuum Renaissance Drama series, ed. Helen Ostovich and Erin Julian (London: Continuum, forthcoming).

17 For survey histories of *The Alchemist* see Robert Gale Noyes, *Ben Jonson on the English Stage, 1660–1776*, Harvard Studies in English 17 (New York and London: Benjamin Blom, 1935), and Ejner J. Jensen, *Ben Jonson's Comedies on the Modern Stage* (Ann Arbor, MI: UMI Research Press, 1985), which covers the period 1899–1972. My history here is grounded in my own survey of approximately 110 productions of *The Alchemist*.

18 Geoffrey Tillotson, *Times Literary Supplement*, 20 July 1933, 494.

19 *Times Educational Supplement*, 18 October 1996.

20 See, for example, the prompt copy from Hersov's 1987 Manchester Royal Exchange production (Manchester Royal Exchange archive).

21 For more on this production see Jensen, *Ben Jonson's Comedies*, 94–7.

22 James Loehlin, review of *The Alchemist*, *Shakespeare Bulletin* 28:1 (spring 2010), 185.

23 Loehlin, review of *The Alchemist*, 186.

24 Barbara Hodgdon, 'Photography, Theater, Mnemonics; or, Thirteen Ways of Looking at a Still', in *Theorizing Practice: Redefining Theatre History*, ed. W. B. Worthen and Peter Holland (Basingstoke: Palgrave, 2003), 88–119.

25 See, for example, *Re-Presenting Ben Jonson: Text, History, Performance*, ed. Martin Butler (Basingstoke: Macmillan, 1999). Despite this book's subtitle and the photograph from the RSC production of *The Devil Is an Ass* on the book jacket, only two of the twelve essays show any interest at all in performance.

26 See Laura Higgins, 'Staging Geographies and the Geographies of Staging – Space and Place in Shakespeare's *Richard II*: Text and Production', unpublished PhD thesis, Royal Holloway 2012.

27 This picked up on Subtle's description of Drugger's 'olive-coloured face' (1.3.46); *The Alchemist*, ed. Elizabeth Cook (London: A. & C. Black, 1991).

28 *International Herald Tribune* 26 September 2006.

29 Robert Butler, who wrote the A–Z guide to *The Alchemist* in the programme also wrote *'The Alchemist' Exposed* (London: Oberon Books, 2007), which contains more detail on the production.

30 See M. L. Wine's introduction to his edition of *The Tragedy of Master Arden of Faversham* (London: Methuen, 1973). All references to *Arden of Faversham* are to this text.

31 Wine lists sources of the play, introduction to *Arden of Faversham*, xxxv–xliii.

32 Littlewood is one of the few British women theatre practitioners whose work is regularly discussed in theatre histories; however, her work on Renaissance drama is almost completely ignored. Exceptions are Elizabeth Schafer, who looks at Littlewood's Jonson productions in 'Daughters of Ben', in *Ben Jonson and Theatre: Performance, Practice and Theory*, ed. Richard Cave, Elizabeth Schafer and Brian Woolland (London and New York: Routledge, 1999), 154–78; and Nadine Holdsworth, who examines Littlewood's *Edward II* in *Joan Littlewood's Theatres: Staging Class, Community and Nation* (Cambridge University Press, 2011), 97–103. The following discussion of Littlewood's *Arden of Faversham* originated in an interview with Littlewood by the author in June 1996.

33 Kenneth Tynan, '*Arden of Faversham*', in *Curtains: Selections from the Drama Criticism and Related Writings* (London: Longmans, 1961), 82.

34 Wine's edition uses only scene divisions; stopping at 'V.1' would mean stopping at the end of scene 14 (of 18).

35 Tynan, '*Arden of Faversham*', (82).

36 Quotations from the 1955 Paris reviews are from translations in the Theatre Royal archive, Stratford East.

37 This reviewer also claimed that the production muddled some class issues as 'David Bailie's attenuated, dignified Mosbie looks if anything the social cut or two above Emrys James's stocky, thick set Arden.'

38 Billington's comment is partly a reaction to Andrei Serban's *Arden of Faversham* of the previous year, a La MaMa touring production, which Billington described, in this review, as a 'confused, blood-boltered mess'.

39 For example, for clarity 'whores' was used for 'trugs' (1.1.498). The prompt copy indicates deepest cutting in scenes 2, 3, 5, 9 and 12, around Shakebag.

40 The production ran from 9 August to 2 September 1990. I am grateful to Paul Allain for access to his archive of material from *Arden of Faversham*, especially the script and 'Introduction'.

41 For Mitchell's career before *Arden of Faversham*, see Dan Rebellato, 'Katie Mitchell: Learning from Europe', in *Contemporary European Theatre Directors*, ed. Maria M. Delgado and Dan Rebellato (London and New York: Routledge, 2010), 317–38. Two years after *Arden*, Mitchell directed *A Woman Killed With Kindness* for the RSC, exploring similar theatrical and thematic territory to *Arden of Faversham*. In 1997 Mitchell became artistic director of the RSC's The Other Place, the space Buzz Goodbody made famous.

42 Susan spoke the lines of Adam of the Flower-de-luce in scene 1; and brought in the letter instead of Bradshaw in scene 8. See Paul Allain's script.

43 Quotation taken from Katie Mitchell's 'Introduction' in Paul Allain's production archive which also contains a reading list including works by, for example, Keith Thomas, Lawrence Stone, Alan McFarlane, Alexander Leggatt and Catherine Belsey. For Mitchell's seriousness about research, see her emphasis on it in *The Director's Craft: A Handbook for the Theatre* (London and New York: Routledge, 2009).

44 This is marked as 'feminism' on Allain's working script. While she was at Oxford University, Mitchell was in a feminist theatre company called Medusa. See Maria Shevstsova, 'On Directing: A Conversation with Katie Mitchell', *New Theatre Quarterly* 22:1 (February 2006), 3–18 at 3.

45 Mitchell, 'Introduction', Allain's production archive.

46 Other notable responses to Alice by women directors includes Australian playwright and director Cath McKinnon's play *A Rose by Any Other Name* which tells Alice's story alongside that of a 1980s Australian woman, Rose McClements, driven by abuse to murder her husband.

SELECT BIBLIOGRAPHY

Bibliographies and reference

Arber, Edward, *A Transcript of the Registers of the Company of Stationers of London, 1554–1640.* 5 vols. London, 1875–94, rpt, Gloucester, MA: Peter Smith, 1967.

Arnott, James Fullarton, and John William Robinson, *English Theatrical Literature, 1559–1900: A Bibliography.* London: Society for Theatre Research, 1970.

A Short-Title Catalogue of Books Printed in England, Scotland, and Ireland and of English Books Printed Abroad, 1475–1640. 2nd edn, ed. A.W. Pollard, G. R. Redgrave, W. A. Jackson, F. S. Ferguson and Katharine F. Pantzer. 3 vols. London: Bibliographical Society, 1976–91.

Bawcutt, N. W., ed., *The Control and Censorship of Caroline Drama: The Records of Sir Henry Herbert, Master of the Revels, 1623–73.* Oxford: Clarendon Press, 1996.

Beach, Vincent W., *George Chapman: An Annotated Bibliography of Commentary and Criticism.* New York: G. K. Hall, 1995.

Bentley, Gerald Eades, *The Jacobean and Caroline Stage.* 7 vols. Oxford: Clarendon Press, 1941–68.

Berger, Thomas L., and William C. Bradford, Jr, *An Index of Characters in English Printed Drama to the Restoration.* Englewood, CO: Microcard Editions Books, 1975.

Berger, Thomas L., William C. Bradford, and Sidney L. Sondergard, *An Index of Characters in Early Modern English Drama: Printed Plays, 1500–1660.* Rev. edn. Cambridge University Press, 1998.

Bergeron, David M., ed., *Twentieth-Century Criticism of English Masques, Pageants and Entertainments, 1558–1642. With a Supplement on Folk-Play and Related Forms* by H. B. Caldwell. San Antonio, TX: Trinity University Press, 1972.

Chambers, E. K., *The Elizabethan Stage.* 4 vols. Oxford: Clarendon Press, 1923.

Dean, James Seay, *Robert Greene: A Reference Guide.* Boston, MA: G. K. Hall, 1984.

Dessen, Alan C., and Leslie Thomson, *A Dictionary of Stage Directions in English Drama, 1580–1642.* Cambridge University Press, 1999.

Foakes, R. A., *Illustrations of the English Stage, 1580–1642.* Stanford University Press, 1985.

Fordyce, Rachel, *Caroline Drama: A Bibliographic History of Criticism.* 2nd edn. New York: G. K. Hall, 1992.

Greg, W. W., *A Bibliography of the English Printed Drama to the Restoration.* 4 vols. London: The Bibliographical Society, 1939–59.

Dramatic Documents from the Elizabethan Playhouses: Stage Plots, Actors' Parts, Prompt Books. 2 vols. Oxford: Clarendon Press, 1931.

Harbage, Alfred, *Annals of English Drama, 975–1700.* Philadelphia: University of Pennsylvania Press, in cooperation with The Modern Language Association of America, 1940

  Annals of English Drama, 975–1700. 2nd edn, revised by S. Schoenbaum. Philadelphia, PA, 1964.

  Annals of English Drama, 975–1700. Supplement by S. Schoenbaum. Evanston, IL: Northwestern University Press, 1966.

  Annals of English Drama, 975–1700. 3rd edn, revised by Sylvia S. Wagonheim. London and New York: Routledge, 1989.

Harner, James L., *Samuel Daniel and Michael Drayton: A Reference Guide.* Boston, MA: G. K. Hall, 1980.

Henslowe, Philip, *Henslowe's Diary*, ed. R. A. Foakes and R. T. Rickert. 2nd edn. Cambridge University Press, 2002.

Holzknecht, Karl J., *Outlines of Tudor and Stuart Plays, 1497–1642.* New York: Barnes and Noble, 1947.

Honigmann, E. A. J., and Susan Brock, eds., *Playhouse Wills, 1558–1642: An Edition of Wills by Shakespeare and His Contemporaries in the London Theatre.* Manchester University Press, 1993.

Hoy, Cyrus, 'The Shares of Fletcher and his Collaborators in the Beaumont and Fletcher Canon.' *Studies in Bibliography* 8 (1956), 129–46; 9 (1957), 143–62; 11 (1958), 55–106; 12 (1959), 91–116; 13 (1960), 77–108; 14 (1961), 45–67; and 15 (1962), 71–90.

Kawachi, Yoshiko, *Calendar of English Renaissance Drama, 1558–1642.* New York and London: Garland Publishing, 1986.

Lidman, Mark J., *Studies in Jacobean Drama, 1973–1984: An Annotated Bibliography.* New York: Garland, 1986.

Logan, Terence P., and Denzell S. Smith, eds., *The Later Jacobean and Caroline Dramatists: A Survey and Bibliography of Recent Studies in English Renaissance Drama.* Lincoln, NE: University of Nebraska Press, 1978.

  The New Intellectuals: A Survey and Bibliography of Recent Studies in English Renaissance Drama. Lincoln, NE: University of Nebraska Press, 1977.

  The Popular School: A Survey and Bibliography of Recent Studies in English Renaissance Drama. Lincoln, NE: University of Nebraska Press, 1975.

  The Predecessors of Shakespeare: A Survey and Bibliography of Recent Studies in English Renaissance Drama. Lincoln, NE: University of Nebraska Press, 1973.

Stratman, Carl J., ed., *Bibliography of English Printed Tragedy 1565–1900.* Carbondale, IL: Southern Illinois University Press, 1966.

Sugden, E. H., *A Topographical Dictionary to the Works of Shakespeare and His Fellow Dramatists.* Manchester University Press, 1925.

Tannenbaum, Samuel Aaron, and Dorothy R. Tannenbaum, *Elizabethan Bibliographies.* 41 vols. in 39. New York, 1937–50, rpt, 10 vols. Port Washington, NY: Kennikat, 1967.

Tucker, Kenneth, *A Bibliography of Writings by and about John Ford and Cyril Tourneur.* Boston, MA: G. K. Hall, 1977.

Wentworth, Michael, *Thomas Heywood: A Reference Guide*. Boston, MA: G. K. Hall, 1986.

White, D. Jerry, *Early English Drama, 'Everyman' to 1580: A Reference Guide*. Boston, MA: G. K. Hall, 1986.

Wickham, Glynne, *Early English Stages 1300–1660*. 3 vols. in 4 parts. New York: Columbia University Press, 1959–81.

Williams, Franklin B., Jr, *Index of Dedications and Commendatory Verses in English Books Before 1641*. London: Bibliographical Society, 1962.

Wing, Donald, ed., *Short-Title Catalogue of Books Printed in England, Scotland, Ireland, Wales, and British America, and of English Books Printed in Other Countries, 1641–1700*. 2nd edn. 4 vols. New York: MLA, 1972–98.

Zimmer, Ruth, K., *James Shirley: A Reference Guide*. Boston, MA: G. K. Hall, 1980.

Biographies and criticism

Aebischer, Pascale, *Jacobean Drama*. Basingstoke: Palgrave Macmillan, 2010.

Aggeler, Geoffrey, *Nobler in the Mind: The Stoic–Skeptic Dialectic in English Renaissance Tragedy*. Newark, DE, and London: University of Delaware Press, 1998.

Altieri, Joanne, 'Against Moralizing Jacobean Comedy: Middleton's *Chaste Maid*.' *Criticism* 30 (1988): 171–87.

Anderson, D. K., Jr, ed., '*Concord in Discord': The Plays of John Ford, 1586–1986*. New York: AMS Press, 1986.

Andrews, C. E., *Richard Brome: A Study of His Life and Works*. 1913, rpt, Hamden, CT: Shoe String Press, 1972.

Astington, John, *English Court Theatre, 1558–1642*. Cambridge University Press, 1999.

Axelrad, A. José, *Un Malcontent Elizabéthain: John Marston, 1576–1634*. Paris: Didier, 1955.

Ayers, P. K., 'Plot, Subplot, and the Uses of Dramatic Discord in *A Mad World My Masters* and *A Trick to Catch the Old One*.' *Modern Language Quarterly* 47 (1986): 3–18.

Bacquet, Paul, *Un contemporain d'Elisabeth I: Thomas Sackville, l'homme et l'œuvre* Geneva: Droz, 1966.

Baines, Barbara J., *Thomas Heywood*. Boston, MA: Twayne Publishers, 1984.

Barber, C. L., *Creating Elizabethan Tragedy: The Theater of Marlowe and Kyd*. Chicago and London: University of Chicago Press, 1988.

Barish, Jonas, *The Anti-Theatrical Prejudice*. Berkeley and Los Angeles: University of California Press, 1981.

Bartels, Emily C., *Spectacles of Strangeness: Imperialism, Alienation, and Marlowe*. Philadelphia: University of Pennsylvania Press, 1993.

Barton, Anne, *Ben Jonson, Dramatist*. Cambridge University Press, 1984.

Bednarz, James, *Shakespeare and the Poets' War*. New York: Columbia University Press, 2001.

Bennett, Susan, 'Not-Shakespeare, Our Contemporary: Transgression, Dissidence, and Desire', in her *Performing Nostalgia: Shifting Shakespeare and the Contemporary Past*. London and New York: Routledge, 1996, 79–118.

Bentley, Gerald Eades, *The Profession of Dramatist in Shakespeare's Time, 1590–1642.* Princeton University Press, 1971.

Bergeron, David Moore, *Twentieth-Century Criticism of English Masques, Pageants, and Entertainments: 1558–1642.* San Antonio, TX: Trinity University Press, 1972.

Bergeron, David M., ed., *Pageantry in the Shakespearean Theater.* Athens, GA: University of Georgia Press, 1985.

Bevington, David M., *From 'Mankind' to Marlowe: Growth of Structure in the Popular Drama of Tudor England.* Cambridge, MA: Harvard University Press, 1962.

  Tudor Drama and Politics: A Critical Approach to Topical Meaning. Cambridge, MA: Harvard University Press, 1968.

Bevington, David, ed., *George Peele.* The University Wits. Aldershot, UK, and Burlington, VT: Ashgate, 2011.

Bevington, David, and Peter Holbrook, eds., *The Politics of the Stuart Court Masque.* New York: Cambridge University Press, 1998.

Bevington, David, Martin Butler and Ian Donaldson, eds., *The Cambridge Edition of the Works of Ben Jonson.* 7 vols. Cambridge University Press, 2012.

Bliss, Lee, *Francis Beaumont.* Boston, MA: Twayne Publishers, 1987.

  The World's Perspective: John Webster and the Jacobean Drama. New Brunswick, NJ: Rutgers University Press, 1983.

Bluestone, Max, and Norman Rabkin, *Shakespeare's Contemporaries: Modern Studies in English Renaissance Drama.* 2nd edn. Englewood Cliffs, NJ: Prentice-Hall, 1970.

Boas, F. S., *Shakspeare and His Predecessors.* London: John Murray, 1896.

Bowers, Fredson, *Elizabethan Revenge Tragedy, 1587–1642.* 1940, rpt, Princeton University Press, 1966.

Boyd, Brian, ed., *Words That Count: Essays on Early Modern Authorship in Honor of MacDonald P. Jackson.* Newark, DE, and London: University of Delaware Press, 2004.

Bradbrook, M. C., *John Webster: Citizen and Dramatist.* London: Weidenfeld and Nicolson, 1980.

Braunmuller, A. R., *Natural Fictions: George Chapman's Major Tragedies.* Newark, DE, and London: University of Delaware Press, 1990.

Braunmuller, A. R., and Michael Hattaway, eds., *The Cambridge Companion to English Renaissance Drama.* Cambridge University Press, 1990. 2nd edn, Cambridge University Press, 2003.

Brinkley, R. F., *Nathan Field, The Actor-Playwright.* New Haven, CT: Yale University Press, 1928.

Brooke, Nicholas, *Horrid Laughter in Jacobean Tragedy.* New York: Barnes & Noble, 1979.

Brooks, Douglas A., *From Playhouse to Printing House: Drama and Authorship in Early Modern England.* Cambridge University Press, 2000.

Brown, Georgia, ed., *Thomas Nashe.* The University Wits. Aldershot, UK, and Burlington, VT: Ashgate, 2011.

Brown, Pamela Allen, and Peter Parolin, eds., *Women Players in England, 1500–1660.* Burlington, VT: Ashgate, 2006.

Burks, Deborah G., *Horrid Spectacle: Violation in the Theater of Early Modern England*. Pittsburgh, PA: Duquesne University Press, 2003.

Burner, Sandra A., *James Shirley: A Study of Literary Coteries and Patronage in Seventeenth-Century England*. Lanham, MD: University Press of America, 1988.

Butler, Martin, *Theatre and Crisis, 1632–1642*. Cambridge University Press, 1984.

Callaghan, Dympna, *Women and Gender in Renaissance Tragedy*. London and New York: Harvester Wheatsheaf, 1989.

Caputi, Anthony, *John Marston, Satirist*. Ithaca, NY: Cornell University Press, 1961.

Carrère, Félix, *Le Théâtre de Thomas Kyd: Contribution à l'étude du drame élizabéthain*. Toulouse, privately published, 1951.

Carson, Neil, *A Companion to Henslowe's Diary*. Cambridge University Press, 1988.

Cartwright, Kent, *Theatre and Humanism: English Drama in the Sixteenth Century*. Cambridge University Press, 1999.

Cathcart, Charles, *Marston, Rivalry, Rapprochement, and Jonson*. Aldershot, UK, and Burlington, VT: Ashgate, 2008.

Cerasano, S. P., and Marion Wynne-Davies, eds., *Readings in Renaissance Women's Drama: Criticism, History, and Performance, 1594–1998*. London and New York: Routledge, 1998.

Renaissance Drama by Women: Texts and Documents. London and New York: Routledge, 1996.

Chakravorty, Swapan, *Society and Politics in the Plays of Thomas Middleton*. Oxford: Clarendon Press, 1996.

Charney, Maurice, 'Shakespeare and the Others.' *Shakespeare Quarterly* 30 (1979): 321–42.

Chartier, Roger, *Cardenio entre Cervantès et Shakespeare: Histoire d'une pièce perdue*. Paris: Éditions Gallimard, 2011.

Cheney, Patrick, *Marlowe's Counterfeit Profession*. Toronto: University of Toronto Press, 1997.

Cheney, Patrick, ed., *The Cambridge Companion to Christopher Marlowe*. Cambridge University Press, 2004.

Clare, Janet, *'Art made tongue-tied by authority': Elizabethan and Jacobean Censorship*. 2nd edn. Manchester University Press, 1999.

Clark, A. M., *Thomas Heywood: Playwright and Miscellanist*. Oxford: Basil Blackwell, 1931.

Clark, Ira, *Professional Playwrights: Massinger, Ford, Shirley, and Brome*. Lexington, KY: University Press of Kentucky, 1992.

Clark, Sandra, *The Plays of Beaumont and Fletcher: Sexual Themes and Dramatic Representations*. Hemel Hempstead: Harvester Wheatsheaf, 1994.

Renaissance Drama. Oxford: Polity Press, 2007.

Cohen, Walter, *Drama of a Nation: Public Theater in Renaissance England and Spain*. Ithaca, NY, and London: Cornell University Press 1985.

Cone, Mary, *Fletcher without Beaumont: A Study of the Independent Plays of John Fletcher*. Salzburg: Institut für Englische Sprache und Literatur, Universität Salzburg, 1976.

Conover, James H., *Thomas Dekker: An Analysis of Dramatic Structure*. The Hague: Mouton, 1969.

Cook, Judith, *At the Sign of the Swan: An Introduction to Shakespeare's Contemporaries*. London: Harrap, 1986.

Cotton, Nancy, *Women Playwrights in England, 1363–1750*. Lewisburg, PA: Bucknell University Press, 1980.

Cox, John D., and David Scott Kastan, eds., *A New History of Early English Drama*. Foreword by Stephen J. Greenblatt. New York: Columbia University Press, 1997.

Craig, D. H., *Ben Jonson: The Critical Heritage, 1599–1798*. London: Routledge, 1990.

Craig, Hugh, and Arthur F. Kinney, eds., *Shakespeare, Computers, and the Mystery of Authorship*. Cambridge University Press, 2009.

Cromwell, Otelia, *Thomas Heywood: A Study in the Elizabethan Drama of Everyday Life*. 1928, rpt, Hamden, CT: Archon Books, 1969.

Cudar-Domínguez, Pilar, *Stuart Women Playwrights, 1613–1713*. Aldershot, UK, and Burlington, VT: Ashgate, 2010.

Cuvelier, Eliane, *Thomas Lodge: Témoin de son temps (c. 1558–1625)*. Paris: Didier Erudition, 1984.

Davis, J. L., *The Sons of Ben: Jonsonian Comedy in Caroline England*. Detroit, MI: Wayne State University Press, 1967.

Davril, Robert, *Le Drame de John Ford*. Paris: Didier, 1954.

Dolan, Frances E., *Dangerous Familiars: Representations of Domestic Crime in England, 1550–1700*. Ithaca, NY: Cornell University Press, 1994.

Dollimore, Jonathan, *Radical Tragedy: Religion, Ideology and Power in the Drama of Shakespeare and His Contemporaries*. Brighton: Harvester Press, 1984.

Donaldson, Ian, *Ben Jonson: A Life*. Oxford: Oxford University Press, 2011.

Drábek, Pavel, Klára Kolinská and Matthew Nicholls, eds., *Shakespeare and His Collaborators over the Centuries*. Newcastle upon Tyne: Cambridge Scholars Publishing, 2008.

Dunn, T. A., *Philip Massinger: The Man and the Playwright*. London: Thomas Nelson and Sons, 1957.

Dutton, Richard, *Licensing, Censorship and Authorship in Early Modern England: Buggeswords*. Basingstoke: Palgrave Macmillan, 2000.

Mastering the Revels: The Regulation and Censorship of English Renaissance Drama. University of Iowa Press, 1991.

Dutton, Richard, ed., *The Oxford Handbook to Early Modern Theatre*. Oxford: Oxford University Press, 2010.

Edmond, Mary, *Rare Sir William Davenant*. Manchester University Press, 1987.

Edwards, Philip, 'Massinger's Men and Women', in *Philip Massinger: A Critical Reassessment*, ed. Douglas Howard. Cambridge University Press, 1985, 39–49.

Erne, Lukas, *Shakespeare as Literary Dramatist*. Cambridge University Press, 2003.

Shakespeare's Modern Collaborators. London: Continuum, 2008.

Esche, Edward J., ed., *Shakespeare and His Contemporaries in Performance*. Aldershot, UK, and Burlington, VT: Ashgate, 2000.

Evans, G. B., *Shakespeare: Aspects of Influence*. Cambridge, MA: Harvard University Press, 1976.

Farley-Hills, David, *Shakespeare and the Rival Playwrights, 1600–1606.* London and New York: Routledge, 1990.

Farr, D. M., *John Ford and the Caroline Theater.* New York: Barnes and Noble, 1979.

Findlay, Alison, *A Feminist Perspective on Renaissance Drama.* Oxford: Blackwell, 1999.

Finkelpearl, Philip J., *Court and Country Politics in the Plays of Beaumont and Fletcher.* Princeton University Press, 1990.

  John Marston of the Middle Temple: An Elizabethan Dramatist and His Social Setting. Cambridge, MA: Harvard University Press, 1969.

Fischlin, Daniel, and Mark Fortier, eds., *Adaptations of Shakespeare: A Critical Anthology of Plays from the Seventeenth Century to the Present.* London and New York: Routledge, 2000.

Forker, C. R., *The Skull Beneath the Skin: The Achievement of John Webster.* Carbondale and Edwardsville, IL: Southern Illinois University Press, 1986.

Fraser, Russell A., and Norman Rabkin, eds., *Drama of the English Renaissance, I: The Tudor Period.* London: Macmillan, 1976.

  Drama of the English Renaissance, II: The Stuart Period. London: Macmillan, 1976.

Friedenreich, K., ed., *'Accompaninge the Players': Essays Celebrating Thomas Middleton 1586–1980.* New York: AMS Press, 1982.

Frost, David L., *The School of Shakespeare: The Influence of Shakespeare on English Drama, 1600–42.* Cambridge University Press, 1968.

Garrett, Martin, ed., *Philip Massinger: The Critical Heritage.* London and New York: Routledge, 1991.

Geckle, George L., *John Marston's Drama: Themes, Images, Sources.* Rutherford, NJ: Fairleigh Dickinson University Press, 1980.

Gibbons, Brian, *Jacobean City Comedy.* 2nd edn. London and New York: Methuen, 1980.

Gill, Roma, 'Collaboration and Revision in Massinger's *A Very Woman.*' *Review of English Studies* 18 (1967): 136–48.

Goldberg, Jonathan, *James I and the Politics of Literature: Jonson, Shakespeare, Donne, and Their Contemporaries.* Baltimore, MD: Johns Hopkins University Press, 1983.

Gossett, Suzanne, 'Editing Collaborative Drama.' *Shakespeare Survey* 59 (2006): 213–24.

  'Marston, Collaboration, and *Eastward Ho!*' *Renaissance Drama* 33 (2004): 181–200.

Gossett, Suzanne, ed., *Thomas Middleton in Context.* Cambridge University Press, 2011.

Grantley, Darryll, and Peter Roberts, eds., *Christopher Marlowe and English Renaissance Culture.* Aldershot: Scolar Press, 1996.

Gray, J. C., ed., *Mirror up to Shakespeare: Essays in Honour of G. R. Hibbard.* University of Toronto Press, 1984.

Greenblatt, Stephen, Ines Županov, Reinhard Meyer-Kalkus, Heike Paul, Pál Nyíri and Frederick Pannewick, *Cultural Mobility: A Manifesto.* Cambridge University Press, 2010.

Grivelet, Michel, *Thomas Heywood et le drame domestique élizabéthain.* Paris: Didier, 1957.

Gurr, Andrew, *Playgoing in Shakespeare's London*. 3rd edn. Cambridge University Press, 2004.

    The Shakespearean Stage, 1574–1642. 3rd edn. Cambridge University Press, 1992.

    The Shakespeare Company, 1594–1642. Cambridge University Press, 2004.

    Shakespeare's Opposites: The Admiral's Company, 1595–1625. Cambridge University Press, 2009.

    The Shakespearian Playing Companies, 1574–1642. Oxford: Clarendon Press, 1996.

Gurr, Andrew, and Mariko Ichikawa, *Staging in Shakespeare's Theatres*. Oxford University Press, 2000.

Hadfield, Andrew, ed., *Amazons, Savages, and Machiavels: Travel and Colonial Writing in English 1550–1630: An Anthology*. Oxford University Press, 2001.

Harbage, Alfred, *Cavalier Drama*. New York: Modern Language Association of America, 1936.

    Shakespeare and the Rival Traditions. New York: Macmillan, 1952.

Harp, Richard, and Stanley Stewart, eds., *The Cambridge Companion to Ben Jonson*. Cambridge University Press, 2000.

Hattaway, Michael, *Elizabethan Popular Theatre: Plays in Performance*. London: Routledge & Kegan Paul, 1982.

Heinemann, Margot, *Puritanism and Theatre: Thomas Middleton and Opposition Drama under the Early Stuarts*. Cambridge University Press, 1980.

Henze, Catherine, 'How Music Matters: Some Songs of Robert Johnson in the Plays of Beaumont and Fletcher.' *Comparative Drama* 34 (2000): 1–32.

    'Unraveling Beaumont from Fletcher with Music, Misogyny, and Masque.' *Studies in English Literature* 44 (2004): 379–404.

Hibbard, G. R., *Thomas Nashe: A Critical Introduction*. Cambridge, MA: Harvard University Press, 1962.

Hirschfeld, Heather, 'Collaboration: Sustained Partnerships', in *Thomas Middleton in Context*, ed. Suzanne Gossett. Cambridge University Press, 2011, 219–28.

    '"For the Author's Credit": Issues of Authorship in English Renaissance Drama', in *The Oxford Handbook to Early Modern Theatre*, ed. Richard Dutton. Oxford University Press, 2010, 441–55.

    Joint Enterprises: Collaborative Drama and the Institutionalization of English Renaissance Theatre. Amherst, MA: University of Massachusetts Press, 2004.

Honigmann, E. A. J., *Shakespeare's Impact on His Contemporaries*. London and Basingstoke: Macmillan Press, 1982.

Honigmann, E. A. J., ed., *Shakespeare and His Contemporaries: Essays in Comparison*. Manchester University Press, 1986.

Hope, Jonathan, *The Authorship of Shakespeare's Plays: A Socio-Linguistic Study*. Cambridge University Press, 1994.

Hopkins, Lisa, *Christopher Marlowe: A Literary Life*. Basingstoke: Palgrave, 2000.

    John Ford's Political Theatre. Manchester University Press, 1994.

Howard, Douglas, ed., *Philip Massinger: A Critical Reassessment*. Cambridge University Press, 1985.

Howard, Jean E., *Theater of a City: The Places of London City Comedy, 1598–1642*. Philadelphia: University of Pennsylvania Press, 2007.

Hoy, Cyrus, 'Critical and Aesthetic Problems of Collaboration.' *Research Opportunities in Renaissance Drama* 19 (1976): 6.

Introductions, Notes and Commentaries to Texts in 'The Dramatic Works of Thomas Dekker.' 4 vols. Cambridge University Press, 1980.

'Shakespeare and the Drama of His Time', in *Shakespeare: Aspects of Influence*, ed. G. B. Evans. Cambridge, MA: Harvard University Press, 1976, 21–41.

Hunter, G. K., *Dramatic Identities and Cultural Tradition: Studies in Shakespeare and His Contemporaries*. Liverpool University Press, 1978.

English Drama, 1586–1642: The Age of Shakespeare. Oxford: Clarendon Press, 1997.

John Lyly: The Humanist as Courtier. London: Routledge & Kegan Paul, 1962.

Hunter, G. K., and S. K. Hunter, eds., *John Webster*. Harmondsworth: Penguin, 1969.

Hutchings, Mark, and A. A. Bromham, *Middleton and His Collaborators*. Horndon: Northcote House, 2008.

Ingram, William, *The Business of Playing: The Beginnings of the Adult Professional Theater in Elizabethan London*. Ithaca, NY: Cornell University Press, 1992.

Ioppolo, Grace, *Dramatists and Their Manuscripts in the Age of Shakespeare, Jonson, Middleton, and Heywood: Authorship, Authority, and the Playhouse*. London and New York: Routledge, 2006.

Jacquot, Jean, *George Chapman (1559–1634), sa vie, sa poésie, son théâtre, sa pensée*. Paris: Société d'Édition les Belles Lettres, 1951.

Jenkins, Harold, *The Life and Work of Henry Chettle*. London: Sidgwick and Jackson, 1934.

Johnson, Nora, *The Actor as Playwright in Early Modern Drama*. Cambridge: Cambridge University Press, 2003.

Jones-Davies, M.-T., *Un Peintre de la vie londonienne: Thomas Dekker (circa 1572–1632)*. 2 vols. Paris: Librairie Marcel Didier, 1958.

Kastan, David Scott, and Peter Stallybrass, eds., *Staging the Renaissance: Reinterpretations of Elizabethan and Jacobean Drama*. New York and London: Routledge, 1991.

Kaufmann, R. J., *Richard Brome, Caroline Playwright*. New York: Columbia University Press, 1961.

Kernan, Alvin, ed., *Two Renaissance Mythmakers: Christopher Marlowe and Ben Jonson*. Baltimore, MD, and London: Johns Hopkins University Press, 1977.

Kerr, Mina, *Influence of Ben Jonson on English Comedy: 1598–1642*. New York: J. F. Tapley, 1912.

King, T. J., *Casting Shakespeare's Plays: London Actors and Their Roles, 1590–1642*. Cambridge University Press, 1992.

Kinney, Arthur F., ed., *A Companion to Renaissance Drama*. Oxford: Blackwell, 2002.

Kirk, Andrew M., *The Mirror of Confusion: The Representation of French History in English Renaissance Drama*. New York: Garland, 1996.

Klein, David, *The Elizabethan Dramatists as Critics*. New York: Philosophical Library, 1963.

Knapp, Jeffrey, *Shakespeare Only*. Chicago and London: University of Chicago Press, 2009.

'What Is a Co-Author?' *Representations* 89:1 (Winter 2005): 1–29.

Knights, L. C., *Drama and Society in the Age of Jonson*. London: Chatto & Windus, 1937.

Knutson, Roslyn Lander, *Playing Companies and Commerce in Shakespeare's Time*. Cambridge University Press, 2001.

The Repertory of Shakespeare's Company, 1594–1613. Lafayetteville: University of Arkansas Press, 1991.

Koestenbaum, Wayne, *Double Talk: The Erotics of Male Literary Collaboration*. London and New York: Routledge, 1989.

Kuriyama, Constance B., *Christopher Marlowe: A Renaissance Life*. Ithaca, NY: Cornell University Press, 2002.

Lancashire, Ian, *Dramatic Texts and Records of Britain: A Chronological Topography to 1558*. University of Toronto Press, 1984.

Lagarde, Fernand, *John Webster*. 2 vols. Toulouse: Publications de la Faculté des Lettres et Sciences Humaines de Toulouse, 1968.

Leech, Clifford, 'Three Times *Ho* and a Brace of Widows: Some Plays for the Private Theatre', in *The Elizabethan Theatre III: Papers given at the Third International Conference on Elizabethan Theatre held at the University of Waterloo, Ontario, in July 1970*, ed. and with an introduction by David Galloway. Toronto: Macmillan of Canada, 1973, 14–32.

Leggatt, Alexander, *Citizen Comedy in the Age of Shakespeare*. Toronto: University of Toronto Press, 1973.

Leinwand, Theodore B., *The City Staged: Jacobean Comedy, 1603–1613*. Madison: University of Wisconsin Press, 1986.

Theatre, Finance and Society in Early Modern England. Cambridge University Press, 1999.

Leishman, J. B., ed., *The Three Parnassus Plays*. London: Nicolson and Watson, 1949.

Levin, Harry, *The Overreacher: A Study of Christopher Marlowe*. Cambridge, MA: Harvard University Press, 1952.

Levin, Richard, *The Multiple Plot in English Renaissance Drama*. Chicago and London: University of Chicago Press, 1971.

Limon, Jerzy, *The Masque of Stuart Culture*. Newark, DE, and London: University of Delaware Press, 1990.

Lindley, David, ed., *The Court Masque*. Manchester University Press, 1984.

Court Masques, 1605–1640. Oxford University Press, 1995.

Loewenstein, Joseph, *Ben Jonson and Possessive Authorship*. Cambridge University Press, 2002.

Loftis, John, *Renaissance Drama in England and Spain: Topical Allusion and History Plays*. Princeton University Press, 1987.

Logan, Robert A., ed., *Christopher Marlowe*. The University Wits. Aldershot, UK, and Burlington, VT: Ashgate, 2011.

Lomax, Marion, *Stage Images and Traditions: Shakespeare to Ford*. Cambridge University Press, 1987.

Loomba, Ania, *Gender, Race, Renaissance Drama*. Manchester University Press, 1989.

Lopez, Jeremy, *Theatrical Convention and Audience Response in Early Modern Drama*. Cambridge University Press, 2003.

Love, Harold, *Attributing Authorship: An Introduction*. Cambridge University Press, 2002.

Lucow, Ben, *James Shirley*. Boston, MA: Twayne Publishers, 1981.

Lunney, Ruth, ed., *John Lyly*. The University Wits. Aldershot, UK, and Burlington, VT: Ashgate, 2011.

MacIntyre, Jean, *Costumes and Scripts in the Elizabethan Theatres*. Edmonton: University of Alberta Press, 1992.

MacLure, Millar, *George Chapman: A Critical Study*. University of Toronto Press, 1966.

MacLure, Millar, ed., *Christopher Marlowe: The Critical Heritage*. London and New York: Routledge, 1979.

Malcolmson, Cristina, '"As Tame as the Ladies": Politics and Gender in *The Changeling*.' *English Literary Renaissance* 20 (1990): 320–39.

Martin, Matthew R., *Between Theater and Philosophy: Skepticism in the Major City Comedies of Ben Jonson and Thomas Middleton*. Newark, DE, and London: University of Delaware Press, 2001.

Masten, Jeffrey, 'Beaumont and/or Fletcher: Collaboration and the Interpretation of Renaissance Drama.' *English Literary History* 59 (1992): 337–56.

    'Playwrighting: Authorship and Collaboration', in *A New History of Early English Drama*, ed. John D. Cox and David Scott Kastan. New York: Columbia University Press, 1997, 357–82.

    Textual Intercourse: Collaboration, Authorship, and Sexualities in Renaissance Drama. Cambridge University Press, 1997.

Maus, Katharine Eisaman, *Inwardness and Theater in the English Renaissance*. Chicago and London: University of Chicago Press, 1995.

McDonald, Russ, 'High Seriousness and Popular Form: The Case of *The Maid of Honour*', in *Philip Massinger: A Reassessment*, ed. Douglas Howard. Cambridge University Press, 1985, 83–116.

    Shakespeare and Jonson, Jonson and Shakespeare. Lincoln: University of Nebraska Press, 1988.

McEuen, Kathryn Anderson, *Classical Influence upon the Tribe of Ben: A Study of Classical Elements in the Non-Dramatic Poetry of Ben Jonson and His Circle*. 1939, rpt, New York: Octagon Books, 1968.

McLuskie, Kathleen, 'Collaboration', in *The Revels History of Drama in English*, vol. IV: *1613–1660*, ed. Philip Edwards, Gerald Eades Bentley, Kathleen McLuskie and Lois Potter. London and New York: Methuen, 1981, 169–82.

    Dekker and Heywood: Professional Dramatists. New York: St Martin's Press, 1993.

    Renaissance Dramatists: Feminist Readings. Hemel Hempstead: Harvester Wheatsheaf, 1989.

McManus, Clare, *Women on the Renaissance Stage: Anna of Denmark and Female Masquing in the Stuart Court (1590–1619)*. New York: Manchester University Press, 2002.

McMillin, Scott, and Sally-Beth MacLean, *The Queen's Men and Their Plays*. Cambridge University Press, 1998.

McMullan, Gordon, '"Our Whole Life Is Like a Play": Collaboration and the Problem of Editing.' *Textus* 9 (1996): 437–60.

The Politics of Unease in the Plays of John Fletcher. Amherst, MA: University of Massachusetts Press, 1994.

McMullan, Gordon, and Jonathan Hope, eds., *The Politics of Tragicomedy: Shakespeare and After*. London and New York: Routledge, 1992.

Melnikoff, Kirk, ed., *Robert Greene. The University Wits*. Aldershot, UK, and Burlington, VT: Ashgate, 2011.

Moore, Don D., ed., *John Webster: The Critical Heritage*. London and New York: Routledge, 1981.

Morris, Brian, ed., *John Webster*. London: Benn, 1970.

Muir, Kenneth, *Shakespeare as Collaborator*. London: Methuen, 1960.

Mullaney, Steven, *The Place of the Stage: License, Play, and Power in Renaissance England*. Ann Arbor, MI: University of Michigan Press, 1995.

Mulryne, J. R., and Margaret Shewring, eds., *Theatre and Government under the Early Stuarts*. Cambridge University Press, 1993.

Munro, Lucy, *Children of the Queen's Revels: A Jacobean Theatre Repertory*. Cambridge University Press, 2005.

Murray, P. B., *A Study of Cyril Tourneur*. Philadelphia: University of Pennsylvania Press, 1964.

Nason, A. H., *James Shirley, Dramatist: A Biographical and Critical Study*. New York: A. H. Nason, 1915.

Neill, Michael, *Issues of Death, Mortality and Identity in English Renaissance Tragedy*. Oxford: Clarendon Press, 1997.

Putting History to the Question: Power, Politics, and Society in English Renaissance Drama. New York: Columbia University Press, 2000.

'"The Tongues of Angels": Charity and the Social Order in *The City Madam*', in *Philip Massinger: A Critical Reassessment*, ed. Douglas Howard. Cambridge University Press, 1985, 193–220.

Neill, Michael, ed., *John Ford: Critical Re-Visions*. Cambridge University Press, 1988.

Nethercot, Arthur H., *Sir William Davenant: Poet Laureate and Playwright-Manager*, re-issued with additional notes. New York: Russell & Russell, 1967.

Newman, Karen, '*A Chaste Maid in Cheapside* and London', in *Early Modern English Drama: A Critical Companion*, ed. Garrett A. Sullivan, Patrick Cheney and Andrew Hadfield. Oxford University Press, 2006, 237–47.

Fashioning Femininity and English Renaissance Drama. Chicago and London: University of Chicago Press, 1991.

Nordlund, Marcus, *The Dark Lantern: A Historical Study of Sight in Shakespeare, Webster, and Middleton*. Göteborg: Acta Universitatis Gothoburgensis, 1999.

O'Callaghan, Michelle, *Thomas Middleton, Renaissance Dramatist*. Edinburgh University Press, 2009.

Oliphant, E. H. C., *The Plays of Beaumont and Fletcher. An Attempt to Determine Their Respective Shares and the Shares of Others*. Oxford University Press, 1927.

Orgel, Stephen, *The Illusion of Power: Political Theatre in the English Renaissance*. Berkeley: University of California Press, 1975.

Impersonations: The Performance of Gender in Shakespeare's England. Cambridge University Press, 1996.

The Jonsonian Masque. Cambridge, MA: Harvard University Press, 1965.

'What Is a Text?' (1981), in *Staging the Renaissance: Reinterpretations of Elizabethan and Jacobean Drama*, ed. David Scott Kastan and Peter Stallybrass. New York and London: Routledge, 1991, 83–7.

Orgel, Stephen, and Roy Strong, *Inigo Jones: The Theatre of the Stuart Court.* 2 vols. Berkeley: University of California Press, 1973.

Orlin, Lena Cowen, *Private Matters and Public Culture in Post-Reformation England.* Ithaca, NY: Cornell University Press, 1994.

Ostovich, Helen, Mary V. Silcox and Graham Roebuck, eds., *Other Voices, Other Views: Expanding the Canon in English Renaissance Studies.* Cranbury, NJ: University of Delaware Press, 1999.

Palfrey, Simon, and Tiffany Stern, *Shakespeare in Parts.* Oxford University Press, 2007.

Paster, Gail Kern, *The Body Embarrassed: Drama and the Disciplines of Shame in Early Modern England.* Ithaca, NY: Cornell University Press, 1993.

The Idea of the City in the Age of Shakespeare. Athens, GA: University of Georgia Press, 1985.

Patterson, Annabel, *Censorship and Interpretation.* Madison: The University of Wisconsin Press, 1984.

Peery, William, *The Plays of Nathan Field.* Austin, TX: University of Texas Press, 1950.

Pincombe, Michael, *The Plays of John Lyly: Eros and Eliza.* Manchester University Press, 1996.

Pogue, Kate Emery, *Shakespeare's Friends.* Westport, CT, and London: Praeger, 2006.

Prest, W. R., *The Inns of Court under Elizabeth I and the Early Stuarts, 1590–1640.* London: Longman, 1972.

Prouty, C. T., ed., *The Life and Works of George Peele.* 3 vols. New Haven, CT: Yale University Press, 1952–70.

Rabkin, Norman, 'Problems in the Study of Collaboration.' *Research Opportunities in Renaissance Drama* 19 (1976): 7–13.

Rasmussen, Eric, 'The Revision of Scripts', in *A New History of Early English Drama*, ed. John D. Cox and David Scott Kastan. New York: Columbia University Press, 1997, 441–60.

Rees, Ennis, *The Tragedies of George Chapman: Renaissance Ethics in Action.* Cambridge, MA: Harvard University Press, 1954.

Rees, Joan, *Samuel Daniel: A Critical and Biographical Study.* Liverpool University Press, 1964.

Robson, Ian, *The Moral World of John Ford's Drama.* Salzburg: Institut für Englische Sprache und Literatur, Universität Salzburg, 1983.

Rochester, Joanne, *Staging Spectatorship in the Plays of Philip Massinger.* Farnham: Ashgate, 2010.

Rowe, George E., Jr, *Thomas Middleton and the New Comedy Tradition.* Lincoln, NE: University of Nebraska Press, 1979.

Rowe, Katherine, *Dead Hands: Fictions of Agency, Renaissance to Modern.* Stanford University Press, 1999.

Rowland, Richard, *Thomas Heywood's Theatre, 1599–1639.* Aldershot, UK, and Burlington, VT: Ashgate, 2010.

Rubik, Margarete, *Early Women Dramatists, 1550–1800*. Basingstoke: Macmillan, 1998.

Saccio, Peter, *The Court Comedies of John Lyly: A Study in Allegorical Dramaturgy*. Princeton University Press, 1969.

Sanders, Julie, *Caroline Drama: The Plays of Massinger, Ford, Shirley, and Brome*. Plymouth: Northcote House, 1999.

Sanders, Julie, Kate Chedgzoy and Susan Wiseman, eds., *Refashioning Ben Jonson: Gender, Politics, and the Jonsonian Canon*. New York: St Martin's Press, 1998.

Sanders, Wilbur, *The Dramatist and the Received Idea: Studies in the Plays of Marlowe and Shakespeare*. Cambridge University Press, 1968.

Senn, Werner, *Studies in the Dramatic Construction of Robert Greene and George Peele*. Berne: Francke, 1973.

Shapiro, James S., *Rival Playwrights: Marlowe, Jonson, Shakespeare*. New York: Columbia University Press, 1991.

Shapiro, Michael, *Children of the Revels: The Boy Companies of Shakespeare's Time and Their Plays*. New York: Columbia University Press, 1977.

  Gender in Play on the Shakespearean Stage: Boy Heroines and Female Pages. Ann Arbor, MI: University of Michigan Press, 1994.

Shaw, Catherine, *Richard Brome*. Boston, MA: Twayne Publishers, 1980.

Sisson, Charles J., *Lost Plays of Shakespeare's Age*. Cambridge University Press, 1936.

Smith, David L., David Strier and David Bevington, eds., *The Theatrical City: Culture, Theatre and Politics in London, 1576–1649*. Cambridge University Press, 1995.

Southern, Antonia, *Player, Playwright and Preacher's Kid: The Story of Nathan Field, 1587–1620*. Twickenham: Athena Press 2009.

Spivack, Charlotte, *George Chapman*. New York: Twayne Publishers, 1967.

Stachniewski, John, 'Calvinist Psychology in Middleton's Tragedies', in *Three Jacobean Revenge Tragedies: A Casebook*, ed. R. V. Holdsworth. Basingstoke: Macmillan, 1990, 226–47.

Stallybrass, Peter, 'Reading the Body and the Jacobean Theater of Consumption: *The Revenger's Tragedy* (1606)', in *Staging the Renaissance: Reinterpretations of Elizabethan and Jacobean Drama*, ed. David Scott Kastan and Peter Stallybrass. New York and London: Routledge, 1991, 210–20.

Steggle, Matthew, *Richard Brome: Place and Politics on the Caroline Stage*. Manchester University Press, 2004.

Stern, Tiffany, *Making Shakespeare: From Page to Stage*. London and New York: Routledge, 2004.

  Rehearsal from Shakespeare to Sheridan. Oxford University Press, 2000.

Sturgess, Keith, *Jacobean Private Theatre*. London: Routledge, 1987.

Swinburne, Algernon, *Contemporaries of Shakespeare*, in *The Complete Works of Algernon Charles Swinburne*, ed. Edmund Gosse and Thomas James Wise, vol. XII (Prose Works vol. II). London: Heinemann, 1926, 125–368.

Taylor, Gary, 'Forms of Opposition: Shakespeare and Middleton.' *English Literary Renaissance* 24 (1994): 283–314.

Taylor, Gary, and John Jowett, *Shakespeare Reshaped, 1603–1623*. Oxford University Press, 1997.

Taylor, Gary, and John Lavagnino, eds., *Thomas Middleton and Early Modern Textual Culture: A Companion to the Collected Works*. Oxford: Clarendon Press, 2007.

Taylor, Gary, and John Lavagnino, eds., *Thomas Middleton: The Collected Works*. Oxford: Clarendon Press, 2007.

Thomson, Lesley, '"*Enter Above*": The Staging of *Women Beware Women.*' *Studies in English Literature* 26 (1986): 331–43.

Turner, Celeste, *Anthony Mundy, an Elizabethan Man of Letters*. Berkeley: University of California Press, 1928.

Vickers, Brian, *Shakespeare, Co-Author: A Historical Study of Five Collaborative Plays*. Oxford University Press, 2004.

Waith, Eugene M., *The Herculean Hero in Marlowe, Chapman, Shakespeare and Dryden*. New York: Columbia University Press, 1962.

  Ideas of Greatness: Heroic Drama in England. New York: Barnes & Noble, 1971.

  The Pattern of Tragicomedy in Beaumont and Fletcher. New Haven, CT: Yale University Press, 1952.

Wall, Wendy, *Staging Domesticity: Household Work and English Identity in Early Modern Drama*. Cambridge University Press, 2002.

Walls, Peter. *Music in the English Courtly Masque, 1604–1640*. New York: Oxford University Press, 1996.

Wells, Stanley, *Shakespeare & Co.: Christopher Marlowe, Thomas Dekker, Ben Jonson, Thomas Middleton, John Fletcher, and the Other Players in His Story*. London: Penguin, 2006.

Wells, Stanley, and Gary Taylor, with John Jowett and William Montgomery, *William Shakespeare: A Textual Companion*. Oxford: Clarendon Press, 1987.

Welsford, Enid, *The Court Masque: A Study in the Relationship between Poetry and the Revels*. New York: Russell & Russell, 1962.

Wharton, T. F., *The Critical Fall and Rise of John Marston*. Columbia, SC: Camden House, 1994.

Wharton, T. F., ed., *The Drama of John Marston: Critical Re-Visions*. Cambridge University Press, 2000.

White, Martin, *Renaissance Drama in Action: An Introduction to Aspects of Theatre Practice and Performance*. London and New York: Routledge, 1998.

White, Paul Whitfield, *Theatre and Reformation: Protestantism, Patronage and Playing in Tudor England*. Cambridge: Cambridge University Press, 1993.

Whitney, Charles C., ed., *Thomas Lodge*. The University Wits. Aldershot, UK, and Burlington, VT: Ashgate, 2011.

Wickham, Glynne, Herbert Berry and William Ingram, *English Professional Theatre, 1530–1660*. Cambridge University Press, 2000.

Wiggins, Martin, *Shakespeare and the Drama of His Time*. Oxford University Press, 2000.

Wikander, Matthew H., *The Play of Truth and State: Historical Drama from Shakespeare to Brecht*. Baltimore, MD: Johns Hopkins University Press, 1986.

Williams, William Proctor, 'Not *Hornpipes* and *Funerals*: Fletcherian Tragicomedy', in *Renaissance Tragicomedy: Explorations in Genre and Politics*, ed. Nancy Maguire. New York: AMS, 1987, 139–54.

Wilson, F. P., *Marlowe and the Early Shakespeare*. Oxford: Clarendon Press, 1953.

Wilson, John Harold, *The Influence of Beaumont and Fletcher on Restoration Drama*. New York: Haskell House, 1969.

Womack, Peter, *English Renaissance Drama*. Oxford: Blackwell, 2006.

Wymer, Rowland, *Webster and Ford*. New York: St Martin's Press, 1995.

Zimmerman, Susan, ed., *Erotic Politics: Desire on the Renaissance Stage*. London and New York: Routledge, 1992.

Zucker, Adam, and Alan B. Farmer, eds., *Localizing Caroline Drama: Politics and Economics of the Early Modern English Stage, 1625–1642*. Basingstoke: Palgrave Macmillan, 2006.

Cambridge companions to ...

AUTHORS